11-30-59
3-17-60

Lift Up Your Eyes

THE
RELIGIOUS WRITINGS
OF
LEO TOLSTOY

LIFT
UP
YOUR
EYES

Introduction by Stanley R. Hopper

THE JULIAN PRESS, INC., NEW YORK

1960

PUBLISHED BY THE JULIAN PRESS, INC.
80 East 11th Street, New York 3

© Copyright 1960 by The Julian Press, Inc.

Library of Congress Card Number 59-15567

Manufactured in the United States of America

The Tolstoy material has been reproduced for the most part from *The Collected Works of Leo Tolstoy* published by Thomas Y. Crowell & Co. in 1899 and which was translated from the original Russian by several translators authorized by the author.

LITHOGRAPHED FOR THE PUBLISHERS BY
NOBLE OFFSET PRINTERS, INC., NEW YORK

Contents

INTRODUCTION

THESE pages from the religious writings of Tolstoy are among the most fascinating in all literature. Not only do they abound in forthright, provocative challenges to religious interpreters of all beliefs and backgrounds, but they reveal the earnest and impassioned probings of one of the world's greatest writers in search of a sustaining meaning for life. One might go further: they reveal the impassioned probings of a soul in quest of itself—a quest that results in a unique revision of the religious consciousness. Since this is also the characteristic quest of our times—in existentialism, depth psychology, Zen Buddhism, and much apologetic theology—the work of Tolstoy suddenly renews its relevance in a manner and dimension totally unsuspected twenty years ago.

Everything depends on whether Tolstoy is read from the center or from the periphery. According to Epictetus, "Everything has two handles: one by which it may be borne, another by which it cannot." By either metaphor, this alternative is supremely applicable to the reading of Tolstoy. By one reading he is a dreamer, a utopist, a sublime mountebank, an incomparable artist who turned Rousseauist and social reformer, and whose passionate prophecies have long since shattered and fallen away with the general collapse of nineteenth-century vision. A few days after the death of Tolstoy (November 20,

1910) Paul Claudel wrote to André Gide: "The news of Tolstoy is very moving. Unhappy sower of the wind, who reaped nothing but the whirlwind and dies at the age of eighty on the public highway in a waiting-room!"[1]

But much has happened since 1910. A "world of things" (as we say with unconscious candor) has passed away. The adequate rationalisms of that day, whether sociological or theological or epistemological, are no longer serviceable to us. We perceive dimly that Western culture, in its "European" and classical phase, has passed. We are diminished, and feel that our knowledge is partial. The smugness of 1910 is the emptiness of 1960. Somewhere in the interim of fifty years a world has ended; a great deal is finished and we have stepped across a threshold into what's next to be in the world. But we do not know what this next is to be. We are engaged in the search for it, meanwhile fending off the collapse of our "knowledge" by propping up the forms and symbols that were useful hitherto. Yet we know that it is we ourselves who have sown the wind and reaped the great whirlwinds, and are even now being driven in mounting isolations of spirit toward some unplotted depot of ultimate meanings. In the pathos of Tolstoy's dying in the station-master's house at Astapovo, someone reported that he had two books by his bedside: the *Essais* of Montaigne and *The Brothers Karamazov*. This also is symbolic of our quest, for we too are flanked by these influences.

Let us note quickly, however, the vast advantage of our present position. We are released from an entire congeries of biases, predilections, and uncriticized commitments, "points of view" that presided, either by authority or custom, over our ways of seeing things (of given meaning to experience). Ours is, by necessity, an epoch of "reconsiderations," a time when the whole of

---

[1] *The Correspondence between Paul Claudel and Andre Gide*, Tr. by John Russell, New York, Pantheon Books, Inc., 1952, p. 143.

our supposed fixed knowledge is up for review, when it is subject to revision in the light of new data and radically altered perspectives. It is this precisely that permits us to take up Tolstoy's work by another handle, one by which he may be borne, and to reread him from his own center, which we have scarcely managed to do heretofore.

This "center" of Tolstoy's work is religious (in the sense in which Tolstoy himself, over a long period of time, sought to define it); it will correspond, as we shall see, with the much discussed phrase of Paul Tillich, our "ultimate concern." It has points of contact with existentialism. Religion, as deep quest and ultimate concern, is the one handle by which Tolstoy's work may be borne; it is also the center from which his work may be grasped and seen as a whole. This is why the republication of these religious works, long out of print and unavailable, is timely and salutary: timely, because their burden coincides strikingly with the deep concern of sensitive spirits in our time, and salutary because Tolstoy's lifelong quest for authentic self-knowledge and truth is like our own.

I must confess that I have come to this view somewhat reluctantly, perhaps even grudgingly. For it has become patent amongst theologians that Tolstoy's eloquent abridgment of the Gospels sideslips with almost sophistical ease from traditional Christian realism to Rousseauistic humanitarian unrealism. It is easy to parallel in Tolstoy that same "naturalization of the Gospel" which numerous religious critics have noted in Rousseau. Tolstoy has himself confessed his indebtedness to Rousseau, at the age of fifteen, at the beginning of his career, and again at age seventy-seven, in the maturity of his religious consciousness. When first I explored the religious writings of Tolstoy some twenty-five years ago, I was struck with the ease with which one could document the covert commutation of terms, from "God" to "love" to "humanity" to "the service of humanity," as though these were equivalent meanings. The same pattern was observable in Gandhi, whose early correspondence with Tolstoy is well known, and whose famous "Tolstoy Farm" experiment in South Africa bears eloquent witness to the centrality of Tolstoy's teachings in the young Indian reformer. All three, Rousseau, Tolstoy, Gandhi, wrote "Confessions"; the persistence in doctrine from the "Profession of Faith of the Savoyard Vicar" to the professions of Tolstoy to those of Gandhi is easily traceable. Only the emergence of the tenet of passive nonresistance in Tolstoy and of nonviolent noncooperation in Gandhi marks the progression of social concern. What we have in all this is the flowering of humanitarian liberalism in the early twentieth century upon the stem of nineteenth-century rationalism. This was the aspect of Tolstoy's religious works that was caught up by devotees of the "social Gospel" and by the liberal pacifists of the same period. It is useless to try to pick up Tolstoy by this handle. It misconceives the true center of his religious concern. Not that I would play down these features of his polemical writings, for there is much in them that we have still to acknowledge and come to terms with. Even so conservative a critic as Paul Elmer More remarked: "I know not how we shall escape his ruthless conclusions unless we deny resolutely his premises. . . ."[2] But the careful reader of these pages will discover that it is Tolstoy's minor premises rather than his major ones that we have, up to this point, resolutely denied.

There is a second cliché of criticism that has obscured Tolstoy's authentic center. It is simply that a great artist was lost to the world when Tolstoy became a great moralist. Not only is this point of view dramatized by Tolstoy himself in his extravagant if rhetorical preference for *Uncle Tom's Cabin* over the plays of Shakespeare; but it has had the support of men of letters and

[2] *Shelburne Essays*, First Series, Boston, Houghton Mifflin Co., The Riverside Press, Cambridge, 1904, p. 194.

critics who have set the style for it. There is, above all, the oft-cited letter of Turgenev (1883): "My Dear and Beloved Leo Nicholayevitch!—I have not written to you for such a long time because, putting it bluntly, I was, and am, on my death-bed. I cannot recover,—it would be useless to entertain any hopes. I am writing to you chiefly to tell you how glad I was to have been your contemporary and to address my last request to you. My friend, return to artistic work! This gift of yours comes from the same source from which all other things come. Oh, how glad I would be if only I knew that my request will impress you. . . ."

There was a very good reason why this plea to Tolstoy did not impress him. His entire angle of vision on life and its meaning was radically different from that of Turgenev, as it was also from that of Dostoievsky. He never stood *apart* from his work, so as to create it as an aesthetic something unrelated to himself as its executor. His novels were one mode of his way of experiencing things: just as riding and hunting and ploughing and soldiering and fraternizing with peasants and attempting educational reforms were other modes of it. The truth is that his celebrated "renunciation of literature" never was a fact at all. As one of his biographers has put it, "Tolstoy did not give up literature, and never made shoes *instead of writing.*"[3] More important, however, is the fact that his novels are deeply as well as extensively autobiographical. They are one with his life quest, and they exhibit it. Just as Kierkegaard was able to inscribe an essay on the point of view for his work as an author and show that the "indirect" and "fictional" writings *and* the "edifying discourses" with their direct assaults and polemics were but two facets of one authorship, so Tolstoy's aesthetic writings *and* his religious and polemic writings are but two aspects of a single quest. This quest is religious. As with Kierkegaard, the cate-

[3] Alexander I. Nazaroff: *Tolstoy, the Inconstant Genius,* New York, Frederick A. Stokes Company, 1929, p. 245.

gory within which his work may be viewed as a whole is the religious. As with Kierkegaard, the aesthetic works become, from the religious point of view, "frivolous." This is the category that W. H. Auden continues distressingly to insist upon in the face of his own fine achievements. But it must be stressed that they are "frivolous" *from the religious point of view*. Just as Thomas Aquinas, following his climactic vision of God, appraised his theological works as "rubbish" and refused to write more, so Tolstoy, following a similar crisis in his own life, tended to devote less time to the fictional parables of the human situation and more time to a variety of attempts to witness through direct forms of deed and utterance to the truth of life as he now saw it. The polemics into which this later mode led him were, again, not unlike those of Kierkegaard, in that both were convinced that Christianity had been betrayed by Christendom, and that official Christianity must submit to radical revision, almost from the beginning, if it is to become once more a source of life to us and not a prime agency for the stifling of the spirit. At this point his polemics are one with those of Nietzsche and Dostoievsky, as well as with Kierkegaard.

Matthew Arnold (one of the first to recognize his greatness in English) glimpsed this from quite another point of view when he published his famous essay on Count Leo Tolstoy in the *Fortnightly Review* for December, 1887. In speaking of *Anna Karenina* he wrote: ". . . the truth is we are not to take (it) as a work of art; we are to take it as a piece of life. . . . The author has not invented and combined it, he has seen it. . . ." This is, to be sure, one of those dubious Arnoldian distinctions irritating to contemporary critics. But it is perfectly true all the same: Tolstoy's great masterpieces, those fictional works that have made him one of the greatest novelists of all time, are as Arnold puts it, "pieces of life." They are parables of existence. There are many things of a "purely aesthetic" kind in them that attest to their author's artistic skills; but that which makes them "great" is what we should today call their "existential dialectic," those inevitable dialectics of the human situation that thrust us forward upon those onto-logic crossroads (or railroad stations) toward which our decisions vis-a-vis reality predestinate us. This is the burden of Tolstoy's great *War and Peace,* in which the intricate web of human circumstance, woven in the woof of compounding human choices, exhibits a philosophy of history that is dialectical and existential from begin-ning to end. As the reader of these pages will discover, these perspectives in the novels are one with his direct religious writings. He was driven, as he tells us in his *Confession,* by "the conviction that a knowledge of truth can be gained only by living," and that he "must live, not the life of a parasite, but a real life"; but what that feeling of being driven meant for him he could not describe otherwise "than as a searching after God." His life and his novels were one with this search. Merezhkov-sky recognized this: "The artistic work of Leo Tolstoy is at bottom nothing else than one tremendous diary, kept for fifty years, one endless, explicit confession."[4]

But the "bottom" is a long way down, as T. S. Eliot once remarked of Matthew Arnold's use of this expres-sion. It may be deeper even than Eliot himself knows. For him it is the "mystery of Iniquity, a pit too deep for mortal eyes to plumb"; or, it is

the backward half-look
Over the shoulder, towards the primitive terror.[5]

Since we take but a half-look over the shoulder the "primitive terror" remains undefined for us. We permit

---

[4] Quoted in Thomas Mann, *Essays of Three Decades,* "Goethe and Tolstoy," New York, Alfred A. Knopf, 1947, p. 100.

[5] First citation from Choruses from "The Rock." X, from *Collected Poems,* 1909-1935, New York, Harcourt, Brace and Company, First American Edition, 1936, p. 208; the second from The Dry Salvages, II, in *The Four Quartets,* New York, Harcourt, Brace and Company, 1934, p. 24.

it to trouble us for a moment only, and hurry on into the structure of motions and compatibilities built up for us and by us to protect us from this very anxiety.

Another passage of Eliot's probes more deeply. In East Coker,[6] he describes a moment in the subway, in the tube, when the train

6 III, *op. cit.,* p. 14.

> stops too long between stations
> And the conversation rises and slowly fades into silence
> And you see behind every face the mental emptiness deepen
> Leaving only the growing terror of nothing to think about. . . .

Here the sense of "growing terror" is much more realistic than in the foregoing; but it is not the "nothing to think about" that brings on the terror as much as the temptation to think about nothing—about not being.

Tolstoy is much more direct about all this. In *Anna Karenina,* Karenin, her husband, has suddenly come face to face with the fact of his own jealousy:

He felt that he was standing face to face with something illogical and irrational, and did not know what was to be done. Alexey Alexandrovitch was standing face to face with life, with the possibility of his wife's loving some one other than himself. . . .

This was disconcerting and baffling to him, as he had been protected hitherto by mores of breeding, official life, and the rational precepts that dictated what "one" ought to expect and do.

. . . every time he had stumbled against life itself he had shrunk away from it. Now he experienced a feeling akin to that of a man who, while calmly crossing a bridge over a precipice, should suddenly discover that the bridge is broken, that there is a chasm below. That chasm was life itself, the bridge that artificial life in which Alexey Alexandrovitch had lived. For the first time the question presented itself to him of the possibility of his wife's loving some one else, and he was horrified at it.

We may note in passing how sharply this argument impinges upon those *Pensées* of Pascal in which he notes how men run toward a precipice while holding a cover over their eyes; and how he was terrified at the eternal silences of the infinite spaces; but most directly how, though contrary to our wish, "nothing stays for us. . . . We burn with desire to find solid ground and an ultimate sure foundation whereon to build a tower reaching to the Infinite. But our whole groundwork cracks, and the earth opens to abysses."[7]

It is, however, Tolstoy's superb narrative of *The Death of Ivan Ilyitch* that brings us straight upon the problem. The plot is simple. It is about a man who discovers that *he* has an incurable malady and is going to die. Death, to this point, had been something that happens to others, or to men generally; but it is also the socially postponed question or the socially dissolved question. Ivan discovers that his life and the lives of those about him had been meaningless and futile. All acknowledge that "people die," but none has ever confronted himself with the fact that he himself must die. In the concluding pages of the narrative, Ivan's pretensions fall away. He accepts the fact of death for himself. "From that moment began that shriek that did not cease for three days!" But the facing of death became for him the facing of life. He learned to see his friends for the first time, and to care for them. He learned a new sympathy and understanding for his wife. For the first time in his life he had learned to love. "What joy!" he exclaimed. He had been forced back upon himself by the threat of death. He had been forced upon the primary questions: Who am I? What is the meaning of my

[7] *Pensées*, pp. 183, 206, 72 (Brunschrig edition).

life? He has had to come to terms with the threat of nothingness and annihilation.

This story, which, as William Barrett pointed out some years ago, "has become something of a basic scripture for existential thought,"[8] dramatizes that social con-
edition, New York, Harper & Brothers, Publishers, 1957, p. 143.
spiracy into which all men enter, whereby we hide from ourselves the primary questions, and obscure the issue of death and life in such a way as that "it will take nothing less than the presence of death to restore [the] sense of life."[9]

Heidegger's use of this narrative is by this time widely recognized. The entire second chapter of the second part of his *Being and Time* is, as Walter Kaufmann has recently noted, "for the most part an unacknowledged commentary on *The Death of Ivan Ilyitch*."[10] Heidegger has at one point, in connection with the popular generalization that "people die," remarked in a footnote that "L. N. Tolstoy has portrayed in his story, *The Death of Ivan Ilyitch*, the phenomenon of shock and collapse of this 'one dies' attitude."[11] Heidegger goes on to argue that our existence as a being-toward-death is the prime root of our essential anxiety (p. 266); and that implicit in the method of existential analysis are the questions of a biology, psychology, theodicy, and theology of death. The attempt to grasp the meaning of death by the usual structures of intellectualist reflection will fail; it will only reveal the eternally formal and empty character of all speculative ontology. At the same time it is in the existential truth of "existence-toward-death" that the essence of all ontological inquiry will be seen to lie (p. 248, *passim*).

[8] In *Spiritual Problems in Contemporary Literature*, ed. by Stanley R. Hopper; essay on "Existentialism a Symptom of Man's Contemporary Crisis." First, published 1952; first Harper Torchbook
[9] *Ibid.*
[10] "Existentialism and Death," in the *Chicago Review*, 13: 2: 81, Summer, 1959.
[11] *Sein und Zeit*, Neomarius Verlag, Tübingen, 1949, p. 254n.

Tolstoy himself was never as abstruse as this. His language is always simple, clear, and direct. Especially in his polemical writings and in the pages of religious reflection that follow, he seeks always very simple analogies or illustrations with which to carry his arguments. Indeed, his controlling ideas are few. They recur again and again in his writings. But they reach into these difficult centers that we have been trying to evoke, and in terms of which alone, I am persuaded, the unity and deep contemporary significance of his work are to be grasped. The reader may be slightly irked at times by a certain repetitiousness of these themes; but it must be borne in mind that Tolstoy, after his "conversion," is doing his best to speak these ideas on every occasion, and that these occasions are many and they are various. Both the variety and the repetitiousness will be seen, in the long run, to confirm the internal unity of all his writings: novels, essays, autobiography, polemical tracts, and religious studies. What we note here is the existential and psychologic root of these ideas in Tolstoy's haunting sense of death.

The reader will find the full account of this crucial transition in Tolstoy's life in the all-important document entitled *My Confession*. This is not a superficial document. It is projected along grand lines. It solicits comparison much less with the *Confessions* of Jean-Jacques Rousseau than with those of Augustine. The experience here recorded occurred to him shortly before his fiftieth year, at a time when all his circumstances were favorable and "eminently happy ones." He had wife, family, estates, exuberant physical health, the universal praise of men for his aesthetic works. Yet

I felt that the ground on which I stood was crumbling, that there was nothing for me to stand on, that what I had been living for was nothing, that I had no reason for living.

My life had come to a stop. . . .

The truth was, that life was meaningless. Every day

of life, every step in it, brought me, as it were, nearer the precipice, and I saw clearly that before me there was nothing but ruin.

The thought of suicide occurred to him. He found himself hiding away a cord from himself, and ceasing to hunt because of the gun he carried. He was "afraid of life"; life seemed like "a foolish and wicked joke" that someone had played on him. Then follows his dramatic account of "an old Eastern fable" concerning a traveler in the steppes attacked suddenly by a wild beast. To escape from the beast he climbs into a waterless well; but at the bottom of the well he sees a great dragon with its jaws wide open ready to devour him. Since he can neither get out for fear of the beast nor descend farther for fear of the dragon, he clutches a branch of a wild plant growing from a crevice in the well. With death awaiting him above and below, his muscles tire; but he hangs on. Then he sees two mice, one white and one black, circling the branch and gradually nibbling it through! He knows that soon the branch will break off and he will be devoured by the dragon. Then he finds some drops of honey on the plant leaves, and, still clinging, reaches out to lick them with his tongue.

Thus do I cling to the branch of life, knowing that the dragon of death inevitably awaits me, ready to tear me to pieces, and I cannot understand why such tortures have fallen to my lot. I also strive to suck the honey which once comforted me, but this honey no longer rejoices me, while the white mouse and the black, day and night, gnaw through the branch to which I cling. . . .

The panic aspect of this experience he describes vividly in a figure reminiscent of Dante:

I was like a man lost in a forest, and who, terrified by the thought that he is lost, rushes about trying to find a way out, and, though he knows each step leads him still farther astray, cannot help rushing about.

It was this that was terrible!

William James was not slow to single out this confession for inclusion in his *Varieties of Religious Experience*.[12] He describes it as a "well-marked case of anhedonia, of passive loss of appetite for all life's values"—what Hugo von Hofmannsthal somewhere describes as "lassitude of spirit." But James goes on to note, secondly, how our worlds are all compounded of our projections, how the values and meanings of our worlds are "pure gifts of the spectator's mind." When these projections fall away or drop back upon the consciousness that projected them, we feel at once estranged, isolated, and suffer that "ontological shock" that the stark anonymity of things presents to us. In Tolstoy's case it thrust him back, as in contemporary existentialism, upon the primary ontological questions: Who am I? Why am I? Why is anything at all? What is its intent or meaning?

He reacts to these questions precisely as Augustine did. "I sought in all directions." He sought in the several branches of knowledge. He turned to Socrates, Buddha, "Solomon," and Schopenhauer. Here he found that "life is what it ought not to be, an evil; and a passage from it into nothingness is the only good in life" (Schopenhauer).

Then he turned to "life itself." Here he found four main patterns of escape whereby men avoid the issue. The first is by the way of ignorance, by which people blind their eyes to the absurdity of life, perceiving neither the dragon nor the mice, but licking away the honey. The second is the way of the Epicurean—the escape into pursuits of pleasure; what Pascal compounded adroitly under the term *divertissement*. The third pattern of escape is more realistic. Recognizing the absurd, these persons have the courage and the energy to "put an end at once to the stupid joke"; while the fourth class are those who, though recognizing the evil

12 Modern Library Edition, pp. 146 ff.

and absurdity of life, continue "to drag it out, though aware that nothing can come of it." These people "live on, through weakness, in despair."

The analysis here is by no means as acute or perceptive as that of Kierkegaard; nor is the notion of the "absurd" developed with anything like the philosophical adequacy of an existentialist like Camus; but the basic movement of mind is much the same. It leads Tolstoy to a rejection of Cartesian "reason" and to a restatement of the problem along existential or experiential lines: "I understood that it was useless to seek an answer to my question from knowledge founded on reason, and that the answer given by this form of knowledge is only an indication that no answer can be obtained *till the question is put differently. . . .*"

This statement is of considerable importance; for Tolstoy is often charged with being a "rationalist," and it is quite true that in many of his papers he makes an appeal to the "rational consciousness" and to "reason." But, while he is not always precise and not always consistent, it is important to note that this "rational consciousness" lies nearer to Pascal than to Voltaire. The question, says Tolstoy, must "be made to include the relation between the finite and the infinite." This led him, as it led Pascal, to a recognition of a kind of knowledge founded upon faith, namely, religious knowledge, and to "the conviction that a knowledge of truth can be gained only by living."

We shall have to observe now that Tolstoy has undergone a deep reorientation of his life. What was formerly great and public and exuberant and superficial—the outward movement of his early years—has recoiled upon him in its hollowness. The *Thanatos* principle of Freud is in clear evidence here, as Tolstoy is thrown back upon himself in such a way as to compel his coming to terms with reality. William James describes the process as one of redemption, of being saved, "by what seems to him a second birth, a deeper kind of conscious being than he

could enjoy before." [13] We note again that this new consciousness is, for Tolstoy, a religious consciousness; but
it is a religious consciousness that he will define increasingly in terms of life, love, meaning, balance, security,
well-being, and wholeness. These are the vital terms that
hold the clues to his deepest religious consciousness. Not
that he would come up with a new speculative system
that would provide either rational or dogmatic explanations for things. He had come to know "that the explanation of the whole, like the beginning of all things, was
hidden in infinity." [14] It began rather with the simple
witness that "the true office of any faith is to give to life
a meaning which death cannot destroy." [15] His *Confession* is a witness to the fact that he had experienced an
inner change, a change in depth, an experience that it
would take the remaining years of his life to construe.

At the end of his *Confession* he appends a dream,
which came to him some three years after the *Confession*
proper was written. "This dream repeated for me in a
condensed form all that I had lived through and described. . . ." he comments. In his account of the dream,
he portrays himself as lying on a bed made of interlaced
cords. Striving for greater comfort on this bed, the cords
begin to slip away, until he is holding himself up pre-
cariously by the upper part of the back only. "I now
begin to ask myself what I had not thought of before. I
ask myself where I am, and on what I am lying." Then
he looks below, for the first time, and to his horror discovers that he is hanging over a bottomless abyss. "My
heart ceases to beat, and horror fills my mind. . . . I
feel that if I look down I shall slip the last cord, and
perish." Then he looks above, and feels sustained. "The
infinite depth repels and horrifies me; and the infinite
height attracts and satisfies me. . . . I know that I am
hanging thus, but I look only upwards, and my terror

13 *Ibid.,* p. 154.
14 *My Confession,* 106.
15 *My Confession,* 95.

leaves me." Still mystified by this sustaining power, he looks further and discovers under the middle of his body "a stay," "and on looking up I find that I am lying perfectly balanced, and that it was this stay alone that held me up before." The dream imagery shifts a little, and he perceives at his bedside a pillar, the "solidity of which is beyond doubt, though there is nothing for it to stand on." From the pillar runs a cord; if he lies across the cord and looks upward there is no question of his falling. This became clear to him, and he was "glad and easy in [his] mind."

Much might be made of this dream. The cord is provocatively suggestive of the cord that he hid from himself lest he should hang himself on the transom of his bedroom. The language concerning the infinites is reminiscent of Pascal's *Pensees* already referred to (especially the 72nd[16]); but it parallels Nietzsche also, surprisingly enough:

Not the height, it is the declivity that is terrible!
The declivity, there the gaze shooteth *downwards*, and the hand graspeth *upwards*. There doth the heart become giddy through its double will. . . .[17]

Attractive as these parallels might be, however, there is a really startling revelation here of the way in which Tolstoy's unconscious self has made over the "old Eastern fable" of the well, the mice, and the dragon. The regressive symbol of the well has become the firm and solid pillar; while the branch that is about to break and drop him into the jaws of the dragon has become the cord of life attached to the pillar of life, and which now upholds him and sustains him like "a stay." This is in contrast to his earlier fear lest he should "slip from the last cord"—combining "slip the cord" and "the last cord (chord)—as well as the "or ever the silver cord be

---

[16] *Life*, p. 161, where Tolstoy paraphrases Pascal's definition of the universe to make man the "center of a sphere, whose surface is everywhere and nowhere."

[17] *Thus Spake Zarathustra*, II, xliii.

loosed" of Ecclesiastes, which he had been reading.

The psychological terrors of this period of his life must have been great. To his credit it must be said that he did not contemplate a break with Orthodoxy. He sought first in the Church for a confirmation of his experience. But "when I looked around me at all that was done in the name of religion, I was horrified." [18] He turned also to the theologians and to the commentaries on Scripture. But he was again thwarted. He "was unwillingly forced to see that the doctrines of faith destroy the very thing which they should produce." [19]

Thus was Tolstoy thrust agonistically upon the dilemma of all revealers and prophets. Like Jeremiah, like Job, he has made the discovery that God is no longer livingly present in the forms and symbols and doctrinal structures of conventional religion; and he must therefore, like Job or like Hölderlin's poet, go out into the open and there seek for the new name of God. "That God, whom one knew, has become familiar, and one no more believes in Him. We entirely believe in God only when He discloses Himself afresh to us. And he discloses Himself to us from a new side when we seek Him with all our soul." [20] But it is always terrifying to step out from under the approved ways of knowing "God." Nevertheless the "cords" of the bed that heretofore had sustained Tolstoy had been slipping away one by one: and suddenly he was exposed to the Ground of Being, to the God beyond "God." "Surely," remarked Gorky, "he has some thoughts of which he is afraid." In his *What I Believe* Tolstoy remarked:

It is terrible to say, but it sometimes appears to me that if Christ's teaching, with the Church teaching that has grown out of it, had not existed at all, those who now call themselves Christians would have been nearer

18 *My Confession*, p. 104.
19 *Ibid.*, p. 102.
20 *Thoughts on God*, XIV, pp. 383-84.

to the truth of Christ—that is to say, to a reasonable understanding of what is good in life—than they are now.

A deeper terror is revealed by Gorky, when, on reading a page of Tolstoy's diary, he came across the statement: "God is my desire." Puzzled by this, he asked Tolstoy what it meant.

"An unfinished thought," he said, glancing at the page and screwing up his eyes. "I must have wanted to say: God is my desire to know him. . . . No, not that. . . ." He began to laugh, and rolling up the book into a tube, he put it into the big pocket of his blouse.

This laughter is doubtless a cover for the sudden panic involved either in coming to "know" God (or being known of Him), or of treading the paranoiac brink of confounding the deep Self with God in the simple affirmation "God is my desire." And yet again, one might well recoil before the rejections and isolations of misunderstanding that must follow upon the proclamation of a fresh way of apprehending God and His will for us.

That is the one side of it. The other lies in Jeremiah's recognition that one must pluck up before one can plant. "Before one can pour anything into a vessel one must first empty it of what it already contains. So also it is necessary to free men from the deceit in which they are held in order that they may accept true religion, that is, a true relation to the source of all—God. . . ."[21]

This negative aspect of his task might be documented extensively. It will be found to run throughout these pages. But before he can tell what religion is, he must tell what it is not.

For Tolstoy the true religion is not to be found in creeds, in rites and rituals, in sacraments, or in the Church. He falls back upon the Gospels. The teaching of the Gospels was, he holds, so plain that one would

[21] *What is Religion*, p. 304.

think it impossible to distort them. "But the human mind is ingenious" and it invented a new trick for obscuring their contents.

This "dodge" consisted in attributing infallibility not only to certain words but also to a certain body of men called The Church, which has the right to transmit this infallibility to other men elected by it. A little addition to the Gospel was also invented,—that Christ when leaving for heaven transmitted to certain men the exclusive right not only of teaching others the divine truth . . . but also of making men saved or unsaved, and, above all, of transmitting this right to others (*What Is Religion,* pp. 279-280).

Tolstoy undertakes a radical demythologizing both of ecclesiastical and Biblical extravagances.

. . . the foundations of this religion, established by the Nicene Creed, and recognized by every one, are so absurd and immoral, and are developed to such a degree of contradiction to normal human feeling and reason, that men cannot believe them (*What Is Religion,* p. 281).

He concedes that men may repeat certain beliefs with their lips, such as that the world was created six thousand years ago, or that Jesus ascended into heaven and is sitting at the right hand of the Father, or that God is One and also Three—

. . . but no one can believe it, because the words have no sense. And therefore the men of our modern world who profess distorted Christianity, in reality believe in nothing.
And it is in this that the peculiarity of our time consists (*What is Religion,* pp. 281, 282).

We are today, of course, pretty well agreed on all this. Professor Bultmann has pointed out the impossibility of retaining those images which functioned in the myth structures of a two-storied or three-storied universe; and, as Tolstoy sought to do, we are attempting to focus upon the *kerygma* or central core of the Gospels.

It would be easy to dismiss Tolstoy's complaints, how-ever, as thrashing once more what has by this time be-come pretty much old straw. But we ought not to do this too hastily. When Tolstoy argues that "men today are without faith," he speaks to us also. And when he argues that there are those, on the one hand, who have freed themselves from the influence of the Church and believe in nothing, and there are those on the other hand who, still under "the hypnotic influence" of the tradition, believe that what is held out to them as faith really is faith, but in reality is not and only confuses them the more, he still speaks to us. For "this is terrible," and on both hands it compounds the perplexities of the con-temporary agony and pain.

At this point we may note two perspectives in Tolstoy that make his case most formidable. The first is his clear recognition of the fact that "dogmas about 'revelations' *disunite* men more and more."[22] They are essentially divisive, and in the long run destroy the very thing they seek to protect. "Never," he remarks in his Preface to *The Gospel in Brief* (p. 290), "since the time of Arius, has a single dogma arisen from other cause than the desire to contradict an opposing dogma." Secondly, not only is the doctrinal faith divisive, but it delivers the believer into impotence and contradiction, and sets the self against itself and reality. "Once one has admitted as positive truth all the absurdities and horrors which are accepted as the revelation of God in the Scriptures, one has to keep on distorting common sense more and more in order to justify all these horrors and absurdi-ties."[23]

These arguments will acquire greater force if we con-

[22] Private Letters from *The Complete Works of Leo Tolstoy*, New York, Thomas Y. Crowell Co., 1899, p. 366.

[23] *Ibid.*, p. 364.

sider briefly the positive side of Tolstoy's view, namely, what religion is. Here we must bear in mind his earlier insistence that no adequate answer to the religious question can be obtained until the question is put differently. It cannot be provided secondhand in a doctrine, nor in anything objective whatsoever. It must be experienced within as the "establishment by man of his relation to the Infinite Existence of which he feels himself a part."[24] God is the Infinite Source of all Being. Man must learn how to serve this Source, for "this is the will of the Father."[25] It is also, as Schleiermacher and Feuerbach held, "man's consciousness of his dependence on God."[26] But it is also "what in mathematics is called integration: besides his relations to his immediate circumstances, he must establish his relation to the whole universe. And such an establishment by man of his relation to that whole of which he feels himself a part . . . is called Religion."[27]

But it is obviously psychological integration rather than mathematical with which Tolstoy is deeply concerned here. Like Augustine[28] he recognizes that every man lives for his own good and desires to attain "happiness";[29] hence "God is for me what I strive for" and that which "constitutes (his) my life"; yet He is such "that I cannot comprehend or name Him." He is always more than and beyond my experience or comprehension of Him, and this is good, for "if I understood Him, I should have reached Him, and there would be nothing to strive after and there would be no life . . . yet at the same time I know Him and the direction toward Him. . . . I am always anxious when I am without Him, and only when I am with Him am I not anxious."[30] "The chief thing

[24] *What Is Religion*, p. 273.
[25] *Gospel in Brief*, Preface, p. 410.
[26] *What Is Religion*, p. 272.
[27] *Ibid.*, p. 272.
[28] *Confessions*, Bk. X, ch. xx. p. 29.
[29] *Life*, Ch. I, p. 124.
[30] *Thoughts on God*, p. 370.

in this feeling is a consciousness of entire security, a consciousness that He is, that He is good, that He knows me, and that I am entirely surrounded by Him, that I have come from Him, and am going to Him, form a part of Him, am His child."[31]

These aphoristic *perçus* on religion might be extended indefinitely. God is also life and love; and when one is in God he is in love and evokes God in others, for love evokes love. Faith is the understanding of the meaning of human life, that understanding whereby man does not destroy himself, but lives.

The important clue, perhaps, is the word "direction"; religion is not a doctrine, but a way. The decisive importance of Jesus and the Gospels is that He shows us the way. Once again we are warned that not only is there nothing in common between the official Church and authentic Christianity, apart from the name, but their principles are absolutely opposed and hostile. It was in the teaching of the Gospels, not in theories about God and Christ, that Tolstoy "found the explanation of the spirit which animates the life of all who really live."[32] "I sought a solution to the problem of life, and not a theological or historical question; and that is why I was indifferent to know whether Jesus Christ is or is not God, and from whom proceeds the Holy Spirit, etc."[33] The important thing is that "Christianity . . . is the only doctrine which gives a meaning to life."

Tolstoy's *Gospel in Brief,* in which he has presented his own harmony of the Gospels and has translated very freely to bring out the meaning that he feels is to be found there, would merit a careful study on its own account. Two texts, however, will suffice to illustrate his method and the ways in which the Gospel speaks to him.

Whoever commits his life to him (the heavenly Son in man) does not die; but he who does not commit his life

[31] *Ibid.,* p. 383.
[32] *Gospel in Brief,* Preface, pp. 414, 415.

to him destroys himself thereby, in that he has not trusted to that which is life. Death consists in this, that life is come into the world, but men themselves go away from life.

—John 3:18, 19

The emphasis here falls upon the opposition of life and death. In the same way he translates Matthew 12:30: "It is necessary to be at one with the spirit of life. He who is not at one with it, is against it." Tolstoy is impressed with Christ's realism. He "spoke of life as it is, as it always will be; (but) we speak of an imaginary life [he has just spoken of the Fall, and Paradise, and Adam, entirely unknown to Christ and never mentioned by him] which has never existed. How, then, can we understand Christ's teaching." [34]

From these fragments alone it is easy to see that Tolstoy has driven a very firm wedge between the Gospels, as he sees them, and historical Christianity. To call Christ God would be, for him, idolatrous and blasphemous: it would destroy the inwardness of religion and would be, at bottom, a symptom of a deep lack of faith in God and in Christ's teaching. "I believe it to be the greatest sacrilege and an evident proof of heathenism, to regard him as God. To consider Jesus as God is to renounce God." [35]

In this Tolstoy is consistent, for "salvation," in the sense of some external power acting upon us in some miraculous way, is to him unnecessary. Our alienation from ourselves is one with our alienation from reality. Nevertheless, the life power is within us. "All that we require is given us": [36] we have only to be shown our true condition, our "misery without God," and to be shown the true way, and to walk in it.

[33] *Ibid.*
[34] My Religion from *The Collected Works of Leo Tolstoy*, Vol. IX, New York, Thomas Y. Crowell Co., 1899, p. 196.
[35] *Ibid.*, p. 366.
[36] *Ibid.*, p. 363.

Now it is just here that Tolstoy's religious outlook tends to become defective: as though an incomplete understanding of his own psychologic crisis prevented his probing deeply enough the dynamics of the human condition, of man's misery without God. His insight seems to teeter uncertainly between depth perceptions of a profound and psychologic kind and the rather superficial forms of rationalistic optimism concerning man that prevailed in his time. We must therefore note with some care two or three of the points where the *direction* of his thought anticipates much that we have since come to take for granted concerning the self.

In a very remarkable essay on Emile Zola entitled "Stop and Think!" Tolstoy points out that before Christ told men to love one another he told them to repent: "change (*mètanoeite*) your conception of life, said He, or you will all perish." One's well-being cannot consist in the pursuit of personal goods and gratifications. "Know then that the meaning of our life can lie only in fulfilling the will of Him who sent you into this life, and who demands from you . . . the accomplishment of His own purpose: the establishment of the Kingdom of Heaven." Tolstoy then goes on to urge that the very ills of our time result from the fact that we have not changed. If men would but cease their business for a moment, and reflect, they would see that their whole lives and all their actions "are in incessant and outrageous contradiction" to their reason and their heart. These men "who run singing toward a precipice" (again Pascal) "must cease their hubbub and stop short" (pp. 158-59).

But *metanoia* coincides with a deep crisis of the self, in which the eccentric, superficial life rotating about some Ego-image must be collapsed and the new being, based upon the deep Self, permitted to emerge. "We have only to stop in the efforts we are now making" to see that we must "Seek the Kingdom of Heaven and all other things will be added unto you" (p. 160). But while no one can by simple rational intent decrease his egocentricity, there is wisdom nevertheless in Tolstoy's appeal to Lao-Tze: "All the ills besetting mankind arise, not from man's neglect to do what is necessary, but because he does what is unnecessary" (p. 147).

Tolstoy is on securer ground in his *Preface to Amiel's Journal.* Classifying the book with those left by Marcus Aurelius, Pascal, and Epictetus, he quotes from Pascal:

There are only three kinds of men: first, those who, finding God, serve Him; secondly, those who, not finding Him, are occupied in the search for Him; and thirdly, those who neither find Him nor seek for Him.

The first are reasonable and happy; the last are unreasonable and unhappy; those between are unhappy but reasonable.

Tolstoy comments:

I think that the distinction established by Pascal between the first and second classes . . . does not even exist at all. I think that those who with all their hearts and with agony,—*en gémissant,* as Pascal says,—seek God, are already serving Him. They are serving Him by the fact that by these sufferings their searchings 'trace out and open t he way for others to reach God' (p. 190).

He then applies this to Amiel's life-long search for God, quoting at length that "interior soliloquy" of the man condemned to death "when the execution of the sentence is delayed."

He collects himself in his inmost tribunal. He no longer radiates, he psychologizes. . . . Like the hare he returns to his 'form' to die, and this 'form' is his conscience, his thought. It is also his *journal intime.* As long as he can hold his pen, and while he has a moment of solitude, he collects himself before this echo of himself, and converses with his God.

Tolstoy understands this in 1893; and he observes by way of Amiel that "we are all condemned to death and our execution is only postponed" (p. 369).

Once again we note how proximately the thought of death stands to his religious reflections. We have seen how it threw him back upon himself desperately and forced the major religious crisis of his life. Here he encountered the dragon, but emerged by way of "a stay" that helped him maintain his balance, and by means of which he recognized that the encounter with the deep Self is at the same time an encounter with Reality—with God. But God could not be known otherwise than from within; and He must be experienced as the life-giving relation of one's Self to the Infinite, which relation is one of power and love and joy. But this relation imposes upon me the obligation of fulfilling God's will for me. I must therefore walk in His way, observe the direction of this calling, and seek Him constantly in order to know through experience the God whom I cannot comprehend or name. My relation to Him is, therefore, a dynamic one; it is the going of a way.

The difference between the Christian and pagan teaching of goodness lies in this: that the heathen teaching is one of final perfection, while the Christian teaching is one of infinite perfecting, . . . the infinite perfecting of love. *"Be ye perfect, even as your Father in Heaven is perfect."*

This is, for Tolstoy, another pivotal text. The search for God becomes one with his sense of vocation and this in turn with the infinite perfecting of oneself in love. But when he goes on to say that this pursuit requires the renunciation of self, and yet also holds in his *Thoughts On God* (p. 372) that "by fulfilling God's will I realize God in myself, what He is" and therefore "my life should be the realization of what is highest in the flesh, of what He produces in me," we have to ask how these two views are to be reconciled. The answer will be found in his essay on *Life*.

This is rather a remarkable document. It contains all the perspectives that we have observed up to this point. But it adds something, something that might be called a plea for a maturing rational consciousness. Its argument cannot well be summarized in a few paragraphs; but the primary burden of it is contained in its first epigraph from Pascal:

Man is only a reed, the feeblest in nature; but he is a thinking reed. It is not necessary that the whole universe should rise in arms to crush him. A vapor, a drop of water, suffices to kill him. But if the entire universe were to crush him, man would still be more noble than that which slays him, because he knows that he is dying; and of the advantage which the universe possesses over him the universe knows nothing. Thus all our dignity consists in thought. It is that upon which we must take our stand, not upon space and duration. Let us, then, labor to think well; that is the principle of morals.

This is one thing in the mouth of Pascal; it may be quite another in that of Tolstoy. But the genius of Pascal presides over much of this writing. Tolstoy, as Pascal, is interested to establish the true order of thought (p. 112). He inveighs once more against those who violate this order through the purveying of false knowledge or false doctrines. By virtue of false teachers men submit to external guides rather than to reason. It is only the false doctrines of human life, compounded into customs, sacred duties, etc., which produce "that torturing condition of division into which men enter on the discovery in them of their rational consciousness' (p. 148). When he begins to think for himself he finds himself "alone in all the world, with all the terrible questions which rend his soul" (p. 144). But in spite of this curious conspiracy of suppression, "man cherishes in the depths of his soul an ineffaceable demand that his life shall be happy and have a rational meaning. . . . The time will come when a rational consciousness will outgrow the false doctrines, and man will come to a halt in the midst of life, and demand explanations" (pp. 142, 143).

This is a curious concept in Tolstoy, but all important to any appraisal of his religious consciousness. He distinguishes three orders, reminiscent of Pascal's "three orders": those of (1) rational beings; (2) animals; and (3) lifeless matter. The animal part, the animal personality, ought to be subordinated to the rational part, which is the true life of man. This true life is preserved in man as in a seed; and there comes a time when it makes its appearance. Tolstoy interestingly holds that it comes about the time when his animal personality is pointing him toward his own individual happiness. But now the rational consciousness points him towards another happiness. He cannot see at first just what this newer happiness is; but his awareness of it indubitably destroys his individual happiness, "and in the man there begins to form a new relation of his animal to his rational consciousness" (pp. 150, 151).

These are awkward terms in our current vocabulary. Tolstoy is obviously reflecting the emergence of a new consciousness in himself. It is like every birth. There is the same "annihilation of the germ of the previous form of life, and the appearance of a new shoot." Something drops away in order that the new may come into being. We do not perceive all this because we ourselves are living it; but "our life is nothing else than the birth of this being, invisible to us." Yet when the birth of the new comes, and the rational consciousness "emerges from its concealed condition" we seem to experience a painful contradiction, but it is merely the birth of a new being.

Tolstoy himself hardly knows what to do with this notion. It is obviously not "reason" in its discursive or analytical form. It is, indeed, that consciousness which transcends the reason and roots, as we should today say, in the Unconscious. At the same time it is "that law in accordance with which (one's) life is perfected" (p. 153). If we ignore it or refuse to make way for it and suppress it, "we deprive ourselves of our true happiness and our true life." Thus Tolstoy relates it on the one hand to the *Logos* of the Gospel of John; and on the other he recognizes it as the presupposition of all knowing: like Max Scheler's "capacity for self-transcendence" this consciousness is something "we do not see because we do not possess that highest point from which we might be able to observe it" (p. 166).

The simile of the *seed* carries implicitly a teleologic element. It reveals a new direction to the one who experiences it. He will more than likely take fright at this, at what it lays open before him. He may try to escape from it: but eventually he will come to recognize that "his life consists only in the movement upward" (p. 346). "He must understand that he has wings which raise him above the abyss." It is only a lack of faith that produces in him a division of consciousness.

It is in this wise that Tolstoy understands the imperative, "ye must be born again," as also the injunction "whoso saveth his life shall lose it. And he that loseth his life for my sake, shall find it." Or, in terms of the parable of the Talents,[37] "the meaning is that men must fulfill the will of Him that sent them into life." To refuse this burgeoning is, Tolstoy believes, what is meant by the sin against the Holy Spirit.

Two corollaries follow: (1) a man can no longer live for his personal happiness alone, his life reaches out to all mankind; and (2) true love becomes possible.

True love, before it becomes an active sentiment, must be a certain condition. The beginning of love, its root, is not a burst of feeling, clouding the reason, as is generally imagined, but is the most rational, luminous, and

[37] Private Letters from *The Collected Works of Leo Tolstoy,* Vol. XI, New York, Thomas Y. Crowell Co., 1899, p. 359.

therefore tranquil and joyous state, peculiar to children and to reasonable people (p. 204). . . . Love, according to the doctrine of Christ, is life itself (208).

Now it must be confessed that Tolstoy's ideas, at almost every point, tremble on the brink of nineteenth-century extravagances. When he speaks of the "divine spark" in each of us, he sounds like a Stoic; when he talks of God as all and in everything, he seems to echo Spinoza and the German romantics; when he dons his peasant's blouse, he may call back recollections of Rousseau in Armenian garb. He may have been an essentially pagan genius, like Goethe, as Thomas Mann contends, or he may have been, as Maxim Gorky saw him, an old and frustrated alchemist:

The old magician stands before me, alien to all, a solitary traveller through all the deserts of thought in search of an all-embracing truth which he has not found....[38]

Certainly he was a seeker, and a passionate one. He was also a Prodigal; but he was able to say, "When I came to myself." There are also points where his passion for happiness for all men passes over into a sort of Benthamite service to the greatest number. And I suspect that his translation of Luke 16: 16, "But, from John and to the present time, it is announced that the Kingdom of God is on earth, and that he who makes an effort enters into it," suppresses something, and that he himself was, perhaps, one of the "violent ones" who would have taken it by force. It is related that "the old magician" was standing one day at a railroad station, clad in his peasant's blouse, when a lady of means, descending from the train, summoned him to carry her luggage. Tolstoy readily complied; but when the lady paid him she recog-

[38] Quoted in George Steiner: *Tolstoy or Dostoievsky*, An Essay in the Old Criticism, New York, Alfred Knopf, 1959, p. 246.

nized the famous features of Russia's great man, and apologized. But Tolstoy merely laughed at the episode, which he had greatly enjoyed, forgave the woman, but said he would keep the coins for he had earned them. The peasant's blouse of Tolstoy will continue, no doubt, to be paid off in the small coin of our criticisms, still directed at his minor premises rather than at the major ones.

We have chosen, rather, to point to some things in these pages which may be of continuing interest to us. "Men have lost their way and are suffering in consequence," he wrote.[39] There is no doubt that we inherit a time of dearth, as Hölderlin called it, when many of our sustaining symbols and image structures have dropped away. We too, like Tolstoy, have been thrust abruptly upon ourselves.

As for the religious problem set forth bluntly by Tolstoy, a superbly fine word has been spoken by Abraham Heschel:

It is customary to blame secular science and antireligious philosophy for the eclipse of religion in modern society. It would be more honest to blame religion for its own defeats. Religion declined not because it was refuted, but because it became irrelevant, dull, oppressive, insipid. When faith is completely replaced by creed, worship by discipline, love by habit; when the crisis of today is ignored because of the splendor of the past; when faith becomes an heirloom rather than a living fountain; when religion speaks only in the name of authority rather than with the voice of compassion, its message becomes meaningless.[40]

We must be reminded of this from time to time. But there is that in Tolstoy which, read from our contemporary vantage point, strikes more deeply, and suggests that

[39] *Three Parables,* III, p. 324.
[40] *Between God and Man,* An Interpretation of Judaism, Ed. by Fritz A. Rothschild, New York, Harper & Brothers, 1959, p. 35.

our renewal of life's meanings must come about by way of the hero's quest and the prophet's courage—an adventure in depth through the eonian fire.

Tolstoy's oldest brother, Nicholas, came to Tolstoy once when he was a lad of nine, and told him solemnly that he had discovered a great secret. He had learned how to make the whole world happy. He had written the secret on a green stick, a magical stick, which he had buried near the highroad where it turned into the Zakaz Forest. The little Leo was much impressed with the story, so much so that he burst into tears in his excitement. Two or three years before his death, Count Leo Tolstoy dictated his will to his secretary: "Although it is unimportant, I should like to tell of one thing which I wish to be done after my death. . . . It is a trifle of trifles; yet, I wish that no ceremonies be performed at my burial. Let them put my body into a wooden coffin and, if it is not too much trouble, bury it near Zakaz Forest, at the place of "the green stick. . . ." When he spoke the name of the "green stick" the gray-haired Tolstoy burst into tears.

And his wishes were carried out. He was buried there, near the Zakaz Forest. The well, the pillar, and the little green stick—these, and the cruciform tree.

Stanley R. Hopper

Drew University
September 1959

The Religious Writings of Leo Tolstoy

MY CONFESSION

CHAPTER I

I WAS christened and educated in the Orthodox Christian Faith; I was taught it in my childhood, and in
my boyhood and youth. Nevertheless, when, at eighteen
years of age, I left the university in the second year, I
had discarded all belief in anything I had been taught.

To judge by what I can now remember, I never had
a serious belief; I merely trusted in what my elders
made their profession of faith, but even this trust was
very precarious. 1695261

I remember once in my twelfth year, a boy, now long
since dead, Volodinka M——, a pupil in the gymnasium,
spent a Sunday with us, and brought us the news of the
last discovery in the gymnasium. This discovery was
that there was no God, and that all we were taught on
the subject was a mere invention (this was in 1838). I
remember well how interested my elder brothers were
in this news; I was admitted to their deliberations, and
we all eagerly accepted the theory as something particularly attractive and possibly quite true.

I remember, also, that when my elder brother, Dmitri,
then at the university, with the impulsiveness natural to
his character, gave himself up to a passionate faith, began to attend the church services regularly, to fast, and
to lead a pure and moral life, we all of us, and some
older than ourselves, never ceased to hold him up to
ridicule, and for some incomprehensible reason gave him
the nickname of Noah. I remember that Musin-Push-
kin, then curator of the University of Kazan, having invited us to a ball, tried to persuade my brother, who had

refused the invitation, by the jeering argument that even David danced before the Ark.

I sympathized then with these jokes of my elders, and drew from them this conclusion, — that I was bound to learn my catechism, and go to church, but that it was not necessary to take all this too seriously.

I also remember that I read Voltaire when I was very young, and that his tone of mockery amused without disgusting me.

This estrangement from all belief went on in me, as it does now, and always has done, in those of the same social position and culture. This falling off, as it seems to me, for the most part goes on thus: people live as others live, and their lives are guided, not by the principles of the faith that is taught them, but by their very opposite; belief has no influence on life, nor on the relations among men — it is relegated to some other sphere apart from life and independent of it; if the two ever come into contact at all, belief is only one of the outward phenomena, and not one of the constituent parts of life.

By a man's life, by his acts, it was then, as it is now, impossible to know whether he was a believer or not. If there be a difference between one who openly professes the doctrines of the Orthodox Church, and one who denies them, the difference is to the advantage of the former. Then, as now, the open profession of the Orthodox doctrines was found mostly among dull, stern, immoral men, and those who think much of their own importance. Intellect, honor, frankness, good nature, and morality are oftener met with among those who call themselves disbelievers.

The school-boy is taught his catechism and sent to church; chinovniks, or functionaries, are required to show a certificate of having taken the holy communion. But the man belonging to our class, who is done with school and does not enter the public service, may now live a dozen years — still more was this the case formerly — without being once reminded of the fact that he lives among Christians, and is reckoned as a member of the Orthodox Christian Church.

Thus it happens that now, as formerly, the influence of early religious teaching, accepted merely on trust and upheld by authority, gradually fades away under the knowledge and practical experience of life, which is opposed to all its principles, and that a man often believes for years that his early faith is still intact, while all the time not a trace of it remains in him.

A certain S——, a clever and veracious man, once related to me how he came to give up his belief.

Twenty-six years ago, while he was off on a hunting expedition, he knelt down to pray before he lay down to rest, according to a habit of his from childhood. His elder brother, who was of the party, lay on some straw and watched him. When S—— had finished, and was preparing to lie down, his brother said to him :—

" Ah, so you still keep that up ? "

Nothing more passed between them, but from that day S—— ceased to pray and to go to church. For thirty years S—— has not said a prayer, has not taken the communion, has not been in a church, — not because he shared the convictions of his brother, or even knew them, — not because he had come to any conclusions of his own, — but because his brother's words were like the push of a finger against a wall ready to tumble over with its own weight; they proved to him that what he had taken for belief was an empty form, and that consequently every word he uttered, every sign of the cross he made, every time he bowed his head during his prayers, his act was unmeaning. When he once admitted to himself that such acts had no meaning in them, he could not continue them.

Thus it has been, and is, I believe, with the large majority of men. I am speaking of men of our class, I am speaking of men who are true to themselves, and not of those who make of religion a means of obtaining some temporal advantage. (These men are truly absolute unbelievers; for if faith be to them a means of obtaining any worldly end, it is most certainly no faith at all.) Such men of our own class are in this position : the light of knowledge and life has melted the artifi-

cially constructed edifice of belief within, and they have
either observed that and cleared away the superincumbent
ruins, or they have remained unconscious of it.

The belief instilled from childhood in me, as in so
many others, gradually disappeared, but with this difference; that as from fifteen years of age I had begun to
read philosophical works, I became very early conscious
of my own disbelief. From the age of sixteen I ceased
to pray, and ceased, from conviction, to attend the services of the church and to fast. I no longer accepted
the faith of my childhood, but I believed in something,
though I could not exactly explain in what. I believed
in a God, — or rather, I did not deny the existence of a
God, — but what kind of God I could not have told; I
denied neither Christ nor His teaching, but in what that
teaching consisted I could not have said.

Now, when I think over that time, I see clearly that all
the faith I had, the only belief which, apart from mere
animal instinct, swayed my life, was a belief in the possibility of perfection, though what it was in itself, or
what would be its results, I could not have said.

I tried to reach intellectual perfection; my studies
were extended in every direction of which my life afforded me a chance; I strove to strengthen my will,
forming for myself rules which I forced myself to follow; I did my best to develop my physical powers by
every exercise calculated to give strength and agility,
and by way of accustoming myself to patient endur-
ance; I subjected myself to many voluntary hardships
and trials of privation. All this I looked on as necessary to obtain the perfection at which I aimed.

At first, of course, moral perfection seemed to me the
main end, but I soon found myself contemplating in its
stead an ideal of general perfectibility; in other words,
I wished to be better, not in my own eyes nor in God's,
but in the sight of other men. And very soon this striving to be better in the sight of men feeling again changed
into another, — the desire to have more power than
others, to secure for myself a greater share of fame, of
social distinction, and of wealth.

CHAPTER II

AT some future time I may relate the story of my life, and dwell in detail on the pathetic and instructive incidents of my youth. I think that many and many have had the same experiences as I did. I desired with all my soul to be good; but I was young, I had passions, and I was alone, wholly alone, in my search after goodness. Every time I tried to express the longings of my heart to be morally good, I was met with contempt and ridicule, but as soon as I gave way to low passions, I was praised and encouraged.

Ambition, love of power, love of gain, lechery, pride, anger, vengeance, were held in high esteem.

As I gave way to these passions, I became like my elders, and I felt that they were satisfied with me. A kind-hearted aunt of mine, a really good woman with whom I lived, used to say to me that there was one thing above all others which she wished for me — an intrigue with a married woman: "*Rien ne forme un jeune homme, comme une liaison avec une femme comme il faut.*" Another of her wishes for my happiness was that I should become an adjutant, and, if possible, to the Emperor; the greatest piece of good fortune of all she thought would be that I should find a very wealthy bride, who would bring me as her dowry as many slaves as could be.

I cannot now recall those years without a painful feeling of horror and loathing.

I put men to death in war, I fought duels to slay others, I lost at cards, wasted my substance wrung from the sweat of peasants, punished the latter cruelly, rioted with loose women, and deceived men. Lying, robbery, adultery of all kinds, drunkenness, violence, murder. .... There was not one crime which I did not commit, and yet I was not the less considered by my equals a comparatively moral man.

Such was my life during ten years.

During that time I began to write, out of vanity, love of gain, and pride. I followed as a writer the same path which I had chosen as a man. In order to obtain the fame and the money for which I wrote, I was obliged to hide what was good and to say what was evil. Thus I did. How often while writing have I cudgeled my brains to conceal under the mask of indifference or pleasantry those yearnings for something better which formed the real thought of my life. I succeeded in this also, and was praised.

At twenty-six years of age, on the close of the war, I came to Petersburg and made the acquaintance of the authors of the day. I met with a hearty reception and much flattery.

Before I had time to look around, the prejudices and views of life common to the writers of the class with which I associated became my own, and completely put an end to all my former struggles after a better life. These views, under the influence of the dissipation of my life, supplied a theory which justified it.

The view of life taken by these my fellow-writers was that life is a development, and the principal part in that development is played by ourselves, the thinkers, while among the thinkers the chief influence is again due to us, the artists, the poets. Our vocation is to teach men.

In order to avoid answering the very natural question, "What do I know, and what can I teach?" the theory in question is made to contain the formula that it is not necessary to know this, but that the artist and the poet teach unconsciously.

I was myself considered a marvelous artist and poet, and I therefore very naturally adopted this theory. I, an artist and poet, wrote and taught I knew not what. For doing this I received money; I kept a splendid table, had excellent lodgings, women, society; I had fame. Naturally what I taught was very good.

The faith in poetry and the development of life was a true faith, and I was one of its priests. To be one of its priests was very advantageous and agreeable. I long remained in this belief, and never once doubted its truth.

But in the second, and especially in the third year of

this way of life, I began to doubt the infallibility of the doctrine, and to examine it more closely. What first led me to doubt was the fact that I began to notice the priests of this belief did not agree among themselves. Some said : —

"We are the best and most useful teachers; we teach what is needful, and all others teach wrong."

They disputed, quarreled, abused, deceived, and cheated one another. Moreover, there were many among us who, quite indifferent to the question who was right or who was wrong, advanced only their own private interests by the aid of our activity. All this forced on me doubts as to the truth of our belief.

Again, having begun to doubt the truth of our literary faith, I began to study its priests more closely, and became convinced that almost all the priests of this faith were immoral men, most of them worthless and insignificant, and beneath the moral level of those with whom I associated during my former dissipated and military career; but conceited and self-satisfied as only those can be who are wholly saints, or those who know not what holiness is.

I grew disgusted with mankind and with myself, and I understood that this belief was a delusion. The strangest thing in all this was that, though I soon saw the falseness of this belief and renounced it, I did not renounce the rank given me by these men, — the rank of artist, poet, teacher. I was simple enough to imagine that I was a poet and artist, and could teach all men without knowing what I was teaching. But so I did.

By my companionship with these men I had gained a new vice, —·a pride developed to a morbid extreme, and an insane self-confidence in teaching men what I myself did not know.

When I now think over that time, and remember my own state of mind and that of these men (a state of mind common enough among thousands still), it seems to me pitiful, terrible, and ridiculous; it excites the feelings which overcome us as we pass through a madhouse.

We were all then convinced that it behooved us to

speak, to write, and to print as fast as we could, as much as we could, and that on this depended the welfare of the human race. And thousands of us wrote, printed, and taught, and all the while confuted and abused one another. Quite unconscious that we ourselves knew nothing, that to the simplest of all problems in life — what is right and what is wrong — we had no answer, we all went on talking together without one to listen, at times abetting and praising one another on condition that we were abetted and praised in turn, and again turning upon one another in wrath — in short, we reproduced the scenes in a madhouse.

Thousands of laborers worked day and night, to the limit of their strength, setting up the type and printing millions of words to be spread by the post all over Russia, and still we continued to teach, unable to teach enough, angrily complaining the while that we were not much listened to.

A strange state of things indeed, but now it is comprehensible to me. The real motive that inspired all our reasoning was the desire for money and praise, to obtain which we knew of no other means than writing books and newspapers, and so we did. But in order to hold fast to the conviction that while thus uselessly employed we were very important men, it was necessary to justify our occupation to ourselves by another theory, and the following was the one we adopted : —

Whatever is, is right; everything that is, is due to development; development comes from civilization; the measure of civilization is the diffusion of books and newspapers; we are paid and honored for the books and newspapers which we write, and we are therefore the most useful and best of men!

This reasoning might have been conclusive had we all been agreed; but, as for every opinion expressed by one of us there instantly appeared from another one diametrically opposite, we had to hesitate before accepting it. But we did not notice this; we received money, and were praised by those of our party, consequently we — each one of us — considered that we were in the right.

It is now clear to me that between ourselves and the inhabitants of a madhouse there was no difference: at the time I only vaguely suspected this, and, like all madmen, thought all were mad except myself.

CHAPTER III

I LIVED in this senseless manner another six years, up to the time of my marriage. During this time I went abroad. My life in Europe, and my acquaintance with many eminent and learned foreigners, confirmed my belief in the doctrine of general perfectibility, as I found the same theory prevailed among them. This belief took the form which is common among most of the cultivated men of our day. This belief was expressed in the word "progress." It then appeared to me this word had a real meaning. I did not as yet understand that, tormented like every other man by the question, "How was I to live better?" when I answered that I must live for progress, I was only repeating the answer of a man carried away in a boat by the waves and the wind, who to the one important question for him, "Where are we to steer?" should answer, "We are being carried somewhere."

I did not see this then; only at rare intervals my feelings, and not my reason, were roused against the common superstition of our age, which leads men to ignore their own ignorance of life.

Thus, during my stay in Paris, the sight of a public execution revealed to me the weakness of my superstitious belief in progress. When I saw the head divided from the body, and heard the sound with which they fell separately into the box, I understood, not with my reason, but with my whole being, that no theory of the wisdom of all established things, nor of progress, could justify such an act; and that if all the men in the world from the day of creation, by whatever theory, had found this thing necessary, I knew it was not necessary, it was a bad thing, and that therefore I must judge of what was right and necessary, not by what men said and did, not by progress, but what I felt to be true in my heart.

Another instance of the insufficiency of this super-stition of progress as a rule for life was the death of my brother. He fell ill while still young, suffered much during a whole year, and died in great pain. He was a man of good abilities, of a kind heart, and of a serious temper, but he died without understanding why he had lived, and still less what his death meant for him. No theories could give an answer to these questions, either to him or to me, during the whole period of his long and painful lingering.

But these occasions for doubt were few and far be-tween; on the whole, I continued to live in the profes-sion of the faith of progress. "Everything develops, and I myself am developing; and why this is so will one day be apparent," was the formula I was obliged to adopt.

On my return from abroad I settled in the country, and occupied myself with the organization of schools for the peasantry. This occupation was especially dear to my heart, because it was free from the spirit of false-ness so evident to me in the career of a literary teacher.

Here again I acted in the name of progress, but this time I brought a spirit of critical inquiry to the system on which the progress rested. I said to myself that progress was often attempted in an irrational manner, and that it was necessary to leave a primitive people and the children of peasants perfectly free to choose the way of progress which they thought best. In reality I was still bent on the solution of the same im-possible problem, — how to teach without knowing what I had to teach. In the highest spheres of literature I had understood that it was impossible to do this be-cause I had seen that each taught differently, and that the teachers quarreled among themselves, and scarcely succeeded in concealing their ignorance from one another. Having now to deal with peasants' children. I thought that I could get over this difficulty by allow-ing the children to learn what they liked. It seems now absurd when I remember the expedients by which I carried out this whim of mine to teach, though I knew in my heart that I could teach nothing useful, because I myself did not know what was necessary.[1]

After a year spent in this employment with the school I again went abroad, for the purpose of finding out how I was to teach without knowing anything.

I believed that I had found a solution abroad, and, armed with all that essence of wisdom, I returned to Russia, the same year in which the peasants were freed from serfdom; and, accepting the office of arbitrator,[2] I began to teach the uneducated people in the schools, and the educated classes in the journal which I began to publish. Things seemed to be going on well, but I felt that my mind was not in a normal state and that a change was near. I might even then, perhaps, have come to that state of despair to which I was brought fifteen years later, if it had not been for a new experience in life which promised me safety — family life.

For a year I was occupied with arbitration, with the schools, and with my newspaper, and got so involved that I was harassed to death; the struggle over the arbitration was so hard for me, my activity in the schools was so dubious to me, my shuffling in the newspaper became so repugnant to me, consisting as it did in forever the same thing, — in the desire to teach all people and to hide the fact that I did not know how or what to teach, — that I fell ill, more with a mental than physical sickness, gave up everything, and started for the steppes to the Bashkirs to breathe a fresher air, to drink kumiss, and live an animal life.

After I returned I married. The new circumstances of a happy family life completely led me away from the search after the meaning of life as a whole. My life was concentrated at this time in my family, my wife and children, and consequently in the care for increasing the means of life. The effort to effect my own individual perfection, already replaced by the striving

[1] See "School Scenes from Yasnaya Polyana," Vol. XV.
[2] *Posrednik,* sometimes translated Justice of the Peace.

after general progress, was again changed into an effort to secure the particular happiness of my family.

In this way fifteen years passed.

Notwithstanding that during these fifteen years I looked upon the craft of authorship as a very trifling thing, I continued all the time to write. I had experienced the seductions of authorship, the temptations of an enormous pecuniary reward and of great applause for valueless work, and gave myself up to it as a means of improving my material position, and of stifling in my soul all questions regarding my own life and life in general. In my writings I taught what for me was the only truth, — that the object of life should be our highest happiness and that of our family.

Thus I lived; but, five years ago, a strange state of mind began to grow upon me: I had moments of perplexity, of a stoppage, as it were, of life, as if I did not know how I was to live, what I was to do, and I began to wander, and was a victim to low spirits. But this passed, and I continued to live as before. Later, these periods of perplexity began to return more and more frequently, and invariably took the same form. These stoppages of life always presented themselves to me with the same questions: "Why?" and "What after?"

At first it seemed to me that these were aimless, unmeaning questions; it seemed to me that all they asked about was well known, and that if at any time when I wished to find answers to them I could do so without much trouble — that just at that time I could not be bothered with this, but whenever I should stop to think them over I should find an answer. But these questions presented themselves to my mind with ever increasing frequency, demanding an answer with still greater and greater persistence, and like dots grouped themselves into one black spot.

It was with me as it happens in the case of every mortal internal ailment — at first appear the insignificant symptoms of indisposition, disregarded by the patient; then these symptoms are repeated more and more frequently, till they merge in uninterrupted suffering. The sufferings increase, and the patient, before he has time to look around, is confronted with the fact that what he took for a mere indisposition has become more important to him than anything else on earth, that it is death!

This is exactly what happened to me. I became aware that this was not a chance indisposition, but something very serious, and that if all these questions continued to recur, I should have to find an answer to them. And I tried to answer them. The questions seemed so foolish, so simple, so childish; but no sooner had I taken hold of them and attempted to decide them than I was convinced, first, that they were neither childish nor silly, but were concerned with the deepest problems of life; and, in the second place, that I could not decide them — could not decide them, however I put my mind upon them.

Before occupying myself with my Samara estate, with the education of my son, with the writing of books, I was bound to know why I did these things. As long as I do not know the reason "why" I cannot do anything, I cannot live. While thinking about the management of my household and estate,[1] which in these days occupied much of my time, suddenly this question came into my head : —

"Well and good, I have now six thousand desyatins in the government of Samara, and three hundred horses — what then?"

I was perfectly disconcerted, and knew not what to think. Another time, dwelling on the thought of how I should educate my children, I asked myself, "*Why?*" Again, when considering by what means the well-being of the people might best be promoted, I suddenly exclaimed, "But what concern have I with it?" When I thought of the fame which my works were gaining me, I said to myself : —

"Well, what if I should be more famous than Gogol, Pushkin, Shakespear, Molière — than all the writers of the world — well, and what then?"....

I could find no reply. Such questions will not wait :

[1] All this expressed in the one word *khozyaïstvo*.

they demand an immediate answer; without one it is impossible to live; but answer there was none.

I felt that the ground on which I stood was crumbling, that there was nothing for me to stand on, that what I had been living for was nothing, that I had no reason for living.

CHAPTER IV

My life had come to a stop. I was able to breathe, to eat, to drink, to sleep, and I could not help breathing, eating, drinking, sleeping; but there was no real life in me because I had not a single desire, the fulfilment of which I could feel to be reasonable. If I wished for anything, I knew beforehand that, were I to satisfy the wish, or were I not to satisfy it, nothing would come of it. Had a fairy appeared and offered me all I desired, I should not have known what to say. If I had, in moments of excitement, I will not say wishes, but the habits of former wishes, at calmer moments I knew that it was a delusion, that I really wished for nothing. I could not even wish to know the truth, because I guessed in what it consisted.

The truth was, that life was meaningless. Every day of life, every step in it, brought me, as it were, nearer the precipice, and I saw clearly that before me there was nothing but ruin. And to stop was impossible; to go back was impossible; and it was impossible to shut my eyes so as not to see that there was nothing before me but suffering and actual death, absolute annihilation.

Thus I, a healthy and a happy man, was brought to feel that I could live no longer, — some irresistible force was dragging me onward to escape from life. I do not mean that I wanted to kill myself.

The force that drew me away from life was stronger, fuller, and more universal than any wish; it was a force like that of my previous attachment to life, only in a contrary direction. With all my force I struggled away from life. The idea of suicide came as naturally to me as formerly that of bettering my life. This thought was so attractive to me that I was compelled to practise upon myself a species of self-deception in order to avoid carrying it out too hastily.   I was unwilling to act hastily, only because I wanted to employ all my powers in clearing away the confusion of my thoughts; if I should not clear them away, I could at any time kill myself. And here was I, a man fortunately situated, hiding away a cord, to avoid being tempted to hang myself by it to the transom between the closets of my room, where I undressed alone every evening; and I ceased to go hunting with a gun because it offered too easy a way of getting rid of life.   I knew not what I wanted; I was afraid of life; I struggled to get away from it, and yet there *was* something I hoped for from it.

Such was the condition I had to come to, at a time when all the circumstances of my life were pre-eminently happy ones, and when I had not reached my fiftieth year.   I had a good, loving, and beloved wife, good children, and a large estate, which, without much trouble on my part, was growing and increasing; I was more than ever respected by my friends and acquaintances; I was praised by strangers, and could lay claim to having made my name famous without much self-deception.   Moreover, I was not mad or in an unhealthy mental state; on the contrary, I enjoyed a mental and physical strength which I have seldom found in men of my class and pursuits; I could keep up with a peasant in mowing, and could continue mental labor for eight or ten hours at a stretch, without any evil consequences.   And in this state of things it came to this, — that I could not live, and as I feared death I was obliged to employ ruses against myself so as not to put an end to my life.

The mental state in which I then was seemed to me summed up in the following: My life was a foolish and wicked joke played on me by some one.   Notwithstanding the fact that I did not recognize a "Some one," who may have created me, this conclusion that some one had wickedly and foolishly made a joke of me in bringing me into the world seemed to me the most natural of all conclusions.

I could not help reasoning that *there*, somewhere, is some one who is now diverting himself at my expense, as he watches me, as after from thirty to forty years of a life of study and development, of mental and bodily growth, with all my powers matured and having reached that summit of life from which it is seen in its completeness, I stand like a fool on this height, understanding clearly that there is nothing in life, that there never was anything, and never will be. To him it must seem ridiculous.

But whether there is, or is not, such a being, in either case it did not help me. I could not attribute a reasonable motive to any single act in my whole life. I was only astonished that I could not have realized this at the very beginning. All this had so long been known to me! Illness and death would come (indeed, they had come), if not to-day, then to-morrow, to those whom I loved, to myself, and nothing remains but stench and worms. All my acts, whatever I did, would sooner or later be forgotten, and I myself be nowhere. Why, then, busy one's self with anything? How could men fail to see this, and live? How wonderful this is! It is possible to live only as long as life intoxicates us; as soon as we are sober again we see that it is all a delusion, and a stupid delusion! In this, indeed, there is nothing either ludicrous or amusing; it is only cruel and stupid!

There is an old Eastern fable about a traveler in the steppes who is attacked by a furious wild beast. To save himself the traveler gets into a waterless well; but at the bottom of it he sees a dragon with its jaws wide open to devour him. The unhappy man dares not get out for fear of the wild beast, and dares not descend for fear of the dragon, so he catches hold of the branch of a wild plant growing in a crevice of the well. His arms grow tired, and he feels that he must soon perish, death awaiting him on either side, but he still holds on; and he sees two mice, one black and one white, gradually making their way round the stem of the wild plant on which he is hanging, nibbling it through. The plant will soon give way and break off, and he will fall into the jaws of the dragon. The traveler sees this, and knows that he must inevitably perish; but, while still hanging, he looks around him, and, finding some drops of honey on the leaves of the wild plant, he stretches out his tongue and licks them.

Thus do I cling to the branch of life, knowing that the dragon of death inevitably awaits me, ready to tear me to pieces, and I cannot understand why such tortures have fallen to my lot. I also strive to suck the honey which once comforted me, but this honey no longer rejoices me, while the white mouse and the black, day and night, gnaw through the branch to which I cling. I see the dragon plainly, and the honey is no longer sweet. I see the dragon, from which there is no escape, and the mice, and I cannot turn my eyes away from them. It is no fable, but a living, undeniable truth, to be understood of all men.

The former delusion of happiness in life which hid from me the horror of the dragon no longer deceives me. However I may reason with myself that I cannot understand the meaning of life, that I must live without thinking, I cannot do this, because I have done so too long already. Now I cannot help seeing the days and nights hurrying by and bringing me nearer to death. I can see but this, because this alone is true — all the rest is a lie. The two drops of honey, which more than anything else drew my eyes away from the cruel truth, my love for my family and for my writings, to which latter I gave the name of art, were no longer sweet to me.

"My family," I said to myself; "but a family — a wife and children — are also human beings, and subject to the same conditions as I myself; they must either be living in a lie, or they must see the terrible truth. Why should they live? Why should I love them, care for them, bring them up, and watch over them? To bring them to the despair which fills myself, or to make dolts of them? As I love them, I cannot conceal from them the truth — every step they take in knowledge leads them to it, and that truth is death."

"Art, poetry?" ....

Under the influence of success, and flattered by praise, I had long been persuading myself that this was a work which must be done notwithstanding the approach of death, which would destroy everything — my writings, and the memory of them; but I soon saw that this was only another delusion, I saw clearly that art is only the ornament and charm of life. Life having lost its charm for me, how could I make others see a charm in it? While I was not living my own life, but one that was external to me was bearing me away on its billows, while I believed that life had a meaning, though I could not say what it was, the reflections of life of every kind in poetry and art gave me delight, it was pleasant to me to look at life in the mirror of art; but when I tried to discover the meaning of life, when I felt the necessity of living myself, the mirror became either unnecessary, superfluous, and ridiculous, or painful. I could no longer take comfort from what I saw in the mirror — that my position was stupid and desperate.

It was a genuine cause of rejoicing when in the depths of my soul I believed that my life had a meaning. Then this play of lights, the comic, the tragic, the pathetic, the beautiful, and the terrible in life, amused me. But when I knew that life was meaningless and terrible, the play in the mirror could no longer entertain me. No sweetness could be sweet to me when I saw the dragon, and the mice nibbling away my support.

Nor was that all. Had I simply come to know that life has no meaning, I might have quietly accepted it, might have known that was my allotted portion. But I could not rest calmly on this. Had I been like a man living in a forest, out of which he knows that there is no issue, I could have lived on; but I was like a man lost in a forest, and who, terrified by the thought that he is lost, rushes about trying to find a way out, and, though he knows each step leads him still farther astray, cannot help rushing about.

It was this that was terrible! And to get free from this horror, I was ready to kill myself. I felt a horror of what awaited me; I knew that this horror was more horrible than the position itself, but I could not patiently await the end. However persuasive the argument might be that all the same a blood-vessel in the heart would be ruptured or something would burst and all be over, still I could not patiently await the end. The horror of the darkness was too great to bear, and I longed to free myself from it as speedily as possible by a rope or a pistol ball. This was the feeling that, above all, drew me to think of suicide.

CHAPTER V

" But is it possible that I have overlooked something, that I have failed to understand something," I asked myself; "may it not be that this state of despair is common among men?"

And in every branch of human knowledge I sought an explanation of the questions that tormented me; I sought that explanation painfully and long, not out of mere curiosity; I did not seek it indolently, but painfully, obstinately, day and night; I sought it as a perishing man seeks safety, and I found nothing.

I sought it in all branches of knowledge, and not only did I fail, but, moreover, I convinced myself that all those who had searched like myself had likewise found nothing; and not only had found nothing, but had come, as I had, to the despairing conviction, that the only absolute knowledge man can possess is this, — that life is without meaning.

I sought in all directions, and thanks to a life spent in study, and also to my connections with the learned world, the most accomplished scholars in all the various branches of knowledge were accessible to me, and they did not refuse to open to me all the sources of knowledge both in books and through personal intercourse. I knew all that learning could answer to the question, "What is life?"

It was long before I could believe that human learning had no clear answer to this question. For a long time it seemed to me, as I listened to the gravity and seriousness of tone wherewith Science affirmed its positions on matters unconnected with the problem of life, that I must have misunderstood something. For a long time I was timid in the presence of learning, and I fancied that the insufficiency of the answers which I received was not its fault, but was owing to my own gross ignorance; but this thing was not a joke or pastime with me, but the business of my life, and I was at last forced, willy-nilly, to the conclusion that these questions of mine were the only legitimate questions underlying all knowledge, and that it was not I that was in fault in putting them, but science in pretending to have an answer to them.

The question, which in my fiftieth year had brought me to the notion of suicide, was the simplest of all questions, lying in the soul of every man, from the undeveloped child to wisest sage; a question without which, as I had myself experienced, life was impossible. That question was as follows : —

"What will come from what I am doing now, and may do to-morrow? what will come from my whole life?"

Otherwise expressed, the question will be this : —

"Why should I live? why should I wish for anything? why should I do anything?"

Again, in other words, it is :

"Is there any meaning in my life which will not be destroyed by the inevitable death awaiting me?"

To this question, one and the same though variously expressed, I sought an answer in human knowledge, and I found that with respect to this question all human knowledge may be divided as it were into two opposite hemispheres with their two opposite poles, the one negative, the other positive; but that at neither pole is to be found any answer to the problems of life.

One system of knowledge seems to deny that there is such a question, but, on the other hand, has a clear and exact answer to all its own independent inquiries; this is the system of experimental science, at the extreme end of which is mathematics. Another system accepts the question, but does not answer it; it is that of abstract philosophy, and at its extremity is metaphysics.

I had been addicted from my early youth to abstract studies, but later, mathematics and the natural sciences attracted me; and till I came to put clearly to myself this question as to the meaning of life, until it grew up in me, as it were, of itself, and demanded an immediate answer, I was content with the artificial and conventional answers given by learning.

In the domain of experience I said to myself:—

"Everything develops and becomes differentiated, tends to complication and perfection, and there are laws which govern this process. You are a part of the whole. If you learn as much as possible of this whole, and if you learn the law of its development, you will then know your own place in the great unity, and know yourself as well."

I am ashamed to confess it, but there was a time when I was satisfied with this. It was the very time when I was myself developing,—when my muscles were growing stronger, my memory was becoming enriched, my powers of thinking and understanding were on the increase,—and I, being conscious of this growth, very naturally thought that the law of my own growth was the law of the universe and explained the meaning of my own life.

But the time came when I had ceased to grow, and I felt that I was not developing, but drying up; my muscles grew weaker, my teeth began to fall out, and I saw that this law of growth not only explained nothing, but that such a law did not and could not exist; that I had taken for a general law what only affected myself at a certain age.

I looked more closely into the nature of this law and it became clear to me that there could be no laws of eternal development; it became clear to me, that to say everything in infinite space and time is developed, complicated, differentiated, and perfected, is to talk nonsense. Such words have no meaning, for in the infinite there can be no simple or compound, or past or future, or better or worse.

The main thing was that my personal question, "What am I with my desires?" remained absolutely without an answer. I understood that these branches of knowledge were very interesting, very attractive, but that they were clear and exact in inverse proportion to their applicability to the questions of life. The less they had to do with these questions, the clearer and more exact they were; the more they attempted to answer these questions, the obscurer and less attractive they became. If we turn to those branches of knowledge which have attempted to answer the problems of life, to physiology, psychology, biology, sociology, we meet with a striking poverty of thought, with the greatest obscurity, with an utterly unjustifiable pretension to decide questions beyond their competence, and a constant contradiction of one thinker by another, and even by himself. If we turn to the branches of knowledge which are not concerned with the problems of life, but find an answer to their own particular scientific questions, we are lost in admiration of human intellect; but we know beforehand that we shall get no answer to our questions about life itself, for these branches of knowledge directly ignore the question of life.

They say : —

"We cannot tell you what you are and why you live; such questions we do not study. But if you wish to know the laws of light, of chemical affinities, of the development of organisms; if you wish to know the laws that govern different bodies, their forms, and relations to number and size ; if you wish to know the laws of your own mind, — we can give you clear, exact, and absolutely certain answers."

The relation of experimental science to the question of the meaning of life may be put thus : —

Question. " Why do I live ? "

Answer. " Infinitely small particles, in infinite combinations, in infinite space and infinite time, change their forms in infinite combinations, and when you have learned the laws of these changes, you will know why you live."

I used to say to myself when theorizing, " Spiritual causes lie at the root of man's life and development, and they are the ideals which govern him. These ideals find expression in religion, in the sciences, in the arts, and in the forms of government. These ideals rise ever higher and higher from one stage to another, till man at last reaches his highest good. I am a part of humanity, and am therefore called upon to assist in making the ideals of humanity known and accepted."

In the days of my mental weakness I was satisfied with this reasoning ; but as soon as the problem of life really, as it were, arose within me, the whole theory fell to pieces at once. Not to speak of the dishonest inaccuracy, by which learning of this kind is made to give as general results those due to the study of but a small part of mankind ; not to speak of the many contradictions among the various champions of this theory, as to what are the ideals of humanity, — the strangeness, if it be not the silliness, of this way of thinking is that, in order to answer the question which occurs to every man, — " What am I ? " or " Why do I live ? " or " What am I to do ? " — a man must first answer this other question : —

" What is the life of that humanity, to us unknown, mankind, of which we are acquainted with but one minute part in one minute period of time ? "

In order to understand what he himself is, a man must first know what that mysterious humanity is which is formed of other men like himself, ignorant of what they are.

I must confess there was a time when I believed this. That was the time when I had my own cherished ideals which determined my caprices, and I strove to evolve a theory which should enable me to look on my fancies as a law of humanity. But as soon as the question of the meaning of life made itself clearly felt within me, this answer was scattered in dust. And I understood that, as in the experimental sciences there are real sciences and semi-sciences which try to give answers to questions not appropriate to them, so in the domain of theoretical knowledge is there a whole series of widely diffused philosophies which attempt to answer questions not appropriate to them. The semi-sciences of this domain, jurisprudence and historical sociology, endeavor to decide the questions concerning man and his life, by deciding, each in his own way, another question, that of the life of humanity as a whole.

But, as in the domain of the experimental sciences, a man who earnestly asks, "How am I to live?" cannot be satisfied with the answer, "Study in infinite space and time the infinite combinations and changes of infinite particles, and thou wilt know what thy own life means;" so a sincere man cannot be satisfied with this other answer, "Study the life of humanity as a whole, and then, though we know neither its beginning nor its end, and are ignorant of its parts, thou wilt know what thy life means."

It is the same with these semi-sciences as with the semi-experimental ones; they are full of obscurities, inaccuracies, stupidities, and contradictions, exactly in proportion to their divergence from their proper sphere. The problem of experimental science is the succession of cause and effect in material phenomena. If the question of a finite cause is raised, experimental science stumbles against an absurdity. The problem of speculative science is the conception of the uncaused existence of life. If the question of the cause of phenomena is raised, — as, for instance, of social and historical phenomena, — speculative science lands also in an absurdity.

Experimental science has positive significance, and shows the greatness of man's intellect, only when it does not inquire into finite causes; while, on the contrary, speculative science shows the greatness of man's intellect, is a science at all only when it entirely puts aside all questions of the succession of phenomena, and looks upon man only in relation to finite causes. Such in this department of science, constituting its pole, is metaphysics, or philosophy.

This science puts the question clearly, "What am I, and what is the whole universe? Why do I and the universe exist?" and it has always answered it in the same way. Whatever name the philosopher may give to the principle of life existing in me and in all other living beings, whether he call it an idea, a substance, a spirit, or a will, he still says ever that it is a reality, and that I have a real existence; but why this is so he does not know, and does not try to explain if he is an exact thinker.

I ask: "Why should this reality be? What comes of the fact that it is and will be?" Philosophy not only cannot answer, but it can only put the same question. And if it be a true philosophy, then its whole labor consists in this, — that it should put this question clearly. And if it keep firmly to its proper sphere, it can only answer the question, "What am I and the whole universe?" by saying, "All and nothing," and to the question, "Why?" by adding, "I do not know."

Thus, however I examine and twist the speculative replies of philosophy, I never receive an answer to my question; and that, not as in the sphere of experimental knowledge, because the answer does not relate to the question, but because here, although great mental labor has been applied directly to the question, there *is* no answer, and instead of an answer I get back my own question repeated in a complicated form.

CHAPTER VI

In my search for a solution of the problem of life, I experienced the same feeling as a man who is lost in a forest. He comes to an open plain, climbs up a tree, and sees around him a space without end, but nowhere a house — he sees clearly that there can be none; he goes into the thick of the wood, into the darkness, and sees darkness, but again no house.

Thus had I lost my way in the forest of human knowledge, in the light of the mathematical and experimental sciences which opened out for me clear horizons where there could be no house, and in the darkness of philosophy, plunging me into a greater gloom with every step I took, until I was at last persuaded that there was, and could be, no issue.

When I followed what seemed the bright light of learning, I saw that I had only turned aside from the real question. However alluring and clear were the horizons unfolded before me, however alluring it was to plunge into the infinity of these kinds of knowledge, I saw that the clearer they were the less did I need them, the less did they give me an answer to my question.

"Well," said I to myself, "I know now all that science so obstinately seeks to learn; but an answer to my question as to the meaning of my life is not to be obtained in this way."

I saw that philosophy, notwithstanding that, or perhaps because an answer to my question had become the direct object of its inquiries, gave no answer but the one I had given to myself : —

"What is the meaning of my life?"

"It has none."

Or, "What will come of my life?"

"Nothing."

Or, "Why does all that is exist, and why do I exist?"

"Because it does exist."

When I turned to one branch of human science, I obtained an endless number of exact answers to questions I had not asked : about the chemical elements of the stars, about the movement of the sun toward the constellation Hercules, on the origin of species and of man, about the infinitely small and imponderable particles of ether; but the only answer to my question as to the meaning of my life was this : —

"You are what you call your life; that is, a temporary and accidental agglomeration of particles. The mutual action and reaction of these particles on one another has produced what you call your life. This agglomeration will continue during a certain time, then the reciprocal action of these particles will cease, and with it will end what you call your life, and with it will end all your questions as well. You are an accidentally combined lump of something. The lump undergoes decomposition, this decomposition men call life; the lump falls asunder, decomposition ceases, and with it all doubting."

This is the answer from the clear and positive side of human knowledge, and if true to its own principles it can give no other.

Such an answer proves that the answer does not answer the question. I want to know the meaning of my life; but that it is a particle of the infinite not only does not give a meaning to it, but destroys any possibility of a meaning.

The obscure compromises which this branch of experimental exact science makes with speculative science, when it is said that the meaning of life consists in development, and the concurrent efforts made toward this development from their obscurity and inaccuracy cannot be considered an answer.

The speculative side of human knowledge, when it keeps firmly to its own principles, has everywhere and through all time given and still gives one and the same answer : —

"The world is something eternal and incomprehensible. The life of man is an inconceivable part of this inconceivable *whole*."

Again I set aside all the compromises between the speculative and experimental sciences that constitute all the ballast of the semi-sciences, of so-called jurisprudence, of political economy, and of history. In these sciences we have again a false conception of development and perfection, with this difference, that formerly it was a development of everything, and now it is a development of human life. The inaccuracy is again the same ; development and perfection in infinity can have no object, no direction, and therefore can give no answer to my question.

Whenever speculative science is exact, where philosophy is true to itself, and does not simply serve, after the manner of what Schopenhauer calls "professorial philosophy," to divide all existing phenomena into new columns, and give to them new names — wherever the philosopher does not overlook the great question of all, the answer is always the same, the answer given by Socrates, Schopenhauer, Solomon, and Buddha.

"We approach truth only in the proportion as we are farther from life," said Socrates, when preparing to die. Why do we who love truth strive for death? In order to be free from the body and all the ills that accompany life in it. If so, then, how shall we not be glad of the approach of death?

A wise man seeks death all his life, and therefore death has no terrors for him.

This is what Schopenhauer says : —

"Accept the ultimate principle of the universe as will, and in all phenomena, from the unconscious tendencies of the obscure forces of nature to the conscious activity of man, acknowledge only the objectivity of that will, and still we can never get rid of this logical consequence, that with the free denial and annihilation of that will, all phenomena also disappear, there is an end to the constant efforts and impulses now going on, without aim and without intermission, in every degree of the objectivity in which and through which the universe exists, there is an end to the varieties of successive forms, and with form vanish its postulates, space and time, even to the last and fundamental elements of form, the subject and the object. If there is no will, no phenomenal appearance, then there is no universe. The only thing that remains to us is nothing. But this passage to annihilation is opposed by our own nature, by our will to live — *Wille zum Leben* — which causes our own existence and that of the universe. That we so fear annihilation, or, what is the same, that we so wish to live, only shows that we ourselves are nothing but that wish — life —

and know nothing beyond it. Consequently, after the perfect annihilation of will, what remains to us who are full of wishes is assuredly nothing; on the other hand, for those in whom will has transformed itself and repudiated itself, the whole of this too material universe of ours, with all its suns and milky ways, is *nothing*."

"Vanity of vanities," says Solomon, "vanity of vanities; all is vanity. What profit hath a man of all his labor which he taketh under the sun? One generation passeth away, and another generation cometh: but the earth abideth forever. .... The thing that hath been, it is that which shall be; and that which is done is that which shall be done: and there is no new thing under the sun. Is there anything whereof it may be said, See, this is new? it hath been already of old time, which was before us. There is no remembrance of former things; neither shall there be any remembrance of things that are to come with those that shall come after.

"I the Preacher was king over Israel in Jerusalem. And I gave my heart to seek and search out by wisdom concerning all things that are done under heaven: this sore travail hath God given to the sons of man to be exercised therewith. I have seen all the works that are done under the sun; and behold, all is vanity and vexation of spirit. .... I communed with mine own heart, saying, Lo, I am come to great estate, and have gotten more wisdom than all they that have been before me in Jerusalem: yea, my heart had great experience of wisdom and knowledge. And I gave my heart to know wisdom, and to know madness and folly: I perceived that this also is vexation of spirit. For in much wisdom is much grief: and he that increaseth knowledge increaseth sorrow.

"I said in mine heart, Go to now, I will prove thee with mirth, therefore enjoy pleasure: and, behold, this also is vanity. I said of laughter, It is mad: and of mirth, What doeth it? I sought in mine heart to give myself unto wine (yet acquainting mine heart with wisdom), and to lay hold on folly, till I might see what was that good for the sons of men, which they should do

under the heaven all the days of their life. I made me
great works; I builded me houses; I planted me vine-
yards; I made me gardens and orchards, and I planted
trees in them of all kind of fruits; I made me pools of
water, to water therewith the wood that bringeth forth
trees: I got me servants and maidens, and had servants
born in my house; also I had great possessions of great
and small cattle above all that were in Jerusalem before
me: I gathered me also silver and gold, and the peculiar treasure of kings and of the provinces: I gat me
men singers and women singers, and the delights of the
sons of men, as musical instruments, and that of all
sorts. So I was great, and increased more than all
that were before me in Jerusalem: also my wisdom remained with me. And whatsoever mine eyes desired I
kept not from them, I withheld not mine heart from any
joy. .... Then I looked on all the works my hands had
wrought, and on the labor that I had labored to do:
and behold, all was vanity and vexation of spirit, and
there was no profit under the sun.

"And I turned myself to behold wisdom, and madness, and folly. .:... And I myself perceived also that one
event happeneth to them all. Then said I in my heart,
As it happeneth to the fool, so it happeneth even to
me; and why was I then more wise? Then I said in
my heart, that this also is vanity. For there is no remembrance of the wise more than of the fool forever;
seeing that which now is in the days to come shall be
forgotten. And how dieth the wise man? as the fool.

"Therefore I hated life; because the work that is
wrought under the sun is grievous unto me: for all is
vanity and vexation of spirit. Yea, I hated all my labor
which I had taken under the sun: because I should
leave it unto the man that shall be after me. .... For what
hath man of all his labor, and of the vexation of his
heart, wherein he hath labored under the sun? For all
his days are sorrows, and his travail grief; yea, his
heart taketh not rest in the night. This is also vanity.
There is nothing better for a man than that he should
eat and drink, and that he should make his soul enjoy

good in his labor.   This also I saw, that it was from the hand of God. ....

"All things come alike to all : there is one event to the righteous, and to the wicked ; to the good, and to the clean, and to the unclean ; to him that sacrificeth, and to him that sacrificeth not : as is the good, so is the sinner ; and he that sweareth, as he that feareth an oath.   This is an evil among all things that are done under the sun, that there is one event unto all : yea, also the heart of the sons of men is full of evil, and madness is in their heart while they live, and after that they go to the dead.

"For to him that is joined to all the living there is hope : for a living dog is better than a dead lion.   For the living know that they shall die : but the dead know not anything, neither have they any more a reward ; for the memory of them is forgotten.   Also their love, and their hatred, and their envy, is now perished ; neither have they any more a portion forever in anything that is done under the sun."

Thus speaks Solomon, or the one who wrote those words ; and this is what an Indian sage says : —

"Sakya Muni, the young and happy heir to a great throne, from whom had been kept the sight of illness, old age, and death, once while out driving saw a horrible-looking, toothless, slavering old man.   The prince from whom till then old age had been concealed was much astonished, and asked the driver what it meant, and why the man was in such a pitiable and disgusting state. When he learned that this was the common lot of all men, and that he himself, prince and young though he was, must inevitably one day be the same, he was unable to continue his drive, and ordered the carriage to be driven home, that he might have time to think it all over.   He shut himself up alone and thought it over. He probably thought of something which consoled him, for again he went out for a drive, merry and happy. This time he was met by a sick man.   He sees a worn-out, tottering man, who is quite blue in the face, and has dim eyes.   The prince, from whom all sicknesses had been concealed, stopped and asked what it was. When he was told that it was illness, that old men are subject to it, and he himself, sound and happy prince though he was, might fall ill the next day, he again lost all desire for amusement, and gave orders to drive home. There he again sought peace of mind, and probably found it, for soon after he started again, for the third time, in his carriage. This time, however, he saw something new also — some men were carrying something by.

"'What is that?'

"'A dead man.'

"'What does dead mean?' asked the prince; and he was told that to become one meant to become what the man before him now was.

"The prince descended and approached the body, uncovered it, and looked at it.

"'What will become of him?' asked the prince.

"He was told that the body would be buried in the earth.

"'Why?'

"'Because he will never be alive again, and only stench and worms can come from him.'

"'And that is the lot of all men? And it will be so with me? I shall be put underground to stink and have worms come from me?'

"'Yes.'

"'Back! I will not go for the drive, and never will go again.'"

So Sakya Muni could find no comfort in life, and he decided that life was a very great evil, and applied all his energies to freeing himself and others from it, so that after death life should in no way be renewed, and the very root of life should be destroyed. Thus speak all the Indian sages.

Here we have the only direct answers which human wisdom can give to the problem of life.

"The life of the body is evil and a lie, and so the annihilation of that life is a good for which we ought to wish," says Socrates.

" Life is what it ought not to be, an evil; and a passage from it into nothingness is the only good in life,"
says Schopenhauer.

" Everything in the world, both folly and wisdom,
both riches and poverty, rejoicing and grief, — all is vanity
and worthless. Man dies and nothing is left of him,
and this again is vanity," says Solomon.

"To live, knowing that sufferings, illness, old age,
and death are inevitable, is not possible; we must get
rid of life, get rid of the possibility of living," says
Buddha.

And what these powerful intellects have said, millions on millions of men have thought and felt. I also
have thought and felt the same.

Thus my wanderings over the fields of knowledge
not only failed to cure me of my despair, but increased
it. One branch of knowledge gave no answer at all to
the problem of life; another gave a direct answer which
confirmed my despair, and showed that the state to
which I had come was not the result of my going astray,
of any mental disorder, but, on the contrary, it assured
me that I was thinking rightly, that I was in agreement
with the conclusions of the most powerful intellects
among mankind.

I could not be deceived. All is vanity. A misfor
tune to be born. Death is better than life; life's burden
must be got rid of.

CHAPTER VII

HAVING failed to find an explanation in knowledge, I
began to seek it in life itself, hoping to find it in the
men who surrounded me; and I began to watch men
like myself, to observe how they lived, and how they
practically treated the question that had brought me to
despair.

And this is what I found among those of the same
social position and culture as myself.

I found that for the people of my class there were

four means of escape from the terrible state in which we all were.

The first means of escape is through ignorance. It consists in not perceiving and understanding that life is an evil and an absurdity. People of this class — for the greater part women, or very young or very stupid men — have not understood the problem of life as it presented itself to Schopenhauer, to Solomon, and to Buddha. They see neither the dragon awaiting them, nor the mice eating through the plant to which they cling, and they lick the drops of honey. But they only lick the honey for a time; something directs their attention to the dragon and the mice, and then there is an end to their tasting. From these I could learn nothing: we cannot unknow what we do know.

The second means of escape is the Epicurean. It consists, even while we know the hopelessness of taking advantage of every good there is in life, in avoiding the sight of the dragon and mice, and in the meantime in seeking the honey as best we can, especially wherever there is most of it. Solomon points out this issue from the difficulty thus : —

" Then I commended mirth, because a man hath no better thing under the sun, than to eat, and to drink, and to be merry : for that shall abide with him of his labor the days of his life, which God giveth him under the sun..... Go thy way, eat thy bread with joy, and drink thy wine with a merry heart. .... Live joyfully with the wife whom thou lovest all the days of the life of thy vanity, which he hath given thee under the sun, all the days of thy vanity : for that is thy portion in this life, and in thy labor which thou takest under the sun. Whatsoever thy hand findeth to do, do it with thy might ; for there is no work, nor device, nor knowledge, nor wisdom, in the grave, whither thou goest."

Thus most of the people of our circle maintain the possibility of living. The conditions in which they are placed cause them to know more of the good than the evil of life, and their moral obtuseness enables them to

forget that all the advantages of their position are accidental, and that not all men can have harems and
palaces, like Solomon; that for one man who has a
thousand wives, there are a thousand men who have
none, and for each palace there must be thousands of
men to build it in the sweat of their brow, and that the
same chance which has made me a Solomon to-day may
make me Solomon's slave to-morrow.   The dullness of
their imagination enables these men to forget what
destroyed the peace of Buddha, the inevitable sickness,
old age, and death, which if not to-day, then to-morrow,
must be the end of all their pleasures.

Thus think and feel the majority of the men of our
time and class.   That some of them call their dullness
of thought and imagination by the name of positive
philosophy, does not, in my opinion, separate them from
those who, in order not to see the real question, lick the
honey.   I could not imitate such as these; not having
their obtuseness of imagination, I could not artificially
prevent its action.   Like every man who really lives,
I could not turn my eyes aside from the mice and the
dragon, when I had once seen them.

The third means of escape is through strength and
energy.   It consists in destroying life when we have
perceived that it is an evil and an absurdity.   Only the
rare men, strong and logical, act thus.   Understanding
all the stupidity of the joke that is played on us, and
understanding that the happiness of the dead is more
than the happiness of the living, and that it is better
not to be, they thus act and put an end at once to the
stupid joke, using any means of doing it — a rope round
the neck, water, a knife in the heart, or a railway train.
The number of those in my own class acting thus continually increases, and those that do this are for the
most part in the very prime of life, with their intellectual
powers in their flower, and with but few of the habits
that undermine man's reason as yet formed.

I saw that this means of escape was the worthiest, and
wished to make use of it.

The fourth means of escape is through weakness.   It

consists, though the evil and absurdity of life are well known, in continuing to drag it out, though aware that nothing can come of it.   People of this class know that death is better than life, but have not the strength of character to act as their reason dictates, to have done with deceit and kill themselves; they seem to be waiting for something to happen.   This way of escape is due solely to weakness, for if I know what is better, and it is within my reach, why not seize it?.... To this class of men I myself belonged.

Thus do people of my own class, in four different ways, save themselves from a terrible contradiction.   However earnestly I strained my reasoning faculties I could not find any other than these four ways.   The first way is to ignore the fact that life is absurdity, vanity, and evil, — is not to know that it is better not to live.   For me not to know this was impossible, and when I once saw the truth, I could not shut my eyes to it.

The second way is to make the best of life as it is, without thinking of the future.   This, again, I could not do.   Like Sakya Muni, I could not drive for pleasure, when I knew there were such things as old age, suffering, and death.   My imagination was too lively for that.   Moreover, I could not enjoy chance pleasures which fell for a few rare instants to my lot.

The third way is, knowing that life is an evil and a foolish thing, to put an end to it, to kill one's self.   I understood this, but still for some reason I did not kill myself.

The fourth way is to accept life as described by Solomon and Schopenhauer, to know that it is a stupid and ridiculous joke played on one, and yet live on, to wash, dress, dine, talk, and even write books.   This position was revolting and painful to me, but I remained in it.

I now see that I did not kill myself because I had, in a confused sort of way, an inkling that my ideas were wrong.   However plausible and unanswerable appeared to me the idea, which I shared with the wisest on earth, that life has no meaning, I still felt a confused doubt

of the truth of my conclusions, which formed itself
thus : —

"My reason tells me that life is contrary to reason.
If there is nothing higher than reason — and there is
nothing, and nothing can prove it — then reason is the
creator of life for me ; were there no reason there would
be no life for me. How can this reason deny life, and
at the same time be its creator? Again, from the other
side, if there were no life, I should have no reason, consequently reason is the son of life. Life is all. Reason is
the fruit of life, and this same reason denies life itself."

I felt that something here was wrong. I said to
myself : —

"Life undoubtedly has no meaning, and is evil, but I
have lived and am still alive, and so also have lived and
are living the whole human race. How is this? Why
do all men live when all men are able to die? Is it that
I and Schopenhauer alone are wise enough to have
understood the unmeaning emptiness and evil of life?"

To see the inanity of life is a simple matter enough,
and it has long been apparent to the simplest, but men
have lived and still live on. Why is it men live on, and
never think of calling in question the reasonableness of
life?

My acquired knowledge, confirmed by the wisdom of
the wisest in the world, showed me that everything on
earth, organic or inorganic, was arranged with extraordinary wisdom, and that my own position alone was a
foolish one. But those fools, the enormous masses of
simple people, know nothing of the organic and inorganic
structure of the world, but live on, and it seems to
them that their lives are subjected to perfectly reasonable conditions! ....

Then I thought to myself : "But what if there be
something more for me to know? Surely this is the
way in which Ignorance acts. Ignorance always says
exactly what I do now! When Ignorance does not
know anything it calls that which it does not know
stupid! It really comes to this, that mankind as a
whole have always lived, and are living, as if they

understood the meaning of life, for not doing so they could not live at all; whereas I say that all this life is meaningless, and that I cannot live."

No one prevents us from denying life by suicide, but, then, kill yourself and you will no longer argue about it. If you dislike life, kill yourself. If you live and cannot comprehend the meaning of life, put an end to it, and do not go on talking and writing about being unable to understand life. You have got into a gay company, in which all are well satisfied, all know what they are doing, and you alone are wearied and repelled; then get out of it!

And after all, then, what are we who, persuaded of the necessity of suicide, still cannot bring ourselves to the act, but weak, inconsistent men, — to speak more plainly, stupid men, who carry about with them their stupidity, like the fool with the placarded basket?

Our wisdom, indeed, however firmly it be grounded on truth, has not imparted to us a knowledge of the meaning of life, yet all humanity sharing in life — millions — doubt not that life has a meaning.

It is certainly true that, from the far, far distant time when that life began of which I know something, men have lived who, though they knew all the arguments about the inanity of life such as proved to me that life had no meaning, still lived on, and gave to life a meaning of their own.

Since any sort of life began for men, they have had some conception of their own about it, and have so lived down to my own time. All that is in and around me, physical or immaterial, it is all the fruit of their knowledge of life.[1] The very tools of thought with which I have judged life, and condemned it, were fashioned, not by me, but by them. I was born, and bred, and have grown up, thanks to them. They dug out the iron, taught how to hew down the forests, to tame the cows and the horses, to sow corn, to live one with another;

---

[1] An untranslatable pun: *plotskoye i nyeplotskoye, vsyo eto-plod* (pronounced *plot*): "Material and immaterial is all the material;" literally, "fleshly and unfleshly is all the fruit." — ED.

they gave order and form to our life; moreover, they taught me how to think and how to speak. And I, the work of their hands, their foster-child, the pupil of their thoughts and sayings, have proved to them they themselves had no meaning!

"There must be something wrong here," said I. "I have made some mistake."

I could not, however, discover where the mistake lay.

CHAPTER VIII

ALL these doubts, which I am now able to express more or less clearly, I could not then explain. Then I only felt that, however logical and unavoidable were my conclusions as to the inanity of life, confirmed as they were by the greatest thinkers, there was something wrong in them. Whether in the conclusion itself, or in the way of putting the question, I did not know; I only felt that, though my reason was entirely convinced, that was not enough.

All my reasoning could not induce me to act in accordance with my convictions, *i.e.* to kill myself.

I should not speak the truth, if I said that my reason alone brought me to the position in which I was and prevented me from suicide. Reason had been at work, no doubt, but something else had worked too, something which I can only call the consciousness of life. There also worked in me a force, which determined my attention to one thing rather than to another, and it was this that drew me out of my desperate position, and completely changed the current of my thoughts. This force led me to the idea that I, with hundreds of other men like me, did not form the whole of mankind, — that I was still ignorant of what human life was.

When I watched the narrow circle of those who were my equals in social position, I saw only people who did not understand the question, people who understood the question but kept down their understanding of it by the intoxication of life, people who understood it and put an end to life, and people who, understanding, lived on through weakness, in despair. And I saw no others. It seemed to me that the narrow circle of learned, rich, and idle people, to which I myself belonged, formed the whole of humanity, and that the milliards living outside it were animals, not men.

However strange, improbable, and inconceivable it now seems to me, that I, reasoning about life, could overlook the life of mankind surrounding me on all sides, and fall into such an error as to think that the life of a Solomon, a Schopenhauer, and my own, was the real normal life, and the life lived by unconsidered milliards a circumstance unworthy of attention — however strange this appears to me now, I see that it was so. Led away by intellectual pride, it seemed to me beyond a doubt that I, with Solomon and Schopenhauer, had put the question so exactly and truly that there could be no other form of it ; it seemed unquestionable that all these milliards of men had failed to conceive the depth of the question, that I had sought the meaning of my life ; and it never once occurred to me to think : —

"But what meaning has been given, what meaning is given now, by the milliards of those who have lived and are living in the world?"

I long lived in this state of mental aberration, which, though not always openly expressed in words, is not the less common among the most learned and most liberal men. But whether, owing to my strange kind of instinctive affection for the laboring classes, which impelled me to understand them, and to see that they are not so stupid as we think, or owing to the sincerity of my conviction that I could know nothing beyond the advisability of hanging myself, I felt that, if I wished to live and understand the meaning of life, I must seek it not amongst those who have lost the meaning of life, and wish to kill themselves, but amongst the milliards of the living and the dead who have made our life what it is, and on whom now rests the burden of our life and their own.

So I watched the life common to such enormous numbers of the dead and the living, the life of simple, unlearned, and poor men, and found something quite different. I saw that all these milliards, who are alive and have lived, with rare exceptions, did not come into my classification; I could not count them among those who do not understand the question, because they not only put it, but answer it, with extraordinary clearness. I could not call them Epicureans, because their life has far more of privation and suffering than of enjoyment; to count them amongst those who, against their reason, live through a life without meaning, was still less possible, because every act of their lives, and death itself, is explained by them. Self-murder they regard as the greatest of crimes. It appeared that throughout mankind there is a knowledge of the meaning of life which I had neglected and despised. It resulted, that the knowledge based on reason denies a meaning to life, and excludes life; while the meaning given to life by the milliards that form the great whole of humanity is founded on a despised and fallacious knowledge.

The knowledge based on reason, the knowledge of the learned and the wise, denies a meaning in life, while the great mass of men, all humanity, have an unreasoning knowledge of life which gives a meaning to it.

This unreasoning knowledge is the faith which I could not but reject. This is a God, one and yet three; this is the creation in six days, devils and angels, — and all that I cannot accept while I keep my senses!

My position was terrible. I knew that from the knowledge which reason has given man, I could get nothing but the denial of life, and from faith nothing but the denial of reason, which last was even more impossible than the denial of life. By the knowledge founded on reason it was proved that life is an evil and that men know it to be so, that men may cease to live if they will, but that they have lived and they go on living — I myself lived on, though I had long known that life was meaningless and evil. If I went by faith it resulted that, in

order to understand the meaning of life, I should have
to abandon reason, the very part of me that required a
meaning in life!

CHAPTER IX

I WAS stopped by a contradiction from which there
were only two ways of escape: either what I called
reasonable was not so reasonable as I thought it, or what
I called unreasonable was not so unreasonable as I
thought it. I began to verify the process of thinking
through which I had been led to the conclusions of
reasoning knowledge.

On doing this, I found the process complete and flaw-
less. The conclusion that life was nothing was unavoidable; but I discovered a mistake. The mistake was that
I had not confined my thoughts to the question proposed.
The question was, why should I live, *i.e.* what of real
and imperishable will come of my shadowy and perishable life — what meaning has my finite existence in the
infinite universe? And I had tried to answer this by
studying life.

It was evident that the decision of any number of
questions concerning life could not satisfy me, because
my question, however simple it seemed at first, included
the necessity of explaining the finite by infinity, and the
contrary.

I asked myself what meaning my life had apart from
time, causation, and space. But I replied to my question: what is the meaning of life in respect to time,
causation, and space? The result was that after long
and earnest efforts of thinking, I could only answer —
none at all.

Through all my reasoning with myself I constantly
compared, and I could not do otherwise, the finite with
the finite, and the infinite with the infinite, and the
conclusion was consequently inevitable: a force is a
force, matter is matter, will is will, infinity is infinity,
nothing is nothing, — and there was no getting beyond

that. It was like what happens in mathematics, when thinking to resolve an equation we get identical terms. The process of solution is correct, but our answer is $a = a$, or $x = x$, or $0 = 0$. This happened to me in my inquiries into the meaning of my life. The answers given by all science to the question were " identity."

And in reality knowledge founded strictly on reason, which, like that carried on by Descartes, begins with absolute doubt of everything, throws aside all knowledge founded on faith, and reconstructs all in accordance with the laws of reason and experience, and it can give no other answer to the question about the meaning of life than the one which I myself obtained — an indefinite one.

It seemed to me at first that science did give a positive answer, the answer of Schopenhauer: life has no meaning, it is an evil; but, when I inquired more closely into the matter, I perceived that the answer was not positive, that it was my own feeling alone made me think it so. The answer boldly expressed in the same terms as that given by the Brahmins, and Solomon, and Schopenhauer, is only an indefinite one, — the identity of 0 and 0, life is nothing. Thus philosophical knowledge denies nothing, but merely answers that the question cannot be decided by it, — that the matter remains indefinite.

When I had come to this conclusion, I understood that it was useless to seek an answer to my question from knowledge founded on reason, and that the answer given by this form of knowledge is only an indication that no answer can be obtained till the question is put differently, — till the question be made to include the relation between the finite and the infinite. I also understood that, however unreasonable and monstrous the answers given by faith, they have the advantage of bringing into every question the relation of the finite to the infinite, without which there can be no answer.

However I may put the question, How am I to live? the answer is, " By the law of God."

Will anything real and positive come of my life,
and what?

Eternal torment, or eternal bliss.

What meaning is there not to be destroyed by death?

Union with an infinite God, paradise.

In this way I was compelled to admit that, besides
the reasoning knowledge, which I once thought the
only true knowledge, there was in every living man
another kind of knowledge, an unreasoning one, — faith,
— which gives a possibility of living.

All the unreasonableness of faith remained for me
the same as ever, but I could not help acknowledging that
faith alone gave man answers as to the questions of life,
and consequently the possibility of living.

Reasoning knowledge brought me to the conclusion
that life was meaningless, and my life stood still, and I
wished to put an end to myself. When I looked at the
men around me, at humanity as a whole, I saw that men
lived, and that they know the meaning of life. For
other men, as for myself, faith gave a meaning to life
and a possibility of living.

On examining farther into life in other countries than
my own, as well among my contemporaries as among
those who have passed away, I found the same thing.
From the beginning of the human race, wherever there
is life there is faith which makes life possible, and
everywhere the leading characteristics of faith are the
same.

Whatever answers any kind of faith ever gives to any
one, every one of these answers gives an infinite meaning
to the finite life of man, a meaning which is not destroyed
by suffering, privation, and death. In faith, therefore,
alone is found the possibility of living and a meaning in
life. What is this faith? I understood that faith is not
only the manifestation of things unseen, is not only a
revelation (that is only a description of one of the signs
of faith), is not the relation of man to God (faith must
first be determined, and then God, and not faith through
God), and is not only acquiescence with what has been
told to man, as faith is most frequently understood to

be, — but faith is the knowledge of the meaning of human life, in consequence of which man does not destroy himself, but lives. Faith is the force of life.

If a man lives, he believes in something. If he did not believe that there was something to live for, he would not live. If he does not see and understand the unreality of the finite, he believes in the finite; if he sees that unreality, he must believe in the infinite. Without faith it is impossible to live.

I then went back over all the past stages of my mental state, and was terrified. It was now clear to me that for any one to live, it was necessary for him either not to see infinity, or to accept an explanation of the meaning of life which should equalize the finite and the infinite. Such an explanation I had, but I had no need of it while I believed in the finite, and I began to apply to my explanation the tests of reason, and in the light of reason all former explanations were shown to be worthless. But the time when I ceased to believe in the finite passed, even then I tried to raise on the foundations of reason and out of what I knew an explanation which should give a meaning to life, but I tried in vain. In company with the greatest intellects among men I came only to the conclusion that $0 = 0$, and, though nothing else could have come of it, I was much astonished to have obtained such an answer to my problem.

What did I do when I sought an answer in the study of experimental science? I wanted to know why I lived, and to that end I studied everything outside myself. Clearly in this way I might learn much, but nothing of that which I needed.

What did I do when I sought an answer in the study of philosophy? I studied the thoughts of others in the same position as myself, and who had no answer to the question — "Why do I live?" Clearly I could in this way learn nothing but what I myself knew, namely, that it was impossible to know anything.

What am I? — a part of the infinite. In those few words lay the whole problem.

Could it be that mankind had only now begun to put this question? Could it be that no one before myself had asked this simple question, that must occur to the mind of every intelligent child?

Why! since men have been this question has been put, and since men have been it has been assuredly understood that the decision of this question is equally unsatisfactory, whether the finite be compared with the finite, and the infinite with the infinite, and since men have been, the relations of the finite to the infinite have been sought and expressed.

All these conceptions of the equality of the finite and the infinite, through which we receive the ideas of life, of God, of freedom, of good, we submit to logical analysis. And these conceptions will not bear the tests of reason.

If it were not so terrible, it would be laughable to think of the pride and self-confidence with which we, like children, pull out our watches, take away the spring, make a plaything of them, and are then astonished that they will no longer keep time.

The decision of the contradiction between the finite and the infinite, and such an answer to the question of what is life as shall enable us to live, is essential and precious to us. The only answer is the one to be found everywhere, always, and among all nations, an answer which has come down to us from the times in which the origin of human life is lost, an answer so difficult that we could never ourselves have come to it — this answer we in our careless indifference get rid of, by again raising the question which presents itself to every one, but which no one can answer.

The conception of an infinite God, of the divinity of the soul, of the way in which the affairs of men are related to God, of the unity and reality of the spirit, man's conception of moral good and evil, — these are conceptions worked out through the infinite mental labors of mankind; conceptions without which there would be no life, without which I should not myself exist, and yet I reject all this, the labor of the whole human race, and venture on working out the problem again in my own way alone.

I did not at the time think so, but the germs of these thoughts were already within me. I understood (1) that the position assumed by Schopenhauer, Solomon, and myself, notwithstanding all our wisdom, was foolish: we understand that life is an evil, and yet we live. This is clearly foolish, because if life is foolish, and I care so much for reason, life should be put an end to, and then there would be no one to deny it.

(2) I understood that all our arguments turned in a charmed circle, like a cog-wheel the teeth of which no longer catch in another. However much and however well we reason, we get no answer to our question; it will always be 0 = 0, and consequently our method is probably wrong.

(3) I began to understand that in the answers given by faith was to be found the deepest source of human wisdom, that I had no reasonable right to reject them on the ground of reason, and that these principle answers alone solved the problem of life.

CHAPTER X

I UNDERSTOOD this, but it did not make it any easier for me.

I was now ready to accept any faith that did not require of me a direct denial of reason, for that would be to act a lie; and I studied Buddhism and Mohammedanism in their books, and especially also Christianity, both in its writings and in the lives of its professors around me.

I naturally turned my attention at first to the believers in my own immediate circle, to learned men, to orthodox divines, to the older monks, to the orthodox divines of a new shade of doctrine, the so-called New Christians, who preach salvation through faith in a Redeemer. I seized upon these believers, and asked them what they believed in, and what for them gave a meaning to life.

Notwithstanding that I made every possible conces-
sion, that I avoided all disputes, I could not accept the
faith of these men. I saw that what they called their
faith did not explain, but obscured, the meaning of life,
and that they professed it, not in order to answer the
questions as to life which had attracted me toward faith,
but for some other purpose to which I was a stranger.

I remember the painful feeling of horror with which
I returned to the old feeling of despair, after the hopes
which I experienced many, many times in my relations
with these people.

The more minutely they laid their doctrines before
me, the more clearly I perceived their error, the more I
lost all hope of finding in their faith an explanation of
the meaning of life.

I was not so much revolted by the unnecessary and
unreasonable doctrines which they mingled with the
Christian truths always so dear to me, as by the fact
that their lives were like my own, the only difference
being that they did not live according to the principles
which they professed. I was clearly conscious that they
deceived themselves, and that for them, as for myself,
there was no other meaning to life than to live while
they lived, and take each for himself all that his hands
could lay hold on. I saw this, because if the ideas of
life which they conceived had done away with the fear
of privation, suffering, and death, they would not have
feared them. But these believers of our class, the same
as I myself, lived in comfort and abundance, struggled
to increase and preserve it, were afraid of privation,
suffering, and death ; and again, like myself and all the
rest of us unbelievers, satisfied the lusts of the flesh, and
led lives as evil as, if not worse than, those of infidels
themselves.

No arguments were able to convince me of the sincerity of the faith of these men. Only actions, proving
their conception of life to have destroyed the fear of
poverty, illness, and death, so strong in myself, could
have convinced me, and such actions I could not see
among the various believers of our class. Such actions,

I saw, indeed, among the open infidels of my own class in life, but never among the so-called believers of our class.

I understood, then, that the faith of these men was not the faith which I sought; that it was no faith at all, but only one of the Epicurean consolations of life. I understood that this faith, if it could not really console, could at least soothe the repentant mind of a Solomon on his deathbed; but that it could not serve the enormous majority of mankind, who are born, not to be comforted by the labors of others, but to create a life for themselves. For mankind to live, for it to continue to live and be conscious of the meaning of its life, all these milliards must have another and a true conception of faith. It was not, then, the fact that Solomon, Schopenhauer, and I had not killed ourselves, which convinced me that faith existed, but the fact that these milliards have lived and are now living, carrying along with them on the impulse of their life both Solomon and ourselves.

I began to draw nearer to the believers among the poor, the simple, and the ignorant, the pilgrims, the monks, the raskolniks, and the peasants. The doctrines of these men of the people, like those of the pretended believers of my own class, were Christian. Here also much that was superstitious was mingled with the truths of Christianity, but with this difference, that the superstition of the believers of our class was entirely unnecessary to them, and never influenced their lives beyond serving as a kind of Epicurean distraction; while the superstition of the believing laboring class was so interwoven with their lives that it was impossible to conceive them without it — it was a necessary condition of their living at all. The whole life of the believers of our class was in flat contradiction with their faith, and the whole life of the believers of the people was a confirmation of the meaning of life which their faith gave them.

Thus I began to study the lives and the doctrines of the people, and the more I studied the more I became convinced that a true faith was among them, that their faith was for them a necessary thing, and alone gave them a meaning in life and a possibility of living. In direct opposition to what I saw in our circle — where life without faith was possible, and where not one in a thousand professed himself a believer — amongst the people there was not a single unbeliever in a thousand. In direct opposition to what I saw in our circle — where a whole life is spent in idleness, amusement, and dissatisfaction with life — I saw among the people whole lives passed in heavy labor and unrepining content. In direct opposition to what I saw in our circle — men resisting and indignant with the privations and sufferings of their lot — the people unhesitatingly and unresistingly accepting illness and sorrow, in the quiet and firm conviction that all these must be and could not be otherwise, and that all was for the best. In contradiction to the theory that the less learned we are the less we understand the meaning of life, and see in our sufferings and death but an evil joke, these men of the people live, suffer, and draw near to death, in quiet confidence and oftenest with joy. In contradiction to the fact that an easy death, without terror or despair, is a rare exception in our class, a death which is uneasy, rebellious, and sorrowful is among the people the rarest exception of all.

These people, deprived of all that for us and for Solomon makes the only good in life, and experiencing at the same time the highest happiness, form the great majority of mankind. I looked more widely around me, I studied the lives of the past and contemporary masses of humanity, and I saw that, not two or three, or ten, but hundreds, thousands, millions had so understood the meaning of life that they were able both to live and to die. All these men, infinitely divided by manners, powers of mind, education, and position, all alike in opposition to my ignorance, were well acquainted with the meaning of life and of death, quietly labored, endured privation and suffering, lived and died, and saw in all this, not a vain, but a good thing.

I began to grow attached to these men. The more I learned of their lives, the lives of the living and of the dead of whom I read and heard, the more I liked them, and the easier I felt it so to live. I lived in this way during two years, and then there came a change which had long been preparing in me, and the symptoms of which I had always dimly felt: the life of our circle of rich and learned men, not only became repulsive, but lost all meaning. All our actions, our reasoning, our science and art, all appeared to me in a new light. I understood that it was all child's play, that it was useless to seek a meaning in it. The life of the working-classes, of the whole of mankind, of those that create life, appeared to me in its true significance. I understood that this was life itself, and that the meaning given to this life was true, and I accepted it.

CHAPTER XI

WHEN I remembered how these very doctrines had repelled me, how senseless they had seemed when professed by men whose lives were spent in opposition to them, and how these same doctrines had attracted me and seemed reasonable when I saw men living in accordance with them, I understood why I had once rejected them and thought them unmeaning, why I now adopted them and thought them full of meaning. I understood that I had erred, and how I had erred. I had erred, not so much through having thought incorrectly, as through having lived ill. I understood that the truth had been hidden from me, not so much because I had erred in my reasoning, as because I had led the exceptional life of an epicure bent on satisfying the lusts of the flesh. I understood that my question, "What is my life," and the answer, "An evil," were in accordance with the truth of things. The mistake lay in my having applied to life in general an answer which only concerned myself. I had asked what my own life was, and the answer was "An evil and absurdity." Exactly so, my life — a life of indulgence, of sensuality — was an absurdity and an evil; and the answer, "Life is meaningless and evil," therefore, referred only to my own life, and not to human life in general.

I understood the truth which I afterwards found in the Gospel: "That men loved darkness rather than light because their deeds were evil. For every man that doeth evil hateth the light, neither cometh to the light, lest his deeds should be reproved."

I understood that, for the meaning of life to be understood, it was necessary first that life should be something more than evil and meaningless, and afterwards that there should be the light of reason to understand it. I understood why I had so long been circling round this self-evident truth without apprehending it, and that if we would think and speak of the life of mankind, we must think and speak of that life as a whole, and not merely of the life of certain parasites on it.

This truth was always a truth, as $2 \times 2 = 4$, but I had not accepted it, because, besides acknowledging $2 \times 2 = 4$, I should have been obliged to acknowledge that I was evil. It was of more importance to me to feel that I was good, more binding on me, than to believe $2 \times 2 = 4$. I loved good men, I hated myself, and I accepted truth. Now it was all clear to me.

Now if the question, "What is life?" were asked of himself by an executioner, who passes his life in torturing and cutting off heads, or by a confirmed drunkard, or by a crazy man who has spent his whole life in a darkened chamber, hating that chamber and imagining that he would perish if he left it, evidently he could get no other answer to his question, "What is life?" than that life is the greatest of evils, and the crazy man's answer would be a true one, but only for himself. Here, then, was I such a crazy man? Were all of us rich, clever, idle men, crazy like this?....

I understood at last that we actually were; that I, at any rate, was. In fact the bird is so constituted that it must fly, pick up its food, build its nest, and when I see the bird doing this I rejoice in its joy. The goat, the hare, the wolf, are so constituted that they must feed and multiply, and bring up their young; and when they do this, I have a firm conviction that they are happy, and that their life is reasonable.

What, then, must man do? He also must gain his living like the animals, but with this difference, that he will perish if he attempt it alone; he must labor, not for himself, but for all. And when he does so, I am firmly convinced he is happy, and his life is reasonable.

What had I done during my thirty years of conscious life? I had not only not helped the life of others, I had done nothing for my own. I had lived the life of a parasite, and when I asked myself why I lived at all I received the answer, "There is no reason why." If the meaning of the life of man lies in his having to work out his life himself, how could I, who during thirty years had done my best to ruin my own life and that of others, expect to receive any other answer than this, — that my life was an evil and an absurdity? ....

It was an evil, an absurdity.

The life of the world goes on through the will of some one. Some one makes our own life and that of the universe his own inscrutable care. To have a hope of understanding what that will means, we must first fulfil it, we must do what is required of us. Unless I do what is required of me, I can never know what that may be, and much less know what is required of us all and of the whole universe.

If a naked, hungry beggar be taken from the cross-roads into an enclosed space in a splendid establishment, to be well clothed and fed, and made to work a handle up and down, it is evident that the beggar, before seeking to know why he has been taken, why he must work the handle, whether the arrangements of the establishment are reasonable or not, must first move the handle. If he move the handle he will find that the handle works a pump, the pump draws up water, and the water flows over garden beds. Then he will be taken from the covered well and set to other work; he will gather fruits and enter into the joy of his lord, and as he passes from less to more important labors, he will understand better and better the arrangements of the whole estab-

lishment; and he will take his share in them without
once stopping to ask why he is there, nor will he ever
think of reproaching the lord of that place.

And thus it is with those that do the will of their
master; no reproaches come from simple untaught
working-men, from those we regard as brutes. But we
the while, wise men that we are, devour the goods of
the master, and do nothing of that which he wills us to
do; but instead, seat ourselves in a circle to argue why
we should move the handle, for that seems to us stupid.
And when we have thought it all out, what is our conclusion? Why, that the master is stupid, or that there
is none, while we ourselves are wise, only we feel that we
are fit for nothing, and that we must somehow or other
get rid of ourselves.

CHAPTER XII

MY conviction of the error into which all knowledge
based on reason must fall assisted me in freeing myself
from the seductions of idle reasoning. The conviction
that a knowledge of truth can be gained only by living,
led me to doubt the justness of my own life; but I had
only to get out of my own particular groove, and look
around me, to observe the simple life of the real working-
class, to understand that such a life was the only real
one. I understood that, if I wished to understand life
and its meaning, I must live, not the life of a parasite,
but a real life; and, accepting the meaning given to it
by the combined lives of those that really form the
great human whole, submit it to a close examination.

At the time I am speaking of, the following was my
position : —

During the whole of that year, when I was asking
myself almost every minute whether I should or should
not put an end to it all with a cord or a pistol, during
the time my mind was occupied with the thoughts which
I have described, my heart was oppressed by a torment

ing feeling. This feeling I cannot describe otherwise than as a searching after God.

This search after a God was not an act of my reason, but a feeling, and I say this advisedly, because it was opposed to my way of thinking; it came from the heart. It was a feeling of dread, or orphanhood, of isolation amid things all apart from me, and of hope in a help I knew not from whom.

Though I was well convinced of the impossibility of proving the existence of God — Kant had shown me, and I had thoroughly grasped his reasoning, that this did not admit of proof — I still sought to find a God, still hoped to do so, and still, from the force of former habits, addressed myself to one in prayer, whom I sought, and did not find.

At times I went over in my mind the arguments of Kant and of Schopenhauer, showing the impossibility of proving the existence of the Deity; at times I began to test their arguments and refute them.

I would say to myself that causation is not in the same category of thought as space and time. If I am, there is a cause of my being, and that the cause of all causes. That cause of all things is what is called God; and I dwelt on this idea, and strove with all my being to reach a consciousness of the presence of this cause.

As soon as I became conscious that there is such a power over me, I felt a possibility of living. Then I asked myself : —

"What is this cause, this power? How am I to think of it? What is my relation to what I call God?"

And only the old familiar answer came into my mind, "He is the creator, the giver of all."

This answer did not satisfy me, and I felt that what was necessary for life was failing me, a great horror came over me, and I began to pray to Him whom I sought, that He would help me. But the more I prayed, the clearer it became that I was not heard, that there was no one to whom one could turn. With despair in my heart that there was no God, I cried : —

"Lord, have mercy on me, and save! O Lord, my God, teach me!"

But no one had mercy on me, and I felt that my life had come to a standstill.

But again and again, from various other directions, I came back to the same conviction that I could not have appeared on earth without any motive or meaning, — that I could not be such a fledgling dropped from a nest as I felt myself to be. What if I cry, as the fallen fledgling does on its back in the high grass? It is because I know that a mother bore me, cared for me, fed me, and loved me. Where is she, where is that mother? If I have been thrown out, then who threw me? I cannot help seeing that some one who loved me brought me into being. Who is that some one? Again the same answer — God. He knows and sees my search, my despair, my struggle. "He is," I said to myself. I had only to admit that for an instant to feel that life rearose in me, to feel the possibility of existing and the joy of it.

Then, again, from the conviction of the existence of God, I passed to the consideration of our relation toward Him, and again I had before me the triune God, our Creator, who sent His Son, the Redeemer. Again, this God, apart from me and from the world, melted from before my eyes as ice melts; again there was nothing left, again the source of life dried up. I fell once more into despair, and felt that I had nothing to do but to kill myself, while, worst of all, I felt also that I should never do it.

Not twice, not three times, but tens, hundreds, of times did I pass through these alternations, — now of joy and excitement, now of despair and of consciousness of the impossibility of life.

I remember one day in the early springtime I was alone in the forest listening to the woodland sounds, and thinking only of one thing, the same of which I had constantly thought for two years — I was again seeking for a God.

I said to myself : —

"Very good, there is no God, there is none with a reality apart from my own imaginings, none as real as my own life — there is none such. Nothing, no miracles can prove there is, for miracles only exist in my own unreasonable imagination."

And then I asked myself : —

"But my idea of the God whom I seek, whence comes it?"

And again at this thought arose the joyous billows of life. All around me seemed to revive, to have a new meaning. My joy, though, did not last long. Reason continued its work : —

"The idea of a God is not God. The idea is what goes on within myself; the idea of God is an idea which I am able to rouse in my mind or not as I choose ; it is not what I seek, something without which life could not be."

Then again all seemed to die around and within me, and again I wished to kill myself.

After this I began to retrace the process which had gone on within myself, the hundred times repeated discouragement and revival. I remembered that I had lived only when I believed in a God. As it was before, so it was now ; I had only to know God, and I lived ; I had only to forget Him, not to believe in Him, and I died.

What was this discouragement and revival? I do not live when I lose faith in the existence of a God ; I should long ago have killed myself, if I had not had a dim hope of finding Him. I really live only when I am conscious of Him and seek Him. "What more, then, do I seek?" A voice seemed to cry within me, "This is He, He without whom there is no life. To know God and to live are one. God is life."

Live to seek God, and life will not be without God. And stronger than ever rose up life within and around me, and the light that then shone never left me again.

Thus I was saved from self-murder. When and how this change in me took place I could not say. As gradually, imperceptibly as life had decayed in me, till I reached the impossibility of living, till life stood still,

and I longed to kill myself, so gradually and imperceptibly I felt the glow and strength of life return to me.

And strangely enough this power of life which came
back to me was not new; it was old enough, for I had
been led away by it in the earlier part of my life.

I returned, as it were, to the past, to childhood and
my youth. I returned to faith in that Will which
brought me into being and which required something of
me; I returned to the belief that the one single aim of
life should be to become better, that is, to live in accordance with that Will; I returned to the idea that the
expression of that Will was to be found in what, in the
dim obscurity of the past, the great human unity had
fashioned for its own guidance; in other words, I returned to a belief in God, in moral perfectibility, and in
the tradition which gives a meaning to life. The difference was that formerly I had unconsciously accepted
this, whereas now I knew that without it I could not
live.

The state of mind in which I then was may be
likened to the following: It was as if I had suddenly
found myself sitting in a boat which had been pushed
off from some shore unknown to me, had been shown
the direction of the opposite shore, had had oars put
into my inexperienced hands, and had been left alone.
I had used the oars as best I could and rowed on; but
the farther I went toward the center, the stronger became the current which carried me out of my course,
and the oftener I met other navigators, like myself,
carried away by the stream. There were here and
there solitary navigators who had continued to row hard,
there were others who had thrown down their oars,
there were large boats, and enormous ships crowded
with men; some struggled against the stream, others
glided on with it. The farther I got, the more, as I
watched the long line floating down the current, I forgot the course pointed out to me as my own.

In the very middle of the stream, amid the crowd of
boats and vessels floating down, I had altogether lost
the course and thrown down my oars. From all sides the

joyful and exulting navigators, as they rowed or sailed down-stream, with one voice assured me and one another that there could be no other direction. And I believed them, and let myself go with them. I was carried far, so far that I heard the roar of the rapids in which I was bound to perish, and I already saw boats that had been broken up within them.

Then I came to myself. It was long before I clearly comprehended what had happened. I saw before me nothing but the destruction toward which I was hurrying, which I dreaded, and I saw no salvation and knew not what I was to do! But on looking back, I saw a countless multitude of boats engaged in a ceaseless struggle against the force of the torrent, and then I remembered all about the shore, the oars, and the course, and at once I began to row hard up the stream and again toward the shore.

That shore was God, that course was tradition, those oars were the free will given me to make for the shore to seek union with the Deity.

CHAPTER XIII

AND thus the vital force was renewed in me, and I began again to live. I renounced the life of our class, for I had come to confess that it was not life, but only the semblance of life, that its superfluous luxuries prevent the possibility of understanding life, and that in order to understand life, I must understand not the life of exceptional people, the parasites, but the life of the simple working-classes, the life that fashions life, and gives it the meaning which the working-classes accept. The simple laboring men around me were the Russian people, and I turned to this people and to the meaning which it gives to life.

This meaning, if it can be expressed, was as follows: —

Every man has come into this world by the will of God, and God has so created man that every man is able to ruin or to save his soul. The problem of man's

life being to save his soul, in order to save his soul, he
must live after God's word : to live after God's word,
he must renounce all the pleasures of life, must labor,
be humble, endure, and be meek.   This, to the people,
is the meaning of the whole system of faith, as it has
come down to them through, and is now given them by,
the pastors of their Church and the traditions which
exist among them.

   This meaning was clear to me, and dear to my heart.
This popular faith, however, among the non-dissenting
communities in which I lived, was inextricably bound
up with something else so incapable of being explained
that it repelled me : the sacraments, the services of the
Church, the fasts, and the bowing before relics and
images.   The people were unable to separate these
things, and no more could I.   Though many things belonging to the faith of the people appeared strange to
me, I accepted everything, I attended the church services, prayed morning and evening, fasted, prepared for
the communion ; and, while doing all this, for the first
time felt that my reason found nothing to object to.
What had formerly seemed to me impossible, now roused
no opposition in me.

   The position which I occupied with relation to questions of faith had become quite different to what it once
was.   Formerly, life itself had seemed to me full of
meaning, and faith an arbitrary assertion of certain useless and unreasonable propositions which had no direct
bearing on life.   I had tried to find out their meaning ;
and once convinced they had none, had thrown them
aside.   Now, on the contrary, I knew for certain that
my life had not and could not have any meaning, and
that the propositions of faith not only appeared no
longer useless to me, but had been shown beyond dispute by my own experience to be that which alone gave
a meaning to life.   Formerly I looked on them as a
worthless, illegible scrawl; but now if I did not understand them, still I knew that they had a meaning, and
I said to myself that I must learn to understand them.
   I reasoned thus : —

" Faith springs, like man and his reason, from the mysterious first cause. That first cause is God, the cause of the body and the mind of man. As my body proceeded through successive gradations from God to me, so have my reason and my conception of life proceeded from Him, and consequently the steps of this process of development cannot be false. All that men sincerely believe in must be true; it may be differently expressed, but it cannot be a lie, and consequently, if it seem to me a lie, that must be because I do not understand it."

Again, I said to myself : —

" The true office of any faith is to give to life a meaning which death cannot destroy. It is only natural that for faith to give an answer to the question of the king dying amid every luxury, of the old and labor-worn slave, of the unthinking child, of the aged sage, of the half-witted old crone, of the happy woman full of the strong passions of youth, of all men under all possible differences of position and education, — it is only natural that, if there be but one answer to the one eternally repeated question — 'Why do I live, and what will come of my life ? ' — the answer, though one and the same in reality, should be infinitely varied in its phenomena ; that, in exact proportion to its unvarying unity, to its truth, and its depth, it should appear strange, and even monstrous, in the attempts to find due expression, which are owing to the bringing-up and the social state of each individual answerer."

But these arguments, which justified the oddities of the ritual side of faith, were still insufficient to make me feel that I had a right, in a matter like faith, now become the one business of my life, to take part in acts of which I was still doubtful. I desired, with all the powers of my soul, to be in a condition to unite with the people, conforming to the rites which they practised, but I could not do it. I felt that I should lie to myself, and mock what I held most sacred, if I did this thing.

At this point our new Russian theologians came to my assistance.

According to the explanation of these divines, the fundamental dogma of faith is the infallibility of the Church. From the acceptance of this dogma follows, as a necessary consequence, the truth of all that is taught by the Church. The Church, as the assembly of believers united in love, and consequently possessing true knowledge, became the foundation of my faith. I said to myself: " Divine truth cannot be attained by any one man, — it can be reached only by the union of all men through love. In order to attain the truth, we must not go each his own way; and, to avoid division, we must have love one to the other, and bear with things which we do not agree with. Truth is revealed in love, and, therefore, if we do not obey the ordinances of the Church, we destroy love; but if love is destroyed we are deprived of the possibility of knowing the truth."

At the time I did not perceive the sophism involved in this reasoning. I did not then see that union through love may develop love to the highest degree, but can never give the Divine Truth, as stated in the words of the Nicene Creed, — I did not see that love can never make any particular form of creed binding on all believers. I did not then see error in this reasoning, and, thanks to it, I was able to accept and practise all the rites of the Orthodox Church, but without understanding the greater part of them. I struggled then, with all the powers of my soul, to avoid all discussions, all contradictions, and endeavored to explain, as reasonably as I could, all the Church doctrines that presented any difficulty.

While thus fulfilling the ordinances of the Church, I submitted my reason to the tradition adopted by the mass of my fellow-men. I united myself to my ancestors, — to those I loved, — my father, mother, and grandparents. They and all before them lived, and believed, and brought me into being. I joined the millions of the people whom I respect. Moreover, there was nothing bad in all this, for bad with me meant the indulgence of the lusts of the flesh. When I got up early to attend divine service, I knew that I was doing well, if it were only because I tamed my intellectual pride for the sake of a closer union with my ancestors and contemporaries, and, in order to seek for a meaning in life, sacrificed my bodily comfort.

It was the same with preparing for the communion, the daily reading of prayers, with genuflections, and the observance of all the fasts. However insignificant the sacrifices were, they were made in a good cause. I prepared for the communion, fasted, and observed regular hours for prayer both at home and at church. While listening to the church service, I weighed every word, and gave it a meaning whenever I could. At mass the words which appeared to me to have most importance were the following : —

"*Let us love one another in unity.*" What follows — the confession of belief in the unity of the Father, the Son, and the Holy Ghost — I passed over, because I could not understand it.

CHAPTER XIV

IT was so necessary for me at that time to believe in order to live, that I unconsciously concealed from myself the contradictions and the obscurities in the doctrines.

But this interpretation of the ritual had its limits. If the Liturgy became clearer and clearer to me in its principal expressions; if I gave a kind of meaning to such expressions as " Remembering our Sovereign Lady, the most Holy Mother of God, and all the Saints, let us devote ourselves, each other, and our whole lives to the Christ God "; if I explained the frequent repetition of prayers for the Tsar and his family by the fact that they were more exposed to temptation than others, and were therefore more in need of prayer, and the prayers for victory over our enemies and opponents to mean victory over the principle of evil; these prayers and others like the hymn of the Cherubim, and all the mystery of the

bread and wine, the adoration of the Virgin and others—
in short, two-thirds of the whole service—either remained
for me without an explanation at all, or made me feel
that the only one I could apply to them was false, while
to·lie was to break off my connection with God, and lose
utterly the possibility of believing.

I felt the same at the celebration of the principal
Church holidays. To " remember the Sabbath day,"
that is, to consecrate one day to communion with God,
was comprehensible to me. The great holiday, however, was in remembrance of the Resurrection, the
reality of which I could neither imagine nor understand. This gave a name to the holiday in each week,
to the Sunday. And on this day the sacrament of the
Eucharist was celebrated, a mystery which to me was
utterly inconceivable. The other twelve holidays, with
the exception of Christmas, were all in remembrance of
miracles, which I tried not to think of in order not to
deny : the Ascension, Pentecost, Epiphany, the Inter-
cession of the Virgin, and so on.

On these holidays I felt that the greatest importance
was given to what I believed to be of the least, and I
either held fast to the explanation that quieted me most,
or else shut my eyes so as not to see what disquieted
me.

This feeling came upon me strongest whenever I
took part in the most ordinary, and, generally considered, the most important, sacraments, as christening
and the holy communion. Here I had to do with
nothing incomprehensible, but with what was easy to
understand : such acts appeared to me a delusion, and
I was on the horns of a dilemma—to lie, or to reject.

I shall never forget the painful feeling I experienced
when I took the communion for the first time after many
years. The service, the confession, the collects, all this
was understood by me, and produced the glad conviction
that the meaning of life lay open to me. The communion I explained to myself as an action done in remembrance of Christ, and as signifying a cleansing
from sin and a complete acceptance of Christ's teach-

ing. If this explanation was artificial, I, at least, was
not troubled by its artificiality. It was such happiness
for me to humble myself with a quiet heart before the
confessor, a simple and mild priest, and, repenting of
my sins, to lay bare all the mire of my soul; it was
such happiness to be united in spirit with the meek
Fathers of the Church who composed these prayers;
such happiness to be one with all who have believed
and who do believe, that I could not feel my explanation
was artificial.

But when I drew near to the *tsarskiya dveri*, "the holy
gates," and the priest called on me to repeat that I believed that what I was about to swallow was the real
body and blood, it cut me to the heart; it was a false
note, though small; it was no unconsidered word; it was
the cruel demand of one who had evidently never known
what faith was.

I now allow myself to say that it was a cruel demand,
but then I did not think so; it was only unspeakably
painful. I was no longer in that position where I
had been in my youth, thinking that all was clear in
life; I had been drawn toward faith because outside it
I had found nothing, assuredly nothing but ruin; and as
I could not throw faith aside, I had submitted. I had
found in my soul a feeling which had helped me to do
this. It was a feeling of self-abasement and submission.
I humbled myself, I swallowed the blood and the body
without any mocking thoughts in the wish to believe,
but the shock had been received, and knowing beforehand what awaited me, I could never go a second time.

I still continued an exact observance of the rites of
the Church, and I still believe that there was truth in
the doctrines I followed; and then there happened to
me a thing which now is clear enough, but which then
appeared to me very strange.

I was at one time listening to the discourse of an unlettered muzhik, a pilgrim. He spoke of God, of faith,
of life, and of salvation, and a knowledge of what faith
was seemed open to me.

I went amongst the people, familiarizing myself with

their ideas of life and faith, and the truth became clearer and clearer to me. It was the same when I read the " Martyrology " and " Prologues "; they be came my favorite books. With the exception of the miracles, and looking on these as fables to bring out forcibly the thought, the reading of these books revealed to me the meaning of life. There I found the lives of Macarius the Great; of Ioasaph the Prince (the story of Buddha); the discourses of St. John Chrysostom; the story of the traveler in the well; of the Monk who found gold; of Peter the Publican; — this is the history of the martyrs, of those who have all testified the same, that life does not end with death; here we have the story of unlettered foolish men, who knew nothing of the doctrines of the Church.

But no sooner did I mix with learned believers, or consult their books, than doubts, uneasiness, and irritation came over me once more, and I felt that the more I studied their discourses the more I wandered from the truth, the nearer I came to the precipice.

CHAPTER XV

How often have I envied muzhiks their inability to read and write, their lack of learning. The very doctrines of faith which to me were manifest nonsense contained for them nothing that was false; they were able to accept them and to believe in truth, the same truth in which I also believed; only to me, unhappy, it was clear that truth was connected with falsehood by the finest threads of difference, and that I could not receive it in such a form.

In this condition I lived for three years, and when I first, like a new convert, little by little drew nearer to truth, and, led by an instinct, groped my way to the light, these obstacles seemed to me less formidable. When I failed to understand anything, I said, " I am wrong, I am wicked." But the more I became imbued with the spirit of the truths which I studied, the more surely I saw them to be the substratum of life, the greater and more formidable became the obstacles, the more clearly defined the line between what I did not understand; and because I was unable to understand, I could understand only through lying unto myself.

Notwithstanding all my doubts and sufferings, I still clung to Orthodoxy; but practical questions arose and had to be settled, and the decisions of these questions by the Church, contrary to the elementary principles of the faith by which I lived, compelled me finally to abandon all communion with it.

The questions were, in the first place, the relation of the Orthodox Church to other churches, to Catholicism and the so-called Raskolniks or Dissenters. The interest which I took in this great question of faith led me at this time to form acquaintance with the professors of different creeds, Catholics, Protestants, Old Believers, Molokans [1] and others, and among them I found many who sincerely believed and obeyed the highest moral standard. I desired to be a brother to these men, and what came of it? The doctrines which had seemed to promise me the union of all men in one faith and love, these doctrines, in the persons of their best representa- tives, told me that all these men were living in a lie; that what gives them strength to live is a temptation of the devil, that we alone possess the possibility of know- ing truth.

And I saw that the members of the Orthodox Church consider all those who do not profess the same faith as themselves to be heretics, exactly as Catholics and others account our Orthodoxy to be heresy; I saw that Orthodoxy considers others who do not adopt the same outward symbols and the same formulas of faith as her- self as her enemies, though she tries to conceal it; and it must be so, in the first place, because the assertion that you live a lie and I am in the truth is the hardest thing that one man can say to another; in the second place, because a man who loves his children and his brethren cannot but feel at enmity with those who

[1] " Milk-drinkers," who do not believe in fasting.

desire to convert his children and brethren to a false
faith. Moreover, this enmity increases as men learn
more of the particular doctrines which they adopt.
Even I, who had believed faith was to be found in the
union of love, was unwillingly forced to see that the
doctrines of faith destroy the very thing which they
should produce.

This snare is so evident, to men living like ourselves
in countries where differing faiths are professed, and wit-
nessing the contemptuous and self-confident exclusive-
ness with which the Catholic treats the Protestant and
Orthodox, repaid by the scorn of the Orthodox for the
Catholic and the Protestant, and that of the latter for
both the others, while the same relation of enmity includes the Old Believers, the Revivalists, the Shakers,
and all other creeds, that at first it perplexes us.

We say to ourselves: —

"No, it cannot be so simple as that, and yet these
men have not seen that when two propositions contradict each other they cannot both have the one truth
on which faith should rest. There was some cause for
this, there was some explanation."

I myself thought there was, and sought for it; and
with this object in view I read everything I could
get on the subject, and consulted with as many as I
could, but the only explanation I obtained was that in
accordance with which " Sumsky " hussars account their
"Sumsky" regiment the first in the world, while the
yellow Uhlans consider that the first regiment in the
world is that of the yellow Uhlans.

Clergymen of all the different religions, the best
representatives of them, without exception, all told me
of their belief that they alone were right and all others
wrong, and that all they could do for those who were in
error was to pray for them. I went to archimandrites,
bishops, priors, and ascetic monks, and asked them; but
no one made the slightest attempt to explain this snare
to me. Only one among them all explained everything
for me, but his explanation was such that I asked nothing
more of any one.

I said that, for every unbeliever who returns to belief
(in which category I place the whole of the present
young generation) the principal question is, Why is
truth to be found in the Orthodox Church and not in
the Lutheran or the Catholic Church? He is taught in
his gymnasium, and he cannot but know what the peasant is ignorant of, that Protestants and Catholics equally
affirm their own faith to be the only true one.

Historical proofs, twisted by each sect to serve their
own purpose, are insufficient. Is it not possible, as I
have already said, for a higher knowledge to issue from
the disappearance of these differences, as they do already disappear for those who sincerely believe? Can
we not go farther on the way on which we and the Old
Believers start out together? They affirm that our way
of signing the cross, of singing hallelujah, and of moving
round the altar, is not the same as theirs. We say : —

"You believe in the Nicene Creed, in the seven sacraments, and we also believe. Keep to that, and for the
rest do as you will."

We shall then be united to them by this, that we both
place the essential points of faith above the unessential.
Again, can we not say to Catholics : —

"You believe in this and in that, in certain things
which are essential, but in what concerns the dispute
about the procession of the Trinity and the Pope, do
as you please "?

Can we not say the same to the Protestant, and unite
with him in what is really important?

My fellow-disputant agreed with me, but added that
such concessions draw down the reproach that the clergy
have receded from the faith of their forefathers and
favor dissent, while the office of those in authority in the
Church is to preserve the purity of the Russian Greek
Orthodox faith as handed down from our ancestors.

Then I understood it all. I am in search of faith,
the staff and strength of life, while these men seek the
best means of fulfilling in the sight of men certain
human obligations, and having to deal with human affairs, they fulfil them as ordinary men ever do. How-

ever much they may talk of their pity for the errors of their brethren, of praying for them at the throne of the Most High, for the accomplishment of earthly affairs force is needed, and force always has been, is, and will be, applied.

If two religious sects each believe that truth resides in themselves, and that the faith of the other is a lie, they will preach their doctrines in the hope of converting their brethren to the truth, and, if false doctrines are taught to the inexperienced sons of the Church who still tread in the ways of truth, she cannot but burn the books and banish the man who seduces her sons. What can be done with the Sectary, who in his fiery enthusiasm for a faith which the Church pronounces false, seduces her sons? What can be done with him, but to cut off his head or imprison him? In the time of Alexis Mikhaïlovitch men were burnt at the stake; in other words, the severest punishment of the time was applied, and in our days also the severest punishment is applied; men are condemned to solitary confinement. When I looked around me at all that was done in the name of religion, I was horrified, and almost entirely withdrew from the Orthodox Church.

The second point which concerned the relations of the Church to the problems of life was her connection with war and executions. At this time Russia was engaged in war, and, in the name of Christian love, Russians were engaged in slaying their brethren. Not to think of this was impossible. Not to see that murder is an evil, contrary to the very first principles of every faith, was impossible. But at the same time in the churches men were praying for the success of our arms, and the teachers of religion were accepting these murders as acts which were the consequence of faith. Not only murder in actual warfare was approved, but, during the troubles which ensued, I saw members of the Church, her teachers, monks, and ascetics, approving of the murder of erring and helpless youths. I looked round on all that was done by men who professed to be Christians, and I was horrified.

CHAPTER XVI

I CEASED from this time to doubt, and became firmly convinced that not all was truth in the faith which I had joined. Formerly I should have said that all in this faith was false, but now it was impossible to say so.

The people as a whole had a knowledge of truth, this was incontestable, for otherwise they could not live. Moreover, this knowledge of truth was open to me; I was already living by it, and felt all its force, but in that same knowledge there was also error. Of that again I could not doubt. All, however, that had formerly repelled me now presented itself in a vivid light. Although I saw that there was less of what had repelled me as false among the people than among the representatives of the Church, I also saw that in the belief of the people what was false was mingled with what was true.

Whence, then, came this truth and this falsehood? Both the falsehood and the truth came to them from what is called the Church; both the falsehood and the truth are included in the traditions, the so-called sacred traditions and writings.

I was thus, whether I would or not, brought to the study and analysis of these writings and traditions, a study which up to that time I had feared, and I turned to the study of theology, which I had once thrown aside with such contempt as useless. Then theology had seemed to me but profitless trifling with nonsense; then I was surrounded by the phenomena of life, which seemed to me clear and full of meaning; now I should have been glad to throw off ideas unsuited to a healthy state of mind, but I could not.

On this doctrinal basis was founded, or at least with it was very intimately bound up, the only explanation of the meaning of the life I had so lately discovered. However strange it might seem to my old practised intellect, it was the only hope of salvation. To be understood, it must be cautiously and carefully examined,

even though the result might not be the certain knowledge of science, which, aware as I was of the special
character of religious inquiry, I did not and could not
seek to obtain.

I could not attempt to explain everything. I knew
that the explanation of the whole, like the beginning of
all things, was hidden in infinity. I wished to be
brought to the inevitable limit where the incomprehensible begins; I wished that what remained uncompre-
hended should be so, not because the mental impulse to
inquiry was not just and natural (all such impulses are
just and without them I could understand nothing), but
because I had learned the limits of my own mind. I
wished to understand so that every unexplained proposition should appear to my reason necessarily unexplain-
able, and not an obligatory part of belief.

That the doctrines contained truth was unquestionable; but it was also unquestionable that they contained
also falsehood, and I was bound to find the truth and
the falsehood and separate the one from the other. I
began to do this. What I found of false, what I found
of true, and to what results I came, forms the following
part of this work,[1] which, if it be thought worth while,
and if it can be useful to any one, will probably be some
day published.

1879.

The above was written by me three years ago.

The other day, on looking over this part again, on
returning to the train of thought and to the feelings
through which I had passed while writing it, I saw a
dream.

This dream repeated for me in a condensed form all
that I had lived through and described, and I therefore
think that a description of it may, for those who have
understood me, serve to render clearer, to refresh the
remembrance of, and to collect into one whole, all that
has been described at so much length in these pages.
The dream was as follows.

[1] My Religion.

I see myself lying in bed, and I feel neither particularly well and comfortable, nor the contrary. I am lying on my back. I begin to think whether it is well for me to lie, and something makes me feel uncomfortable in the legs; if the bed be too short or ill-made, I know not, but something is not right. I move my legs about, and at the same time begin to think how and on what I am lying, a thing which previously had never troubled me. I examine my bed, and see that I am lying on a network of cords fashioned to the sides of the bedstead. My heels lie on one of these cords, my legs on another, and this is uncomfortable. I am somehow aware that the cords can be moved, and with my legs I push the cord away, and it seems to me that thus it will be easier.

But I had pushed the cord too far; I tried to catch it with my legs, but this movement causes another cord to slip from under me, and my legs hang down. I move my body to get right again, convinced that it will be easy, but this movement causes other cords to slip and change their places beneath me, and I perceive that my position is altogether worse; my whole body sinks and hangs, without my legs touching the ground. I hold myself up only by the upper part of the back, and I feel now not only discomfort, but horror. I now begin to ask myself what I had not thought of before. I ask myself where I am, and on what I am lying. I begin to look round, and first I look below, to the place toward which my body sank, and where I feel it must soon fall. I look below, and I cannot believe my eyes.

I am on a height far above that of the highest tower or mountain, a height beyond all my previous powers of conception. I cannot even make out whether I see anything or not below me, in the depths of that bottomless abyss over which I am hanging, and into which I feel drawn. My heart ceases to beat, and horror fills my mind. To look down is horrible. I feel that if I look down I shall slip from the last cord, and perish. I stop looking, but not to look is still worse, for then I think of what will at once happen to me when the last cord breaks. I feel that I am losing, in my terror, the last remnant of my strength, and that my back is gradually sinking lower and lower. Another instant, and I shall fall.

Then all at once comes into my mind the thought that this cannot be true — it is a dream — I will awake.

I strive to wake myself, and cannot. " What can I do ? what can I do ? " I ask myself, and as I put the question I look above.

Above stretches another gulf. I look into this abyss of heaven, and try to forget the abyss below, and I do actually forget it. The infinite depth repels and horrifies me ; the infinite height attracts and satisfies me. I still hang on the last cords which have not yet slipped from under me, over the abyss ; I know that I am hanging thus, but I look only upwards, and my terror leaves me. As happens in dreams, I hear a voice saying, " Look well ; it is there ! " My eyes pierce farther and farther into the infinity above, and I feel that it calms me. I remember all that has happened, and I remember how it happened — how I moved my legs, how I was left hanging in air, how I was horrified, and how I was saved from my horror by looking above. I ask myself, " And now, am I not hanging still ? " and I feel in all my limbs, without looking, the support by which I am held. I perceive that I no longer hang, and that I do not fall, but have a fast hold. I question myself how it is that I hold on. I touch myself, I look around, and I see that under the middle of my body there passes a stay, and on looking up I find that I am lying perfectly balanced, and that it was this stay alone that held me up before.

As happens in dreams, the mechanism by which I am supported appears perfectly natural to me, a thing to be easily understood, and not to be doubted, although this mechanism has no apparent sense when I am awake. In my sleep I was even astonished that I had not understood this before. At my bedside stands a pillar, the solidity of which is beyond doubt, though there is nothing for it to stand on. From this pillar runs a cord,

somehow cunningly and at the same time simply fixed, and if I lie across this cord and look upward, there cannot be even a question of my falling. All this was clear to me, and I was glad and easy in my mind. It seemed as if some one said to me, "See that you remember!"
And I awoke.

1882.

LIFE

LET us picture to ourselves a man whose only means of livelihood is a mill. This man is the son and grandson of a miller, and knows thoroughly, by tradition, how to deal with every part of the mill so that it shall grind well. This man, though ignorant of mechanics, adjusts all the parts of the mill to the best of his ability, so that the product may be profitable and good, and that men may live and eat.

But it has chanced that this man has begun to reflect upon the construction of the mill, to hear some confused statements about its mechanism, and he has begun to observe what part is turned by what other part.

And, from the fly-wheel to the grindstone, from the grindstone to the mill-race, from the mill-race to the wheel, from the wheel to the gate, the dam, and the water, he has come clearly to comprehend that the whole matter lies in the dam and the river. And the man has rejoiced so greatly in this discovery of his, that instead of scrutinizing, as heretofore, the quality of the flour which comes forth, instead of raising and lowering the millstones, of shoeing them, of tightening and slackening the belt, he has begun to study the river. And his mill has been thrown entirely out of gear. People have begun to tell the miller that he is not behaving rightly. He has disputed, and continued to reason about the river. And he has worked so much, so very much, over this, he has disputed so much and so hotly with those who have proved to him the falsity of his premises, that he has, at last, become convinced that the river is the mill itself.

To every proof of the falsity of his course of reasoning such a miller will reply : " No mill grinds without water. Consequently, in order to know the mill, it is

requisite to know how to admit the water, to know the force
of its current and whence it is derived ; hence, in order to
know the mill, it is necessary to know the river."

The miller cannot be logically controverted in his line
of argument. The only means of dispelling his illusion
lies in showing him that, in every course of reasoning,
the reasoning itself is not so important as the place
occupied by the reasoning, *i.e.* that, in order to meditate
fruitfully, it is indispensable to know upon what to
meditate first, and what afterward ; to demonstrate to
him that sensible activity is distinguished from senseless activity only in this, — that sensible activity disposes
its meditations in the order of their importance, deciding
which reasoning must come first, second, third, tenth,
and so on. But senseless activity consists in reasoning
without order. It must be demonstrated to him that
the order of this arrangement is not accidental, but that
it depends upon the object for which the reasoning is
conducted.

The object of all courses of reasoning determines the
order in which the separate trains of thought must be
arranged in order to be understood.

And reasoning not bound together by a common aim
of all the arguments is foolish, no matter how logical it
may be.

The aim of the miller consists in producing good
flour, and this aim, if he will keep it in view, will determine for him the most unquestionable regularity and
order of sequence for his reasoning about the millstones,
the wheel, the dam, and the river.

But without this relation to the aim of his reasoning,
the miller's arguments, no matter how fine and logical
they may be, will be inherently irregular and, what is
the principal consideration, vain ; they will be like the
reasoning of Kifa Mokeevitch,[1] when he argued as to
what should be the thickness of the shell of an ele-
phant's egg, if elephants were produced from the egg,
like birds.

[1] An incoherent reasoner, introduced in Part Second of Gogol's "Dead
Souls." — TRANS.

And such in my opinion are the arguments of our contemporary science about life.

Life is the mill which man desires to investigate. The mill is necessary to grind well; life is necessary only in order that it may be good. And this branch of investigation man cannot abandon for a single moment with impunity. If he does abandon it, his deliberations infallibly lose their place, and become like the reasoning of Mokeevitch as to how much powder would be required to break the shell of elephants' eggs.

Man studies life only in order that it may become better. In this manner have those men studied life who have advanced humanity in the path of knowledge. But, by the side of these true teachers and benefactors of humanity, there always have existed, and there exist now, reasoners who have abandoned the aim of reasoning, and who, in its stead, investigate the question as to the origin of life, — as to why the mill turns. Some assert that it is by reason of the water; others, that it is in consequence of the arrangement. The dispute waxes hot, and the subject of discussion moves farther and farther away, and is completely replaced by utterly foreign topics.

There is an ancient jest regarding the dispute of a Jew and a Christian. The story runs that the Christian, replying to the confused subtleties of the Jew, slapped the latter on his bald pate with his palm, so that it cracked, and put the question : " Did the crack come from the pate or the palm ?" And the dispute about faith was replaced by a fresh and insoluble problem.

Something of the same sort has been in progress since the most ancient times, side by side with men's true wisdom, and in connection with the question about life.

Discussions are known to have arisen in the most ancient times as to the origin of life? whether from an immaterial beginning, or from the combination of various materials? And these discussions have continued down to the present day, so that no end to them can be foreseen, because the aim of all discussion has been abandoned, and life is reasoned upon apart from its aim, and by the word life — life itself is not understood, but that from which it proceeds, or that which accompanies it.

Now, not only in scientific books, but even in conversation, when life is mentioned, the discussion is not about what we all know, — about life; about life of which I am conscious by those sufferings which I fear and which I hate, and by those joys and pleasures which I desire; but of something which came into existence, perhaps, through the play of chance according to some physical laws, and, perhaps, because it possesses in itself some secret cause.

Now the word "life" is ascribed to something contestable, which does not contain within itself the chief signs of life: the consciousness of suffering and of enjoyment, and of aspirations toward goodness.

"La vie est l'ensemble des fonctions, qui resiste à la mort. La vie est l'ensemble des phénomènes, qui se succédent pendant un temps limité dans un être organisé." Life is the sum total of the functions which resist death. Life is the sum total of the phenomena which follow each other in the course of a limited time in an organic being.

Setting aside the inaccuracy, the tautology, with which these definitions are filled, the substance of them all is identical, namely, — that which all men in common understand incontestably by the word "life" is not defined by them, but some processes or other which are accompanied by life and other phenomena.

Under the majority of these definitions comes the activity of the crystal in process of formation; under some comes the activity of fermentation, decomposition; and under all comes the life of each separate cell in my body, for which there nothing exists—neither good nor evil. Some of the processes that take place in the crystal, in the protoplasm, in the germ of the protoplasm, in the cells of my body and of other bodies, are called by a word which is indissolubly connected in me with the consciousness of an aspiration toward my welfare.

Arguments upon some of the conditions of life, as life itself, are precisely the same as the argument about the river, as about the mill. These arguments are, possibly, very necessary for some purpose or other. But they do not touch the subject which they intend to discuss. And, therefore, all deductions as to life drawn from such arguments cannot fail to be false.

The word "life" is very short and very clear, and every one understands what it signifies, and we are bound always to employ it in that sense which is comprehensible to every one. Surely this word is comprehensible to every one, not because it is very accurately defined by other words and ideas, but, on the contrary, because this word expresses a fundamental conception, from which are deduced many, if not all, other conceptions, and therefore, in order to draw deductions from this conception, we are bound, first of all, to accept that conception in its central signification which is undisputed by every one. And precisely this, it seems to me, has been neglected by the contending parties in connection with the conception of life. It has come to pass that the fundamental conception of life, taken at first, not in its central significance, in consequence of disputes about it, and departing ever more and more from its fundamental meaning, accepted by every one, has finally lost the thought upon which it is based, and has received another meaning, which does not correspond to it. This has come to pass, that the very center from which the figure was drawn has been deserted and transferred to another point. Men dispute over the question, whether life lies in the cell or in the protoplasm, or, still lower, in inorganic matter.

But, before disputing, we should ask ourselves, have we a right to attribute the conception of life to a cell?

We say, for instance, that there is life in the cell, that the cell is the living being. But the fundamental conception of human life and the conception of life which is contained in the cell are two conceptions which are not only utterly different, but which cannot be united. One conception excludes the other. I discover that the whole of my body, without exception, consists of cells. These cells, I am informed, possess the same sort of life as myself, and are precisely such living beings as myself; but I acknowledge that I am alive only because I am conscious that I, with all the cells which constitute me, am one living, indivisible being. But I am informed that the whole of me, without exception, is composed of living cells. To whom am I to attribute the property of life, to the cells or to myself? If I admit that the cells have life, then from the idea of life I must obtain the chief indication of my life, the consciousness that I am a single, living being; but if I do not admit that I have life as an independent being, then it is evident that I can by no means attribute that property to the cells of which my body is composed, and of whose consciousness I know nothing.

Either I am alive, and there are portions of me which are not alive, called cells, or there exists an assemblage of living cells, and my consciousness of life is not life, but merely an illusion.

For we do not say that there is in the cells anything that we call *bryzn*, but we say that there is "life" (Zhizn). We say "life" because by this word we understand, not some indefinite *x*, but a thoroughly well-defined dimension, which we all call by the same name, and know only through ourselves as the consciousness of ourselves with our own unit of body, indivisible from ourselves,—and hence such a conception is inapplicable to those cells of which my body is composed.

In whatever investigations or observations a man engages, he is bound, in stating his observations, by every word to mean that which every one indisputably understands alike, and not some conception or other which is necessary to him, but wholly incompatible with its fundamental conception comprehensible to all.

If the word "life" can be used so that it designates, indifferently, both the property of an object as a whole, and entirely different properties of all its component parts, as is done in the case of the cell and the animal composed of cells, then other words may also be employed in the same way. We may say, for example, that, as all thoughts are composed of words, and all words are composed of letters, and letters are made up of lines, the drawing of lines is the same as the exposition of thoughts, and that, therefore, lines may be called thoughts.

The most ordinary phenomenon in the scientific world is to hear and to read discussions upon the origin of *life* from the play of physical, mechanical powers.

But it is doubtful if the majority of the scientific people hold to this — I find it difficult to express it — opinion which is not an opinion, this paradox which is not a paradox, but rather a jest or a riddle.

It asserts that life proceeds from the play of physical and mechanical forces, of those physical forces which we have named physical and mechanical merely in contradistinction to the conception of life.

It is evident that the word "life," improperly applied to conceptions which are foreign to it, departing farther and farther from its fundamental signification, has abandoned its center to such a degree that life is already assumed to be where, according to our conceptions, life cannot exist. The assumption is equivalent to asserting that there exists a circle or sphere whose center lies outside of its periphery.

In fact, life, which I cannot imagine as otherwise than as a striving from evil toward good, proceeds from those regions where I can discern neither good nor evil. It is evident that the center of the conception of life has been entirely shifted. Moreover, following up the investigations into that something called life, I even see that these investigations touch hardly any of the conceptions with which I am acquainted. I perceive an entire series of new conceptions, and of words which possess their conventional meaning in the scientific jargon, but which have nothing in common with existing conceptions.

The conception of life which is familiar to me is not understood as every one understands it, and the conceptions deduced from it do not accord with the usual conceptions, but present themselves as new, conventional conceptions, having received manufactured names to correspond.

The human language is becoming more and more supplanted in scientific investigations, and instead of language, the means of expression of existing objects and ideas, a scientific volapük reigns, distinguished from the real volapük only in this, that the real volapük calls existing objects and conceptions by universal words, but the scientific volapük calls, by words which do not exist, conceptions which do not exist.

The sole means of mental communication between men is language, and, in order that this communication may be possible, it is necessary so to employ language that every word shall infallibly evoke, in every one, corresponding and accurate conceptions. But if it be possible to use language at random, and by that language to understand whatever occurs to us, it is better not to speak, but to indicate everything by signs.

I admit that to settle the laws of the world from the deductions of the mind alone, without experience or observation, is a false and unscientific course — that is to say, it cannot afford true knowledge ; but will it not be still worse to study the phenomena of the world by experiments and observations, and at the same time be guided in these experiments and observations by conceptions which are not fundamental and common to all men, but conventional, and to describe the results of these experiments in words to which a varying significance can be attached? The best apothecary's shop is productive of the greatest injury if the labels are pasted on the bottles not according to their contents, but to suit the convenience of the apothecary.

But men say to me : "Science does not set itself the task of examining all the combinations of life (including within it, will, the desire for good, and the spiritual world); it makes only an abstract from the ideas of life of those phenomena which are subject to its experimental investigations.

This would be very good and lawful. But we know that this is not at all the case in the representations of the scientific men of our times. If, first of all, the conception of life were admitted in its central significance, in that in which every one understands it, it would afterward be clearly settled that science, having made from this conception an abstraction of all its sides, except of the one subject to external observation, looks upon the phenomena from that side only for which it has its own peculiar methods of investigation, it would all be very well, and it would be quite another thing ; then the place which science would have occupied, and the results to which we should have arrived on the foundation of science, would have been entirely different. That which is must be said, and we must not conceal that which we all know. Do we not know that the majority of experimental scientific investigators are fully convinced that they are studying, not one side only of life, but all life ?

Astronomy, mechanics, physics, chemistry, and all the other sciences, together and separately, work over the side of life appertaining to each without coming to any results as to life in general. Only during the period of their savagery, that is to say, of their indistinctness, their ill-defined state, did some of these sciences endeavor from their own point of view to grasp all the phenomena of life, and became confused, through inventing for themselves new conceptions and new words. Thus it was with astronomy when it was astrology, thus it was with chemistry when it was alchemy. The same thing now takes place with that experimental science of evolution which, surveying one side or several sides of life, brings forward a claim to the study of all life.

Men with such a false view of science by no means wish to admit that only a few sides of life are subject to their investigation, but they affirm that all life, with all its phenomena, will be studied by them, by the path of external experiment. "If," say they, "*psychics*" (they are fond of this indefinite word of their volapük) "are still unknown to us, they will yet be known to us. By following up one side or several sides of the phenomena of life, we shall learn to know all sides. That is to say, in other words, that, if we gaze very long and earnestly upon an object from one side, we shall see the object from all sides, and even from its interior."

Amazing as is this strange doctrine, — explicable only by the fanaticism of superstition, — it does exist, and, like every whimsical, fanatical doctrine, it produces its destructive effect, directing the activity of human thought in a false and frivolous path. Conscientious toilers perish, having consecrated their lives to the study of an almost utterly worthless thing. The material forces of people perish from being turned in a direction which is useless. The young generations perish, being directed to the same idle activity as Kifa Mokeevitch, erected into the rank of the highest service to humanity.

It is generally said : Science studies life from all sides. And here lies the point, that every subject has as many sides as there are radii in a sphere, that is to say, they are innumerable, and it is impossible to study from all sides; but one must know from which side it is most important and necessary, and from which it is less important and less useful. As it is impossible to approach an object from all sides at once, so it is impossible to study the phenomena of life from all sides and at once. And, willy-nilly, an order of succession is established. And herein lies the gist of the matter. But this order of succession is furnished only by an understanding of life.

Only a right understanding of life imparts the proper significance and direction to science in general, and to each science in particular, regulating them according to the importance of their significance in connection with life. But if the understanding of life is not such as is implanted within all of us, then science itself will be erroneous.

Not what we call science determines life, but our conception of life determines what should be acknowledged as science. And therefore, in order that science may be science, the question must first be settled as to what is and what is not science, and to this end our idea of life must be elucidated.

I will express the whole of my thought frankly; we all know the fundamental dogma of faith of this false experimental science.

Matter and its energy exist! Energy moves; mechanical movement is converted into molecular; molecular movement is expressed by heat, electricity, nervous, and brain movement. And all the phenomena of life, without exception, present themselves as relations of energy. Everything is thus beautiful, simple, clear, and, chief of all, convenient. So that, if there is nothing of all that which we so much desire, and which so simplifies our life, then all this must be invented in some manner or other.

And here is the whole of my audacious thought : the chief portion of the energy, zeal, and activity of experimental science is founded on the desire to invent everything that is necessary for the firm establishment of so comfortable a representation.

In all the activity of this science we behold, not so much a desire to investigate the phenomena of life, as the one ever present anxiety to prove the veracity of its fundamental tenet. That force is wasted on experiments to explain the origin of organic from inorganic and psychical activity from the processes of organism. The organic does not pass into the inorganic : let us seek at the bottom of the sea, we shall find a bit of stuff which we will call the kernel, a monera.

And it is not there; we shall believe that it is to be found, — the more so as the whole infinity of centuries stands at our service, into which we can thrust everything that ought to be in our creed, — but which is not there in reality.

It is the same with the transition from organic to psychical activity. It does not yet exist. But we believe that it will exist, and we bend all the powers of our intelligence to prove the possibility of this at least.

Disputes as to that which does not concern life, namely, as to whence life proceeds — whether it is animism or vitalism, or, again, the idea of some special force — have concealed from men the principal question of life — that question without which the conception of life loses its coherence, and have gradually led scientific men — those who should guide others — into the position of a man who walks along, and even hastens his steps, but who has forgotten precisely whither he is going.

But perhaps I am deliberately endeavoring not to see the vast results afforded by science in its present course? But, surely, no results can correct a false course? Let us concede the impossible, — that all that contemporary science desires to know of life, and of which it asserts (though it does not believe this itself) — that all this will be revealed; let us concede that all has been revealed, that all is as clear as day. It is clear how organic material arises from inorganic through adaptations; it is clear how physical energy is converted into feeling, will, thought, and that all this is known, not only to students in the gymnasiums, but to village schoolboys.

I am aware that such and such thoughts and feelings proceed from such and such movements. Well, and what then? Can I or can I not direct these movements, in order to arouse in myself such and such thoughts? The question as to how I must awaken thoughts and feelings in myself and in others remains not only unsettled, but even untouched.

I know that scientific men do not trouble themselves to answer this question. The solution of this problem seems to them very simple, as the solution of a difficult problem always seems to a man who does not understand it. The answer to the question, how to regulate our life when it is in our power, seems very easy to men of science. They say: Regulate it so that people may satisfy their wants; science provides means, in the first place, for the proper determination of wants, and, in the second, means to produce so easily and in such abundance that all wants can be easily satisfied, and then people will be happy.

But if we inquire what they call needs, and where lie the limits of needs, they simply reply: "Science — that is what science is for — to portion them out into physical, mental, æsthetic, even moral, and plainly to define what needs are legitimate and in what measure they are illegitimate. It will define this in course of time." But if they are asked how one must guide one's self in the decision as to the legitimacy and illegitimacy of needs, they reply boldly: "By the study of the needs." But the word *need* has only two meanings: either a condition of existence, and the conditions of existence of every object are innumerable in quantity, and hence all the conditions cannot be studied; or the need of happiness for human beings can be known and determined only by consciousness, and is therefore even less susceptible of investigation by contemporary science.

There is an institution, a corporation, an assembly of some sort, either of people or of minds, which is infallible, and which is called science. It will determine all this in course of time.

Is it not evident that all this settlement of the question is merely a paraphrase of the kingdom of the Messiah, in which the part of the Messiah is played by science, and that, for the sake of having the explanation explain anything, it is necessary to believe in the dogmas of science as indisputably as the Hebrews believe in the Messiah, which is what the orthodox scientists do, with this difference only, that the orthodox Jew, representing to himself the Messiah as the envoy of God, can believe that all that the Messiah will establish by his power will be excellent, but the orthodox believer in science cannot, from the nature of things, believe that by means of the external investigation of needs the chief and only question concerning life can be decided?

CHAPTER I

EVERY man lives only for his own good, for his personal welfare. If man feels no desire for happiness, he is not even conscious that he is alive. Man cannot imagine life without the desire for happiness. To live is, for every man, the same thing as to desire and to attain happiness; to desire and to attain happiness is synonymous with living. Man is conscious of life only in himself, only in his own personality, and hence, at first, man imagines that the happiness which he desires for himself personally is happiness, and nothing more.

At first, it seems to him that he and he alone really lives.

The life of other beings seems to him not in the least like his own. He imagines it as merely the semblance of life. Man only observes the life of other beings, and learns from observation only that they are alive. Man knows about the life of other beings when he is willing to think of them, but he *knows* of his own, he cannot for a single moment cease to *know* that he lives, and hence to every man his own life only appears real life. The life of other beings about him seems to him to be merely one of the conditions of his own existence. If he does not desire evil to others, it is only because the sight of the sufferings of others interferes with his happiness. If he desires good to others, it is not at all the same as for himself — it is not in order that the person to whom he wishes good may be well placed, but only in order that the happiness of other beings may augment the happiness of his own life. Only that happiness in this life is important and necessary to a man which he feels to be his own, *i.e.* his own individual happiness.

124

And behold, in striving for the attainment of this, his own individual happiness, man perceives that his happiness depends upon other beings. And upon watching and observing these other beings, man sees that all of them, both men and even animals, possess precisely the same conception of life as he himself. Each one of these beings, precisely like himself, is conscious only of his own life and his own happiness, considers his own life alone of importance and real, and the life of all other beings only as a means to his individual happiness. Man sees that every living being, precisely like himself, must be ready, for the sake of his petty happiness, to deprive all other beings of greater happiness and even of life.

And, having comprehended this, man involuntarily makes this calculation; that if this is so, — and he knows that it is indubitably so, — then, not one being or not half a score of beings only, but all the innumerable beings in the world, for the attainment, each of his own object, are ready every moment to annihilate him, — that man for whom alone life exists. And, having apprehended this, man sees that his personal happiness, in which alone he understands life, is not only not to be easily won by him, but that it will assuredly be taken from him.

The longer a man lives, the more firmly is this conviction confirmed by experience, and the man perceives that the life of the world in which he shares, composed of individualities bound together, desirous of exterminating and devouring each other, not only cannot be a happiness for him, but will, assuredly, be a great evil.

But this is not all : if the man is placed in such favorable conditions that he can successfully contend with other personalities, fearing nothing for his own, both experience and reason speedily show him that even those semblances of happiness which he wrests from life, in the form of enjoyment for his own personality, do not constitute happiness, and are but specimens of happiness as it were, vouchsafed him merely in order that he may be the more vividly conscious of the suffer ing which is always bound up with enjoyment.

The longer man lives, the more plainly does he see that weariness, satiety, toils, and sufferings become ever greater and greater, and enjoyments ever less and less.

But this is not all: on beginning to become conscious of a decline of strength, and of ill-health, and gazing upon ill-health, age, and the death of others, he perceives this also in addition, that even his existence, in which alone he recognizes real, full life, is approaching weakness, old age, and death, with every hour, with every movement; that his life, besides being subject to thousands of chances of annihilation from other beings warring with him, and from ever increasing sufferings, is, in virtue of its very nature, nothing else than an incessant approach to death, to that condition in which, together with the life of the individual, will, assuredly, be annihilated every possibility of any personal happiness. The man perceives that he, his own personality, — that in which alone he feels life, does nothing but struggle with those with whom it is impossible to struggle — with the whole world ; that he is in search of enjoyments which give only the semblances of happiness, and which always terminate in sufferings, and he wishes to hold back life, which it is impossible to hold back. The man perceives that he himself, his own personality, that for which, alone, he desires life and happiness, can have neither life nor happiness. And that which he desires to have — life and happiness — is possessed only by those beings who are strangers to him, whom he does not feel, and cannot feel, and of whose existence he cannot know and does not wish to know.

That which for him is the most important of all, and which alone is necessary to him, that which — as it seems to him — alone possesses life in reality, his personality, that which will perish, will become bones and worms, is not he; but that which is unnecessary for him, unimportant to him, which he does not feel to be alive, all that world of ever changing and struggling beings, that is to say, real life, will remain, and will exist forever

So that the sole life which is felt by man, and which evokes all this activity, proves to be something deceptive and impossible; but the inward life, which he does not love, which he does not feel, of which he is ignorant, is the one real life.

That of which he is not conscious, — that alone possesses those qualities of which he would fain be the sole possessor. And this is not that which presents itself to a man in the evil moments of his gloomy moods, this is not a representation which it is possible for him not to have, but it is, on the contrary, such a palpable, indubitable truth, that if this thought once occurs to man, or if others explain it to him, he can never again free himself from it, he can never more force it out of his consciousness.

CHAPTER II

THE SOLE AIM OF LIFE

The contradiction of life has been admitted by mankind from the most ancient times. The enlighteners of mankind expounded to men the definition of life, solving the problem of this inward contradiction, but the Scribes and Pharisees conceal it from the people.

THE sole aim of life, as it first presents itself to man, is the happiness of himself as an individual, but individual happiness there cannot be; if there were anything resembling individual happiness in life, then that life in which alone happiness can exist, the life of the individual, is borne irresistibly, by every movement, by every breath, toward suffering, toward evil, toward death, toward annihilation.

And this is so self-evident and so plain that every thinking man, old or young, learned or unlearned, will see it.

This argument is so simple and natural that it presents itself to every reasoning man, and has been known to mankind ever since the most ancient times.

" The life of man as an individual, striving only toward

his own happiness, amid an endless number of similar individuals, engaged in annihilating each other and in annihilating themselves, is evil and absurdity, and real life cannot be like that." This is what man has been saying to himself from the most ancient times down to the present day, and this inward inconsistency of the life of man was expressed with remarkable force and clearness by the Indian, and the Chinese, and the Egyptian, and the Greek, and the Jewish sages ; and from the most ancient times the mind of man has been directed to the study of such a happiness for man as should not be canceled by the contest of beings among themselves, by suffering, and by death. In the increasingly better solution of this indubitable, unavoidable happiness for man inviolable by contest, by sufferings, and by death, lies the whole progress of mankind during the period of our acquaintance with its life.

From the most ancient times, and among the most widely varying peoples, the great teachers of mankind have revealed to men more and more the clear definitions of life, solving its inward contradictions, and have pointed out the true happiness and true life which is proper to men.

And, since the position of all men in the world is identical, since the contradiction of his strivings after his personal happiness, and the consciousness of its impossibility is identical for every man, all the definitions of true happiness, and therefore of true life, revealed to men by the grandest minds of humanity, are identical in their nature.

" Life is the diffusion of that light which, for the happiness of men, descended upon them from heaven," said Confucius, six hundred years before Christ.

" Life is the peregrination and the perfection of souls, which attain to greater and ever greater happiness," said the Brahmins of the same day.

" Life is the abnegation of self, with the purpose of attaining blessed Nirvana," said Buddha, a contemporary of Confucius.

" Life is the path of peacefulness and lowliness, for

the attainment of happiness," said Lao-dzi, also a contemporary of Confucius.

" Life is that which God breathed into man's nostrils, in order that he, by fulfilling his law, might receive happiness," says the Hebrew sage, Moses.

" Life is submission to the reason, which gives happiness to man," said the Stoics.

" Life is love toward God and our neighbor, which gives happiness to man," said Christ, summing up in his definition all those which had preceded it.

Such are the definitions of life, which, thousands of years before our day, pointing out to men real and indestructible happiness in the place of the false and impossible happiness of the individual, solve the contradictions of human life and impart to it a reasonable sense.

It is possible not to agree with these definitions of life, it is possible to assume that these definitions can be expressed more accurately and more clearly; but it is impossible not to see that these definitions are such that the acknowledgment of them, since it does away with the inconsistencies of life, and replaces the aspiration for the unattainable happiness of the individual, by another aspiration, — for a happiness indestructible by suffering and death, imparts to life a reasonable sense. It is impossible not to see this also, that these definitions, while theoretically correct, are also confirmed by the experience of life, and that millions and millions of men, who have accepted and who do accept such definitions of life, have, in fact, proved, and do prove, the possibility of replacing the aspiration toward individual welfare by an aspiration toward another happiness, of a sort which is not to be destroyed by suffering and death.

But, in addition to those men who have understood and who do understand the definitions of life, revealed to men by the great enlighteners of humanity, and who live by them, there always have been and there are now an immense number of people who, during a certain period of their life, and sometimes their whole life long, have led and do lead a purely animal existence, being not only ignorant of those definitions which serve to

solve the contradictions of human life, but not even perceiving that contradiction of it which they solve.   And
there always have been and there now exist among those
people, men who, in consequence of their exclusively
external position, regard themselves as called upon to
guide mankind, and who, without themselves comprehending the meaning of human life, have taught and do
teach other people life, which they themselves do not
understand ; to the effect that human life is nothing but
individual existence.

Such false teachers have existed in all ages, and exist
in our day also.   Some confess in words the teachings
of those enlighteners of mankind, in whose traditions
they have been brought up, but not comprehending
their rational meaning, they convert these teachings into
supernatural revelations as to the past and future life
of men, and require only the fulfilment of ceremonial
forms.

This is the doctrine of the Pharisees in the very
broadest sense, *i.e.* of the men who teach that a life
preposterous in itself can be amended by faith in a
future life, obtained by the fulfilment of external forms.

Others, who do not acknowledge the possibility of
any other life than the visible one, reject all marvels and
everything supernatural, and boldly affirm that the life
of man is nothing but his animal existence from his
birth to his death.   This is the doctrine of the Scribes
— of men who teach that there is nothing preposterous
in the life of man, any more than in that of animals.

And both the former and the latter false prophets, in
spite of the fact that the teaching of both is founded
upon the same coarse lack of understanding of the
fundamental inconsistency of human life, have always
been at enmity with each other, and are still at enmity.
Both these doctrines reign in our world, and, contending
with each other, they fill the world with their dissensions — by those same dissensions concealing from men
those definitions of life which reveal the path to the
true happiness of men, and which were given to men
thousands of years ago.

The Pharisees, not comprehending this definition of life, which was given to men by those teachers in whose traditions they were brought up, replace it with their false interpretations of a future life, and, in addition to this, strive to conceal from men the definition of life of other enlighteners of humanity, by presenting the latter to their disciples in the coarsest and harshest aspect, assuming that, by so doing, they will uphold the absolute authority of that doctrine upon which they found their interpretation.[1]

And the Scribes, not even suspecting in the teachings of the Pharisees those rational grounds from which they took their rise, flatly reject all doctrines concerning a future life, and boldly affirm that all these doctrines have no foundation whatever, but are merely remnants of the coarse customs of ignorance, and that the forward movement of mankind consists in not putting any questions whatever to one's self concerning life which overleap the bounds of the animal existence of man.

CHAPTER III

THE ERROR OF THE SCRIBES

AND, marvelous to relate! the fact that all the teachings of the great minds of mankind so startled men by their grandeur that the rude populace attributed to them, for the most part, a supernatural character, and accepted their authors as demigods, — the very fact which serves as the chief indication of the importance of these doctrines, — that very fact serves the Scribes, so they think, as their best proof of the incorrectness and antiquated character of these doctrines.

The fact that the insignificant teachings of Aristotle, Bacon, Comte, and others have remained, and will al-

[1] The unity of the rational idea of the definition of life by other enlighteners of mankind does not present itself to them as the best proof of the truth of their teaching, since it injures faith in the senseless, false interpretations with which they replace the substance of doctrine.

ways remain, the property of a small number of their
readers and admirers, and on account of their falsity,
never could influence the masses, and hence were never
subjected to superstitious distortions and excrescences,
— this mark of their insignificance is recognized as a
proof of their truth.   But the teachings of the Brahmins,
of Buddha, of Zoroaster, Lao-dzi, Confucius, Isaiah, and
Christ are accounted superstitious and erroneous, merely
because these teachings have effected a change in the
lives of millions.

The fact that millions of men have lived, and do still
live, according to these superstitions, because even in
their mutilated form they furnish men with answers to
questions about true happiness; the fact that these doctrines not only are shared by, but serve as a foundation
for the thoughts of the best men of all ages, and that the
theories professed by the Scribes alone are shared only
by themselves, are always contested, and sometimes do
not live ten years, and are forgotten as quickly as they
were evolved, — does not disturb them in the least.

On no point does that false direction of learning followed by contemporary society express itself with such
clearness as on the place which is held in this society by
the doctrines of those great teachers of life by which
mankind has lived and developed, and by which it still
lives and develops itself.   It is affirmed in the calen-
dars, in the department of statistical information, that
the creeds now professed by the inhabitants of this globe
number one thousand.   Among the list of these creeds
are reckoned Buddhism, Brahmanism, Confucianism,
Laodism, and Christianity.   There are a thousand creeds,
and the people of our day believe this implicitly.   There
are a thousand creeds, they are all nonsense — why study
them ?   And the men of our time consider it a disgrace
if they do not know the latest apothegms of wisdom
of Spencer, Helmholtz, and others; but of Brahma,
Buddha, Confucius, Mentizus, Lao-dzi, Epictetus, and
Isaiah they sometimes know the names, and sometimes
they do not even know that much.   It never enters their
heads that the creeds professed in our day number not

one thousand, but three, in all : the Chinese, the Indian, and the European-Christian (with its offshoot, Mahometanism), and that the books pertaining to these faiths can be purchased for five rubles, and read through in two weeks, and that in these books, by which all mankind has lived and now lives, with the exception of seven per cent, almost unknown to us, is contained all human wisdom, all that has made mankind what it is.

But not only is the populace ignorant of these teachings, the learned men are not acquainted with them, unless it is their specialty; philosophers by profession do not not consider it necessary to glance into these books. And why, indeed, study those men who have solved the inconsistency of his life admitted by the sensible man, and have defined true happiness and the life of men?

The Scribes, not understanding this contradiction or inconsistency which constitutes the beginning of rational life, boldly assert that there is no contradiction, because they do not perceive it, and that the life of man is merely his animal existence.

Those who do see, understand and define that which they see before them — the blind man fumbles before him with a cane, and asserts that nothing exists except that which the touch of his cane reveals to him.

CHAPTER IV

THE TEACHING OF THE SCRIBES, UNDER THE CONCEPTION OF THE WHOLE LIFE OF MAN, PRESENTS THE VISIBLE PHENOMENA OF HIS ANIMAL EXISTENCE, AND FROM THEM DRAWS DEDUCTIONS AS TO THE AIM OF HIS LIFE

" LIFE is what takes place in a living being from the time of his birth to his death. A man, a dog, a horse is born ; each one has his special body ; and this special body of his lives and then dies ; the body decomposes, passes into other beings, but will never be the former being again. Life was, and life came to an end ; the heart beats, the lungs breathe, the body does not decompose, — which means that the man, the horse, the dog, is alive; the heart has ceased to beat, breathing has come to an end, the body has begun to decompose, — which means that it is dead, and that there is no life. Life is that process which goes on in the body of man, as well as in that of the animal, in the interval of time between birth and death. What can be clearer?"

Thus have the very rudest people, who have hardly emerged from animal existence, always looked upon life, and thus do they look upon it now. And lo! in our day, the teaching of the Scribes, entitling itself science, professes this same coarse, primitive presentation of life as the only true one. Making use of all those instruments of inward knowledge which mankind has acquired, this false teaching is systematically desirous of leading man back into that gloom of ignorance from which he has been striving to escape for so many thousand years.

"We cannot define life in our consciousness," says this doctrine. "We go astray when we observe it in ourselves. That conception of happiness, the aspiration toward which in our consciousness constitutes our life, is a deceitful illusion, and life cannot be understood in that consciousness. In order to understand life, it is only necessary to observe its manifestations as movements of matter. Only from these observations, and the laws deduced from them, can we discover the law of life itself, and the law of the life of man." [1]

The science of physics talks of the laws and relations of forces, without putting to itself any questions as to what force is, and without endeavoring to explain the nature of force. The science of chemistry speaks of the relations of matter, without questioning what matter is, and without seeking to define its nature; the science of biology deals with the forms of life, putting to itself no questions as to what life is, and not seeking to define its nature. And force and matter and life are accepted

---

[1] Real science, knowing its proper place and hence its object, modest and hence powerful, never has said and never says this.

as real sciences, not as subjects for study, but adopted as axioms from other realms of learning, as bases of operation upon which is constructed the edifice of every separate science. Thus does real science regard the subject, and this science cannot have any injurious influence upon the masses, inclining them to ignorance. But not thus does the false, philosophizing science look upon the subject. " We will study matter and force and life; and, if we study them, we can know them," say they, not reflecting that they are not studying matter, force, and life, but merely their relations and their forms.

And behold, false science, having placed under the conception of the whole life of man its visible portion which is known to him through his consciousness, — the animal existence, — begins to study these apparent phenomena at first in the animal man, then in animals in general, then in plants, then in matter, constantly asserting, in the meanwhile, that they are studying not a few phenomena, but life itself. Their observations are so complicated, so varied, so confused, so much time and strength have been wasted upon them, that men gradually forget the original error of admitting a portion of the subject as the whole subject, and finally become fully convinced that the study of the visible properties of matter, plants, and animals is study of life itself, of that life which is known to man only through his consciousness.

What takes place is somewhat similar to that which happens when a person is showing something in the dark, and is desirous of upholding that mistake under which the spectators are laboring.

" Look nowhere," says the exhibitor, " except in the direction where the reflections appear, and, most of all, do not look at the object itself; for there is no object, but only its reflection."

This is the very thing which the false science of the Scribes of our day does, conniving with the rude throng, looking upon life without its chief definition, without its aspiration toward happiness, which is discovered only in the consciousness of man.[1] Proceeding directly from the definition of life, independent of the aspiration toward happiness, false science observes the objects of human beings, and, finding in them aims foreign to man, forces them upon him.

The aim of human beings, as presented by these external observations, is the preservation of one's individuality, the preservation of one's species, the production of others similar to one, and the struggle for existence; and this same fancied aim of life is also thrust on man.

False science, having adopted as a base of operation an antiquated presentation of life, in which that contradiction of human life which constitutes its chief property is not visible, — this fictitious science in its most extreme deductions arrives at that point which the coarse majority of mankind requires, — at the admission of the possibility of the happiness of individual life alone, at the admission for humanity of the happiness of the animal existence alone.

False science goes much farther even than the demands of the coarse herd for whom it wishes to find an explanation, — it arrives at the assertion that it rejects the rational consciousness of man from its first flash, it arrives at the deduction that the life of man, like that of every animal, consists in the struggle for the existence of individuality, race, and species.[2]

CHAPTER V

THE FALSE DOCTRINES OF THE SCRIBES AND PHARISEES GIVE NEITHER EXPLANATIONS OF THE MEANING OF REAL LIFE, NOR GUIDANCE THEREIN ; THE INERTIA OF LIFE, WHICH HAS NO RATIONAL EXPLANATION, APPEARS AS THE SOLE GUIDE OF LIFE

"IT is useless to define life; every one knows it, so let us live!" say, in their error, the men who are upheld

[1] See appendix at the end of the book, on "The false definition of life."
[2] See second appendix.

by false teachings. And, not knowing what life and its happiness are, it seems to them that they live, as it may seem to a man who is being borne along by the waves without exercising any control of his course, that he is sailing to the place where he should go, and where he wishes to go.

A child is born in want or in luxury, and he receives the training of the Pharisees or of the Scribes. For the child, for the young man, there exists as yet no contradiction in life nor problems concerning it, and therefore neither the explanations of the Pharisees nor the explanations of the Scribes are necessary to him, and they cannot govern his life. He learns simply from the example of the people who live around him, and this is equally the example of the Scribes and Pharisees; and both the former and the latter live only for personal happiness, and this is what they teach him.

If his parents are poor, he learns from them that the aim of life is the acquisition of as much bread and money as possible, and as little work as possible, so that his animal person may be as comfortable as possible.

If he has been born in luxury, he learns that the aim of life is wealth and honors, so that he may pass his time in the merriest and most agreeable manner possible.

All the knowledge acquired by the poor man is of use to him only for the purpose of improving the comfortable condition of his own person. All the attainments in science and art acquired by the rich man are of use to him only for the combating of ennui, and passing the time pleasantly. The longer both of them live, the more and more strongly do they imbibe the prevailing views of men of the world. They marry, have families, and their thirst for the acquisition of animal welfare of life is augmented by the justificatory excuse of their families; the struggle with others grows fiercer, and the inertia of the custom of life arranges itself solely with a view to the welfare of the individual.

And if there occurs to either the rich or the poor man a doubt as to the reasonableness of such a life, if to either there presents itself the question, "What is the reason for this objectless struggle for my existence, which my children will continue? or why this delusive pursuit of enjoyments, which end in suffering for me and for my children?" then there is hardly any likelihood that he will learn those definitions of life which were given long ago to mankind by its great teachers, who thousands of years before him found themselves in the same situation. The teachings of the Scribes and Pharisees so thickly veil them that he rarely succeeds in seeing them.

The Pharisees alone, to the question, "To what purpose this miserable life?" make reply: "Life is miserable, and always has been so, and must always be so; the happiness of life consists not in its present, but in the past, before life was, and in the future, after life is ended."

Brahmin, and Buddhist, and Lao-dziist, and Jewish, and Christian Pharisees always say one and the same thing. The present life is evil, and the explanation of this evil lies in the past, in the phenomenon of the world and of man; but the correction of the existing evil lies in the future, beyond the grave. All that man can do for the acquisition of happiness, not in this but in a future life, is — to believe in that teaching which we impart to you — to fulfil the ceremonial forms which we prescribe.

And the doubter, perceiving in the life of all men who are living for their own happiness, and in the life of the very Pharisees who live only for the same thing, the falsity of this explanation, and not penetrating the meaning of their reply, flatly refuses to believe them, and betakes himself to the Scribes.

"All teachings about any other life whatsoever than this which we see in the animal is the fruit of ignorance," say the Scribes. "All your doubts as to the reasonableness of your life are empty fancies. The life of worlds, of the earth, of man, of animals, of plants, have their laws, and we are investigating them, we are studying the origin of worlds, and of man, of animals and plants, and of all matter; we are also investigating

what awaits the worlds when the sun shall cool, and so
forth, and what has been and what will be with man,
and with every animal and plant. We can show and
prove that all has been and will be as we say; besides
this, our investigations will contribute to the amelioration of mankind. But of your life and your aspirations
toward happiness, we can tell you nothing more than
what you already know without us : you are alive, so
live as best you can."

And the doubter, having received no reply to his
question from these either, remains as he was before,
without any guidance whatever in life, except the
impulses of his own personality.

Some of the doubters, according to the reasoning of
Pascal, having said to themselves : " What if all
the things with which the Pharisees frighten us for
non-fulfilment of their prescribed forms should be
true ?" and so fulfil *in their leisure time* all the dictates
of the Pharisees (there can be no loss, and there is a
possibility that the profit may be great), while others,
agreeing with the Scribes, flatly reject any other life
and all religious forms, and say to themselves : " Not I
alone, but all the rest, have lived and do live thus, — let
what will be, be." And this discrepancy confers no
superiority on either the one set or the other; and
both the former and the latter remain without any
explanation whatever of the meaning of their present
life.

But it is necessary to live.

Human life is a series of actions from the time a man
rises until he goes to bed ; every day, of actions which
are possible to him, man must incessantly make his
choice out of hundreds of those which he will perform.
Neither the teaching of the Pharisees, which explains
the mysteries of the heavenly life, nor the teaching of the
Scribes, which investigates the origin of worlds and of
man, and draws conclusions concerning their future
fate, furnishes that guidance for actions. But without
guidance in the choice of his action a man cannot live.
And so the man submits, perforce, not to reason, but to

that external guidance of life which has always existed,
and does exist in every community of men.

This guidance has no rational explanation, but it
directs the vast majority of the actions of all men.
This guidance is the habit of life of communities of
men, ruling all the more powerfully over men in proportion as men have less comprehension of the meaning
of their life. This guidance cannot be accurately defined, because it is composed of facts and actions, the
most varied as to place and time. It is : lights upon the
boards of their ancestors for the Chinese; pilgrimages
to certain places for the Mahometan; a certain amount
of prayer words for the Indian; it consists of fidelity
to his flag, and honor to his uniform, for the warrior;
the duel for the man of the world; blood-vengeance for
the mountaineer; it means certain sorts of food on
specified days, a particular mode of education for one's
children; it means visits, a certain decoration of one's
dwelling, specified manners of celebrating funerals,
births, and deaths. It is an interminable number of
facts and actions, filling the whole of life. It is what
is called propriety, custom, and, most frequently of all,
duty, and even sacred duty.

And it is to this guidance that the majority of mankind submit themselves, in spite of the explanations of
life furnished by the Scribes and Pharisees. Man beholds everywhere about him, from his very childhood,
men accomplishing those deeds with complete conviction and outward solemnity, and possessing no rational
explanation of his life, and the man not only begins to
do the same things, but even attempts to ascribe a
rational meaning to these deeds. He wishes to believe
that the people who do these things possess an explanation as to why, and to what end they do what they do.
And he begins to be convinced that these deeds have a
rational meaning, if not wholly known to him, yet known
to these persons at least.

But the majority of the rest of mankind, not being
possessed, any more than himself, of a rational explanation of life, find themselves in precisely the same

situation as himself. They, also, do these things only
because others, who, as it seems to them, have an explanation of these deeds, demand the same from them.
And thus, involuntarily deceiving each other, people become ever more and more accustomed, not only to do
these things without possessing a rational explanation,
but they become accustomed to ascribing to these deeds
some mysterious meaning incomprehensible even to
themselves. And the less they understand the meaning of what they do, the more doubtful to themselves
these acts become, the more importance do they attach
to them, and with all the greater solemnity do they fulfil
them. And the rich man and the poor man do that
which others do round about them, and they call these
acts their duty, their sacred duty, reassuring themselves
by the thought that what has been done so long by so
many people, and is so highly prized by them, cannot
but be the real business of life. And men live on to
hoar old age, to death, striving to believe that if they
themselves do not know why they live, others do know
this — the very people who know precisely as little
about it as those who depend upon them.

New people come into existence, are born, grow up,
and, looking upon this whirlpool of existence called
life, — in which old, gray, respected men, surrounded
by the reverence of the people, assert that this senseless
commotion is life, and that there is no other, — go away
after being jostled at its doors. Such a man, who has
never beheld an assembly of men, having seen a crowd-
ing, lively, noisy throng at the entrance, and having decided that this is the assembly itself, after having been
elbowed at the door, goes home with aching ribs and
under the full conviction that he has been in the
assembly.

We pierce mountains, we fly round the world; electricity, microscopes, telephones, wars, parliaments, phi-
lanthropy, the struggle of parties, universities, learned
societies, museums, — is this life?

The whole of men's complicated, seething activity,
with their trafficking, their wars, their roads of communi-

cation, their science and their arts, is, for the most part,
only the thronging of the unintelligent crowd about the
doorway of life.

CHAPTER VI

DIVISION OF CONSCIOUSNESS IN THE MEN OF OUR WORLD

"BUT verily, verily, I say unto you, the time is at
hand, and is even now come, when the dead shall hear
the voice of the Son of God, and, hearing, shall be made
alive." And this time will come.

However much a man may have assured himself, and
however much others may have assured him of this,—
that life can only be happy and rational beyond the
grave, or that only personal life can be happy and
rational, — man cannot believe it. Man cherishes in the
depths of his soul an ineffaceable demand that his life
shall be happy and have a rational meaning ; but a life
having before it no other aim than the life beyond the
grave, or an impossible bliss of personality, is evil and
nonsense.

"Live for the future life ? " says the man to himself :
"but if this life, the only specimen of life with which I
am acquainted, — my present life, — must be irrational,
then it not only does not confirm in my mind the possibility of another, a rational life, but, on the contrary, it
convinces me that life is, in its very substance, irrational, and that there can be no other life than an
irrational one.

"Live for myself ? But my individual life is evil and
senseless. Live for my family ? For my society ? For
my country or even mankind ? But if my individual
life is miserable and senseless, then the life of every
other human individual is miserable and senseless also ;
and therefore an endless quantity of senseless and irrational persons, collected together, will not form even one
happy and rational life. Live for myself, not knowing
why, doing that which others do ? But, surely, I am

aware that others know no more than I why they do what they do."

The time will come when a rational consciousness will outgrow the false doctrines, and man will come to a halt in the midst of life, and demand explanations.[1]

Only the rare man, who has no connection with people of other modes of life, and only the man who is constantly engaged in an intense struggle with nature for the support of his bodily existence, can believe that the fulfilment of those senseless acts which he calls his duty can be the peculiar duty of his life.

The time is coming, and is already come, when that delusion which sets forth the renunciation — in words — of this life, for the sake of preparing for one's self one in the future, and the admission of the mere individual animal existence alone as life, and so-called duty as the business of life, — when that delusion will become clear to the majority of men, and only those forced by necessity, and dulled by a vicious career, will be able to exist without being conscious of the senselessness and poverty of their existence.

More and more frequent will be men's awakening to a rational sense ; they will in their graves return to life, and the fundamental contradiction of human life will, in spite of all men's efforts to hide it from themselves, present itself before the majority of men with terrible power and distinctness.

" All my life consists of a desire for happiness for myself," says the man to himself, on awakening, " but my reason tells me that this happiness cannot exist for me, and that, whatever I may do, whatever I may attain to, all will end in one and the same thing, — in sufferings and death, in annihilation. I desire happiness, I desire life, I desire a rational sense, but in myself and in all who surround me there is evil, death, and incoherence. How am I to exist ? How am I to live ? What am I to do ? " and there is no reply.

The man looks about him, and seeks an answer to his question, and finds it not. He finds around him doc-

[1] See third appendix at the end of the book.

trines that answer questions which he has never put to
himself; but there is no answer in the world surrounding him to the question which he does put to himself.
There is one anxiety for men who do, without themselves knowing why, the things which others do, when
they themselves know not why.

All live as though unconscious of the wretchedness
of their position and the senselessness of their activity.
"Either *they* are irrational or *I* am," says the awakened
man to himself.   "But all cannot be irrational, so it
must be that the irrational one is myself.   But no — the
rational *I* which says this to me cannot be irrational.
Let it stand alone against all the world, but I cannot do
otherwise than trust it."

And the man recognizes himself as alone in all the
world, with all the terrible questions which rend his
soul.

But it is necessary to live.

One *I*, his individuality, bids him live.

But another *I*, his reason, says, "It is impossible to
live."

The man is conscious that he has been parted in twain.
And this partition rends his soul like torture.

And the cause of this partition and of his suffering
seems to him to be his reason.

Reason, the loftiest of man's faculties, which is indispensable to his life, which gives to him, naked and helpless amid the powers of nature which destroy him, both
means of existence and means of enjoyment, — this faculty poisons his existence.   In all the world which sur-
rounds him, among living beings, the faculties peculiar
to these beings are necessary to them all in common, and
constitute their happiness.   Plants, insects, animals, submitting to the law of their being, live a blissful, joyous,
tranquil life.

But behold, in man, this loftiest faculty of his nature
produces in him such a torturing condition of things that
often — with ever increasing frequency of late days —
man cuts the Gordian knot of his life, and kills himself
simply for the sake of escaping from the torturing in

ward contradictions produced by intelligent consciousness which, in our day, has been carried to the last degree of tension.

CHAPTER VII

THE PARTITION OF CONSCIOUSNESS ARISES FROM THE BLENDING OF THE LIFE OF THE ANIMAL WITH THE LIFE OF MAN

It seems to man that the partition of rational consciousness which has awakened within him shatters his life in fragments, and brings it to a standstill, only because he recognizes as his life that which has not been, is not, and could not be his life.

Having been reared and having grown up in the false doctrines of our world, which have confirmed in him the conviction that his life is nothing else than his individual existence, which began with his birth, it seems to man that he lived when he was a boy, a baby; then it seems to him that he has lived, without a break, when he was a youth and when he had reached full manhood. He has lived a very long time, as it seems to him, and during all that time has never ceased to live, and lo, all at once, he has reached a point where it has become indubitably clear to him that it is impossible for him to continue to live as he has lived before, and that his life has stopped and been shattered.

False teaching has confirmed him in the idea that his life is the period of time from birth to death; and, looking at the visible life of animals, he has confounded the idea of apparent life with his consciousness, and has become quite convinced that this life which he can see is his life.

The intelligent consciousness which has awakened within him, having advanced such demands as are not to be satisfied by the animal life, shows him the error of his conception of life; but the false teaching which has eaten into him prevents his confessing his error; he cannot reject his conception of life as an animal exis-tence, and it seems to him that his life has come to a

standstill through the awakening of intelligent conscious·
ness. But that which he calls his life, his existence
since his birth, has never even existed; his idea that he
has been living all the time from his birth to the present
moment is an illusion of consciousness, similar to the
illusion of the senses in the visions of sleep; up to the
time of his awakening he had no visions, they have all
formed at the moment of his awakening. Before the
awakening of his intelligent consciousness, there was no
life of any sort; his conception of his past life was
formed at the awakening of his intelligent consciousness.

A man has lived like an animal during the period of
his childhood, and has known nothing of life. If the
man had lived only ten months, he would never have
known anything about his own existence or any one
else's; he would have known just as little of life as
though he had died in his mother's womb. And not
only can the baby not know, but the unintelligent grown-
up men and the utter idiot cannot know, that they live,
and that other human beings live. And therefore they
have no human life.

Man's life begins only with the appearance of rational
consciousness, — of that which reveals to man simultaneously his life in the present and the past, and the
life of other individuals, and all that flows inevitably from
the relations of these individuals, sufferings and death,
— of that same thing which calls forth in him the renunciation of personal happiness in life, and the inconsistency which, as it seems to him, brings his life to a
standstill.

Man tries to define his life by dates, as he defines an
existence outside himself which he sees, and all of a
sudden a life awakens in him which does not correspond with the date of his birth in the flesh, and he does
not wish to believe that that which is not defined by a
date can be life. But seek as a man may in time that
point which he can consider as the beginning of his
rational life, he will never find it.[1]

[1] Nothing is more common than to hear discussions as to the birth and
development of man's life, and of life in general, in time. It seems to

He will never find in his reminiscences, that point, that beginning of rational consciousness. He imagines that rational consciousness has always existed in him. But if he does find something which bears a resemblance to the beginning of this consciousness, he does not, by any means, find it in his birth in the flesh, but in a realm which has nothing in common with that birth in the flesh. He recognizes his rational origin not as at all the same as his birth in the flesh seems to him. When questioning himself as to his rational consciousness a man never thinks that he, as a rational being, was the son of his father and mother and the grandson of his grandfathers and grandmothers, who were born in such and such a year; but he always recognizes himself, not as a son, but as joined in one with the consciousness of other reasoning beings, the most remote from him in point of time and place, who have sometimes lived a thousand years before him, and at the other end of the world. In his rational consciousness man does not even perceive his origin at all, but he recognizes his union, independent of time and space, with other rational consciousnesses, so that they enter into him and he enters into them. And this rational consciousness, awakened in man, seems to bring to a halt that semblance of life which the error of men regards as life: to people in error it seems that their life stops just when it has first been aroused.

people who reason thus that they stand on the very firm ground of reality, but, nevertheless, there is nothing more fantastic than discussions of the development of life in time. These discussions resemble the actions of a man who should undertake to measure a line, and who should not place a mark at the one point which he knows, on which he stands, but should take imaginary points on an endless line, at various and indefinite distances from himself, and from them should measure the distance to himself. Is not this the very thing that men do when they discuss the origin and development of life in man? In fact, where can we take on that endless line which represents development — from the past in the life of man, — that arbitrary point, from which it is possible to begin the fantastic history of the development of this life? In the birth or generation of the child or of his parents, or still further back, in the original animal, and protoplasm, in the first bit that broke away from the sun? Surely, all these discussions will be the most arbitrary fantasies — a measuring without measures.

CHAPTER VIII

THERE IS NO DIVISION AND CONTRADICTION, IT ONLY SO APPEARS THROUGH FALSE DOCTRINE

ONLY the false doctrine of human life, as the existence of an animal from birth to death, in which men are reared and abide, produces that torturing condition of division into which men enter on the discovery in them of their rational consciousness.

To a man who finds himself laboring under this error, it seems as though the life within him were being rent in twain.

Man knows that his life is a unit, but he feels that it consists of two parts. A man, when he crooks two fingers, and rolls a little ball between them, knows that there is but one ball, but he feels as though there were two balls. Something of the same sort occurs with the man who has acquired a false idea of life.

A false direction has been imparted to the mind of man. He has been taught to recognize as life his one fleshly, individual existence, which cannot be life.

With the same false conception of life as he imagines it, he has looked upon life and has beheld two lives, — the one which he has imagined to himself, and the one which actually exists.

To such a man it seems as though the renunciation by his rational consciousness of the happiness of individual existence, and the demand for a different happiness, is something sickly and unnatural.

But, for man as a rational being, the renunciation of the possibility of personal happiness and life is the inevitable consequence of the conditions of individual life, and a property of the rational consciousness connected with it. The renunciation of personal happiness and life is, for a rational being, as natural a property of his life as flying on its wings, instead of running on its feet, is for a bird. If the feathered fowl runs on its legs, it does not prove that it is not its nature to fly. If we see around us men with unawakened consciousness, who consider that their life lies in their happiness as individuals, this does not prove that man is incapable of living a rational life. The awakening of man to the true life which is peculiar to him takes place in our society with such a painful effort, merely because the false teaching of the world strives to convince men that the phantom of life is life itself, and that the appearance of true life is the violation of it.

With the people of our society who enter into true life, something of the same sort happens as would take place with a maiden from whom the nature of woman had been concealed. On feeling the symptoms of sexual maturity, such a maiden would take a condition which summons her to the future family life, for an unhealthy and unnatural condition, and be driven to despair.

The self-same despair is felt by the men of our society at the first symptoms of awakening to the real life of man.

The man in whom rational consciousness has awakened, but who, at the same time, understands his life only as an individual, finds himself in that position of torture in which an animal would find itself, which, having acknowledged its life as the movement of matter, should not have recognized its law of individuality, but should have merely seen its life in subjection to laws of matter that would go on even without its efforts. Such an animal would experience a painful inward contradiction and division. By submitting itself to the one law of matter, it would see that its life consists in lying still and breathing, but its individuality would have required something else from it; food for itself, a continuation of its species, — and then it would seem to the animal that it suffered division and contradiction. "Life," it would say to itself, "consists in submitting to the laws of gravity, *i.e.* in not moving, in lying still, and in submitting to the chemical processes which go on in the body, and lo, I am doing that, but I must move, and procure myself food, and seek a male or a female." The animal would suffer, and would perceive in this condition a painful inconsistency and division.

The same thing takes place with a man who has been taught to recognize the lower law of his life, the animal individuality, as the law of his life. The highest law of life, the law of his rational consciousness, demands from him another; and the life surrounding him on all sides, and false doctrines, retain him in a deceptive consciousness, and he feels contradiction and division.

But as the animal, in order that it may cease to suffer, must confess as its law not the lower law of matter, but the law of its individuality, and, by fulfilling it, profit by the laws of matter for the satisfaction of its aims as an individual, exactly so is it only requisite for a man to recognize his life not in the lower law of individuality, but in the higher law, which includes the first law, — in the law revealed to him in his rational sense, — and the inconsistency is annihilated, and he, as an individual, will be free to submit himself to his rational consciousness, and it will serve him.

CHAPTER IX

THE BIRTH OF TRUE LIFE IN MAN

By observing the times, by watching the appearance of life in the human being, we see that true life is preserved in man as it is preserved in the seed; and that a time comes when this life makes its appearance. The appearance of true life consists in the animal personality inclining man to his own happiness, while his rational sense shows him the impossibility of personal happiness, and points him to another happiness. Man looks at this happiness, which is pointed out to him in the distance, is incapable of seeing it, at first does not believe in this happiness, and turns back to personal happiness; but the rational consciousness, which thus indistinctly indicates his happiness to him, so indubitably and convincingly demonstrates the impossibility of individual happiness that man once more renounces individual happiness and takes another look at this new happiness which has been pointed out to him. No rational happiness is visible, but individual happiness is so indubitably destroyed that it is impossible to continue individual existence ; and in the man there begins to form a new relation of his animal to his rational consciousness. The man begins to be born into the true life of mankind.

Something of the same sort takes place which takes place in the material world at every birth. The child is born not because it desires to be born, because it is better for it to be born, and because it knows that it is good to be born, but because it is ready, and can no longer continue its previous existence ; it must yield itself to a new life, not so much because the new life calls it, as because the possibility of the former existence has been annihilated.

Rational consciousness imperceptibly springing up in his person grows to such a point that life in individuality becomes impossible.

What takes place is precisely what takes place at the birth of everything. The same annihilation of the germ of the previous form of life, and the appearance of a new shoot ; the same apparent strife of the preceding form, decomposing the germ, and the increase in size of the shoot, — and the same nourishment of the shoot at the expense of the decomposing germ. The difference for us between the birth of the rational consciousness and the fleshly birth visible to us consists in this, — that, while in the fleshly birth we see, in time and space, from what and how, when and what is born from the embryo, we know that the seed is the fruit, that from the seed, under certain well-known conditions, a plant will proceed, that there will be a flower upon it, and then fruit, of the same sort as the seed (the entire cycle of life is accomplished before our very eyes), — we do not perceive the growth of the rational consciousness in time, and we do not see its cycle. We do not see all the growth of the rational consciousness, and its cycle, because we are ourselves accomplishing it ; our life is nothing else than the birth of this being, invisible to us, which is brought forth within us, and hence we can in no wise see it.

We cannot see the birth of this new being, of this new relation of the rational consciousness to the animal, just as the seed cannot see the growth of its stalk. When the rational consciousness emerges from its concealed condition, and reveals itself to us, it seems to us that we experience a contradiction. But there is no contradiction whatever, as there is none in the sprouting seed. In the sprouting seed we perceive only that the life, which formerly resided only within the covering of the seed, has now passed into its shoot. Precisely the same in man, on the awakening of the rational consciousness there is no contradiction whatever, there is only the birth of a new being, of a new relationship of the rational consciousness to the animal.

If a man exists without knowing that other individuals live, without knowing that pleasures do not satisfy him, that he will die, — he does not even know that *he* lives, and there is no contradiction in him.

But if a man has perceived that other individuals are the same as himself, that sufferings menace him, that his existence is a slow death, he will no longer place his life in that decomposing individuality, but he must inevitably place it in that new life which is opening before him. And again there is no contradiction, as there is no contradiction in the seed which sends forth a shoot and then dies.

CHAPTER X

REASON IS THAT LAW ACKNOWLEDGED BY MAN ACCORDING TO WHICH HIS LIFE MUST BE ACCOMPLISHED

THE true life of man, revealed in the relation of his rational consciousness to his animal individuality, begins only when renunciation of individual happiness begins. But what is this rational sense? It only begins when the renunciation of the happiness of the animal personality begins. But the renunciation of the happiness of the animal individuality only begins when the rational consciousness is aroused.

But what is this rational consciousness? The gospel of John begins by saying that the Word, *Logos* (sense, wisdom, word), is the beginning, and that in it is all and from it comes all; and that therefore reason is that which determines all the rest, and which cannot be determined by anything else.

Reason cannot be determined, and we are not called upon to determine it, because we all of us not only know it, but because reason is the only thing that we do know. Communicating one with another, we are convinced beforehand, more than of anything else, of the identical obligation for all of us of this common reason. We are convinced that reason is the only foundation which unites all of us living beings together in one. We know reason most firmly and earliest of all, so all that we know in the world we know only because that which we know is consonant with the laws of that reason which is indubitably known to us. We know reason, and it is impossible for us not to know it. It is impossible, because reason is that law by which reasoning beings — men — must inevitably live. Reason is for man that law in accordance with which his life is perfected, such a law as is that law for the animal in accordance with which it feeds and reproduces itself, as is that law for the plant in accordance with which grows and blossoms the grass or the tree, as is that law for the heavenly bodies in accordance with which the earth and the stars move. And the law which we know in ourselves as the law of our life is that law in accordance with which are accomplished all the external phenomena of the world ; only with this difference, — that we know this difference, that we know this law in ourselves, as that which *we* ourselves must fulfil, and in external phenomena as that which is fulfilled, in accordance with that law, without our participation. All that we know about the world is only what we see accomplished outside of us, in the heavenly bodies, in animals, in plants, in all the world, subject to reason.

In the outer world we see this subjection to the law
of reason ; but in ourselves we know this law as that
which we are bound to fulfil.

The common error in regard to life consists in this, —
that the subjection of our animal body to the law, not
accomplished by us, but only seen by us, is taken for
human life ; while this law of our animal body, with
which our rational consciousness is bound up, is accomplished in our animal bodies as unconsciously to ourselves as it is accomplished in a tree, a crystal, a
heavenly body.

But the law of our life — the subservience of our
animal body to our reason — is the law which we nowhere see, because it has not yet been accomplished,
but is accomplished by us in our life.   In the fulfilment of this law, in the subjection of our animal part
to the law of reason for the attainment of happiness,
consists our life.   By not understanding that the happiness of our life consists in the subjection of our animal
individuality to the law of reason, and taking happiness
and the existence of our animal individuality for our
whole life, and rejecting the work of life which has
been appointed for us, we deprive ourselves of our true
happiness and our true life ; in place of it we set up
that existence which we can see, of our animal activity,
which operates independently of us, and which cannot,
therefore, be our life.

CHAPTER XI

THE FALSE DIRECTION OF LEARNING

THE error of supposing that the law accomplished in
our animal persons, and visible to us, is the law of our
life, is an ancient one, into which men have always
fallen, and into which they still fall.   This error, concealing from men the chief subject of their knowledge,
the subjection of the animal individual to reason for the
attainment of the happiness of life, sets in its place a

study of the existence of men independent of the happiness of life.

Instead of making a study of that law to which, for the attainment of his happiness, the animal individuality of man must be subjected, and, as soon as this law is learned, studying, with it as a foundation, all the other phenomena of the world, this false knowledge directs its efforts only to the study of happiness, and of the existence of the animal individuality of man, without any relation to the chief subject of knowledge, — the subjection of this animal individuality of man to the law of reason for the attainment of the happiness of true life.

False knowledge directs its efforts to the study of happiness alone, and, not having in view the chief object of knowledge, directs its efforts to the study of the animal existence of past and contemporary people, and to the study of the conditions of existence of man in general, as an animal. It seems to it that from this study there may be derived also a guide for the happiness of human life.

False knowledge reasons thus : " Men exist and have existed before us. Let us see how they have existed, what changes have come about in their existence through time and situation, in what direction these changes point. From these historical alterations in their existence we shall discover the law of their life."

Not having in view the principal aim of learning, the study of that rational law to which the personality of man must submit itself for his happiness, the so-called learned men of this category, by the very aim which they set themselves for their study, pronounce the condemnation on the futility of their study.

In point of fact : if the existence of men alters only in consequence of the general laws of their animal existence, then the study of those laws, to which it is thus subjected, is utterly useless and vain. Whether men know or do not know about the law of change in their existence, this law is accomplished, exactly as the change is accomplished in the life of moles and beavers, in con

sequence of those conditions in which they find them
selves.

But if it is possible for man to know that law of reason to which his life must be subservient, then it is evident that he can nowhere procure the knowledge of that
law of reason, except where it is revealed to him : in his
rational consciousness. And therefore, however much
men may have studied the subject of how men have *existed*
as animals, they will never learn concerning the existence of man anything which would not have taken place
of itself in men without the acquirement of that knowledge ; and no matter how much they have studied the
animal existence of man, they will never learn the law
to which, for the sake of his life's happiness, the animal
existence of man must be subjected.

This is one category of the vain reasonings of men
upon life, called historical and political science.

Another category of reasonings, widely disseminated
in our day, in which the only object of knowledge is
utterly lost sight of, is as follows : —

"Looking upon man as an object of knowledge," say
the wise men, "we see that he is nourished, grows, reproduces his species, becomes old and dies, exactly like
any other animal; but some phenomena (psychical, as
they are designated) prevent accuracy of observation,
present too great complications, and hence, in order the
better to understand man, we will first examine his life
in simpler phenomena, similar to those which we see in
animals and plants, which lack this psychical activity.

"With this aim, we will investigate the life of animals
and plants in general. But, on investigating animals
and plants, we see that in all of them there reveal themselves still more simple laws of matter, which are common to them all. And as the laws of the animal are
simpler than the laws of the life of man, and the laws
of the plant simpler still, investigation must be based
upon the simplest — upon the laws of matter. We see
that what takes place in the plant and the animal is
precisely what takes place in the man," say they, "and
hence we conclude that everything which takes place in

man we can explain to ourselves from what takes place
in the very simplest dead matter that is visible to us,
and open to our investigations, the more so as all the
peculiarities of the activity of man are found in constant
dependence upon powers which act in matter. Every
change of the matter constituting the body of man alters
and infringes upon his whole activity." And hence,
they conclude, the laws of matter are the cause of man's
activity. But the idea that there is in man something
which we do not see in animals or in plants, or in dead
matter, and that this something is the only subject of
knowledge, without which every other is useless, does
not disturb them.

It does not enter their heads that, if the change of
matter in the body of man infringes upon his activity,
—this merely proves that the change of matter is one
of the causes which affects the activity of man, but not
that the movement of matter is one of the causes of
man's activity being interfered with, nor in the least that
the movement of matter is the cause of his activity.
Exactly as the injury done by the removal of earth from
under the root of a plant proves that the earth may or
may not be everywhere, but not that the plant is merely
the product of the earth. And they study in man that
which takes place also in dead matter, and in the plant,
and in animals, assuming that an explanation of the
laws, and the phenomena accompanying the life of man,
can elucidate for them the life of man itself.

In order to understand the life of man, that is to say,
that law to which, for the happiness of man, his animal
person must be subservient, men examine either historical existence, but not the life of man, or the subservience, not acknowledged by man but only seen by him,
of the animal and the plant, and of matter, to various
laws; *i.e.* they do the same thing that men would do if
they studied the situation of objects unknown to them,
for the sake of finding that unknown goal which must
be followed.

It is perfectly true that the knowledge of the phenomenon, visible to us, of the existence of man in

history, may be instructive for us; and that the study
of the laws of the animal individuality of man and of
other animals may be equally instructive for us, as well
as the study of those laws to which matter is subject.
The study of all this is important for man, since it
shows him, as in a mirror, that which is infallibly
accomplished in his life; but it is evident that the
knowledge of that which is already in process of
accomplishment and visible to us, however full it may
be, cannot furnish us with the chief knowledge, which
is necessary to us, the knowledge of that law to which,
for our happiness, our animal individuality must be
subservient. The knowledge of the laws that are
accomplished is instructive for us, but only when we
acknowledge that law of reason to which our animal
personality must be subservient, but not when that law
is not recognized at all.

However well the tree may have studied (if it could
but study) all those chemical and physical phenomena
which take place in it, it can by no means, from these
observations and from this knowledge, deduce for itself
the necessity of collecting sap and of distributing it for
the growth of the bole, the leaf, the flower, and the
fruit.

Precisely this is the case with man; however well he
may know the law which guides his animal personality,
and the laws which control matter, — these laws will
afford him not the slightest guidance as to how he is to
proceed with the bit of bread which is in his hands:
whether he is to give it to his wife, to a stranger, to a
dog, or to eat it himself; to defend this bit of bread, or
to give it to the person who shall ask him for it. But a
man's life consists solely of the decision of these and
similar questions.

The study of laws which guide the existence of
animals, plants, and matter is not only useful but indispensable for the elucidation of the law of the life of
man, but only when that study has as its chief aim the
subject of man's knowledge: the elucidation of the law
of reason.

But on the assumption that the life of man is merely his animal existence, and that the happiness indicated by rational consciousness is impossible, and that the law of reason is but a vision, — such study becomes not only vain but deadly, since it conceals from man the sole object of knowledge and maintains him in the error that, by following up the reflection of the object, he can know the object also. Such study is similar to that which a man should make by attentively studying all the changes and movements of the shadow of the living being, assuming that the cause of the movement of the living being lies in the changes and movements of its shadow.

CHAPTER XII

THE CAUSE OF FALSE KNOWLEDGE IS THE FALSE PERSPECTIVE IN WHICH OBJECTS PRESENT THEMSELVES

"TRUE knowledge consists in knowing that we know that which we know, and that we do not know that which we do not know," said Confucius.

But false knowledge consists in thinking that we know that which we do not know. And it is impossible to give a more accurate definition of that false knowledge which reigns among us. It is assumed by the false knowledge of our day that we know that which we cannot know, and that we do not know that which alone we can know. It seems to a man possessed of false knowledge that he knows everything which presents itself to him in space and time, and that he does not know that which is known to him through his rational consciousness.

To such a man it seems that happiness in general, and his happiness in particular, is the most unfathomable of subjects for him. His reason and his rational consciousness seem to him as almost equally unfathomable subjects. A little more comprehensible subject appears to be himself as an animal; still more comprehensible appear to him animals and plants, and more comprehensible still seems dead, endlessly diffused matter.

Something of the same sort takes place with man's vision. A man always unconsciously directs his sight chiefly on the objects which are more distant, and which therefore seem to him the most simple in color and outline; on the sky, the horizon, the far-off meadows, the forest. These objects present themselves to him as better defined and more simple in proportion as they are more distant, and, *vice versa*, the nearer the object, the more complicated is it in outline and color.

If man did not know how to compute the distance of objects, he would not, as he looked, arrange objects in perspective, but would acknowledge the great simplicity and definiteness of outline and color, their greater degree of visibility ; and to such a man the interminable sky would appear the simplest and most visible, and then as less visible objects would the more complicated outlines of the horizon appear to him, and still less visible would appear to him his own hands, moving before his face, and light would appear to him the most invisible of all.

Is it not the same with the false knowledge of man ? What is indubitably known to him — his rational consciousness — seems to him to be beyond comprehension, while that which is, indubitably, unattainable for him — boundless and eternal matter — seems to him to be within the scope of knowledge, because on account of its distance from him it seems simple to him.

But it is precisely the reverse. First of all, and most indubitably of all, every man can know and does know the happiness toward which he is striving ; then, as indubitably, he knows the reason which points out to him that happiness, — he already knows that his animal part is subject to that reason, and he already sees, though he does not know, all the other phenomena which present themselves to him in space and time.

Only to the man with a false idea of life does it seem that he knows objects better in proportion as they are

more clearly defined by time and space; in point of
fact, we know fully only that which is defined neither
by time nor by space : happiness and the law of reason.
But we know external objects the less in proportion as
our consciousness has less share in the knowledge, in
consequence of which an object is defined only by its
place in time and space.   And hence, the more exceptionally an object is defined by time and space, the less
comprehensible is it to man.

The true knowledge of man ends with the knowledge
of his individuality — of the animal part.   A man
knows his animal part, which seeks happiness and is
subject to the law of reason, quite apart from the
knowledge of that which is not his individuality.   He
actually knows himself in this animal; and knows himself, not because he is something appertaining to time
and space (on the contrary, he never can know himself
as a phenomenon appertaining to time and space), but
because he is something which must, for its own happiness, be subservient to the law of reason.   He knows
himself in this animal as something independent of time
and space.

When he questions himself as to his place in time
and space, it seems to him, first of all, that he stands in
the middle of time, which is endless on both sides of
him, and that he is the center of a sphere, whose surface is everywhere and nowhere.   And this self of his,
exempt from time and space, man actually knows, and
with this, his "*ego*," ends his actual knowledge.   All
that is contained outside of this, his "*ego*," man does
not know, and he can only observe and define it in an
external and conventional manner.

Having departed, for a time, from the knowledge of
himself as a rational center, striving toward happiness,
i.e. as a being independent of time and space, man can,
for a time, conditionally admit that he is part of the
visible world appearing in time and space.   Regarding
himself thus, in time and space, in connection with
other beings, man combines his true inward knowledge
of himself with external observations on himself, and

receives of himself a conception of a man in general, similar to all other men ; through this conventional knowledge of himself man conceives of other men, also, a certain external idea, but he does not know them.

The impossibility, for man, of true knowledge of men, proceeds also from the fact that of such men he sees, not one, but hundreds, thousands, and he knows that there have existed and that there will exist men whom he has never seen and whom he never will see.

Beyond men, still farther removed from himself, man beholds, in time and space, animals differing from men and from each other. These creatures would be utterly incomprehensible to him if he were not possessed of a knowledge of man in general ; but, having this knowledge, and deducing from his conception of man his rational consciousness, he receives some idea concerning animals also ; but this idea is for him less like knowledge than his idea of men in general. He beholds a vast quantity of the most varied animals, and the greater their numbers, the less possible, apparently, is any knowledge of them for him.

Farther removed from himself he beholds plants ; and the diffusion of these phenomena in the world is even greater, and knowledge of them is still more impossible for him.

Still farther from him, beyond animals and plants, in space and time, man beholds living bodies, and forms of matter which are but little or not at all distinguishable from each other. Matter he understands least of all. The knowledge of the forms of matter is already quite indifferent to him, and he not only does not know it, but he only imagines it to himself, the more so as matter already presents itself to him, in space and time, as endless.

CHAPTER XIII

THE RECOGNIZABILITY OF OBJECTS IS AUGMENTED, NOT BECAUSE OF THEIR MANIFESTATION IN SPACE AND TIME, BUT BECAUSE OF THE UNITY OF THE LAW WHERETO WE AND THOSE SUBJECTS WHICH WE STUDY ARE SUBSERVIENT

WHAT can be more clear than the words: the dog is sick; the calf is affectionate; he loves me; the bird rejoices; the horse is afraid; a good man; a vicious animal? And all these most important and comprehensible words are not defined by space and time; on the contrary, the more incomprehensible to us the law to which a phenomenon is subservient, the more accurately is the phenomenon defined by time and space. Who will say that he understands that law of gravity in accordance with which the movements of the earth, moon, and sun take place? Yet an eclipse of the sun is determined in the most accurate manner by space and time.

We know fully only our life, our aspiration for happiness, and the reason which points us to that happiness. The knowledge which stands next to it in point of sureness is the knowledge of our animal personality, striving toward happiness and subservient to the law of reason. In the knowledge of our animal personality there already appear conditions of time and space, visible, palpable, observable, but not accessible to our understanding. After this, in point of sureness of knowledge, is the knowledge of animal personalities, similar to ourselves, in which we recognize an aspiration toward happiness, as well as a rational consciousness, in common with ourselves. In so far as the life of these personalities approaches the laws of our life, of aspiration toward happiness, and submission to the law of reason, to that extent do we know them; in so far as it reveals itself under conditions of time and space, to that extent we do not know them. Thus, more than in any other way, do we know men.

The next thing in point of surety of knowledge is our knowledge of animals, in which we see a personality striving toward welfare, like our own,— though now we hardly recognize a semblance of our rational consciousness,— and with which we cannot communicate through that rational consciousness.

After animals, we behold plants, in which we with difficulty recognize a personality similar to our own, aspiring to happiness. These beings present themselves to us chiefly in phenomena of time and space, and are hence still less accessible to our knowledge.

We know them only because in them we behold a personality, similar to our animal personality, which, equally with ours, aspires to happiness, and matter which subjects itself to the law of reason under the conditions of time and space.

Still less accessible to our knowledge are impersonal, material objects; in them we no longer find semblances of our personality, we perceive no striving at all after happiness, but we behold merely the phenomena of time and space, of the laws of reason, to which they are subject.

The genuineness of our knowledge does not depend upon the accessibility to observation of objects in time and space, but contrariwise; the more accessible to observation the phenomena of the object in time and place, the less comprehensive is it to us.

Our knowledge of the world flows from the consciousness of our striving after happiness, and of the necessity, for the attainment of this happiness, of the subjection of our animal part to reason. If we know the life of the animal, it is only because we behold in the animal a striving toward happiness, and the necessity of subjection to the law of reason, which is represented in it by the law of organism.

If we know matter, we know it only because, in spite of the fact that its happiness is incomprehensible to us, we nevertheless behold in it the same phenomenon as in ourselves — the necessity of subjection to the law of reason, which rules it.

We cannot know ourselves from the laws which rule animals, but we can know animals only by that law which we know in ourselves. And so much the less can we know ourselves from the laws of our life transferred to the phenomena of matter.

All that man knows of the external world he knows only because he knows himself and in himself finds three different relations to the world: one relation of his rational consciousness, another relation of his animal, and a third relation of the matter which enters into his animal body. He knows in himself these three different relations, and therefore all that he sees in the world is always disposed before him in a perspective of three planes, separate from each other: (1) rational beings; (2) animals; and (3) lifeless matter.

A man always sees these three categories in the world, because he contains within himself these three subjects of knowledge. He knows himself: (1) as a rational consciousness, subjecting the animal part; (2) as an animal, subject to the rational consciousness; (3) as matter, subject to the animal part.

Not from a knowledge of the laws of matter, as they think of it, can we learn the law of organisms, and not from the laws of organism can we know ourselves as a rational creation, but *vice versa*. First of all, we may and we must know ourselves, *i.e.* that law of reason to which, for our own happiness, our personality must be subject, and only then can we and must we know also the law of our animal personality, and of other personalities like it, and, at a still greater distance from us, the laws of matter.

We need to know and we do know only ourselves. The animal world is for us a reflection of what we know in ourselves. The material world is, as it were, a reflection of a reflection.

The laws of matter seem peculiarly clear to us, only because they are uniform for us: and they are uniform for us because they are especially far removed from the law of our life as we recognize it.

The laws of organisms seem to us simpler than the

law of our life, also on account of their distance from us. But in them we merely observe laws, but we do not know them, as we know the law of our rational consciousness, which we must fulfil.

We know neither the one being nor the other, but we merely see, we observe outside of ourselves. Only the law of our rational consciousness do we know indubitably, because it is necessary to our happiness — because we live by this consciousness; but we do not see it because we do not possess that highest point from which we might be able to observe it.

Only, if there were higher beings subjecting our rational consciousness as our rational consciousness subjects itself to our animal personality, and as our animal personality (our organism) subjects matter to itself — these higher beings might behold our rational life as we behold our animal existence and the existence of matter.

Human life presents itself as indissolubly bound up with two modes of existence, which it includes within itself: the existence of animals and plants (of organisms), and the existence of matter.

Man himself makes his real life, and lives it; but in the two modes of existence bound up with his life, man cannot take part. Body and matter, of which he consists, exist of themselves.

These forms of existence present themselves to man as preceding lives lived through, included in his life, as reminiscences of former lives.

In the real life of man, these two forms of existence furnish him with implements and materials for his work, but not the work itself.

It is useful for a man to study thoroughly both the materials and the implements of his work. The better he knows them, the better condition will he be in to work. The study of these forms of existence included within his life, of his animal and the material constituting the animal, shows man, as though in a reflection, the universal law of all existence — submission to the law of reason, and thereby confirms, as to his conviction, the necessity of subjecting his animal to its laws; but man cannot and must not confound the material and implements of his work with the work itself.

However much a man may have studied the visible, palpable life, observed by him in himself and in others, the life which is fulfilled without any effort of his, this life will always remain a mystery to him ; he will never understand a life of which he is unconscious, and by observations upon this mysterious life, which is always hiding from him in the infinity of space and time, he will be in no wise enlightened as to his real life, which is revealed to him in his consciousness, and which consists in the subservience of his animal personality, quite peculiar from all and well known to himself, to the law of reason, quite peculiar and well known to himself, for the attainment of his happiness, entirely independent and well known to himself.

CHAPTER XIV

THE TRUE LIFE OF MAN IS NOT THAT WHICH TAKES PLACE IN SPACE AND TIME

MAN knows life in himself as an aspiration toward happiness, to be attained by the submission of his animal personality to the law of reason.

He does not and cannot know any other life of man. For the man recognizes the animal as living only when the matter constituting it is subject, not only to its laws, but to the higher law of organism.

There is in a certain conjunction of matter submission to the higher law of organism ; we recognize life in this conjunction of matter ; no, this submission has not begun or ended ; and that does not yet exist, which distinguishes this matter from all other matter, in which act only mechanical, physical, and chemical laws, — and we do not recognize in it the life of the animal.

In precisely the same manner, we recognize people like ourselves, or even ourselves, as living only when our animal personality, in addition to submission to the law of organism, is subservient to the higher law of our rational consciousness.

As soon as there is none of this submission of the personality to the law of reason, as soon as the law of personality alone acts in man, subjecting to itself the matter which constitutes it, we do not know and we do not see human life either in others or in ourselves, as we do not see the life of the animal in matter, which is subject only to its own laws.

However powerful and rapid may be a man's movements in delirium, in madness, in agony, in intoxication, in a burst of passion even, we do not recognize a man as alive, we do not bear ourselves toward him as to a living man, and we recognize in him only the possibility of life.   But however weak and motionless a man may be, if we see that his animal personality is subservient to his reason, we recognize him as living, and bear ourselves toward him as such.

We cannot understand man's life otherwise than as the subjection of the animal personality to the law of reason.

This life reveals itself in space and time, but is not defined by the conditions of space and time, but only according to the degree of subjection of the animal personality to the reason.   Defining life by conditions of space and time is precisely the same as defining the height of an object by its length and breadth.

The movement upward of an object which is also moving on a plane surface will furnish an accurate simile of the relationship of the true life of man to the life of the animal personality, or of the true life to the life of time and space.   The movement of the object upward does not depend upon its movement on a plane surface, and can be neither augmented nor diminished thereby.   It is the same with the definition of the life of man.   True life always reveals itself in personality, and does not depend upon and cannot be either augmented or diminished by this, that, or the other existence of personality.

The conditions of time and space, in which the

animal personality of man finds itself, cannot wield influence over the true life, which consists of the submission of the animal personality to the rational consciousness.

It is beyond the power of man, who desires to live, to annihilate or to arrest the movement of his existence in time and space; but his true life is the attainment of happiness by submission to reason, independently of those visible movements of time and space. It is only in this increasing attainment of happiness, through submission to reason, that what constitutes the life of man consists. There is none of this augmentation in submission, and man's life proceeds in the two visible directions of time and space, and is one existence.

There is this upward movement, this greater and greater submission to reason, — and between two powers and one a relationship is established; and more or less movement takes place in accordance with the rising existence of man in the realm of life.

The powers of time and space are definite, final, incompatible with the conception of life, but the power of aspiration toward good through submission to reason is a power rising on high, the very power of life, for which there are no bounds of time or space.

Man imagines that his life comes to a standstill and is divided, but these hindrances and hesitations are only an illusion of the consciousness (similar to the illusions of the external senses). Obstacles and hesitations there are not and there cannot be in real life: they only seem such to us because of our false view of life. Man begins to live with real life, *i.e.* he rises to a certain height above the animal life, and from this height he sees the shadowy nature of his animal existence, which infallibly ends in death; he sees that his existence on a plane surface is encompassed on all sides by precipices, and, recognizing the fact that this ascent on high is life itself, he is terrified by that which he has beheld from the height.

Instead of recognizing the power of his life which has raised him on high, and instead of going in the direction revealed to him, he takes fright at what has been laid open before him from the heights, deliberately descends, and lies as low as possible, in order not to see the abysses yawning around him. But the force of rational consciousness raises him once more, again he sees, again he takes fright, and again he falls to earth in order to avoid seeing. And this goes on until he finally recognizes the fact that, in order to save himself from terror before the movement of a pernicious life, he must understand that his movement on a plane surface — his existence in time and space — is not his life, but that his life consists only in the movement upward, that in the submission of his animal personality to the law of reason lies the only possibility of life and happiness. He must understand that he has wings which raise him above the abyss; that, were it not for those wings, he never would have mounted on high, and would not have beheld the abyss. He must believe in his wings, and soar whither they bear him.

It is only from this lack of faith that proceed those phenomena which seem strange to him at first, of the fluctuation of true life, of its arrests, and the division of consciousness.

Only to the man who understands his life in its animal existence, defined by time and space, does it appear that the rational consciousness has revealed itself at times in the animal creature. And, looking thus upon the revelation in himself of rational consciousness, man asks himself when and under what conditions his rational consciousness revealed itself in him? But, scrutinize his past as carefully as he will, man will never discover those times of revelation of the rational consciousness: it will always seem to him either that it has never existed, or that it has always existed. If it appears to him that there have been gaps in rational consciousness, it is only because he does not recognize the life of rational consciousness as life. Comprehending his life only as an animal existence, determined by conditions of time and space, man tries to measure the awakening and activity of rational consciousness by the same measure : he asks himself, "When, for how long a time, under what conditions, did I find myself in possession of rational consciousness ? "

But the intervals between the awakenings of rational life exist only for the man who understands his life as the life of an animal personality. But for the man who understands his life as consisting in the activity of the rational consciousness — there can exist none of these intervals.

Rational life exists. It alone does exist. Intervals of time of one minute or of fifty thousand years are indistinguishable by it, because for it time does not exist.

The true life of man, from which he forms for himself an idea of every other life, is the aspiration toward happiness, attainable by the subjection of his personality to the law of reason. Neither reason nor the degree of his submission to it are determined by either time or space. The true life of mankind arises outside of space and time.

CHAPTER XV

THE RENUNCIATION OF HAPPINESS OF THE ANIMAL PERSONALITY IS THE LAW OF MAN'S LIFE

LIFE is a striving toward happiness.[1] A striving toward happiness is life. Thus all men have understood, do understand, and always will understand life. And hence the life of man is an aspiration toward the happiness of man, and an aspiration toward the happiness of man is human life. The common herd, unthinking men, understand the happiness of man to lie in the happiness of his animal part.

False science, excluding the conception of happiness from the definition of life, understands life in its animal existence, and hence it sees the happiness of life only in animal happiness, and agrees with the error of the masses.

[1] *Blago*, good, happiness, welfare.

In both cases, the error arises from confounding the
personalities, the individualities, as science calls them,
with rational consciousness.   Rational consciousness includes in itself individuality.   But individuality does not
always include in itself rational consciousness.   Individuality is a property of the animal, and of man as well
as of the animal.   Rational consciousness is the property
of man alone.

The animal may live for his own body only — nothing prevents his living thus; he satisfies his individual
and unconsciously plays his part, and does not know
that he is an individual; but reasoning man cannot live
for his own body alone.   He cannot live thus because
he knows that he is an individual, and therefore knows
that other beings are individualities also, as well as himself, and he knows all that must result from the relations of these individualities.

If man aspired only to the happiness of his individuality, if he loved only himself, — his own individuality,
— he would not know that other beings love themselves
also, any more than animals know this; but if man
knows that he is a personality, striving toward the same
thing as all the personalities surrounding him, he can
no longer strive for that happiness which evidently
is evil for his rational consciousness, and his life can
no longer consist in striving for his individual happiness.

It merely seems to man, at times, that his aspiration
toward happiness has, for its object, the satisfaction of
the demands of the animal personality.   This delusion
arises from the fact that man takes that which he sees
proceeding in his animal part for the object of the
activity of his rational consciousness.   What results is
something in the nature of what would take place if a
man were to govern himself, in a waking state, by what
he had seen in dreams.

And if this delusion is upheld by false teachings, there
results in man a confounding of his personality with his
rational consciousness.

But his rational consciousness always shows man that

the satisfaction of the demands of his animal personality cannot constitute his happiness, and hence his life, and therefore it draws him irresistibly toward that happiness, hence toward the life which is proper to him, and it does not become confused with his animal personality.

It is generally thought and said that renunciation of the happiness of personality is a deed worthy of a man. Renunciation of the happiness of personality is not a merit, is not an exploit, but an indispensable condition of the life of man. At the same time that a man recognizes himself as an individual, separated from all the world, he also recognizes other individuals separated from all the world, and their mutual connection, and the transparency of the happiness of his personality, and the sole actuality of happiness to be only of such a sort as may be satisfied by his rational consciousness.

In the case of an animal, activity which does not have for its object its individual welfare, but is directly opposed to that welfare, is renunciation of life ; but in the case of man, it is precisely the reverse. The activity of man, directed solely to the attainment of individual happiness, is a complete renunciation of the life of man.

For the animal, who has no rational consciousness to demonstrate to him the poverty and limited character of his existence, personal happiness, and the reproduction of its species therefrom resulting, constitute the highest aim of life. But for man, personality is merely that step in existence from which the true happiness of his life, which is not synonymous with the happiness of his personality, is revealed to him.

The consciousness of individuality is not life for man, but that boundary from which his life, consisting in ever greater and greater attainment to the happiness which is proper to him, and which does not depend upon the welfare of his animal part, begins.

According to the prevalent conception of life, human life is the fragment of time from the birth to the death of his animal part. But this is not human life ; this is merely the existence of man as an animal personality. But human life is something which only reveals itself in the animal existence, just as organic life is something which only reveals itself in the existence of matter.

First of all, the apparent objects of man's personality present themselves to him as the objects of his life. These objects are visible, and hence they seem to be comprehensible.

But the aims pointed out to him by his rational consciousness seem incomprehensible, because they are invisible to him. And man, at first, finds it terrible to repulse the visible and yield himself to the invisible.

To a man perverted by the false teachings of the world, the demands of the animal which fulfil themselves, and which are visible both in himself and in others, seem simple and clear, but the new, invisible requirements of rational consciousness present themselves as conflicting; the satisfaction of them, which is not accomplished by themselves, but which a man must himself attend to, seem, in some way, complicated and indistinct. It is painful and alarming to renounce the visible idea of life and yield one's self to its invisible consciousness, as it would be painful and alarming to a child to be born, were he able to feel his birth — but there is nothing to be done when it is evident that the visible idea leads to death, while the invisible consciousness alone gives life.

CHAPTER XVI

THE ANIMAL PERSONALITY IS THE INSTRUMENT OF LIFE

SURELY no arguments can conceal from man this patent and indubitable truth, that his personal existence is something which is constantly perishing, hasting on to death, and that there can be, therefore, no life in his animal personality.

Man cannot avoid seeing that the existence of his personality from birth and childhood to old age and death is nothing else than a constant waste and diminution of this animal personality, ending in inevitable death; and hence, the consciousness of one's life in personality, including in itself a desire for enlargement and indestructibility of personality, cannot be otherwise than uninterrupted contradiction, and suffering cannot be otherwise than evil, while the only sense of his life lies in its aspiration toward happiness.

In whatever the genuine happiness of man consists, renunciation of the happiness of his animal person is inevitable for him.

Renunciation of the happiness of the animal personality is the law of man's life. If it is not accomplished freely, expressing itself in submission to rational consciousness, then it is accomplished violently in every man at the fleshly death of his animal, when, in consequence of the burden of suffering, he desires but one thing : to escape from the torturing consciousness of a perishing personality, and to pass into another form of existence.

Entrance into life, and the life of man, is similar to that which takes place with the horse whom his master leads forth from the stable and harnesses. It seems to the horse, on emerging from the stable and beholding the light, and scenting liberty, that in that liberty is life ; but he is harnessed, and driven off. He feels a weight behind him, and if he thinks that his life consists in running at liberty, he begins to kick, falls down, and sometimes kills himself. But if he does not kick he has but two alternatives left to him : either he will go his way and drag his load, and discover that the burden is not heavy, and trotting not a torment, but a joy ; or else he will kick himself free, and then his master will lead him to the treadmill, and will fasten him by his halter, the wheel will begin to turn beneath him, and he will walk in the dark, in one place, suffering ; but his strength will not be wasted ; he will perform his unwilling labor, and the law will be fulfilled in him. The only difference will lie in this : that the first work will be joyful, but the second compulsory and painful.

" But to what purpose this personality, whose happiness I am bound to renounce, in order to receive life ? " say men, who accept their animal existence as life.

"But for what purpose is this consciousness of individuality, which is opposed to the revelation of his true life, given to man?"

This question may be answered by a similar question which might be put by the animal, striving toward his aims, the preservation of his life and species.

"Why," it might ask, "this matter and its laws, mechanical, physical, chemical, and others, with which I must contend in order to attain my ends? If my calling," the animal would say, "be the accomplishment of animal life, then why all these obstacles, which must be overcome?"

It is clear to us that all matter and its laws, with which the animal contends, and which it subjugates to itself for the accomplishment of its animal existence, are not obstacles, but means for the attainment of its ends. Only by working over matter, and by means of its laws, does the animal live. It is precisely the same in the life of man. His animal personality, in which man finds himself, and which he is called upon to subject to his rational consciousness, is no obstacle. but a means whereby he attains the aim of his happiness; his animal personality, is, for man, that instrument with which he works. Animal personality is, for man, the spade given to a rational being in order that he may dig with it, and, as he digs, dull and sharpen it, and wear it out, but not in order that he may polish it up and lay it away. This talent is given to him to increase, and not to hoard. "And whoso saveth his life shall lose it. And he that loseth his life for my sake, shall find it."

In these words it is declared that we must not save but lose, and lose unceasingly; and that only by renouncing what is destined to perish, our animal personality, shall we acquire our true life, which will not and cannot perish. It is declared that our true life begins only when we cease to count as life that which was not and could not be our life, — our animal existence. It is declared that he who will save the spade which he has for the preparation of his food, to sustain his life, — that he, having saved his spade, shall lose both his food and his life.

CHAPTER XVII

BIRTH IN THE SPIRIT

"YE must be born anew," said Christ. It is not that any one has commanded man to be born, but that man is inevitably led to it. In order to see life, he must be born again into that existence through rational consciousness.

Rational consciousness is bestowed upon man in order that he may place life in that happiness which is revealed to him by his rational consciousness. He who has placed his life in that happiness has life; but he who does not place his life therein, but in his animal personality, thereby deprives himself of life. In this consists the definition of life given by Christ.

Men who accept as life their aspiration toward happiness hear these words, and not only do not admit them, but do not understand and cannot understand them. These words seem to them to mean nothing, or very little, as designating some sentimental and mystical mood, which has been let loose upon them. They cannot understand the significance of these words, which furnish the explanation of a condition that is inaccessible to them, just as a dry seed which has not sprouted could not understand the condition of a moist and already growing seed. For the dry seeds, that sun which shines in its rays upon the seed which is being born into life is only an insignificant accident, — something large and warm and light; but for the sprouting seed it is the cause of birth unto life. Just the same, for those people who have not yet attained to the inward inconsistency of the animal personality and rational consciousness, the light of the sun of reason is only an insignificant accident, only sentimental, mystical words. The sun leads to life only those in whom life has already been engendered.

No one has ever learned how, why, when, and where it is engendered; either in men or in animals and plants

Of its origin in man, Christ has said that no one knows or can know it. And, in fact, what can a man know about the manner in which life is engendered within him? Life is the light of men, the beginning of all things; how can man know when it is engendered? That is engendered and perishes for man which does not live, that which is revealed in space and time. But true life *is*, and therefore it cannot either begin or perish.

CHAPTER XVIII

THE DEMANDS OF RATIONAL CONSCIOUSNESS

YES, rational consciousness indubitably, incontrovertibly says to man that, with the constitution of the world which he sees from his personality, he, his personality, can have no happiness. His life is a desire for happiness for himself, for himself in particular, and he sees that this happiness is impossible. But, strange to say, in spite of the fact that he undoubtedly perceives that this happiness is impossible for him, he still lives in the one desire for this impossible happiness — happiness for himself alone.

A man with an awakened (just awakened) rational consciousness, which has not yet, however, subjected to itself his animal personality, if he does not kill himself, lives only for the purpose of realizing that impossible happiness; the man lives and acts only in order that happiness may be his alone, in order that all people, and even all creatures, should live and work to the end that his welfare alone may be provided for, that he may enjoy himself, that for him there may be no suffering and no death.

It is astonishing: in spite of the fact that his experience and observation of life, the life of all about him, and his reason, indubitably point out to each man the inaccessibility of this, show him that it is impossible to make other living beings cease to love themselves, and love him alone; in spite of this, the life of each man consists only in this, — by means of wealth, power, honor, glory, flattery, deceit, in some manner or other, to compel other beings to live, not for themselves, but for him alone; to force all beings to love, not themselves, but him alone.

Men have done and do everything that they can for this object, and at the same time they see that they are attempting the impossible. "My life is a striving after happiness," says man to himself. "Happiness is possible for me only when all shall love me more than themselves, and all creatures love only themselves — hence all that I do to make them love me is useless. It is useless, and I can do nothing more."

Centuries pass; men learn the distance from the planets, determine their weight, learn the structure of the sun and stars, but the question as to how to reconcile the demands of personal happiness with the life of the world, which excludes the possibility of that happiness, remains for the majority of men as insoluble a problem as it was for men five thousand years ago.

Rational consciousness says to every man: "Yes, thou must have happiness, but only on condition that all will love thee more than themselves." And the same rational consciousness demonstrates to men that this cannot be, because they all love themselves alone. And therefore the only happiness which is opened to men by rational consciousness is closed to him again by it.

Centuries pass, and the puzzle as to the happiness of man's life still remains for the majority of men insoluble. But the problem has been solved long ago. And it always seems astonishing to all who have learned the solution of the riddle that they have not themselves solved it, — it seems as though they had known it long ago and had merely forgotten it, so simply and voluntarily does the solution of that riddle, which seemed so difficult amid the false teachings of our world, offer itself.

Dost thou wish that all should live for thee, that all should love thee better than themselves? There is only one condition in which thy desire can be fulfilled, — namely, that all creatures should live for the good of others, and should love others better than themselves.

Then only canst thou and all creatures be loved by all,
and then only canst thou, among their number, receive
that happiness which thou desirest. But if happiness
be possible for thee only when all creatures love others
better than themselves, then thou, a living creature,
must love other creatures more than thyself.

Only under these conditions are the happiness and
the life of man possible, and only under these conditions
will that be annihilated which has poisoned the life of man,
— will the strife of beings, the torment of suffering, and
the fear of death be annihilated.

What, in fact, has constituted the impossibility of the
happiness of personal existence ? In the first place, the
strife among themselves of beings in search of their personal happiness. In the second, the delusion of enjoyment which leads to waste of life, to satiety, to suffering,
and, in the third, — death. But it is worth while to
admit mentally that man may replace the striving for
his own personal happiness by a striving for the happiness of other beings, in order that the impossibility of
happiness may be annihilated, and that happiness may
present itself as attainable to man. Looking upon the
world from his idea of life, as a striving after personal
happiness, man has beheld in the world a senseless conflict of beings engaged in destroying each other. But
it is only requisite that man should recognize the fact
that his life lies in a striving after the good of others,
in order to see the world in quite a different light; to
behold, side by side with chance phenomena of the strife
of beings, a constant, mutual service of each other by
these beings, — a service without which the existence of
the world is inconceivable.

All that is necessary is to admit this, and all previous
senseless activity, directed toward the unattainable happiness of the individual, will be replaced by another activity, in conformity with the law of the world and directed
to the attainment of the greatest possible happiness for
one's self and the whole world.

Another cause of the poverty of personal life, and of
the impossibility of happiness for man, has been the de-

ceitfulness of personal enjoyments, which waste life, and lead to satiety and sufferings. A man need only admit that his life consists in a striving after the good of others, and the delusive thirst for enjoyments will cease; and the vain, painful activity, directed to the filling of the bottomless cask of animal personality, will be replaced by an activity engaged in maintaining the life of other beings, which is indispensable for his happiness, and the torture of personal suffering, which annihilates the activity of life, will be replaced by a feeling of sympathy for others, infallibly evoking fruitful activity which is also the most joyful.

A third cause of the poverty of personal life has been the fear of death. Man has but to admit that his life does not consist in the happiness of his animal personality, but in the happiness of other beings, and the bugbear of death vanishes forever from before his eyes. For the fear of death arises only from the fear of losing the happiness of life with its death in the flesh. But if a man could place his happiness in the happiness of other beings, *i.e.* if he would love them more than himself, then death would not represent to him that discontinuance of happiness and life, such as it does represent to a man who lives only for himself. Death to the man who should live only for others could not seem to be a cessation of happiness and of life, because the happiness and the life of other beings is not only not interrupted with the life of a man who serves them, but is frequently augmented and heightened by the sacrifice of his life.

"But that is not life," replies the troubled and erring consciousness of man. "That renunciation of life is suicide." — "I know nothing about that," replies rational consciousness; "I know that such is the life of man, and that there is no other, and that there can be no other. I know more than that. I know that such a life is life and happiness both for a man and for all the world. I know that, according to my former view of the world, my life and the life of every living being was an evil and without sense; but according to this view, it appears as the realization of that law of reason which is placed in man.

"I know that the greatest happiness of the life of every being, which is capable of being infinitely enhanced, can be attained only through this law of the service of each to all, and, hence, of all to each."

"But if this can exist as an imaginary law, it cannot exist as an actual law," replies the perturbed and erring consciousness of man. "Others do not now love me more than themselves, and therefore I cannot love them more than myself, and deprive myself of enjoyment, and subject myself to suffering, for their sakes. I have nothing to do with the law of reason; I desire enjoyment for myself, and freedom from suffering. But a strife is now in progress between creatures, and if I do not struggle also, the others will crush me. It makes no difference to me by what road in imagination the greatest success for all is attained — all I need at present is my own actual greatest happiness," says false consciousness.

"I know nothing about that," replies rational consciousness. "I only know that what thou callest enjoyment will only become happiness for thee when thou shalt not thyself take, but when others shall give of theirs to thee, and thy enjoyments will become superfluous and sufferings, as they now are, only when thou shalt seize them for thyself. Only then, also, shalt thou free thyself from actual suffering, when others shall release thee from them, and not thou, thyself — as now, when, through fear of imaginary sufferings, thou deprivest thyself of life itself.

"I know that an individual life, a life where it is indispensable that all should love me alone, and that I shall love only myself, and in which I shall receive as much enjoyment as possible, and free myself from suffering and death, is the greatest and most incessant suffering. The more I love myself and strive with others, the more will others hate me, and the more viciously will they struggle with me; the more I hedge myself in from suffering, the more torturing will it be come, and the more I guard myself against death, the more terrible will it become.

"I know that, whatever a man may do, he will attain to no happiness until he lives in harmony with the law of his life. But the law of his life is not contest but, on the contrary, the mutual service of individuals to each other."

"But I know life only in my own person. It is impossible for me to place my life in the happiness of other persons."

"I know nothing about that," replies rational consciousness; "I only know that my life and the life of the world, which has hitherto seemed to me malicious nonsense, now appear to me as one rational whole, alive and striving toward the same happiness, through submission to one and the same law of reason, which I know in myself."

"But this is impossible to me," says erring consciousness, and at the same time there is not a man who would not have done this impossible thing, who would not have placed in this impossibility the best happiness of his life.

"It is impossible to place one's happiness in the happiness of other beings;" yet there is no man who has not known a condition in which the happiness of beings outside himself has become his happiness.

"It is impossible to place one's happiness in labors and sufferings for others;" but a man need only yield to that feeling of compassion, and personal pleasures lose their sense for him, and the force of his life is transferred into toils and sufferings for the happiness of others, and these sufferings and toils become happiness for him.

"It is impossible to sacrifice one's life for the happiness of others;" but a man need only recognize this feeling, and death is not only no longer visible and terrible to him, but it appears as the highest bliss to which he can attain.

A reasoning man cannot fail to see that if we mentally admit the possibility of replacing the striving for

his own happiness, with a striving for the happiness of
other beings, his life will become rational and happy,
instead of senseless and poverty-stricken as before.

He cannot fail, also, to see that, by admitting the
same conception of life in other people and beings, the
life of the whole world, in place of the incoherence and
harshness which were formerly apparent, will become
the most rational, elevated happiness which man can
desire, and that in place of its former incoherence and
aimlessness, it will acquire for him a rational meaning ;
to such a man the aim of life appears as the infinite enlightenment and union of beings in the world, toward
which life leads, and in which men first, and afterward
all other creatures, submitting themselves ever more and
more to the light of reason, will understand (what is at
present granted to man alone to understand) that the
happiness of life is to be attained, not by the striving of
each being toward his own personal happiness, but by a
united striving of each creature for the good of all the
rest.

But this is not all : admitting the mere possibility of a
change of aspiration toward one's own personal happiness, into an aspiration for the good of other beings,
man cannot fail to perceive, also, that precisely this
gradual, ever increasing renunciation of his individuality, and transference of the object of his activity from
himself to other beings, constitutes the whole movement
in advance of mankind, and of those living beings which
stand nearest to man.

Man cannot but see in history that the movement of
life in general lies not in the growth and augmentation
of strife of beings among themselves, but, on the contrary, in the diminution of disagreement and in the miti-
gation of the strife ; that the movement of life consists
only in this, that the world, through submission to the
law of reason, passes from enmity and discord ever
more toward concord and unity.

Having admitted this, man cannot but see that those
who have been in the habit of devouring each other
cease to devour each other ; that those who have been

in the habit of slaying prisoners and their children cease to slay them; that warriors who have taken pride in murder are ceasing to take pride in it; that people who have been in the habit of killing animals are beginning to tame them, and to kill them less; they are beginning to subsist on the eggs and milk of animals, instead of upon their bodies; that they are beginning to restrain their destructiveness, even in the world of plants.

Man perceives that the best representatives of mankind condemn researches for gratification, exhort men to abstinence, and that the very best men, who are lauded by posterity, present examples of the sacrifice of their own existences for the good of others. Man perceives that that which he has only admitted at the demand of reason is the very thing which actually takes place in the world, and is confirmed by the past life of mankind.

But this is not all: more powerfully and convincingly than through either reason or history, and from quite a different source, as it were, does the aspiration of man's heart reveal itself to him, impelling him to immediate happiness; to that very activity which his reason has pointed out to him, and which is expressed in his heart by love.

CHAPTER XIX

THE DEMAND OF THE INDIVIDUALITY APPEARS INCOMPATIBLE WITH THE DEMAND OF RATIONAL CONSCIOUSNESS

REASON and judgment and history and his inward feeling, — all, it would appear, should convince a man of the justice of this conception of life; but to the man educated in the doctrines of the world it appears, nevertheless, as though the satisfaction of the demands of his rational consciousness and of his feeling could not be the law of his life.

" Not contend with others for one's personal happiness, not seek enjoyment, not ward off suffering, and not fear death! But that is impossible, that is equivalent to renouncing the whole of life! And how am I to renounce my individuality, when I feel the demands of my individual self, and when I know, by my reason, the legitimacy of these demands?" say the cultivated men of our world, with full conviction.

And here is a noteworthy phenomenon. Laboring men, simple men, who exercise their judgment but little, hardly ever defend the demands of individuality, and always feel in themselves demands opposed to the demands of individuality; but an almost complete denial of the demands of rational consciousness and, chief of all, a refutation of the legality of those demands and a defense of the rights of the individual, are to be met with only among wealthy, refined people with cultivated judgment.

The cultivated, enervated, idle man will always prove that individuality has its inalienable rights. But the hungry man will not demonstrate that a man must eat: he knows that every one knows that, and that it is impossible either to prove or to controvert it; he will only eat.

This arises from the fact that the simple, so-called uncultivated man, having toiled all his life with his body, has not perverted his judgment, but has preserved it in all its purity and force.

But the man who has thought all his life, not only of insignificant, trivial objects, but even of such things as it is unnatural for a man to think of, has perverted his mind; his mind is no longer untrammeled. His mind is occupied with matter which is foreign to it, with a consideration of the requirements of its individuality, — with the development, the augmentation, of them, and with devising means to gratify them.

" But I am conscious of the demands of my individuality, and therefore those demands are legitimate," say so-called men of culture, brought up in the doctrine of the world.

And it is impossible for them not to feel the demands

of their personality. The whole life of these people is directed toward the imaginary satisfaction of the happiness of the individual. But this happiness of the individual seems to them to lie in the gratification of wants. And they call all those conditions of the existence of the individual upon which they have bent their minds, wants. But the wants recognized — those upon which the mind is bent — always grow to unlimited dimensions in consequence of this recognition. But the satisfaction of these wants veils from them the wants of their real life.

Social science, so-called, places at the foundation of its investigations the doctrine of the requirements of man, forgetful of the circumstance, very inconvenient for this doctrine, that no man has any wants at all, like the man who commits suicide or the man who is dying with hunger, or that they are literally innumerable.

There are as many requirements for the existence of the animal man as there are sides to that existence, and these sides are as numerous as the radii in a sphere. Need of food, of drink, of breathing, of the exercise of all the muscles and nerves ; need of labor, of rest, of pleasure, of family life ; need of science, of art, of religion, of their diversity. Wants, in all these connections, of the child, the youth, the man, the old man, the young girl, the woman, the aged crone, the wants of the Chinese, the Parisian, the Russian, the Laplander. Wants corresponding to the customs of the race, and to maladies. ....

One might go on enumerating them to the end of his days without enumerating all which constitute the wants of the individual existence of man. All the conditions of existence may be wants, and the conditions of existence are innumerable.

Only those conditions which are recognized are called wants. But recognized conditions, as soon as they are recognized, lose their true meaning, and acquire that always exaggerated meaning which is given to them by the mind directed upon them, and which veils from it its true life.

What are called needs, *i.e.* the conditions of man's animal existence, may be compared with countless little balls which are capable of being inflated, of which some body or other should have been formed. All the little spheres are equal to each other, and have their own places, and are not impeded in any way. As long as they are not inflated, all their wants are equal, and have room, and they do not feel painful until they are recognized. But all that is necessary is to begin to inflate one sphere, and it will occupy more space than all the rest, it will crowd the rest, and be crowded itself. It is the same with wants : all that is required is to direct the rational consciousness upon one of them, and this recognized want takes possession of the whole life and makes the man's whole being suffer.

CHAPTER XX

WHAT IS REQUIRED IS, NOT RENUNCIATION OF INDIVIDU-
ALITY, BUT ITS SUBJECTION TO RATIONAL CONSCIOUS-
NESS

YES, the assertion that man does not feel the wants of his rational consciousness, but feels only the wants of his individual part, is nothing else than an assertion that our animal desires, to the satisfaction of which we have devoted all our mind, rule us, and have hidden from us our true life as men. The weeds of our thickly grown vices have stifled the germs of true life.

And how can it be otherwise in our world, when it has been frankly admitted and is admitted, by those who consider themselves teachers of others, that the highest perfection of the isolated man is the development on all sides of the refined wants of his personality, that the happiness of the masses lies in this, that they should have many wants, and that they should be able to satisfy them, that the happiness of men consists in gratifying their wants.

How can men reared in such a doctrine do otherwise

than affirm that they do not feel the demands of rational consciousness, but feel only the wants of the individual? And how are they to feel the wants of reason when their entire mind, without reservation, has gone to the increase of their carnal desires? and how are they to renounce the demands of their desires when these desires have swallowed up their whole life?

"The renunciation of individuality is impossible," these people generally say, endeavoring intentionally to turn the question, and placing, instead of an idea of the subjection of the individuality to the law of reason, the idea of the renunciation of it.

"It is unnatural," they say, "and therefore impossible." But no one is talking about renouncing individuality. Individuality is, to the rational man, the same that breath, the circulation of blood, is to the animal. How is the animal personality to renounce the circulation of its blood? It is impossible to discuss this. Equally impossible is it to talk to the rational man about renouncing individuality. Individuality is, for the reasoning man, as indispensable a condition of his life as the circulation of the blood is a condition of the existence of his animal individuality.

Individuality, as an animal individuality, cannot present and does not present any demands. These demands are presented by a falsely directed mind; a mind directed, not to a guidance of life, not to its enlightenment, but to the inflation of the carnal desires of individuality.

The demands of the animal are always satisfied. Man cannot say, "What shall I eat?" or "Wherewithal shall I be clothed?" All these wants are guaranteed to man, as to the animal and the bird, if he lives a rational life. And, in fact, what thinking man can believe that he could diminish the wretchedness of his position by the guarantee of his individuality?

The wretchedness of man's existence arises, not from the fact that he is an individual, but from the fact that he recognizes the existence of his individuality as life and happiness. Only then do contradiction, division, and the suffering of man make their appearance.

The sufferings of the man begin only when he employs the force of his mind in the strengthening and augmentation to an unlimited extent of the growing demands of his individual, for the sake of concealing from himself the demands of reason.

It is neither possible nor necessary to renounce individuality, any more than in the case of all those conditions under which man exists; but he neither can nor must admit these conditions as life itself. He may and ought to make use of the given conditions of life, but it is impossible to look, and he must not look, upon these conditions as upon the aim of life. It is not necessary to renounce individuality, but to renounce the happiness of the individual, to cease to recognize individuality as life: this is what man must do in order to return to unity, and in order that that happiness, the striving toward which constitutes his life, may be attainable to him.

From the most ancient times the doctrine that the recognition of one's life in personality is the annihilation of life, and that renunciation of the happiness of personality is the only road to the attainment of life, has been preached by the great teachers of mankind.

"Yes, but what is this? This is Buddhism?" say the people of our day, as a rule, in reply to this. "This is Nirvana, this is standing on a pillar." And when they have said this, it seems to the people of our day that they have overthrown in the most successful manner what all know very well, and what it is impossible to conceal from any one: that individual life is poverty-stricken and can have no sense.

"This is Buddhism, Nirvana," they say; and it seems to them that with these words they have overthrown all that has been and is confessed by milliards of people, and what each of us, in the depths of his soul, knows very well, — namely, that life for the aims of the individual is pernicious and senseless, and that if there is any escape from this perniciousness and senselessness, that escape indubitably leads through the renunciation of the happiness for the individual.

The fact that the larger half of mankind has understood and does understand life thus, the fact that the
grandest minds have understood life in the same manner, the fact that it is impossible to understand it otherwise, does not trouble them in the least. They are so
firmly convinced that all the questions of life, if not settled in the most satisfactory manner, are set aside by
the telephone, operettas, bacteriology, electric lighting,
and so on, that the idea of renouncing their individual
life appears to them only as an echo from ancient
ignorance.

But, in the meanwhile, the unhappy men do not suspect that the very roughest Hindu, who stands for years
upon one leg, in the name only of renunciation of individual happiness for Nirvana, is, without any comparison, a more living man than they, the men of our
contemporary European society, who have turned to
beasts, who fly all over the world on railways, and
exhibit to the whole world, by the electric light, their
brutish condition.

That Hindu has understood that in the life of individuality and the life of reason there is a contradiction,
and he is solving it according to his light; but the men
of our cultivated world have not only not comprehended
this contradiction, but do not even believe that it exists.
The proposition that the life of man is not the existence
of the individuality of man, won by the spiritual toil of
all mankind prolonged through thousands of years —
this proposition has become for the man (not for the
animal) not only as indubitable and unalterable a truth
as the revolution of the earth or the laws of gravity, but
even more indubitable and unalterable than these. Every
thinking man, learned or ignorant, child or old man, understands and knows this; it is concealed only from the
savage men of Africa and Australia, and from well-to-do
people in our European towns and capitals who have
become savage.

This truth has become the property of mankind, and if
mankind does not retrograde in its illegitimate branches
of learning, mechanics, algebra, astronomy, still less

can it retrograde in the fundamental and chief learning of the definition of its life. It is impossible to forget and erase from the consciousness of man that which he has gathered from his life of many thousand years — the solution of vanity and senselessness, and the wretchedness of individual life. The attempts to resuscitate the savage, antediluvian view of life as an individual existence, with which the so-called science of our European world is engaged, only exhibit more visibly the growth of rational consciousness in mankind, and demonstrate clearly how mankind has already outgrown its childish garments. And the philosophical theories of self-annihilation, and the practice of suicide, which is growing to fearful proportions, prove the impossibility of a return of mankind to the degrees of consciousness already lived through.

Life, as an individual existence, has been outlived by mankind; and it is impossible to return to it, and to forget that the individual existence of man has no sense is impossible. Whatever we may write or say or discover, to whatever point we may perfect our personal life, the renunciation of possible happiness for the individual remains an incontrovertible truth for every thinking man of our times.

" But, nevertheless, it does revolve."

The point does not lie in overthrowing the proposition of Galileo and Copernicus, and in devising new Ptolemaic circles, — they are no longer to be devised; but the point lies in proceeding further, in drawing the most extreme conclusions from this proposition, which has already passed into the general knowledge of mankind. The same with the proposition relating to the impossibility of personal happiness, enounced by the Brahmins, and by Buddha, and Lao-dzi, and Solomon, and the Stoics, and by all the true thinkers of mankind. We must not conceal from ourselves this proposition, and get around it in every way, but boldly and clearly confess it, and draw from it the most extreme deductions.

CHAPTER XXI

THE FEELING OF LOVE IS A PHENOMENON OF THE INDI-
VIDUAL ACTIVITY BROUGHT INTO SUBJECTION TO RA-
TIONAL CONSCIOUSNESS

IT is impossible for a rational being to live for the
aims of individuality. It is impossible because all roads
are prohibited to it; all aims to which the animal individuality of man is drawn are plainly unattainable.
Rational consciousness points out other aims, and these
aims are not only attainable, but give full satisfaction to the
rational consciousness of man; at first, however, under
the influence of the false teaching of the world, it seems
to man that these aims are opposed to his individuality.

Try as a man may, who has been reared in our world
with cultivated, exaggerated desires of the individual, to
acknowledge himself as an "I" in his reason, he will
not feel in this "I" the aspiration toward life which he
feels in his animal person. The "I" of the reason
contemplates life, as it were, but does not itself live,
and has no aspirations toward life; but the animal "I"
must suffer, and therefore but one thing remains, — to
free itself from life.

Thus, in bad faith, do the negative philosophers of
our times (Schopenhauer, Hartmann) settle the question
— philosophers who deny life and who yet remain in it,
instead of availing themselves of the possibility of quitting it. And thus, in good faith, do suicides decide this
question by quitting a life which offers them nothing
but evil. Suicide presents to them the only escape from
the incoherence of the human life of our times.

The argument of pessimistic philosophy and of the
most commonplace suicides is as follows: there is an
animal *ego* in which there is an inclination for life.
This *ego* and its inclination cannot be gratified. There is
another *ego*, of the reason, in which there is no inclination
for life, which only critically surveys all the false joy of
life, and the passion of the animal *ego*, and rejects all of it.

If I yield myself to the former, I see that I live
senselessly, and that I am on my way to misery, plunging ever deeper and deeper in it.   If I yield myself to
the latter, to the rational *ego*, there remains within me
no inclination for life.   I see that to live for that which
alone it pleases me to live, for my personal happiness,
is awkward and impossible.   It would be possible to
live for rational consciousness, but there is no object in
it, and I do not wish it.   Serve that origin from which
I proceeded — God?   Why?   God — if he exists — will
find other servitors without me.   But why should I?

It is possible to look on at all this game of life until
it becomes tiresome.   And when it does become tiresome, I can leave it — I can kill myself.   And that is
what I am doing.

This is the contradictory representation of life which
mankind had reached before Solomon's day, before
Buddha's, and to which the false teachers of our times
wish to lead it back.

The demands of the individual are pushed to the most
extreme limits of senselessness.   The reason, on awakening, rejects them.   But the demands of the individual
have grown to such proportions, have so encumbered
man's consciousness, that it seems to him that reason
rejects the whole of life.   It seems to him that if he
eradicates from his consciousness of life all that his
reason rejects, nothing will remain.   He does not yet
perceive what will remain.   The remnant, that remnant
in which is life, seems nothing to him.

"But the light shineth in darkness and the darkness
comprehendeth it not."

The teaching of the truth recognizes this dilemma —
either a senseless existence or a renunciation of it —
and "it solves it."

The doctrine which has always been called the doctrine of happiness — the doctrine of the truth — has
pointed out to people that, instead of the deceptive
happiness which they seek for their animal personality,
they always possess, here and now, an inalienable and
actual happiness which is always attainable by them,

not that which they may receive somewhere and at some time.

This happiness is not merely something deduced from reasoning, it is not that something or other which must be sought somewhere, it is not that happiness promised somewhere and at some time, but is that very happiness which is familiar to man, and toward which every unperverted human soul is drawn.

All men know from the earliest years of their childhood that, in addition to the happiness of the animal personality, there is still another and better happiness of life, which is not only independent of the gratification of the carnal desires of the animal personality, but which, on the contrary, becomes all the greater in proportion to the renunciation of the happiness of the animal personality.

This feeling, which solves all the contradictions of human life, and gives the greatest possible happiness to man, these men know. This feeling is *love*.

Life is the activity of the animal personality, subjected to the law of reason. Reason is that law to which, for its own happiness, the animal personality of man must be rendered subservient. Love is the only reasonable activity of mankind.

The animal personality inclines to happiness ; reason demonstrates to man the delusiveness of personal happiness, and leaves but one path. Activity along this pathway is love.

The animal personality of man demands happiness ; rational consciousness shows man the misery of all beings who contend with each other, demonstrates to him that there can be no happiness for his animal individuality, shows him that the only happiness possible to him is one in which there shall be no contest with other beings, no cessation of happiness, no satiety ; in which there shall be no phantom and fear of death.

And lo, like a key made for this one lock alone, man finds in his own soul a feeling which gives him that very happiness which his reason indicates to him as the only possible one. And this feeling not only solves the former contradictions of life, but finds in these very contradictions, as it were, a possibility of manifesting itself.

Animal individualities desire to employ for their ends the individuality of man. But the feeling of love inclines him to give his existence for the good of other beings.

The animal individuality suffers. And this suffering and its alleviation constitute the chief activity of love. The animal individuality, in striving after happiness, strives with every breath toward the greatest evil — toward death, the phantom of which has destroyed every bliss of the individual.

But the feeling of love not only annihilates this fear, but inclines man to the extremest sacrifice of his fleshly existence for the happiness of others.

CHAPTER XXII

THE MANIFESTATION OF THE FEELING OF LOVE IS IMPOSSIBLE FOR MEN WHO DO NOT UNDERSTAND THE MEANING OF THEIR LIFE

EVERY man knows that in the feeling of love there is something peculiar, capable of solving all the contradictions of life, and of giving man that full happiness in the striving for which his life consists.

"But this feeling comes rarely, continues for but a brief time, and its consequences are still worse than suffering," say men who do not understand life.

To these men, love does not present itself as the sole legitimate manifestation of life which it represents to the rational consciousness, but merely as one among thousands of the varied accidents which occur in life; it presents itself as one of those thousands of varied moods in which man finds himself in the course of his existence: there are times when a man parades as a dandy, there are times when he is attracted by science or art, there are times when he is inclined to service, to

ambition, to acquisition; there are times when he loves
some one. The mood of love presents itself to men
who do not understand life, not as the essence of
human life, but as an accidental frame of mind, — and
hence as independent of their will, like all the others
to which man is subject in the course of his life. It
is often possible even to read and to hear arguments to
the effect that love is something irregular, which dis-
turbs the regular current of life, — a torturing state of
mind. Something like what it must seem to the owl
when the sun rises.

It is true that even these people feel that there is in
the state of love something peculiar and more important than in all other frames of mind. But, not understanding life, these people cannot understand love, and
the condition of love seems to them as lamentable and
as deceptive as all other conditions.

"Love? — But whom? It is not worth while to love
for a time; and to love forever is impossible."

These words accurately express the confused knowledge of people that in love there is salvation from the
misery of life, and the only thing resembling true
happiness, and, at the same time, a confession that, for
people who do not understand life, love cannot be an
anchor of safety. There is no one to love, and all love
passes away. And, therefore, love can be happiness
only when there is some one to love, and when it is
some one whom it would be possible to love eternally.
And, as there is nothing of the kind, there is no salvation in love, and love is as much of a delusion and
suffering as everything else.

And thus, and not in any other way, can people
understand love, who have learned and who themselves
teach that life is nothing else than an animal existence.

For such people, life does not even correspond to
that conception which we all involuntarily connect with
the word love. It is not a beneficial activity, giving
happiness to the one who loves, and to the person
loved. It very frequently happens that love, in the
estimation of people who recognize life in the animal

person, is the same feeling in consequence of which one
mother, for the welfare of her child, will deprive another
hungry child of its mother's milk, and suffer with anxiety
for the success of the nursing; that feeling which makes
the father, to his own torture, take the last bit of bread
from starving men in order to provide for his children;
it is the feeling through which he who loves a woman
suffers from this love, and causes her to suffer, seducing
her, or killing both himself and her out of jealousy;
that feeling through which it even happens that a man
violates a woman out of love; it is that feeling through
which men belonging to one association injure other
associations for the sake of upholding their own
fellows; it is that feeling which makes a man torment
himself over his favorite occupations, and by these same
occupations cause grief and suffering to the people
about him; it is the feeling which renders a man unable to endure an insult to his beloved fatherland,
strews the plain with dead and wounded, his own countrymen and others.

But even this is not all: the activity of love, for
people who recognize life as lying in the happiness of
the animal individuality, presents such difficulties that
its manifestations become not only painful, but often
impossible. "Love must not be discussed," is what is
generally said by the people who do not understand
life; "but one must yield to that direct feeling of preference, of passion, for people, which one experiences—
and this is genuine love."

They are right in saying that love must not be argued
about, that every argument about love destroys love.
But the point lies in this,—that only those people can
refrain from discussing love who have already applied
their reason to the understanding of life, and who have
renounced the happiness of individual life; but those
people who have not attained to a comprehension of
life, and who exist for the animal personality, cannot
do otherwise than discuss it. It is indispensable that
they should discuss it, in order to be able to give themselves over to that feeling which they call love. Every

manifestation of this feeling is impossible to them without discussion, without solving insoluble problems.

In point of fact, men prefer their own baby, their
own friends, their own wife, their own children, their
own country, to all other children, wives, friends, countries, and call this feeling love.

To love generally means to wish to do good. Thus
we have all understood love, and we cannot understand
it otherwise. And behold, I love my child, my wife, my
country, *i.e.* I desire the welfare of my baby, my wife,
my country, rather than the welfare of children, wives,
and countries. It never happens, and it never can happen, that I should love only my baby, or wife, or my
own country only. Every man loves his baby, and wife,
and children, and country, and men in general, together.
Meanwhile, those conditions of happiness which, because of his love, he desires for the different objects
of his love, are so connected together that every loving
activity of man, for one of his beloved beings alone, not
only interferes with his activity for others, but accrues
to the detriment of others.

And here the questions present themselves — in the
name of what love, and how to act? In the name of
what love to sacrifice another love, whom to love most,
and to whom to do the most good, — to one's own wife
and children, or to the wives and children of others?
How to serve one's beloved country without infring-
ing upon one's love for one's wife and children and
friends?

How, in short, to decide the question as to how much
I can sacrifice my own personality which is necessary
for the service of others? How much care may I take
of myself, in order to be able, since I love others, to
serve them? All these problems seem very simple to
people who do not know how to account to themselves
for that feeling which they call love; but they are not
only not simple — but they are absolutely insoluble.

And not without a reason did the publican put to Christ
this same question: "Who is my neighbor?" The
answer to these questions seems very easy only to those

people who have forgotten the present conditions of
human life.

Only in case men were gods, as we imagine them,
could they love merely chosen people; then only could
the preference of some over others be true love. But
men are not gods, and find themselves subject to conditions of existence under which all living beings always
live upon each other, devouring each other, both in a
direct and in a figurative sense; and man, as a reasonable being, must know and see this. He must know
that every happiness of the flesh is received by one
being only at the expense of another.

However much religious and scientific superstitions
may assure men of some future golden age, in which
everybody will have enough of everything, the rational
man sees and knows that the law of this temporal existence in space is the struggle of all against each, and of
each against each and against all.

In the pressure and conflict of animal interests which
constitute life, it is impossible for men to love selected
individuals, as those people who do not understand life
imagine. Man, if he loves even selected individuals,
can never love more than one. Every man loves his
mother, and his wife, and his child, and his friends, and
his country, and even all men. And love is not a word
only (as all are agreed that it is), but activity directed
to the good of others. But this activity does not proceed in any definite order, so that at first the demands
of a man's own strong, personal love are the first to present themselves, next the less powerful, and so on. The
demands of love present themselves constantly, all at
once, without any order. Just now a hungry old man,
of whom I am rather fond, comes to me and asks for
the food which I am keeping for the supper of my
dearly loved children. How can I weigh the demands
of a temporary and less powerful love with the future
demands of a stronger love?

These same questions were put by the lawyer to
Christ: "Who is my neighbor?" In fact, how are we
to decide whom it is necessary to serve, and in what

degree; people or our fatherland? our fatherland or our friends? our friends or our own wife? our wife or our father? our father or our children? our children or ourselves? (In order to be in a condition to serve others when this is necessary.)

For all these are the demands of love, and all are so interwoven with each other that the satisfaction of the demands of some deprives a man of the possibility of satisfying the demands of the others. If I admit that it is possible not to clothe a shivering child because my children will be in want, some day, of the garment which is asked of me, then I need not yield to other demands of love in the name of my future children.

It is precisely the same in relation to love for one's country, for chosen occupations, and for all men. If a man can deny the demands of the very smallest present love, in the name of the very greatest love in the future, is it not clear that such a man, even if he desire this with all his heart, will never be in a condition to weigh in what measure he can refuse the demands of the present in the name of the future, and therefore, not being competent to decide this question, he will always choose that manifestation of love which is agreeable to him, *i.e.* he will act, not in the name of his love, but in the name of his individuality. If a man decides that it is better for him to refrain from the demands of the smallest present love in the name of a future and different manifestation of a greater love, then he deceives either himself or others, and loves no one but himself alone.

There is no love in the future. Love is only activity in the present. And the man who manifests no love in the present has no love.

The same thing also comes to pass in the conception of life, in those people who have no life. If men were animals without reason they would exist like animals, and would not discuss life; and their animal existence would be legitimate and happy. It is the same with love; if men were animals without reason, they would love those whom they do love; their wolf-cubs, their flock; and they would not know that they love their wolf-cubs or their flock, and they would not know that other wolves love their cubs, and other flocks their comrades in the flock, and their love would be that love and that life which are possible on that plane of consciousness upon which they find themselves.

But men are reasoning beings, and they cannot help perceiving that others cherish the same love for their own, and that therefore these feelings of love must come in conflict and produce something not favorable, but quite opposed to the conception of love.

But if men employ their reason in justifying and strengthening that animal and ill-disposed sentiment which they call love, communicating to that sentiment monstrous proportions, then that sentiment becomes not only the reverse of good, but it makes of man — a truth long since established — the most malign and terrible of animals. That takes place which is described in the Gospels: "If the light that is in thee be darkness, how great is that darkness!" If there were nothing in man except love for himself and his children, there would not be even ninety-nine hundredths of the evil that now exists among men. Ninety-nine per cent of the evil among men springs from that false feeling which they, lauding it, call love, and which is as much like love as the life of the animal is like the life of man.

What people who do not understand life call love is only the familiar preference of some conditions of their personal happiness to others. When a man who does not understand life says that he loves his wife or his child or his friend, he merely says that the presence in his life of his wife or his child or his friend heightens the happiness of his individual life.

These preferences bear the same relation to love that existence bears to life. And as existence is called life by the people who do not know what life is, so the preference of some conditions of personal existence to others is called love by the same people.

These feelings — preferences for certain beings, as for example, for one's children, or even for certain occupations, for science, for instance, or for art, — we also call love ; but such feelings of preference, infinitely varied, constitute the whole complication of the visible, tangible, animal life of men, and cannot be called love, because they have not the chief mark of love, — activity, which has for its aim and end, happiness.

The violence of manifestation of these preferences only demonstrates the energy of the animal personality. The violence of preference of some people over others, inaccurately called love, is merely the stock upon which true love, and even its fruits, may be grafted. But as the stock is not the apple tree and does not yield fruit, or gives only bitter fruit, instead of sweet, so passion is not love, and does no good to people, or produces still greater evil. And therefore the much vaunted love for wife and children, as well as for friends, brings the greatest evil to the world, not to mention love for science, for art, for one's country, which is nothing else than a preference, for the time being, of certain conditions of the animal life over others.

CHAPTER XXIII

TRUE LOVE IS THE RESULT OF THE RENUNCIATION OF THE HAPPINESS OF THE PERSONALITY

TRUE love, then, becomes possible, only on the renunciation of happiness for the animal personality.

The possibility of true love begins only when a man has comprehended that there is no happiness for his animal personality. Only then will all the sap of his life pass into the one ennobling shoot of genuine love, which has already grown stout with all the powers of the trunk of the wild sapling of the animal person. And the doctrine of Christ is the graft for this love, as He Himself said. He said that He, His love, was the one branch which could bring forth fruit, and that every branch which bringeth not forth fruit is cut off.

Only he who has not only understood, but has also

by his life confessed that he who loves his soul loses it, and that he who hates his soul in this world preserves it to life everlasting, — only he understands genuine love.

"And he who loveth father or mother more than Me is unworthy of Me. And he that loveth son or daughter more than Me is unworthy of Me. If ye love them that love you, that is not love; but love your enemies, love them that hate you."

It is not by love for father, or son, or wife, or friends, or good and amiable people, as it is generally thought, that men renounce their individuality, but only as a result of the recognition of the vain existence of the individual, a recognition of the impossibility of its happiness, and therefore as a result of the renunciation of individual life, that man becomes acquainted with real love, and can really love father, son, wife, children, and friends.

Love is the preference of other beings to one's self, to one's animal personality.

The neglect of the nearest interests of the individual for the attainment of distant aims of the same individual, as is the case with what is generally called love, which has not grown to self-sacrifice, is merely the preference of some beings over others, for one's own individual happiness. True love, before it becomes an active sentiment, must be a certain condition. The beginning of love, its root, is not a burst of feeling, clouding the reason, as is generally imagined, but is that most rational, luminous, and therefore tranquil and joyous state, peculiar to children and to reasonable people.

That state is a state of affection toward all people, which is inherent in children, but which in grown persons arises only on renunciation, and increases only with the degree of renunciation of the happiness of the individuality. How often are we forced to hear the words: "It is all the same to me, I need nothing," and in connection with these words to see an unloving mien toward men. But let every man try, at least once, at a moment when he is ill-disposed toward people, to say to himself honestly and from his soul, " It is all the same to me, I need nothing," and, only for a time, to desire nothing for himself, and every man will learn, through this simple, inward experiment, how instantaneously, in proportion to the honesty of his renunciation, all malevolence will disappear, and how, afterward, affection toward all people will gush from his heart, sealed up to that time.

Love is, in truth, a preference of other beings to one's self — surely that is the way we all understand love, and it is impossible to understand it otherwise. The amount of love is the amount of the fraction whose numerator, my partiality, my sympathy for others, is not in my power; but the denominator, my love for myself, can be augmented or diminished by me, to infinity, in proportion to the significance which I attribute to my animal personality. But the judgment of our world concerning love, concerning its grades, is a judgment as to the size of the fraction according to the numerator alone, without regard to the denominator.

Real love always has as its foundation renunciation of individual happiness, and the affection toward all men which arises therefrom. Only upon this universal affection can spring up genuine love for certain people, — one's own relatives or strangers. And such love alone gives the true bliss of life, and solves the apparent contradictions of the animal and the rational consciousness.

Love which has not for its foundation renunciation of individuality, and, as a consequence, affection for all people, is merely the life of the animal, and is subject to the same miseries as, and to even greater miseries and to still greater folly than, life without this fictitious love. The feeling of partiality called love not only does not remove the conflict of existences, does not free an individual from the pursuit of enjoyments, and does not save from death, but merely darkens life still more, embitters the strife, augments the thirst for pleasures for one's self and others, and increases the terror of death for one's self and others.

The man who places his life in the existence of the animal individuality cannot love, because love must seem to him an activity directly opposed to his life. The life of such a man is only in the happiness of his animal existence; but love demands, first of all, the sacrifice of that happiness. Even if a man who does not understand life should sincerely wish to give himself up to the activity of love, he will not be in a condition to do this, until he understands life, and changes his whole relation to it. The man who sets his life in the happiness of his animal person, who increases, during the whole course of his life, the means of his animal happiness, by acquiring wealth and hoarding it, will make others serve his animal happiness, and will distribute that happiness among those individuals who have been most useful to him for the happiness of his personality. But how is he to give up his life, when his life is supported, not by himself, but by other people? And still more difficult will it be for him to choose to which of the persons whom he prefers he shall give the happiness which he has accumulated, and whom he shall serve.

In order to be in a position to give up his life, he must first give away that superfluity which he takes from others for the happiness of his own life; and more than that, he must accomplish the impossible: decide which of the people he is to serve with his life.

Before he will be in a condition to love, that is, to do good, sacrificing himself, he must cease to hate, that is, to do evil, and he must cease to prefer some people to others for the happiness of his personality.

Only for the man who does not acknowledge happiness in individual life, and who does not, therefore, trouble himself about that false happiness and about that affection toward all men proper to man, which is set free in him, is the activity of love, which always satisfies him and others, possible.

The happiness of the life of such a man in love is like the happiness of the plant in the light; and hence, as the plant which is not in the least covered cannot

inquire, and does not inquire, in what direction it is to
grow and whether the light is good, whether it must
not wait for some other and better light, but takes the
only light that exists in the world, and stretches toward
it, — thus the man who has renounced individual happiness does not argue about what he must give up of that
which he has taken from other people, and to what
beloved beings, and whether there is not some better
love than the one which makes the demand, but gives
himself, his being, to the love which is accessible to
him, and which lies before him. Only such love gives
full satisfaction to the reasoning nature of man.

CHAPTER XXIV

LOVE IS LOVE ONLY WHEN IT IS THE SACRIFICE OF SELF

And there is no other love than this, that a man
should lay down his life for his friend. Love is love
only when it is the sacrifice of one's self. Only when
a man gives to another, not merely his time and his
strength, but when he spends his body for the beloved
object, gives up his life for him, — only this do we all
acknowledge as love; and only in such love do we all
find happiness, the reward of love. And only in virtue
of the fact that there is such love toward men, only in
this, does the world stand. A mother who nurses her
child gives herself directly, her body, for the nourishment of the children, who, were it not for this, would
not be alive. And this is love. Exactly in the same
manner does every laborer for the good of others give
his body for the nourishment of another, when he exhausts his body with toil, and brings himself nearer to
death. And such love is possible only for the man
between whom and the possibility of sacrifice of himself
and other beings whom he loves there stands no limit
to sacrifice. The mother who gives her child to a nurse

cannot love it; a man who acquires and hoards his money cannot love.

"If any man say that he is in the light, and hateth his brother, he is still in darkness. If any man love his brother, that man abideth in the light and there is no deceit in him. But he that hateth his brother dwelleth in darkness, and walketh in darkness, and knoweth not whither he goeth, because darkness hath blinded his eyes. .... Let us love not in word or with the tongue, but in deed and truth. And hereby do we know that we are of the truth, and our hearts are set at rest. .... Love attaineth such perfection in us that we have boldness in the day of judgment, because we so walk in the world even as He walked. There is no fear in love, but perfect love casteth out fear, for in fear there is torment. He that feareth is not made perfect in love."

Only such love gives true life to men.

"Thou shalt love the Lord thy God with all thy heart and all thy soul and all thy mind. This is the first and great commandment." And the second is like unto it: "Thou shalt love thy neighbor as thyself," said the lawyer to Christ. And to this Jesus replied: "Thou hast said rightly, so do," — *i.e.* love God and thy neighbor — and *thou shalt live.*

True love is life itself. "We know that we have passed from death to life, because we love the brethren," says a disciple of Christ. "He that loveth not his brother abideth in death." Only he is alive who loves.

Love, according to the doctrine of Christ, is life itself, but not a senseless, suffering, and perishing life, but a blessed and endless life. And we all know this. Love is not a deduction of the mind, it is not the result of certain activity; but it is itself the joyful activity of the life which encompasses us on all sides, and which we all know in ourselves from the first memories of our childhood to the time when the false teaching of the world veils it in our soul and deprives us of the possibility of testing it.

But love is not a partiality for that which enhances the temporal happiness of man's personality, like love toward selected individuals or objects, but that striving toward the good of that which is within man, which will remain in man after the renunciation of the happiness of the animal individuality.

Who among living people does not know that blissful sensation, — even if but once experienced, and most frequently of all in the earliest childhood, before the soul is yet choked up with all that lie which stifles the life in us, — that blessed feeling of emotion, during which one desires to love everybody, both those near to him, his father, and mother, and brothers, and wicked people, and his enemies, and his dog, and his horse, and a blade of grass; he desires one thing, — that it should be well with everybody, that all should be happy; and still more he desires that he himself may act so that it may be well with all, that he may give himself and his whole life to making others comfortable and happy. And this, and this alone, is that love in which lies the life of man.

This love, in which alone is life, manifests itself in the soul of man as a hardly perceptible, tender shoot, in the midst of the coarse shoots of weeds resembling it, of the various carnal desires of man which we call love. At first, it seems to men, and to the man himself, that this shoot is the one from which must grow that tree in which the birds shall shelter themselves, — and that all the other shoots are the same.

At first, men even prefer the weeds which grow faster, and the only shoot of life is stifled and languishes; but what is even worse is that which most frequently happens: men have heard that among the number of these shoots there is one which is genuine, life-giving, called love, and, trampling it down, they begin to rear another shoot from the weeds, calling it love.

But, what is still worse, men seize the shoot with rough hands and cry: "Here it is, we have found it; now we know it, let us train it up; love, love! the most elevated sentiment; here it is!" and men begin to transplant it, to correct it, and they grasp it, and tread it under foot, until the shoot dies before it has flowered, and these same men or others say: "All this is nonsense, folly, sentimentality."

The shoot of love, when it appears, is tender, it does not bear handling; it is powerful only when it has attained its growth. All that men do to it is but the worse for it. It needs but one thing, — that men should not hide from it the sun of reason, which alone will promote its growth.

CHAPTER XXV

MEN'S EFFORTS, DIRECTED TO THE IMPOSSIBLE AMELIORATION OF THEIR EXISTENCE, DEPRIVE THEM OF THE POSSIBILITY OF THE ONE TRUE LIFE

ONLY the knowledge of the visionary and delusive character of the animal existence, and the setting free within him of the one true life of love, confers happiness upon man. And what steps do men take for the attainment of this happiness? Men, whose existence consists in the gradual annihilation of personality, and in the approach of that personality to inevitable death, and who cannot fail to be aware of this, strive in every way, during the whole period of their existence, to establish that perishing existence, to gratify its desires, and thereby to deprive themselves of the possibility of the only happiness in life — love.

The activity of men who do not understand life is directed, during the entire period of its existence, to a conflict for their own existence, to the acquisition of enjoyments, to emancipating themselves from suffering, and to putting away from them inevitable death.

But the increase of enjoyment increases the strain of the conflict, the sensitiveness to suffering, and brings death nearer. In order to hide from himself the approach of death, there is but one means: still further to augment pleasure. But the augmentation of pleasures reaches its limits, pleasure cannot be further increased, it passes into suffering, and remains only in the form of sensitiveness to suffering and terror before death, which is approaching ever nearer and nearer in the midst of suffering alone. And a vicious circle makes its appearance: one is the cause of the other and one augments the other. The chief horror in the life of people who do not understand life lies in the fact that what they regard as pleasures (all pleasures of a rich life), being of such a nature that they cannot be shared equally among all men, must be taken from others, must be obtained by force, by evil, by annihilating the possibility of that kindly inclination toward people from which springs love. So that pleasure is always directly opposed to love, and the stronger it is, the more opposed is it. So that, the stronger, the more intense the activity for the attainment of pleasure, the more impossible becomes the only happiness accessible to man — love.

Life is understood, not as it is recognized by the rational consciousness — as an invisible but undoubted submission at every moment of one's animal nature to the law of reason, setting free the affection toward all people which is proper to man, and the activity of love which flows from it, but only as an existence in the flesh during a certain period of time under settled conditions arranged by us, which exclude the possibility of kindliness to all men.

To people of the doctrine of the world, who bend their minds to the organization of fixed conditions of existence, it seems that the augmentation of the happiness of life proceeds from the best external arrangement of one's existence. But the best external arrangement depends upon the exercise of greater violence over men, which is directly opposed to love. So that the better their organization, the less possibility of love, the less possibility of life, is there left to them.

Having applied their reason, not to understanding that identical happiness for all men of the animal existence is equal to a cipher, men have recognized this cipher as a quantity which can be augmented or diminished, and

in this supposititious augmentation and diminution of
the cipher they use all the reason which remains unap-
plied in them.

Men do not perceive that nothing, however much it
may be multiplied, remains the same to every other
person a cipher; they do not perceive that the existence of the animal personality of every man is equally
wretched, and cannot be rendered happy by any external
conditions.   Men do not wish to see that no one existence, in the flesh, can be happier than any other, that
this is as much a law as that whereby the water on the
surface of a lake can nowhere rise higher than the
general level.   Men who have perverted their understanding do not see this, and apply themselves to this
impossible work, and in this elevation of the water in
various places above the level of the lake — after the
manner of what is done by children bathing, who call it
"brewing beer" — passes the whole of their existence.

It seems to them that the lives of men are more or
less happy and good; the existence of a poor laborer
or of a sickly man, they say, is evil, unhappy; the existence of a rich or a healthy man is good and happy;
and they bend all the strength of their minds to escaping an evil, unhappy, poor, and sickly existence, and in
constructing for themselves a good, rich, healthy, and
happy one.

They work out for generations the processes for
organizing and maintaining these various and happiest
of lives, and hand down the programmes of these fancied better lives, as they call their animal existence, to
their descendants.   Men vie with each other in endeavoring to maintain as well as possible that happy *life*
which they have inherited from the organization of
their parents, or to organize for themselves a new and
still happier *life*.   It seems to men that, by maintaining
the order of existence which they have inherited, or by
establishing a new one which is better, as they imagine,
they are accomplishing something.

And thus upholding each other in this delusion, men
often become so sincerely convinced that **this senseless**

beating of the water, the absurdity of which is evident
to themselves, constitutes life — they become so convinced of this, that they turn away with scorn from the
summons to true life, which they hear incessantly : both
in the teaching of the truth, and the examples of life
presented by people who are alive, and in their own
suppressed hearts, in which, even to the end, the voice
of reason and of love is never stifled.

A wonderful thing takes place. Men, vast numbers
of men, who possess the possibility of a life of love and
reason, find themselves in the position of those sheep
who are being dragged out of a burning house, while
they, imagining that people want to fling them into the
fire, exert all their strength to contend with those who
are trying to save them.

Through fear of death, men do not wish to escape
from it ; through fear of suffering, men torture themselves, and deprive themselves of the only happiness
and life that are possible for them.

CHAPTER XXVI

THE FEAR OF DEATH IS ONLY A CONFESSION OF THE UNSOLVED CONTRADICTION OF LIFE

"THERE is no death," the voice of truth says to men.
" I am the Resurrection and the Life ; he that believeth
in Me, though he were dead, yet shall he live. And
every one that liveth and believeth in Me shall never
die. Believest thou this ? "

"There is no death," say all the great teachers of
the world ; and the same say millions of men who
understand life, and bear witness to it with their lives.
And every living man feels the same thing in his soul,
at the moment when his consciousness clears up. But
men who do not understand life cannot do otherwise
than fear death. They see it, and believe in it.

" How is there no death ? " cry these people in wrath
and indignation. " This is sophistry ! Death is before

us; it has mowed down millions, and it will mow us down as well. And you may say as much as you please that it does not exist, it will remain all the same. Yonder it is!"

And they see that of which they speak, as a man mentally afflicted sees the vision which terrifies him. He cannot handle the vision, it has never touched him; of its intentions he knows nothing; but he is afraid, and he suffers from this imaginary vision, which is deprived of the possibility of life. And it is the same with death. Man does not know his death, and never can know it; it has never yet touched him; of its intentions he knows nothing. Then what is it that he fears?

"It has never yet seized me, but it will seize me, that I surely know — it will seize me and annihilate me. And that is terrible," say men who do not understand life.

If men with false ideas of life could reason calmly, and think accurately, on the basis of that conception which they have of life, they would be forced to the conclusion that in what is produced in my fleshly existence by the change which I see proceeding, incessantly, in all beings, and which I call death, there is nothing disagreeable or terrible.

I shall die. What is there terrible about that? How many different changes have taken place, and are now in progress, in my fleshly existence, and I have not feared them? Why should I fear this change which has not yet come, and in which there is not only nothing repulsive to my reason and experience, but which is so comprehensible, so familiar, and so natural for me, that during the whole course of my life I have formed fancies, J still form them, in which the death, both of animals and of people, has been accepted by me as a necessary and often an agreeable condition of life. What is there terrible about it?

For there are but two strictly logical views of life: one false — that by which life is understood as those seeming phenomena which take place in my body from my birth to my death; and another, the true one — by which life is understood as that invisible consciousness of it which I bear within myself. One view is false, the other is true; but both are logical, and men may hold either the one or the other; but in neither the one nor the other is the fear of death possible.

The first false view, which understands life as the visible phenomena in the body from birth to death, is as old as the world itself. This is not, as many think, a view of life which has been worked out by the materialistic science and philosophy of our day; the science and philosophy of our times have only carried this view to its extreme limits, by which it becomes more visible than hitherto how little this view corresponds to the fundamental demands of human life; but this is the ancient and primitive view of men who stood upon the lower steps of culture. It is expressed among the Chinese, among the Greeks, and among the Hebrews, in the Book of Job, and in the sentence: " Dust thou art, and to dust shalt thou return."

This view, in its present expression, runs as follows: Life is the fortuitous play of forces in matter, manifesting itself in space and time. And what we call our consciousness is not life, but a certain delusion of the feelings, which makes it appear that life lies in this consciousness. Consciousness is the spark which flashes up from matter under certain conditions of the latter. This spark flashes up, burns, again grows feeble, and finally goes out. This spark, that is to say, consciousness, experienced by matter in the course of a certain time, between two endless spaces of time, is nothing. And in spite of the fact that consciousness sees and passes judgment on itself and on all the infinite world, and beholds all the play of chance of this world, — and *chief of all*, in the contradistinction to something that is not accidental, calls this play accidental, — this consciousness itself is only the product of dead matter, a specter, appearing and disappearing without any trace or reason. All is the product of matter, infinitely varied; and what is called life is only a certain condition of dead matter.

Such is one view of life. This view is utterly false. According to this view, the rational consciousness of man is merely an accident, accompanying a certain condition of matter; and therefore, what we, in our consciousness, call life, is a phantom. What is dead alone exists. What we call life is the play of death. With such a view of life, death should not only not be terrible, but life ought to be terrible, as something unnatural and senseless, as it is among the Buddhists, and the new pessimists, Schopenhauer and Hartmann.

The other view of life is as follows. Life is only that which I recognize in myself. But I am always conscious of my life, not as I have been or as I shall be (thus I meditate upon my life), but I am conscious of my life thus — that I am — that I never begin anywhere, that I shall never end anywhere. No comprehension of time and space is connected with my consciousness of life. My life is manifested in time, in space, but this is merely its manifestation. But the life itself of which I am conscious makes itself perceptible to me outside of time and space; so that, according to this view, it appears, on the contrary, not that the consciousness of life is a phantom, but all that which is dependent upon space and is visionary in time.

And, therefore, a curtailment of the bodily existence, so far as connected with time and space, has nothing wretched about it, according to this view, and can neither shorten nor destroy my true life. And, according to this view, death does not exist.

There could be no fear of death according to either view of life, if men held strictly to either the one or the other.

Neither as an animal nor as a rational being can man fear death. As the animal has no consciousness of life, it does not see death; but the rational being, having a consciousness of life, cannot see in the death of the animal anything except a natural and never ending movement of matter. But if man fears, what he fears is not death, which he does not know, but life, which alone he does know, and his animal and rational existence. That feeling which is expressed in men by the fear of death is only the consciousness of the inward contradiction of life ; just as the fear of ghosts is merely a consciousness of a sickly mental condition.

" I shall cease to be; I shall die; all that which I value in life will die," says one voice to a man.

" I am," says another voice; " and I cannot die, and I ought not to die. I ought not to die, and I am dying."

Not in death, but in this contradiction lies the cause of that terror which seizes upon a man at the thought of death of the flesh : the fear of death lies not in the fact that man dreads the curtailment of his animal existence, but in the fact that it seems to him that that will die which cannot and must not die. The thought of future death is only a transference to the future of the death which takes place in the present. The specter which presents itself of a future death of the flesh is not an awakening of the thought of death, but, on the contrary, an awakening of the thought of the life which a man should have and which he has not.

This feeling is similar to that which a man would experience on awaking to life in his grave, under ground. " There is life, but I am in death ; and this is it — death ! " He imagines that what is and must be will be annihilated. And the mind of man mourns and grows afraid. The best proof of the fact that the fear of death is not the fear of death, but of false life, is this, that men frequently kill themselves from the fear of death.

Men are not terrified by the thought of the death of the flesh because they are afraid that their life will end with it, but because the death of the flesh plainly demonstrates to them the necessity of a true life, which they do not possess. And this is why people who do not understand life are so disinclined to think of death. To think of death is exactly the same with them as to confess that they are not living as their rational consciousness demands.

People who fear death, fear it because it represents emptiness and darkness to them ; but they behold emptiness and darkness because they do not see life.

CHAPTER XXVII

THE DEATH OF THE FLESH ANNIHILATES THE BODY
WHICH BELONGS TO SPACE AND THE CONSCIOUSNESS
WHICH BELONGS TO TIME, BUT IT CANNOT ANNIHILATE
THAT WHICH CONSTITUTES THE FOUNDATION OF LIFE:
THE SPECIAL RELATION OF EVERY CREATURE TO THE
WORLD

BUT if men who do not see life would only approach
nearer to the phantoms which alarm them, and would
examine them, they would perceive that for them also
they are only phantoms, and not realities.

The fear of death always proceeds, in these people,
from the fear of losing, at their death in the flesh, their
special *ego*, which, they feel, constitutes their life. I
shall die, my body will molder and destroy my *ego*.
But my *ego* is that which has lived in my body so many
years.

Men prize this *ego* of theirs; and, assuming that this
ego corresponds with their fleshly life, they draw the deduction that it must be annihilated with the destruction
of their fleshly life.

This is a very common deduction, and it rarely enters
any one's head to doubt it, yet, nevertheless, this deduction is entirely arbitrary. Men — both those who consider themselves materialists, and those who regard
themselves as spiritualists — have become so habituated
to the notion that their *ego* is the consciousness of their
body, which has lived so many years, that it never enters
their heads to verify the authenticity of such a conviction.

I have lived fifty-nine years, and during the whole of
that time I have been conscious of myself in my body, and
this consciousness of myself has, as it seems to me, been my
life. But, as a matter of fact, it only seems so to me. I
have lived neither fifty-nine years, nor fifty-nine thousand
years, nor fifty-nine seconds. Neither my body nor the
length of its existence in any way determines the life of

my *ego*. If I, at every moment of my life, ask myself in my own consciousness, "What am I?" I reply: "Something thinking and feeling," *i.e.* bearing itself to the world in its own entirely peculiar fashion.

Only this *ego* do I recognize as my *ego*, and nothing more. As to when and where I was born, when and where I began to think and to feel as I now think and feel, I know absolutely nothing. My consciousness merely says to me: "I am; I am with that relation of mine to the world in which I find myself at the present moment."

Of my birth, my childhood, of many periods of youth, of middle age, of times not very far past, I often remember nothing at all. But if I do recall anything, or if I am reminded of something in my past, then I remember it — and remember it almost exactly as those things which are told me about others.

On what foundation, therefore, do I assert that, during the whole course of my existence, I have been but *one ego?* My body, assuredly, never has been and is not one: my body has always been, and is ceaselessly wasting substance — through something immaterial and invisible, that recognizes this which flows through it as its body. My whole body has been changed scores of times; nothing has been left of the old: muscles and inward parts, and bones, and brain, — all have undergone a change.

My body is one only because there is something immaterial which acknowledges this changing body as one and its own. This immaterial something is that which we call consciousness: it alone holds the whole body together, and recognizes it as one and its own. Without this knowledge of myself as separate from everything else, I should know nothing of my own or of any other life. And therefore, on first thinking the matter over, it appears that the foundation of all — consciousness — must be constant. But this also is incorrect; and consciousness is not constant. During our whole life, and even now, there is repeated that phenomenon of sleep, which seems to us very simple because we all sleep every

day, but which is decidedly incomprehensible, if we admit, what it is impossible not to admit, that consciousness
is often entirely suspended during sleep.

Every twenty-four hours, during the period of profound slumber, consciousness is entirely suspended, and
is afterward resumed. But, in the meantime, this same
consciousness is the only basis upon which the whole
body is held together, and recognized as its own. It
would seem as though, on the suspension of consciousness, the body should fall apart, and lose its independent existence; but this does not happen either in
natural or artificial sleep.

But not only is the consciousness which binds the
whole body together periodically interrupted, without
the body falling apart, — this consciousness, in addition,
changes like the body. As there is nothing in common
with my body of ten years ago and my present body, —
as it is not one and the same body, so there has not
been one consciousness in me. My consciousness as a
child three years of age, and my present consciousness,
are as different as is the matter of my body now from
what it was thirty years ago. Consciousness is not a
unit, and there is a series of successive states of consciousness which might be subdivided to infinity.

So even that consciousness which holds the whole
body together, and recognizes it as its own, is not a
unit, but something which is suspended and which
undergoes change. Consciousness, a single consciousness of one's self, as we generally imagine it, does not
exist in man, just as there is not one body. There is in
man neither one and the same body nor one of that
thing which sets apart this body from every other —
there is no consciousness which is constantly the same,
throughout the whole life of a man, but there is only
a series of successive states of consciousness, in some
manner united — and, nevertheless, man feels himself
to be himself.

Our body is not one, and that which recognizes this
changing body to be one and ours is not continuous in
point of time, but is merely a series of changing states

of consciousness, and we have already lost both our
body and our consciousness many times; we lose our
body constantly, and we lose our consciousness every
day, when we fall asleep; and every day and hour we
feel in ourselves the alteration of this consciousness, and
we do not fear it in the least.

Hence, if there is any such thing as our *ego*, which
we are afraid of losing at death, then that *ego* cannot
reside in the body which we call ours, nor in that consciousness which we call ours for a certain time, but in
some other, whole series of successive states of consciousness united into one.

What is this something which binds in one all the
states of consciousness which succeed each other in
point of time? What is my same radical and peculiar
ego, which is not composed of the substance of my body
and of the series of states of consciousness which proceed in it, but that fundamental *ego* upon which as upon
a cord are strung, one after the other, the various consciousnesses which follow each other in point of time?
The question seems very profound and wise, but there
is not a child who would not know how to answer it,
and who would not utter the response twenty times a
day.

" But *I* love this and I don't love that."

These words are very simple, but in them lies the
solution of the question as to the peculiar *I* which binds
all consciousness in one. It is that *I* which loves this
thing and does not love that. Why one loves this and
does not love that, no one knows, and, at the same time,
it is this very thing which constitutes the foundation of
life for every man, and it is this which binds in one all
the states of consciousness, varying in point of time, of
every individual man.

The external world acts upon all men alike, but the
impressions of men, even when under the very same
conditions, differ infinitely, both in the number received
and in their capacity for being infinitely subdivided, and
in their strength. From these impressions is formed
the series of successive states of consciousness of every

man. But all these successive consciousnesses are connected only because, even in the present, some impressions act, and others do not act, upon his consciousness.
But certain impressions act or fail to act upon a man
only because he loves this more or less, and does not
love that.

Only in consquence of this greater or lesser degree of
love is a certain series of some judgments, and not of
others, formed. So that only in the property of loving
one more or less, and not loving the other, lies that
peculiar and fundamental *ego* of man, in which all the
scattered and fragmentary senses are united. And this
property, although it is developed in our life, is borne
by us, all ready prepared, into this life, from some past
invisible and unknown to us.

This peculiar property of men, of loving one thing in
a greater or less degree and not loving another, is
usually called character. And by this word the peculiar qualities of each individual man, which have taken
form in consequence of certain conditions of place and
time, are often understood. But this is an error.

The fundamental quality of man, of loving one thing
more or less and not loving another, does not proceed
from conditions of time and space, but, on the contrary,
conditions of time and place act or do not act upon a
man only because man, on his entrance into the world,
already has a very well-defined property of loving one and
not loving another. Only from this cause does it happen that men, born and reared in identical conditions of
time and space, often present the sharpest contrast in
their internal *ego*.

That which unites in one all the scattered states of
consciousness, which, in their turn, bind our body in
one, is a very definite thing, although independent of
conditions of time and place, and is brought into the
world by us from the realm of the spaceless and the
timeless : it is that *something* which lies in my well-
known exceptional relations to the world, and is my
genuine and acting *ego*. I understand myself as that
fundamental quality ; and other men, if I know them, I

know only as some peculiar relations to the world. On entering into serious spiritual communion with men, none of us, surely, is guided by their external marks, but each of us seeks to penetrate into their nature ; that is, to understand what is their relation to the world, what they love, and in what degree, and what they do not love.

Every separate being, — a horse, a dog, or a cow, if I know them, and have any spiritual relations with them, I know, not by their external marks, but by that peculiar relation to the world in which each one of them stands — by the fact that each one of them loves and does not love, and in what degree each loves and does not love. If I know the special and various races of animals, then, strictly speaking, I know them, not so much by their external marks, as because each one of them — the lion, the fish, the spider — presents a general peculiar relation to the world. All lions, as a rule, love one thing, and all fish another, and all spiders a third ; only because they love differently are they distinguished in my imagination as different living creatures.

But what I do not yet distinguish in each of these creatures, his special relation to the world, does not prove that it has not existed, but only that the peculiar relation to the world which constitutes the life of a single individual spider is remote from that relation to the world in which I find myself, and that therefore I have not yet understood him as Silvio Pellico understood his individual spider.

The basis of all I know about myself, and about all the world, is that peculiar relation to the world in which I find myself, and in consequence of which I see other beings, who are in their own peculiar relations to the world. But my special relation to the world has not been settled in this life, and did not begin with this body, nor with the series of consciousnesses which have followed each other in point of time.

And, therefore, my body, bound in one by my temporal senses, may be annihilated, and even my temporal **existence may be annihilated, but** that which cannot be

annihilated is my peculiar relation to the world, which
constitutes my peculiar *ego*, from which has been created
for me all that is.   It cannot be annihilated, because it
alone has existence.   If it did not exist, I should not
know the series of my consecutive states of consciousness, I should not know my body, I should not know
my own life or any other.   And, therefore, the annihilation of the body and the senses cannot serve as a sign
of the annihilation of myself and judgment, cannot
serve as a sign of the destruction of my peculiar relations to the world, which neither began nor arose in
this life.

CHAPTER XXVIII

THE FEAR OF DEATH ARISES FROM THE FACT THAT MEN
ACCEPT AS LIFE ONE SMALL PORTION OF IT LIMITED
BY THEIR OWN FALSE IDEA

WE are afraid of losing, at the death of the flesh, our
special *ego*, uniting the body and a series of conscious
states, which manifest themselves temporally, into one ;
but, nevertheless, this, my peculiar *ego*, did not begin
with my birth, and, therefore, the suspension of a certain temporary consciousness cannot annihilate that
which unites in one all temporal states of consciousness.
    The death of the flesh actually does destroy that which
holds the body together, — the consciousness of temporal
life.   But this happens with us invariably, and every
day when we fall asleep.   The question lies here : does
the death of the flesh destroy that which unites all the
consecutive states of consciousness into one, that is to
say, my special relation to the world ?   In order to
verify this, it is necessary first to demonstrate that this
special relation to the world, which unites in one all
succeeding states of consciousness, was born with my
birth in the flesh, and that it will, therefore, die with it.
But this is not so.
    Reasoning upon the foundation of my consciousness,

I see that what binds all my states of consciousness into one is a certain susceptibility toward one thing, and a coldness toward another, in consequence of which one remains, while the other disappears in me, the degree of my love for good and of my hatred for evil, — that is, my peculiar relation to the world, which constitutes me, my special *me*, is not the result of any external cause, but is the fundamental cause of all the other phenomena of my life.

Reasoning upon the foundation of observation, it seems to me at first that the causes of peculiarity in my *ego* are to be found in the peculiarities of my parents, and in the conditions which have influenced them and me ; but, on proceeding further in this path of reasoning, I cannot fail to perceive that if my special *ego* lies in the peculiarities of my parents, and the conditions which have affected them, then it lies also in the peculiarities of all my ancestors, and in the conditions of their existence, so that my special *ego* has been produced outside the limits of all space, and outside of all time ; that is, that it is the very thing which I recognize it to be.

In this, and only in this timeless and spaceless foundation of my special relation to the world, uniting all the states of consciousness within my memory, and all those states which preceded memory, of my life (as Plato puts it, and as we all feel it in our lives), in this foundation, in my special relation to the world, is there that special *ego*, as to which we fear that it will be annihilated at the death of the flesh.

But it is merely necessary to understand that what unites all states of consciousness in one, that what constitutes the special *ego* of a man, is to be found independent of time, that it always has been and is, and that what can suspend itself is only a series of states of consciousness, within a given time, — in order to make it clear that the destruction of the last state of consciousness in point of time, at the death of the flesh, can as little destroy man's true *ego* as his daily slumber. For no man ever feared to fall asleep, although in sleep precisely the same thing takes place as at death, namely, a temporary suspension of consciousness. But not a single man is afraid of going to sleep, although the suspension of consciousness is precisely the same as in death, — not because he has reasoned it out that he has gone to sleep and waked again, and that therefore he will wake again (this reasoning is inaccurate : he might wake a thousand times and not waken on the thousand and first); — no one ever goes through this reasoning, and this reasoning could not reassure him ; but the man knows that his real *ego* lives independent of time, and that therefore the suspensions of his consciousness which manifest themselves in time cannot destroy his life.

If a man were to fall asleep, as in the fairy tales, for a thousand years, he would go to sleep as tranquilly as for two hours. For consciousness, which is not temporary, but of true life, a break of a million years and of eight hours are all the same, because, for such a life, time does not exist.

The body is annihilated, the consciousness of to-day is annihilated.

But it is surely time for man to become accustomed to the changes of his body, and to the replacement of temporary states of consciousness by others. For these changes began as long ago as man can remember himself, and have proceeded uninterruptedly. Man does not fear the change in his body, and not only is he not terrified, but he often desires to hasten these changes, he desires to grow up, to become a man, to recover health. The person has been a red piece of flesh, and all his consciousness has consisted in the demands of the stomach; now he is a bearded, sensible man, or a woman loving her grown-up children ! ....

For there is nothing similar either in body or mind, and man has not been terrified by these changes which have brought him to his present condition, but he has only welcomed them. What is there terrible about the impending change ? Annihilation ? Why, that in which all these changes are effected — a special relation to the world — that in which consists the consciousness of the true life, did not begin with the birth of the body, but independently of the body and independently of time. Then how can any change connected with time and space destroy that which is not connected with it? A man fixes his eyes upon a small, insignificant bit of his life, does not wish to see all of it, and trembles lest this tiny fragment which is dear to him should be lost. This recalls the anecdote of the madman who imagined that he was made of glass, and who, when he was thrown down, said, "Smash!" and immediately died. In order that a man may have life, he must take the whole of it, and not that small scrap of it which reveals itself in time and space. To him that taketh the whole of life there shall be added, but from him that taketh a portion of it shall be taken away even that which he hath.

CHAPTER XXIX

LIFE IS A RELATION TO THE WORLD. THE MOVEMENT OF LIFE IS THE ESTABLISHMENT OF A NEW, A HIGHER, RELATION, AND THEREFORE DEATH IS THE ENTRANCE UPON A NEW RELATION

WE cannot understand life otherwise than as a certain relation to the world: thus do we understand life in ourselves, and thus do we understand it in other beings.

But we understand life in ourselves not only as a relation to the world once existing, but as the establishment of a new relation to the world through greater and ever greater subjection of the animal personality to the reason, and the appearance of a greater degree of love. The inevitable destruction of fleshly existence, which we see in ourselves, proves to us that the relation in which we stand to the world is not permanent, but that we are compelled to establish another. The establishment of this new relation, *i.e.* the movement of life, also destroys the conception of death. The idea of death presents itself only to the man who has not recognized his life as lying in the establishment of a rational relation to the world, and its manifestation in ever increasing love, and who has remained in this relation, *i.e.* in that degree of love to one thing and dislike to another, with which he entered upon existence.

Life is an unceasing movement, but by remaining in the same relation to the world, by remaining in the same degree of love, with which he entered life, he feels its cessation, and death presents itself to him.

And death is visible and terrible to such a man only. The whole existence of such a man is one constant death. Death is visible and terrible to him, not only in the future, but in the present, at all manifestations of the diminution of animal life, from youth to old age; because the movement of existence from childhood to manhood only seems like a temporary augmentation of strength, while it is, in reality, merely a hardening of the limbs, a decrease of flexibility, of vitality, which never ceases from birth to death. Such a man beholds death constantly before him, and cannot save himself from it by any means whatever. The situation of such a man becomes worse and worse with every day and hour, and nothing can improve it. His special relation to the world, love to one and lack of love for another, seems to such a man only one of the conditions of his existence; and the only business of life, the establishment of a new relation to the world, the increase of love, appears to him as a useless matter. His whole life is passed in the impossible effort to escape from the inevitable diminution of life, the hardening and weakening of it through old age and death.

But it is not thus for the man who understands life. Such a man knows that he brought his peculiar relation to the world into his present life, his love for one and his dislike for the other, from his past, which is concealed from him. He knows that this love of his to one and dislike to another, which has been brought into his existence by himself, is the very essence of his life; that this is not an accidental property of his life, but that this alone possesses the movement of life — and he places his life in this movement alone, in the augmentation of love.

Looking at his past in this life, he perceives, from the series of the conscious states which he understands, that his relation to the world has changed, that his submission to the law of reason has increased, and that the strength and scope of his love have constantly grown — giving him ever more and more happiness, independent of and sometimes directly contrary to it in proportion to the decrease of the personal existence.

Such a man, having received his life from a past that is invisible to him, and recognizing its constant and unbroken growth, transfers it also to the unseen future, not only calmly, but also joyfully.

It is said: sickness, old age, infirmity, relapse into childhood, are annihilation of the consciousness and of the life of man.

For what sort of man?

I imagine to myself, according to tradition, John the Divine fallen into childishness from old age. According to tradition, he merely said: "Brethren, love one another." The old man of a hundred years, who can hardly move, mumbles, with tearful eyes, ever the same words: "Love one another." In such a man the animal existence hardly flickers — it is all devoured by new relations to the world, by a new existence which has not yet succeeded in establishing itself in the fleshly man.

For a man who understands life as lying in that in which it really does lie, to speak of the decrease of his life in sickness and old age, and to grieve over this, is the same as though a man, on approaching the light, were to bewail the decrease in his darkness in proportion to the nearness of his approach to the light. And to believe in the destruction of one's life because the body is destroyed is the same as believing that the destruction of the shadow of an object, after that object has stepped into the full light, is a sure sign of the destruction of the body itself. Such conclusions could be drawn only by a man who has gazed so long upon the shadow alone that he has at last come to imagine that it is the object itself.

But for the man who knows himself, not by his reflection in an existence defined by time and space, but by his growth in a loving relation toward the world, the destruction of the shadow of the conditions of time and space is merely the token of a greater degree of light. The man who, understanding his life as that certain special relation to the world with which he entered into existence, and which has grown in his life by the augmentation of love, believes in his annihilation, is on a level with the man who, being acquainted with the external and visible laws of the world, believes that his mother found him under a cabbage-leaf, and that his body will suddenly fly off somewhere so that nothing will remain of it.

CHAPTER XXX

THE LIFE OF DEAD MEN IS NOT ENDED IN THIS WORLD

But even more plain does the superstition about death become, I will not say when looked at from another side, but according to the very constitution of life as we know it. My friend, my brother, has lived precisely like myself, and he has now ceased to live like me. His life has been his consciousness, and it has been passed under the conditions of his bodily existence; that is to say, there is no place or time for the manifestation of his consciousness, and he does not exist for me. My brother has been, I have had relations with him, but now he is not, and I shall never know where he is.

" All bonds between him and us are broken. He does not exist for us, and, in like manner, we shall not exist for those who remain behind. What is this if not death?" So speak the people who do not understand life.

These people see, in a visible suspension of external communication, an indubitable proof of actual death.

But on no occasion does the visionary character of the conception of death more clearly and more visibly disappear than on the suspension of the fleshly existence of people who are near to us. My brother is dead; what has happened? That has happened which is accessible to my observations in time and space; the manifestation of his relation to the world has disappeared from before my eyes, and nothing has been left behind.

"Nothing has been left behind," — thus would speak a chrysalis, a cocoon, which had not yet released the butterfly, on seeing that the cocoon lying beside it has been left empty. But the cocoon might say this if it could think and speak, because, on losing its neighbor, it would, in reality, no longer feel it in any way. It is not thus with man. My brother has died; his cocoon, it is true, has been left empty. I do not see him in the form in which I have hitherto seen him, but his disappearance from my vision has not destroyed my relations to him. I retain, as the expression goes, a remembrance of him.

A remembrance remains, — not a remembrance of his hands, his face, his eyes, but a remembrance of his spiritual form.

What is this remembrance? such a simple and comprehensible word as it seems! The forms of crystals and animals disappear, — no remembrance of them remains among crystals and animals. But I retain a remembrance of my friend and brother. And this remembrance is all the more vivid in proportion as the life of my friend and brother was more in conformity with the law of reason, and in proportion as it revealed itself more greatly in love.

This recollection is not merely a representation, but this recollection is something of a sort which acts on me, and acts precisely as the life of my brother did during the period of his earthly existence. This memory is that same invisible, immaterial atmosphere of his which encompassed his life and acted upon me and upon others during his earthly existence, exactly as it acts upon me after his death. This remembrance de-

mands of me now, after his death, the same that it
demanded of me during his lifetime.

And this is not all; this recollection has become more
obligatory for me since his death than it was during his
life. That force of life which resided in my brother
has not only not vanished nor suffered diminution, but
has not even remained the same; it has increased, and
acts more powerfully upon me than before.

The force of his life after his death in the flesh has
the same action as before his death, or an even more
powerful one, and acts like every truly living thing.

On what grounds can I, feeling in myself that power
of life, precisely what it was during the existence in the
flesh of this brother, *i.e.* as his relation to the world,
which has elucidated to me my relation to the world,
assert that my dead brother has no longer life? I can
say that he has quitted that lower relation to the world
in which he stood as an animal, and in which I still find
myself, — and that is all; I can say that I do not see
the new center of relation to the world in which he now
stands; but I cannot deny his life, because I am conscious of its power upon me. I have gazed in the
reflecting surface upon the way in which a man holds
me; the reflecting surface has grown dim. I no longer
see how he holds me, but I feel in all my being that he
still holds me as before, and hence that he exists.

But this is not all; this life of my dead brother, which
is invisible to me, not only acts upon me, but enters into
me. His special, living *ego*, his relation to the world,
becomes my relation to the world. In the establishment of his relation to the world, he elevates me, as it
were, to that step to which he has himself risen, and
that succeeding step to which he has already ascended,
vanishing from my vision, but drawing me with him,
becomes clearer to me, to my special, living *ego*. Thus
I am conscious for myself of the life of that brother
who has fallen asleep in the death of the flesh, and,
therefore, I cannot doubt it. But by observing the action in the world of this life which has disappeared from
my sight, I am still more indubitably convinced of the

reality of this life which has passed beyond the reach of my eyes. The man is dead, but his relation to the world continues to act upon men, and not even as during life, but in a vast number of times more powerfully, and this action is heightened, and grows like every living thing, in proportion to its wisdom and love, never ceasing, and knowing no suspension.

Christ died a very long time ago, and His existence in the flesh was brief, and we have a clear idea of His person in the flesh; but the power of His wisely loving life, His relation to the world, and no one else's, acts to the present day upon millions, who receive His relation to the world into themselves, and live accordingly. What is it that acts? What is it that was formerly bound up with the existence of Christ in the flesh, and which constitutes the continuation and the growth of this same life of His? We say that it is not the life of Christ, but its results. And, having uttered these words, utterly destitute of meaning, it seems to us that we have said something clearer and more definite than that this power is the living Christ Himself.

But this is exactly the way in which ants might talk who are clustered about an acorn that has grown up and become an oak; the acorn has sprung up and become an oak, and it tears up the soil with its roots, drops branches, leaves, and fresh acorns; it screens from the light, the rain, completely changes everything that formerly grew around it. "This is not the life of the acorn," say the ants, "but the results of its life, which came to an end when we dragged off the acorn and threw it into a hole."

My brother died yesterday, or a thousand years ago, and the same force of his life which acted during his existence in the flesh continues to act still more powerfully on me and on hundreds, thousands, millions of people, in spite of the fact that the center of the power of his temporary existence in the flesh, which was visible to me, has disappeared from my sight.

What does this mean?

I have seen the light of grass burning before me

This grass has been extinguished, but the light has only increased; I do not see the cause of this light, I do not know what is burning, but I may infer that the same fire which consumed the grass is now consuming the distant forest, or something else which I cannot see.

But the light is such that I not only see it now, but it alone guides me and gives me life. I live by this light. How can I deny it?

I may think that the power of this life has now another center, invisible to me. But deny it I cannot, because I feel it. I live and move in it. What this center, what this life is in itself, I cannot know — I can guess, if I like guessing, and if I am not afraid of becoming entangled. But if I am in search of a rational comprehension of life, I content myself with the clear and indubitable, and I do not wish to spoil the clear and indubitable by combining with it obscure and arbitrary surmises. It is enough for me to know that all that by which I live has been formed from the life of those who have lived before me, and of men who have died long since, and that, hence, every man who fulfils the law of life, submitting his animal personality to reason, and manifesting the power of love, has lived and does live in other people after the disappearance of his corporeal existence, — in order that the clumsy and alarming superstition of death should never again torment me.

We can also observe this in people who have left behind them a force which continues to act, because these people, having submitted their personality to reason and yielded up their lives to love, could never doubt, and have not doubted, the possibility of the annihilation of life.

In the life of such people we can also find the grounds of their faith in life everlasting; and then penetrating into our own life we can find these grounds in ourselves Christ said that He would live after the disappearance of the semblance of life. He said this because already, during the period of His corporeal existence, he had entered upon that true life which cannot end. Already, during the time of his corporeal existence, he lived in the rays of the light from that other center of life, to which he was going, and during his lifetime he saw how the rays of that light illuminated the people about him. The same thing is seen by every man who renounces his personality and lives a rational, loving life.

However contracted may have been the sphere of man's activity, — whether he be Christ or Socrates, a good, obscure, self-sacrificing old man, a youth, a woman, — if he lives, renouncing his personality, for the happiness of others, he already enters here, in this life, upon that new relation to the world which is the business of this life for all men.

The man who has placed his life in subjection to the law of reason, and the manifestation of love, already beholds in this life, on one side, the rays of light from that new center of life toward which he is traveling, and, on the other, the action which this light, passing through him, produces upon those about him. And this gives him an unwavering faith in the impossibility of the decrease of life, in its immortality and in the eternal augmentation of life. It is impossible to receive faith from any one, it is impossible to convince one's self of immortality. In order to have faith in immortality it is necessary that the latter should exist; and in order that the latter should exist, it is necessary to understand one's life in that in which it is immortal. Only he can believe in a future life who has performed his work of life, who has established in that life that new relation to the world which does not, as yet, find a place in the world.

CHAPTER XXXI

THE SUPERSTITION OF DEATH ARISES FROM THIS, THAT
MAN CONFOUNDS HIS DIFFERENT RELATIONS TO THE
WORLD

YES, if we look upon life in its true significance, it becomes difficult even to understand by what the terrible superstition of death is supported.

Thus, if you examine that which has frightened you in the dark as a phantom, you can never again, by any means, revive that visionary fear.

The fear of losing that which alone is, arises only from the fact that life appears to man not only in the relation of his mental consciousness to the world, which is known to him, but invisible, peculiar to him, but also in two relations which are unknown, though visible to him : that of his animal consciousness and that of his body to the world. All that exists presents itself to man : (1) as the relation of his rational consciousness to the world ; (2) as the relation of his animal consciousness to the world ; and (3) as the relation of the matter of his body to the world. Not understanding that the relation of his rational consciousness to the world is his sole life, man imagines his life as still lying in the relation of his animal consciousness to the world, and he is afraid of losing his special relation of rational consciousness to the world, when in his personality the former relations of his animal person and of the matter which constitutes him, to the world, shall have been destroyed.

To such a man it appears that he proceeds from the movement of matter passing to the stage of a personal animal consciousness. It seems to him that this animal consciousness passes into rational consciousness, and that afterward this rational consciousness grows weak, passes back again into the animal, and that the animal finally weakens and passes into the dead matter from which it was derived.

But the relation of his rational consciousness to the

world seems to him, from this point of view, something accidental, unnecessary, perishable. From this point of view it seems to him that the relation of his animal consciousness to the world cannot perish — that his animal will be continued in his species; that the relation of matter to the world cannot be annihilated in any way, and is eternal; but that the most precious thing — his rational consciousness — is not only not eternal, but is merely a gleam of something unnecessary and superfluous.

And man feels that this cannot be. And therein lies the fear of death. In order to save themselves from this fear, some men try to convince themselves that their animal consciousness is their rational consciousness, and that the immortality of the animal man, that is to say, of his race, satisfies the demand for the immortality of the rational consciousness, which they bear within them. Others try to convince themselves that a life which has never previously existed, which suddenly reveals itself in corporeal form, and vanishes in it, will rise again in the flesh and live. But belief in either is impossible for men who do not recognize life as residing in the relation of the rational sense to the world. It is evident to them that the continuation of the human race does not satisfy the ever recurring demand for the immortality of one's individual *ego ;* and the idea of a life which begins again includes in itself an idea of a suspension of life, and if life never existed formerly, has not always existed, then it cannot exist afterward.

For both classes of men, the earthly life is a wave. From dead matter a person is developed, from the person a rational consciousness, the crest of the wave ; having risen to their height, the waves, rational consciousness and individuality, fall back in the same place from which they started, and are annihilated. Human life is the visible life for both classes. Man has grown up and matured and died, and after death there can be nothing for him, — that which is after him and from him remains ; neither posterity nor its deeds can satisfy him. He pities *himself,* he fears the cessation of *his* life.

That this life of his, which has begun here on earth in his body, and which has here come to an end — that this life will revive again of itself he cannot believe.

Man knows that if he has not existed before, and if he has made his appearance from nothing, and has died, that he, his special person, will never exist longer, and that it cannot exist. Man recognizes the fact that he will not die only when he has recognized the fact that he has never been born, that he always has existed, does exist, and always will exist. Man will believe in his immortality only when he comprehends that his life is not a wave, but is that eternal movement which in this life reveals itself only as a wave.

It seems to me that I shall die, and my life will come to an end, and this thought tortures and frightens me because I am sorry for myself. And what will die? For what do I feel compassion? What am I from the ordinary point of view? First of all, I am flesh. What then? Am I afraid for that, am I sorry for that? It seems not : my body, matter, can never be lost anywhere, not a single particle of it. Hence, this part of me is secure; there is nothing to fear for this part. All will be preserved in its entirety.

But no, people say, that is not what I pity. I pity Lyeff Nikolaevitch, Ivan Semyonitch. But no one is any longer what he was twenty years ago, and every day he is a different person. How then do I pity myself? No, they say, that is not it; I do not pity that. I pity my consciousness, my *ego*.

But this consciousness of yours has not always been one, but it has been several ; it was one thing a year ago, it was something still more different ten years ago, and utterly different still earlier. As far back as you can remember, it has kept on changing; does your present consciousness please you so greatly that you are so sorry to lose it?

If it had always been the same in you, then one could understand this ; but it has done nothing but change. You do not see and cannot find its beginning, and, all of a sudden, you desire that there shall be no end to it, that this consciousness now existing in you shall exist forever. You have been moving on ever since you can remember. You came into this life you yourself know not how, but you know that you came as that special *ego* which you are, and then moved on and on until you have reached the half-way point, and, all of a sudden, you do not exactly rejoice or fear, but you have begun to resist, and you do not wish to stir from the spot, because you do not see what there is ahead. But neither did you see the place from which you came; but you came, nevertheless: you have entered at the entrance gate, and you do not wish to go out through the gate of exit.

Your whole life has been a progress through corporeal existence; you have advanced, you have hastened your pace, and all at once you have been seized with pity because that very thing is being accomplished which you have yourself done incessantly. The great change in your position at the death of your body is terrible to you, but the same great change took place with you at your birth, and not only did nothing bad come of it for you, but, on the contrary, so good a thing came of it that you do not wish to part with it.

What can frighten you? You say that you are sorry for yourself, with your present feelings and thoughts, with such views of the world, with your present relations to the world.

You are afraid of losing your present relation to the world. What relation is it? In what does it consist?

If it consists in your eating thus, drinking, reproducing your race, building a dwelling, dressing yourself, bearing yourself this way or that to other people and animals, then this is the relation of every man, as a reasoning animal, to life, and this relation cannot disappear; such have been, and are, and will be millions, and their posterity will be preserved as indubitably as every particle of matter. The instinct for the preservation of their race is inherent in all animals with such force, and therefore in so durable a manner, that there is no occasion to fear for it. If you are an animal, there is noth-

ing for you to fear ; and if you are matter, you are still
surer of your immortality.

But if you are afraid of losing that which is not animal, you fear to lose your special rational relation to
the world — that with which you entered upon this
existence : but you know that this did not have its
source at your birth ; it exists independently of the animal, which is born, and therefore cannot be dependent
upon its death.

CHAPTER XXXII

THE VISIBLE LIFE IS A PART OF THE ENDLESS MOVEMENT OF LIFE

My earthly life and the lives of all other men present
themselves to me thus : —

I and every living man find ourselves in this world
with a certain, well-defined relation to the world, with a
certain degree of love. It seems to us at first that our
life begins with this relation of ours to the world, but
observation of ourselves and others shows us that this
relation to the world, and the degree of love of each
one of us, did not begin with this life, but were brought
into life by us from a past that is concealed from us by
our birth in the flesh ; moreover, we see that the whole
course of our life here is nothing but a never ceasing
augmentation, strengthening of our love, which will
never come to an end, but will only be veiled from our
eyes by the death of the flesh.

Our visible life appears to me like a section of a
cone, the apex and base of which are concealed from
my mental vision. The narrowest portion of the cone
represents my relation to the world, from which I first
recognize myself ; the widest part is that higher relation
to life to which I have now attained. The beginning
of this cone, its apex, is concealed from me in time by
my birth ; the continuation of the cone is hidden from

me, both by my corporeal existence and by my death in the flesh. I see neither the apex of the cone, nor its base; but I recognize its nature without any doubt from that part of it in which my visible life, as it comes within my recollection, passes. It seems to me at first that this section of a cone is the whole of my life; but in proportion to the movement of my true life, I see on one hand that what constitutes the foundation of my life lies behind it, outside of its bounds; according to the measure of my life I feel more clearly and vividly my bond with my past which is visible to me.

On the other hand, I see how this foundation rests upon my future, which is invisible to me. I feel more clearly and vividly my bond with the future, and I come to the conclusion that the life which is visible to me, my earthly life, is but a small portion of my whole life, from both its ends — before birth and after death — undoubtedly existing, but concealed from my present knowledge. And therefore the cessation of the visibility of life, after the death of the flesh, as well as its invisibility before my birth, does not deprive me of the indubitable knowledge of its existence before birth and after death. I enter life with certain ready-prepared qualities of love for the world outside of me; my corporeal existence, short or long, passes in the augmentation of this love, which I brought into life, and hence I conclude, without any doubt, that I lived before my birth, and that I shall live not only after the present moment, in which I now find myself as I meditate, but after every other moment of time, either before or after my corporeal death, as well.

Looking outside of myself at the corporeal beginnings and endings of the existence of other people (even of beings in general), I perceive that one life seems longer, another shorter; one makes its appearance earlier, and continues to be visible to me for a longer time; another makes its appearance later, and is concealed from me again very quickly; but I see in all the revelation of one and the same law, for every true life, — an increase of love, — like the broadening out of the rays of life.

Sooner or later the curtain falls, concealing from me the temporary course of the life of men, but the life of all men is one and the same, and, like every life, it has no beginning and no end. And the fact that a man has lived for a longer or a shorter time in the conditions of this existence which are visible to me cannot present any difference in his true life.

The fact that one man has taken longer to pass across the field which is open to my vision, or that another has passed quickly across it, can by no means cause me to ascribe more reality to the life of the first, or less to the second. I know beyond a doubt that if I have seen a man pass my window, whether fast or slowly, it makes no difference, — I know beyond a doubt that the man existed before the time when I saw him, and that he will continue to exist even when he has disappeared from my sight.

But why do some pass quickly, and others slowly? Why does the old man, dried up and morally hardened, incapable, according to our view, of fulfilling the law of life — the increase in love — live on, while a child, a young man, a maiden, a man in the full strength of his spiritual work, dies, passes beyond the bounds of this fleshly life, when, according to our ideas of the matter, he has only just begun to establish in himself a correct relation to life?

The deaths of Pascal and Gogol are comprehensible; but how about Chenier, Lermontoff, and thousands of other men, who, as it seems to us, had but just begun their inner labor, which might have been, as it seems, completed here?

But this only seems so to us. None of us knows anything about the foundations of life which are brought into the world by another, and about that movement of life which has taken place in him; about those obstacles to the movement of life which exist in that being; and, chief of all of those other conditions of life, possible, but unseen by us, in which, in another existence, the life of that man may be placed.

It seems to us, as we look at the blacksmith's work,

that the horseshoe is completely ready, — that it needs only a couple of blows, — but he breaks it and throws it into the fire again, knowing that it is not thoroughly smelted. We cannot know whether the work of the true life is being accomplished in a man or not. We only know this so far as we ourselves are concerned. It seems to us that a man dies when it is not necessary, but this cannot be so. A man dies only when it is indispensable for his welfare, just as a man grows up and attains to manhood only when that is necessary for his welfare.

And in fact, if by life we mean life and not its semblance, if true life is the foundation of everything, its foundation may depend upon what it produces : — the cause cannot depend upon or proceed from the result, — the course of true life cannot be destroyed by a change in its manifestation. The movement, begun but not completed, of the life of man toward that world, cannot be suspended because he has an abscess, or because bacteria attack him, or because some one shoots him with a pistol.

A man dies only because the happiness of his true life cannot be enhanced, in this world, and not because his lungs pain him, or because he has a cancer, or because a bomb has been thrown at him. It generally appears to us that to live a life in the flesh is natural, and that it is not natural to perish by fire, water, cold, lightning, sickness, a pistol, a bomb; — but it is only necessary to reflect seriously, looking from one side upon the life of men, in order to perceive that, on the contrary, it is quite unnatural for a man to live a corporeal life in the midst of these deadly conditions, in the midst of the wide-spread and, for the most part, deadly and innumerable bacteria. It is natural for him to perish.

And therefore the corporeal existence, in the midst of all these destructive conditions, is, on the contrary, something of the most unnatural sort, in a material sense. If we are alive, it is not in the least because we take care of ourselves, but because we are doing the business of life. The business of life comes to a close, and nothing can arrest any longer the never ceasing destruction of the animal life of man, — this destruction is accomplished, and one of the most intimate causes which always accompany the life of man, the death of the flesh, seems to us its exclusive cause.

Our true life exists; we know it alone; from it alone we know the animal life, and therefore, if its semblance be subjected to immutable laws, then why should not that which this semblance performs be subject to laws also?

But we are troubled because we do not see the causes and effects of our true life as we see causes and effects in external manifestations: we do not know why one person enters life with such and such properties of his *ego*, and another person with others; why the life of one is broken off, and another continues. We ask ourselves: what, before my existence, were the causes of my being born such as I am? And what will be the result after my death, of my living thus or in some other way? And we complain because we receive no answers to these questions.

But to complain because I cannot now understand much that happened before my life, and that will take place after my death, is the same as complaining because I cannot see what is beyond the limits of my vision.

For if I saw what is beyond the limits of my vision, I should not see what is within its bounds. But for the happiness of my animal, it is more necessary that I should see all that is round about me.

And it is the same with the mind, by means of which I know. If I were able to see what is beyond the range of my intellect, I should not see what is within its range. But for the happiness of my true life, it is more necessary that I should know all that to which I must submit *then* and *now* my animal personality, in order to attain the happiness of life. And my mind reveals this to me, reveals to me in this life that sole path along which I do not perceive a cessation of my happiness.

It demonstrates to me indubitably that this life did not begin with birth, but was and is always; but that happiness always exists, — demonstrates to me that the happiness of this life grows and increases here, attaining to such an extent that it cannot be contained, and only then does it pass beyond those conditions which restrict its augmentation, and pass into another existence.

Reason sets a man upon that sole path of life which, like a cone-shaped, widening tunnel, inclosed in the center on all sides by its close walls, opens to him afar off the indubitable immortality of life and its happiness.

CHAPTER XXXIII

THE INEXPLICABILITY OF THE SUFFERINGS OF THE EARTHLY EXISTENCE PROVES TO MAN, MORE CONVINCINGLY THAN ANYTHING ELSE, THAT HIS LIFE IS NOT A LIFE OF PERSONALITY, WHICH BEGAN AT HIS BIRTH AND WHICH ENDS AT HIS DEATH

BUT even if a man could not help fearing death, or thinking of it, the sufferings alone — fearful, aimless, utterly unjustifiable, never to be averted sufferings — to which he is subject, would be sufficient to destroy every rational idea ascribed to life.

I am engaged in a work for others which is undoubtedly good, and all of a sudden I am seized with an illness, which interrupts my undertaking and exhausts and tortures me, without any sense or reason. A screw has grown rusty on the rails, and it must needs be that on that very day when it flies out, in the very train and carriage, a good woman should be traveling,—a mother,— and it must needs be that her children should be crushed before her very eyes. In an earthquake, precisely that spot sinks on which stands Lisbon or Vyerny, and perfectly innocent people plunge headlong, alive, into the earth, and die in terrible agony. What sense is there in this? Why did this happen to these people, and why

thousands of other senseless, frightful cases of suffer
ing, which astound men ?

Argumentative explanations make nothing clear. Argumentative explanations of all such phenomena always
dodge the actual question, and only prove the more con-
clusively its insolubility.   I have fallen ill because such
and such microbes or other have flown to me ; or the
children were crushed before their mother's eyes in the
train because the dampness had acted in such and such
a way on the iron ; or Vyerny sank because of the existence of certain geological laws.   But the real question
is why just these particular people were subjected to
such terrible sufferings, and how I am to avoid such
accidents or sufferings?

To this there is no answer.   Reflection, on the contrary, plainly demonstrates to me that there are no laws
according to which one man is subject, but another man
is not subject to these accidents, that there is and can
be none ; that there is an incalculable quantity of such
accidents, and therefore that whatever I do, my life is
liable every second to all the innumerable chances of the
most terrible suffering.

For if people drew only those deductions which inevitably follow from their view of the world, people who
understand their life as a personal existence would not
remain alive for a minute.   Assuredly, not a single
laborer would live under a master who, on hiring the
laborer, should stipulate for the right, on every occasion
when he should see fit, to roast the laborer alive on a
slow fire, or to flay him alive, or to pull out his sinews,
and in general to commit all those horrors which he
perpetrates upon his laborers, in the presence of the
man hiring himself, without cause or explanation.

If people really did understand life thoroughly, as
they say that they do, not one of them would remain
alive in this world, from pure fear of all those torturing
and utterly inexplicable sufferings which they see around
them, and into which they might fall at any second.

But men, in spite of the fact that they are all acquainted with various easy ways of killing themselves,

of escaping from this life filled with such harsh and inconceivable sufferings, — men live on ; they complain, they weep over the sufferings, and go on living.

It is impossible to say that this arises from the fact that there is more pleasure than suffering in this life, because, in the first place, not only simple reflection, but also philosophical investigations, demonstrate that all earthly life is a series of sufferings, which are far from being redeemed by its enjoyments ; in the second place, we know, both from ourselves and from others, that people in positions which present nothing but a series of increasing sufferings, without any possibility of alleviation except by death itself, do not, nevertheless, kill themselves, but cling to life.

There is but one explanation of this strange contradiction : men all know, in the depths of their own soul, that all sorts of sufferings are always necessary, indispensable to the happiness of their lives, and they only go on living foreseeing them or submitting to them. But they rebel against suffering because, with their false view of life, which demands happiness only for their personality, the interference with that happiness, which does not lead to evident happiness, must appear as something inconceivable, and therefore disturbing.

And people take fright in the face of suffering, they are amazed at it, as though at some utterly unexpected and incomprehensible thing. But, at the same time, every man is reared on sufferings, his whole life is a series of sufferings undergone by him and imposed by him on other beings, and it would seem as though it were time for him to have become accustomed to suffering, and not to quail before it, and not to ask himself why and to what end his sufferings. Every man, if he will but reflect, will see that all his enjoyments are purchased by the sufferings of other beings, that all his sufferings are indispensable for his own enjoyment; that without suffering there is no enjoyment; that suffering and enjoyment are two contrary states, one being evoked by the other, and each indispensable to the other.

Then what mean the questions, " Why ? " — " To

what end is suffering?" which the reasoning man puts
to himself? Why does a man, who knows that suffering
is bound up with enjoyment, ask himself, "Why?" —
"To what end is suffering?" while he does not ask himself, "Why?" — "To what end are enjoyments?"

The whole life of the animal, and of man as an animal,
is an unbroken chain of sufferings. The whole activity
of the animal, and of man as an animal, is called forth
only by suffering. Suffering is a painful sensation
which calls forth activity, that banishes this painful
sensation and calls forth a state of pleasure. And the
life of the animal, and of man as an animal, is not only
not suspended by suffering, but is perfected only by suffering. Suffering, therefore, is that which moves life,
and hence it is what it should be; then what does man
ask about when he asks: "Why and to what end is
suffering?"

The animal does not ask this.

When the perch, in consequence of hunger, torments
the dace, when the spider tortures the fly, the wolf the
sheep, they know that they are doing what must
be, and that they are accomplishing the very thing
which must be fulfilled; and therefore when the perch
and the spider and the wolf fall into the same torments
from those stronger than they, they know, as they flee
and resist and wrench themselves away, that they are
doing what must be done, and therefore there cannot be
the slightest doubt in them that what is happening to
them is precisely that which must be so.

But a man, occupied only with the healing of his legs
when they have been torn off on the battle-field, upon
which he has torn off the legs of others, or occupied only
in passing his time as comfortably as possible in his
solitary cell in jail, after having directly or indirectly
consigned others to that place, or a man who cares only
for fighting himself free and fleeing from the wolves,
who are rending him, after having himself slain thousands of animals and eaten them, — a man cannot regard
what happens to him as what must be, because, in submitting to these sufferings, he did not do all that he

should have done, and therefore it seems to him that something is happening to him which should not be.

But what should a man do, who has been torn by wolves, except flee and fight free from them? — That which it is proper for a man as a rational being to do; confess the sin which has caused suffering, repent of it, and confess the truth.

The animal suffers only in the present, and therefore the activity called forth by the suffering of the animal direct upon itself in the present fully satisfies it. But man suffers not only in the present, but he suffers also in the past, and in the future, and therefore the activity called forth by the sufferings of man, if concentrated only upon the present of the animal man, cannot satisfy him. Only activity directed to the cause as well, and to the results of suffering, both upon the past and upon the future, satisfies the suffering man.

The animal is locked in and tears himself from his cage, or his foot is sore and he licks the spot that pains him, or he devours another and rids himself of him. The law of his life is broken from without, and he concentrates his activity upon restoring it, and he fulfils that which must be. But a man — I myself or some one closely connected with me — is in prison; or I lose my legs, or some one nearly related to me loses his legs in battle, or wolves rend me: the activity devoted to flight from prison, to the healing of my legs, to fighting myself free from wolves, does not satisfy me, because confinement in prison, pain in my leg, and the being torn by wolves, constitute only a very small portion of my suffering.

I perceive the cause of my suffering in the past, in my errors and in the errors of other people, and if my activity is not directed to the cause of the suffering, to the errors, and if I do not try to free myself from it, I do not do that which should be done; and therefore suffering presents itself to me in a way in which it should not, and not only in fact but in imagination does it grow to frightful proportions, which exclude all possibility of life.

The cause of suffering for the animal is the violation
of the law of animal life; this violation makes itself
known by a consciousness of pain, and the activity
called forth by the violation of the law is directed to
the removal of the pain; the cause of pain for rational
consciousness is the violation of the law of life of rational consciousness; this violation reveals itself in a
consciousness of error, of sin, and the activity called
forth by the violation of the law is directed to the removal of the error — the sin.   And as the suffering of
the animal calls forth activity directed to pain, and this
activity deprives suffering of its torture, so the sufferings of a rational being call forth activity directed to
error, and this activity frees suffering from its torture.

The questions, "Why?" and, "To what purpose?"
which make their way into the soul of man, at the
experience or the imagination of suffering, only show
that man has not recognized that activity which should
be called forth in him by suffering, and which frees
suffering from its torture.   And in fact, for the man
who recognizes his life as lying in his animal existence,
there can be none of that activity which frees from
suffering, and the less so in proportion as he already
understands his life.

When a man, who recognizes personal existence as
his life, finds the cause of his personal suffering in his
personal errors, he understands that he has fallen ill
because he has eaten something injurious, or that he has
been beaten because he himself went out to fight, or that
he is hungry and naked because he would not work,
— he knows that he suffers because he has done that
which he should not have done, and in order that he
may do so no more, and that, directing his activity to
the extinction of error, he does not rebel against suffering, but bears it lightly, and often joyously.

But when such a man is attacked by suffering exceed-
ing the bounds of the bond of suffering and error
which are visible to him — as when he suffers from
causes which have always existed in his own personal
activity, or when the results of his suffering can be

in no way advantageous either to himself or to any
other person, — it seems to him that he is overtaken
by that which should not be, and he asks himself:
Why? to what purpose? and, finding no object upon
which to direct his activity, he rebels against suffering,
and his suffering is converted into terrible torture. But
the greater part of man's suffering is always such that
its causes or its consequences — sometimes the one, and
sometimes the other — are concealed from him in space
and time: hereditary diseases, unhappy accidents, bad
harvests, collisions, conflagrations, earthquakes, and so
on, which end in death.

The explanation that this is necessary in order to
furnish a lesson for the people of the future, that they
must not yield to those passions which are reflected in
the diseases of their descendants, or that they must build
trains better, or handle fire with more caution, — all
these explanations give me no answer at all. I cannot admit that the significance of my life lies in the
illustration of the oversights of other people ; my life
is my life, with my aspirations for happiness, and not
an illustration for other lives. And these explanations
are fit only for the purpose of discussion, and do not
alleviate that fear in the presence of the senselessness
of the sufferings which threaten me, and which exclude
all possibility of life.

But even if it were possible to understand in any way
that, while causing other people to suffer through my
errors, I by my sufferings bear the consequences of other
people's errors ; if it were possible also to understand
even remotely that every suffering is a punishment for an
error which must be rectified by men in this life, there
still remains a long series of sufferings which are in no
way explicable.

Wolves rend a man who is alone in the forest, a man
is drowned, frozen, or burned up, or simply falls ill alone
and dies, and no one ever knows how he suffered, and
there are thousands of such cases. Of what use can this
be to any one ?

For the man who understands his life as an animal

existence, there is not, and there cannot be, any explanation, because, for such a man, the connection between
suffering and error lies only in the manifestations which
are visible to him, and this connection is utterly lost
from his mental vision in the sufferings which precede
death.

A man has two alternatives of choice : either, not
recognizing the connection between the sufferings which
he has experienced in his life, to continue to endure the
greater part of his sufferings as tortures, utterly devoid
of reason : or to admit that my errors and the deeds committed in consequence of them — that my sins, whatever
they may be — are the cause of my sufferings, and that
my sufferings are a release and redemption for my sins,
and the sins of other people, whatever may be their
nature.

Only these two attitudes toward suffering are possible : one, according to which suffering is that which
should not exist, because I do not perceive its external
significance ; and the other that it is just what it should be,
because I know its inward significance for my true life.
The first proceeds from the recognition of the happiness
of my separate, individual life as happiness.   The second
proceeds from the recognition as happiness of the happiness of my whole past and future life, in its unbroken
connection with the happiness of other men and
creatures.

According to the first view there is no explanation
for sufferings, and they call forth no other activity than
a constantly increasing despair and bitterness, which are
not to be alleviated.   According to the second, suffering
evokes that same activity which constitutes the movement
of true life, — a consciousness of sin, a release from
error, and submission to the law of reason.

If it is not man's reason, then it is the torture of suffering which forces him, willingly or unwillingly, to confess that his life is not contained in his personality, that
his personality is only the visible part of his whole life,
that the external bond between cause and effect, visible
to him in his personality, does not coincide with that in-

ternal bond of cause and effect which is always known
to man through his rational consciousness.

The connection between error and suffering, visible to
the animal only under conditions of time and space, is
always clear to a man, outside of those conditions in his
consciousness. Suffering of any sort, man always recognizes as the result of his sin, whatever it may have been,
and repentance for his sins as a release from suffering
and the attainment of happiness.

A man's whole life, from the early days of his childhood, consists in this alone: in the acknowledgment,
through suffering, of sin, and in the freeing himself from
error. I know that I came into this life with a certain
knowledge of the truth, and that the greater have been
my errors the greater have been my sufferings and the
sufferings of others, — that the more I have freed myself
from error, the less have been my sufferings, and the
more happiness have I attained. And, therefore, I know
that the greater the knowledge of the truth which I
carry out of this world, and which is given me by my
sufferings, even by my last sufferings which precede
death, the greater is the happiness that I attain.

The torture of suffering is experienced only by the
man who, having separated himself from the life of the
world, and not perceiving those sins of his by which he
brought his sufferings into the world, regards himself as
innocent, and who, therefore, rebels against all those
sufferings which he endures for the sins of the world.

And, strange to say, that very thing which is clear to
the reason, mentally, is confirmed by the sole and true
activity of life, by love. Reason says that a man who
confesses the connection of his sins and his sufferings
with the sins and sufferings of the world, frees himself
from the torture of suffering ; love indeed confirms this.

The half of every man's life is passed in sufferings,
which he not only does not recognize as torture, and
which he does not perceive, but which he regards as his
happiness only because they are borne as the results of
error, and as a means of alleviating the sufferings of
beloved individuals. So that the less love there is, the

more is man subjected to the anguish of suffering; the more love there is, the less acuteness of suffering is there; but a thoroughly rational life, whose entire activity is manifested only in love, excludes the possibility of all suffering. The anguish of suffering is only that pain which men experience on their attempt to break that chain of love to their ancestors, to their descendants, to their contemporaries, which unites the life of a man with the life of the world.

CHAPTER XXXIV

BODILY SUFFERINGS CONSTITUTE AN INDISPENSABLE CONDITION OF THE LIFE AND HAPPINESS OF MEN

" BUT, nevertheless, it is painful, it is corporeally painful. Why this pain?" men ask.

"Because this is not only necessary for us, but because we cannot live without its being painful to us," that man would answer us who has caused our pain, and has rendered it as little painful as possible, and has made as much happiness out of this " pain " as possible.

For who does not know that the very first sensation in us of pain is the first and principal means both of preserving our bodies, and of prolonging our animal life? Bodily pain protects the animal personality. And while pain serves as a protection to the personality, as is the case with the child, pain cannot be that frightful torture, such as we know pain to be, at the times when we are in the full strength of our rational consciousness and resist pain, seeing in it that which it should not be.

Pain in the animal and the child is very well defined and small in size, never attaining that degree of anguish which it reaches in beings endowed with rational consciousness. In the case of the child, we see that he sometimes cries as pitifully from the bite of a flea as from the pain which destroys the internal organs.

And the pain of a being which does not reason leaves no traces whatever in the memory. Let any man endeavor to recall his childish sufferings from pain, and he will see that he not only does not remember these, but that he is incapable of even reconstructing them in his imagination. Our impression at the sight of the suffering of children and animals is our suffering more than theirs. The external expression of suffering in unreasoning beings is immeasurably greater than the suffering itself, and hence it evokes our sympathy in a far greater degree, as can be observed in diseases of the brain, in fevers, in typhus, in all cases of death agony.

At those periods when the rational consciousness has not yet been awakened, and pain serves only as a protection to the person, it is not acute ; but in those periods when there is in a man a possibility of rational consciousness, it is the means of subjugating the animal personality to the reason, and in proportion to the awakening of that consciousness does it become less and less torturing.

In reality, only when we find ourselves the complete master of our rational consciousness can we talk of sufferings, because only with this condition does life begin, and those conditions of it which we call suffering. And in this condition the sensation of pain can increase to the greatest and shrink to the most insignificant dimensions. Who, in fact, does not know, without studying physiology, that there is a limit to sensibility, that, when pain exceeds a certain point, sensibility either comes to an end in a swoon, insensibility, a fever, or that death supervenes ? Hence the augmentation of pain is a very accurately defined quantity, which cannot exceed certain bounds. But the sensation of pain can be infinitely augmented by our relations to it, and in the same way it can be decreased to infinite minuteness.

We all know how a man can, by submitting to pain, by acknowledging it as what must be, reduce it to insensibility, to a sensation of joy, even, in undergoing it.

Not to mention the martyrs, not to mention Huss, who sang in the fire at the stake — simple men, merely out of a desire to exhibit their courage, endure without a cry or a quiver what are considered the most torturing of operations. There are bounds to the augmentation of pain, but to the diminution of sensation under it there is no limit.

The anguish of pain is really frightful for people who consider their lives as consisting in the existence of the flesh. And how can it fail to be terrible to them when the force of reason bestowed upon man for the annihilation of acute suffering is directed only to its augmentation?

As Plato has a myth relating how God first fixed the period of man's existence at seventy years, but afterward, on perceiving that men were the worse for it, altered it to what it now is, that is to say, arranged it so that men do not know the hour of their death, — just so surely would reason have decided upon the present state of things, the myth narrating how men were first created without sensation of pain, but that afterward it was arranged as it is for their happiness.

If the gods had created men without the feeling of pain, men would very soon have begun to beg for it; women lacking the pains of childbirth would have brought forth children under conditions where but few of them would have remained alive; children and young people would have thoroughly spoiled their whole bodies, and grown people would never have known either the errors of those who had lived before them, and of people now living, nor, what is the most important of all, their own errors, — they would not have known what they must do in this life, they would have had no rational object of existence, they could never have reconciled themselves to the idea of impending death in the flesh, and they would have had no love.

For a man who understands life as a submission of his personality to the law of reason, pain is not only not an evil, but is an indispensable condition both of his animal and of his rational life. Were there no pain, this animal personality would have no indication when it had trangressed its laws ; if rational consciousness suffered no pain, man would not know the truth, would not know his own law.

"But you are talking," people retort to this, "about your personal sufferings, but how can you deny the sufferings of others? The sight of these sufferings constitutes the most acute suffering," say people not in full sincerity.

The suffering of others? But the sufferings of others — what you call sufferings — have not ceased, and will not cease. The whole world of men and animals suffers, and has never ceased to suffer. Is it possible that we have learned this only to-day? Wounds, mutilations, cold, diseases, every sort of heart-rending accident, and, chief of all, the pains of birth, without which no one of us made his appearance in this world — surely all these are indispensable conditions of existence.

Surely this is the very thing the alleviation of which, the assistance of which, forms the substance of the rational life of men — the very thing upon which the true activity of life is directed.

An understanding of the sufferings of personality and of men's errors, and activity directed toward their diminution, constitutes the whole business of human life. That is just why I am a man, — an individual,— in order that I may understand the sufferings of other individuals, and that is why I am a rational consciousness, in order that in the sufferings of every other separate individual I may see the general cause of suffering — error — and may eradicate it in myself and in others. How can the material of his work be a cause of suffering to the workman? It is the same as though a plowman were to say that unplowed soil was his suffering.

Unplowed land can be a source of suffering only for him who would like to see the field plowed, but who does not consider it the business of his life to plow it.

Activity directed to the immediate loving service of the suffering and to the diminution of the general cause of suffering — error — is the only joyful labor which lies before a man, and gives him that inalienable happiness in which his life consists.

There is, for a man, but one suffering, and it is that

suffering which makes a man, voluntarily or otherwise, give himself up to that life in which there is for him the only happiness.

This suffering is the consciousness of the contradiction between my own sinfulness and all the world, and not only the possibility, but the obligation, of realizing, not by some one or other, but in my own person, the whole truth in my own life and in that of all the world.

It is impossible to alleviate this suffering, either by sharing the sins of the world, or by perceiving one's own sin, or yet by ceasing to believe not only in the possibility, but also in the duty of any one else, but in my own, to realize all truth in my life and in the life of the world. The first only augments my sufferings, the second deprives me of the force of life. Only the consciousness and activity of true life alleviate this suffering, by annihilating the disproportion between individual life and its aim, as acknowledged by man.

Voluntarily or otherwise, man must acknowledge that his life does not hedge in his person from birth to death, and that the object recognized by him is an object that can be attained, and that, in his striving toward it, in the acknowledgment of his greater and greater sinfulness, and in the greater and greater realization of all the truth in his life, and in the life of the world, consists, has consisted, and always will consist, the business of his life, which is inseparable from the life of the whole world.

If rational consciousness does not drive a man, voluntarily or involuntarily, to the only true path of life on which there are no obstacles, no evil, but only an indestructible, ever growing, never beginning, never ending happiness, then the suffering which flows from error as to the sense of his life will so drive him.

CONCLUSION

THE life of man is a striving after happiness, and what he strives for — that is given to him.

Evil in the form of death and suffering is visible to man only when he takes the law of his corporeal, animal existence from the law of his life. Only when he, being a man, descends to the level of the animal, does he see death and suffering. Death and suffering breathe sighs upon him from all quarters, like bugbears, and drive him upon the one path of human life which is open to him, subservient to his law of reason, and expressing itself in love. Death and suffering are only crimes committed by man against his law of life. For a man who lives according to his law, there is no death and no suffering.

"Come unto Me, all ye that labor and are heavy laden, and I will give you rest.

"Take My yoke upon you, and learn of Me; for I am meek and lowly in heart, and ye shall find rest unto your souls.

"For My yoke is easy, and My burden is light." (Matt. xi.)

The life of man is a striving toward good; what he strives for — that is given to him; since life cannot be death, and good cannot be evil.

APPENDIX I

PEOPLE generally say: "We study life, not from the consciousness of our own life, in general, but outside of ourselves." But this is the same as saying: "We look at an object, not with our eyes, in general, but outside of ourselves."

We behold the objects outside of ourselves because we see them in our eyes, and we know life outside of ourselves only because we know it in ourselves. And we see objects only as we see them in our eyes, and we define life outside of ourselves only as we know it in ourselves. But we know life in ourselves as a striving after happiness. And therefore, without a definition of life as a striving after happiness, it is impossible, not only to observe, but even to see, life.

The first and principal act of our consciousness as living beings consists in our including many different objects in our conception of one living being, and this living being we exclude from every other.

We learn that a man on horseback is not a number of beings, and is not one being, not because we observe all the parts constituting the man and the horse, but because neither in the head, nor in the legs, nor in the other parts of the man and the horse do we see that separate striving after happiness which we know in ourselves. And we know that the man and the horse are not one being, but two beings, because we know in them two separate aspirations toward good, while in ourselves we know only one.

Only from this do we know that there is life in the combination of horse and rider, because there is life in a drove of horses, that there is life in birds, in insects, in trees, in the grass. But if we did not know that the horse and the man each desired his own happiness, that each horse in the drove desired this separately, that such happiness is desired by every bird, beetle, insect, tree, and blade of grass, we should not perceive separateness in the being, and, not perceiving separateness, we could never have understood any living being ; and a regiment of cavalry, and a flock, and birds, and insects, and plants, — all would be like the waves in the sea, and all the world would melt together for us into one indistinguishable movement, in which we could not by any possibility find the secret of life.

If I know that the horse and the dog and the tick that lives upon him are living beings, and if I can observe them, it is only because the horse and the dog and the tick have each their separate aims, — the aim of each being his own happiness. I know this because I know myself as an individual striving after the same happiness.

In this striving after happiness also lies the foundation of every knowledge of life. Without a confession that this striving after good, which man feels within himself, is life, and an image of all life, no study of life is possible, and no observation of life is practicable. And hence, observation begins when life is already known, and no observation upon the manifestations of life can (as it appears to scientific man) define life itself.

Men do not recognize the definitions of life in the striving toward happiness which they find in their consciousness, but they recognize the possibility of the knowledge of this striving in the tick, and on the foundation of that supposititious knowledge, founded upon nothing at all, of this happiness toward which the tick is striving, they make observations and draw deductions even as to the very existence of life.

My every conception as to external life is founded upon the knowledge of my striving toward happiness. And therefore, only through having recognized in what my happiness and my life consist, I shall be in a condition to recognize in what consist the happiness and life of other beings. But the happiness and life of other beings I cannot in any way know without having recognized my own.

Observations upon other beings, striving toward their aims which are unknown to me, constituting semblances of that happiness the striving after which I know in myself, not only can explain nothing to me, but can certainly hide from me my true knowledge of life.

For, to study life in other beings, without having a definition of one's own life is the same as describing a surrounding district without having got its center. Only after having fixed upon an immovable point as a center can the region be described. But, whatever figures we may draw, without a center there will be no surrounding district.

APPENDIX II

FALSE science, studying the manifestations which accompany life, and assuming to study life itself, by this assumption distorts the idea of life: and hence, the longer it studies the manifestations of that which it calls life, the further it gets from the idea of life, which it wishes to study.

At first mammals are studied, then the other creatures, vertebrates, fishes, plants, corals, cells, microscopic organisms, and the matter is carried to such a point that the distinction between living and non-living, between the bounds of organic and of non-organic, between the bounds of one organism and another, are lost.

It is carried to such a point that what cannot be observed seems to be the most important subject of investigation and observation. The secret of life and the explanation of everything seems to lie in comma-shaped and other bacilli, which are not visible, but which are rather assumed, which are discovered to-day and forgotten to-morrow. The explanation of everything is assumed in those beings which are contained in microscopic beings, and in those which are also contained even in these, and so forth, to infinity, as though infinite activity of the little is not the same as infinite activity of the great.

The mystery will be revealed when all the infinity of the little shall have been investigated to the end, that is to say, never. And men do not see this — the idea that the question will attain solution in the infinitely small is an indubitable proof that the question is wrongly stated. And this, the last stage of folly, — that which clearly demonstrates the utter loss of sense in the investigation, — this stage is regarded as a triumph of science; the last degree of blindness appears the highest degree of vision. Men have come to their wits' end, and have thereby clearly proved to themselves the falsity of that path along which they have been journeying; and there are no limits to their rapture. If we can only increase the power of the microscope a little more, we shall understand the conversion of the inorganic into the organic, and of the organic into the psychic, and the whole mystery of life will be laid open to us.

Men who study shadows instead of objects have entirely forgotten the object which they were studying, and, plunging deeper and deeper into the shadows, they have reached utter darkness, and rejoice because the shadow is dense.

The meaning of life is revealed in the consciousness of man as a striving after happiness. The elucidation of this happiness, the more complete definition of it, constitutes the chief aim and work of the life of all mankind, and because this labor is difficult, that is to say, not a plaything, but toil, men come to the conclusion that the definition of this happiness cannot be found in that place where it is situated, that is to say, in the rational consciousness of man, and that, therefore, it is necessary to seek it everywhere, — except where it is indicated.

This is something of the sort that a man would do who had been given an accurate list of all that he required, and who, not knowing how to read it, should fling aside the list, and inquire of every one whom he met whether they did not know what he needed; for men seek everywhere, except in .the consciousness of man itself, for the definition of life, which is inscribed in the soul of man in ineffaceable letters, in his aspiration for happiness. This is all the more strange because all mankind, in the persons of its wisest representatives, beginning with the Greek saying which runs, " Know thyself," has announced it, and continues to announce it, in precisely the opposite sense. All religious teachings are nothing else than definitions of life, than strivings toward that active happiness which is accessible to man, and which cannot lead astray.

APPENDIX III

EVER more and more clearly does the voice of reason become audible to man ; ever more and more frequently does man lend an ear to this voice ; and the time will come, and has already come, when this voice has grown stronger than the voice summoning to personal happiness and to delusive duty.

On the one hand, it becomes ever clearer that the life of personality, with its enticements, cannot be happiness; on the other hand, that the payment of every debt prescribed by men is only a deceit, which deprives man of the possibility of settling the sole debt of man, — to that rational and honorable origin from which he proceeds. That old delusion which demands a belief in that which has no rational explanation has already been worn out, and it is impossible to return to it.

Formerly, men said : " Do not think, but believe in the duty which we prescribe.   Reason will deceive you ; faith alone will disclose to you the true happiness of life."   And man tried to believe, and did believe ; but his relations to men proved to him that other men believe in something entirely different, and assert that this other something gives greater happiness to man.   The decision of the question has become inevitable, as to which faith — out of many — is the more true ; but reason alone can decide this.

Man always learns all things through his reason, and not through faith.   It might be possible to deceive by affirming that he learns all things through faith, and not through reason ; but as soon as man knows two faiths, and sees men confessing another faith, just as he does his own, he is placed under the inevitable necessity of deciding the matter by his reason.   A Buddhist, on becoming acquainted with Mahometanism, if he remains a Buddhist, will remain a Buddhist by faith no longer, but by reason.   As soon as another faith has been presented to him, and the question as to whether he is to reject his own faith, or the one offered him, — that question is inevitably settled by the reason. And if, on becoming acquainted with Mahometanism, he has remained a Buddhist, his former blind faith in Buddha is now infallibly founded on a basis of reason.

Attempts in our day to instil spiritual matters into man by faith, while ignoring his reason, are precisely the same as attempts to feed a man and ignore his mouth.

Men's intercourse with each other has proved to them that they all have a common foundation of knowledge, and men can never more return to their former errors; and the time is coming, and is even now come, when the dead shall hear the voice of the Son of God, and, hearing, shall be made alive.

It is impossible to drown that voice, because that voice is not the single voice of any one person, but the voice of all the rational consciousness of mankind, which is expressed in every separate man, and in the best men of mankind, and now already in the majority of men.

WHAT IS RELIGION

AND WHAT IS ITS ESSENCE?

CHAPTER I

ALWAYS in all human societies, at a certain period of their existence a time comes when their religion begins to diverge from its fundamental meaning, then diverges more and more, loses this fundamental meaning, and finally crystallizes into permanently established forms; — when its influence upon the life of men grows weaker and weaker.

At such periods, the educated minority, though no longer believing in the existing religious teaching, still pretend to believe, finding this religion necessary for holding the masses in the established order of life; whilst the masses, although adhering by the force of inertia to the established religion, are no longer guided in their lives by religious demands, but only by popular customs and state laws.

So it has been, many times, in many human communities. But what is now taking place in our Christian Society has never before occurred. It has never occurred before that the ruling and more educated minority, which has the chief influence on the masses, not only disbelieved in the existing religion, but was certain that in its time religion was no longer necessary at all, and that it taught those who doubted the truth of the accepted faith not some other, more rational and comprehensible religion than that existing, but even

267

persuaded them that religion in general had outlived its time, and had become not only a useless but even a harmful organ of social life, something like the appendix of the cæcum in the human organism.

Religion is studied by this class of men not as something which we know through our inner experience, but as an external phenomenon, a disease as it were to which some people are subject, and which we can understand only in its external symptoms.

Religion, according to some of these men, has sprung from the spiritualization of all the phenomena of nature (animism). According to others, from the idea of the possibility of communicating with departed ancestors. According to others again, from the fear of the powers of nature. And as science has proved — the scientists of our day further argue — that trees and stone cannot be animated, and deceased ancestors are no longer conscious of what the living do, and the phenomena of nature are explicable by natural causes, — therefore the necessity for religion and for all those restraints which people impose upon themselves as the result of religious beliefs has disappeared. In the opinion of scientists there once existed a period of unenlightenment — the religious period. This was outlived by mankind long ago, but occasional atavistic symptoms remain. Then there came the metaphysical period, which also has been outlived. And now, we, the enlightened generations, live in the scientific period, — of positive science, — which replaces religion and leads mankind to a lofty degree of development which it could never have attained whilst it submitted to superstitious religious teaching.

At the beginning of 1901 the celebrated French scientist Berthelot uttered a speech (*Revue de Paris*, January, 1901), in which he communicated to his audience the idea that the age of religion had passed, and that it must now be replaced by science. I cite this speech because it is the first to my hand and because it was uttered in the capital of the cultured world by a universally recognized scientist. But the same idea has been expressed continually and everywhere from philosophical treatises down to newspaper articles.

Mons. Berthelot says in this speech that there were formerly two principles which moved mankind, Force and Religion. These motive powers have become unnecessary now, because their place has been taken by science. By science Mons. Berthelot evidently implies (as all men who believe in it do) a science which embraces the whole sphere of human knowledge, each branch classified according to the degree of its importance, and the whole harmoniously bound together. A science possessing such methods that all the data it discovers present one unquestionable truth. But such a science does not exist, as a matter of fact. What is called science to-day consists of a haphazard heap of information, united by nothing, often utterly unnecessary, and not only failing to present one unquestionable truth, but as often as not containing the grossest errors to-day put forward as truths, and to-morrow overthrown. It is evident, therefore, that the very thing which in Mons. Berthelot's opinion is to replace religion, does not exist. And therefore the assertion of Mons. Berthelot and those who agree with him, that science will replace religion, is entirely arbitrary, and is founded upon an unjustifiable belief in an Infallible Science, exactly resembling the belief in an Infallible Church.

And yet people who call themselves and are regarded as scientists are quite certain that already there exists a science which must and can replace religion, and even has replaced it.

" Religion has outlived its day ; to believe in anything except science is ignorance. Science will arrange all that is necessary, and one should be guided in life by science alone." So think and say both the scientists themselves and the crowd, which, although very far from being scientific, yet believes the scientists and together with them asserts that religion is an outlived superstition and that our life should be guided only by science, — that is, in reality, by nothing, because science, according to its own acknowledged definition as

the investigation of everything that exists, cannot furnish any guidance for man's life.

CHAPTER II

THE scientists of our times have decided that religion
is unnecessary and that science will replace or already has replaced it; and yet, now as before, no human
society or rational man ever has lived or can live without religion. (I say "rational" man, because an irrational man can live as an animal, without religion.) A
rational man cannot live without religion, because religion
alone gives the rational man the necessary guidance as
to what he should do, and what he should do first and
what next.   A rational man cannot live without religion
precisely because reason is an element of his nature.
Every animal is guided in its actions — except those to
which it is attracted by the direct demands of its desires
— by consideration about the immediate results of its
actions.   Having considered these results by the aid of
those means of comprehension which it possesses, the
animal conforms its actions to the results, and always
acts under the influence of these considerations in one
and the same way, without wavering.   Thus, for instance, a bee flies in search of honey and brings it home
into its hive because in winter it will require the food it
has collected for itself and the young ; and beyond these
considerations it knows nothing and is unable to know
anything.   A bird acts in the same way when it makes
its nest, or migrates from the north to the south and *vice
versa*.   And so also does every animal when it commits
any act, not from a direct immediate necessity, but under
the influence of considerations about expected results.
But it is not so with man.   The difference between a
man and an animal consists in this, that the perceptive
faculties in the animal are limited by what we call
instinct, whereas reason is the essential perceptive faculty of man.
A bee collecting its food can have no doubts about

the rightness or wrongness of what it is doing. But a man gathering in the harvest cannot but reflect whether he is destroying for the future the growth of the wheat or fruit, and whether by thus gathering he is not depriving his neighbor of his food. He also cannot but think of the future of the children whom he feeds ; and of many other things. The most important questions of conduct in life cannot be solved definitely by a rational man, precisely because of the multitude of results which he cannot help seeing. Every rational man feels, if he does not know, that in the most important affairs of life he cannot be guided either by the impulse of personal feelings or by considerations of the immediate results of his activity, because he sees too many different results, and often contradictory ones ; results, that is, which with equal probability can be either beneficent or harmful, both to himself and to others.

There is a legend about an angel who descended to earth into a God-fearing family and killed a child in its cradle ; when asked why he had done this, he replied that the child would have become a great malefactor and would have brought misery to its family.

But not only in the question, Which human life is useful, useless, or harmful? — not one of the most important questions of life can be solved, for a rational man, by considerations about immediate relations and results. A rational man cannot be content with the considerations which direct the actions of animals. Man may regard himself as an animal amongst animals, living from day to day ; he may regard himself as a member of a family or of a society or of a nation living from century to century ; he may, and even necessarily must (because his reason irresistibly attracts him to this), regard himself as a part of the whole Infinite Universe existing infinitely. And therefore a rational man is obliged to and always does do, in relation to the infinitely small circumstances of life which influence his actions, what in mathematics is called integration, that is, besides his relations to his immediate circumstances,

he must establish his relation to the whole universe,
infinite in time and space, and conceived as a whole.
And such an establishment by man of his relation to
that whole of which he feels himself a part and from
which he obtains guidance for his actions, is precisely
what was and is called Religion. And therefore religion always has been and cannot cease to be an indispensable and permanent condition of the life of a rational
man and of rational humanity.

CHAPTER III

AND it was in this way that the men who were not
bereft of the capacity of the higher (that is, the religious) consciousness, which distinguishes man from
the animal, always understood religion. The oldest
and most common definition of religion, from which the
word itself is derived (*religio — religare*, to bind back),
is that religion is a connection between man and God.
"*Les obligations de l'homme envers Dieu, voilà la religion*"
("Man's obligations toward God ; that is religion "), says
Vovenargue. A similar meaning is attached to religion
by Schleiermacher and Fehrbach, who recognize as the
foundation of religion man's consciousness of his dependence on God. "*La religion est une affaire entre
chaque homme et Dieu.*"— Beile. ("Religion is a matter
between every man and God.") "*La religion est le
résultat des besoins de l'âme et des effects de l'intelligence.*"
— B. Constant. ("Religion is the result of the needs
of the soul and the effects of the reason.") "*Religion
is a certain method by which man realizes his relation to
the superhuman and mysterious powers from whom he
regards himself dependent.*" — Goblet d'Alviella. "*Religion is the definition of man's life by the connection of
the human with that mysterious spirit, the power of which
over the universe and himself he recognizes and with
which he feels himself united.*" — A. Reville.
So that the essence of religion was always and is still
understood by men who are not bereft of the highest

human capacity, as the establishment by man of his relation to the Infinite Being or Beings whose power he feels over himself. And however different this relation has been for different peoples at different times, it has always determined for man his destination in the world, from which naturally followed the guidance of his actions also. A Jew understood his relation to the Infinite as that of a member of a people chosen by God in preference to all other peoples, and who must therefore keep the Covenant concluded between God and this people. A Greek understood his relation as that of a being dependent upon the representatives of infinity, the gods, and who must therefore do what was pleasing to the gods. A Brahman understood his relation to the Infinite Brahma by considering himself a manifestation of this Brahma, and that it was his duty to strive to unite with this highest being, by the renunciation of life. A Buddhist understood and understands his relation to the Infinite as that of one who, passing from one form of life into another, inevitably suffers, and that as these sufferings proceed from passions and desires, therefore one should strive to destroy all passions and desires and so pass into Nirvana.

Every religion is an establishment by man of his relation to the Infinite Existence of which he feels himself a part, and from which relation he obtains the guidance for his conduct. And therefore any religion which does not establish the relation of man to the Infinite, as, for instance, Idolatry, or Magic, is not a religion, but only a corruption. And if a religion, although establishing a relation of man to God yet establishes it by assertions which disagree with reason and the modern knowledge of man so that man cannot believe such assertions, then this also is not religion, but an imitation. If a religion does not connect the life of man with the Infinite Existence, this also is not religion; and demands of faith in propositions from which no definite direction of man's actions follows, are also not religion.

True religion is the establishment by man of such a relation to the Infinite Life around him, as, while connect-

*ing his life with this Infinitude and directing his conduct,
is also in agreement with his reason and with human
knowledge.*

CHAPTER IV

THE modern scientists, notwithstanding that never
and at no time have people lived, nor do they now
live, without religion, say, like Molière's involuntary
doctor who asserted that the liver is on the left side:
" 'We have changed all that,' and one can and should
live without religion." But religion remains as it always
was, the chief motive power, the heart of the life of
human societies, and without it, as without the heart,
there can be no rational life. There have been, and
there are, many different religions, because the expression of the relation of man to the Infinite, to God, or the
gods, is different at different times, according to the
different degrees of development of different nations;
but no society of men since men have become rational
beings could ever live and therefore never did live and
cannot live without religion.

It is true that there have been (and still occur) periods
in the life of nations when the existing religion was so
distorted and so far behind life that it no longer guided
man. But this cessation of the influence of religion,
which has occurred at certain moments with every religion, has been only temporary. Religion, like everything vital, has the capacity of being born, developing,
growing old, and dying, of reviving again, and reviving
always in a more perfect form than before. After the
period of the highest development of religion there
always follows a period of weakness and lifelessness,
after which again there generally follows a period of
regeneration and of the establishment of a religious
teaching more clear and rational than before. Such
periods of development, decline, and regeneration have
occurred in all religions: in the profound Brahman religion, in which the moment it began to grow old and to
crystallize in coarse, permanently established forms de-

viated from its fundamental conception, there appeared
on the one hand the revival of Brahmanism itself, and
on the other the lofty teaching of Buddhism, which
advanced mankind's understanding of its relation to the
Infinite. A similar decline occurred in the Greek and
Roman religion, and here also, after the decline had
reached its lowest point, Christianity appeared. The
same occurred with Church Christianity, which degenerated in Byzantium into idolatry and polytheism, at
which time, as a counterbalance to this perverted Christianity, there appeared on the one side Paulicianism, and
on the other, in opposition to the teaching of Trinity
and Maryolatry, the severe Mohammedanism, with its
fundamental dogma of One God. The same thing happened also with the Papal Medieval Christianity, which
called forth the Reformation. So that periods of the
decline of religious influence upon the majority of men
present a necessary condition of the life and development of all religious teachings. This proceeds from the
fact that every religious teaching in its true meaning,
however crude it may be, always establishes the relation of man to the Infinite, identical for all men. Every
religion recognizes man as equally insignificant in relation to Infinity; — and therefore every religion always
contains the idea of the equality of all men before that
which it regards as God, whether that be lightning, the
wind, a tree, an animal, a hero, a deceased or even a
live king, as it was in Rome. So that the recognition
of the equality of men is necessarily an essential feature of every religion. But since in reality never and
nowhere has there existed, nor now exists, an equality
between men, therefore the moment a new religion
appeared, which always included the recognition of the
equality of men, then immediately those to whom inequality was advantageous endeavored to conceal this
essential feature, and distorted the teaching itself. And
this was what occurred always and everywhere, when a
new religion appeared.

And this occurred, in the majority of cases, not consciously, but merely because men to whom inequality

was advantageous (those in power, and the wealthy), in order to feel themselves in the right in the face of the accepted teaching without altering their position, tried by every means to attribute to the new religious teaching a meaning which would allow inequality to be possible. And this distortion of the teaching, which allowed those in power over others to consider themselves in the right, being naturally transmitted to the masses, convinced them also that their submission to those in power was a demand of the religion they professed.

CHAPTER V

EVERY human activity is called forth by three influences: Feeling, Reason, and Suggestion (the suggestion which medical men call Hypnotism). Sometimes man acts only under the influence of feeling, and strives to attain his desires. Sometimes he acts under the influence of reason alone, which indicates to him his duties. Sometimes, and most often, man acts because he himself or other men have suggested to him a certain activity and he unconsciously submits to the suggestion. In normal conditions of life all three influences participate in man's activity. Feeling draws man toward a certain activity; reason verifies the agreement of this activity with the surrounding conditions, with the past, and with the anticipated future; and suggestion compels man to fulfil, without feeling, or thinking, the act elicited by feeling and approved by reason. If there were no feeling, man would undertake nothing; if there were no reason, man would simultaneously yield himself to many contradictory feelings, harmful to himself and others; if there were no capacity of submitting to one's own or other people's suggestion, man would have to experience that feeling which prompted him to a certain action, unceasingly, and continually to exert his reason in testing the expediency of his reason. And therefore all these three influences are indispensable to every human activity, however simple. If a man is moving in a certain direction it is because his feeling has prompted him to move from one place to another, his reason has approved of this intention, has indicated the means to realize it (in the given case, walking along a certain road), and the muscles of his body obey. And the man advances in the desired direction. While he is advancing, his feeling and reason become free for another activity, which could not occur if the capacity of submitting to suggestion did not exist. So it is with all human activities, and so also with the most important of all — the religious activity. Feeling calls forth the necessity of establishing the relation of man to God; reason defines this relation; and suggestion prompts man to the activity which follows from this relation. But it takes place thus only while religion has not yet suffered distortion. As soon, however, as this distortion commences, suggestion becomes stronger and stronger, and the activities of feeling and reason weaker and weaker. As to the methods of suggestion, they are everywhere and always the same. They consist in profiting by those conditions of man when he is most susceptible to suggestion (childhood, and during important events in life — deaths, births, marriages), to influence him by works of art: architecture, sculpture, painting, music, dramatic performances, — and in this state of susceptibility, similar to that attained over separate individuals by hypnotic sleep, to incite him to that which is desired by the inciters.

This phenomenon is observable in all the old religious teachings: in the lofty teaching of Brahmanism, degenerated into a gross worship of innumerable images in various temples with singing and incense burning; and in the ancient Hebrew religion as preached by the prophets, transformed into the worship of Jehovah in an imposing temple with solemn hymns and processions; in transcendental Buddhism, degenerated, with its monasteries and images of Buddha, with its innumerable stately rites, into Occult Lamaism; and in Taoism, with its magic and exorcism.

Always, and in all religious teachings, when they begin

to be distorted, their guardians, having brought men
into a state of weakened mental activity, use all their
efforts to instil into them what they think necessary.
And in all religions it was necessary to instil the same
three doctrines which serve as the foundation for all
the distortions to which all degenerating religions are
submitted.   Firstly, that a certain class of men exist
who alone can be the mediators between men and God
or gods ; secondly, that miracles have occurred or are
occurring which prove and corroborate the truth of that
which is asserted by the mediators between men and
God ; and thirdly, that there are certain words, repeated
verbally or written in books, which express the unchangeable will of God or gods, and therefore are
sacred and infallible.   And as soon as these doctrines
are accepted under hypnotic influence, then all which is
asserted by the mediators between God and men is
accepted as sacred truth, and the chief aim of the distortion of religion is attained ; — not only the concealment of the law of human equality, but also the
establishment and confirmation of the greatest inequality, the division of men into castes, into men and Yogi,
into Orthodox and heretics, saints and sinners.   This
has taken place and is taking place with Christianity :
complete inequality has been recognized, and men are
divided not only in the understanding of the teaching,
into clergy and laity, but also in relation to social position, into those who have power and those who must
submit to power ; and this is recognized as established
by God Himself according to the teaching of Paul.

CHAPTER VI

THE inequality of men, not only as clergy and laity,
but also as rich and poor, master and slaves, has
been established by the Christian Church-Religion in as
definite and rigid a form as in other religions.   And yet
to judge by the data we have concerning the primitive
condition of Christianity, and by the teaching expressed

in the Gospels, it would seem that the chief methods of
distortion used in other religions had been foreseen, and
a distinct warning against them uttered. Against a
caste of priests it was distinctly said that no one can be
another's teacher (" Be not ye called Rabbi. . . . And
call no man your father. . . . Neither be ye called
masters "); against attributing a sacred meaning to
books it was said that it is the spirit which is important
and not the letter, and that men should not believe
human traditions, and that all the law and the prophets,
that is, all the books regarded as Holy Writ, are
summed up in this saying, that one should act toward
one's neighbors as one would wish them to act toward
oneself. If nothing is said against the miracles, and if
in the Gospel itself miracles are described as if performed by Jesus, nevertheless from the whole spirit of
the teaching it is evident that Jesus bases the truth of
his teaching not on miracles but on its own merits.
(" If any man willeth to do his will, he shall know of
the teaching, whether it be of God, or whether I speak
of myself.") But above all, the equality of men has
been proclaimed by Christianity no longer as a deduction from man's relation to the Infinite, but as the fundamental teaching of the brotherhood of men, all men
having been recognized as sons of God.

It would seem, therefore, to have been impossible to so
distort Christianity as to destroy the consciousness of
the equality of all men. But the human mind is ingenious, and it invented, perhaps unconsciously, or half
consciously, a new method or *truc*,[1] as the French say,
to render the Gospel warnings and the clear declaration
of the equality of men ineffectual. This " dodge " consisted in attributing infallibility not only to certain words
but also to a certain body of men called The Church,
which has the right to transmit this infallibility to other
men elected by it. A little addition to the Gospel was
also invented, — that Christ when leaving for heaven
transmitted to certain men the exclusive right not only
of teaching others the divine truth (according to the

---

[1] Trick, cunning, dodge. — Tr.

letter of the Gospel, he transmitted also at the same time the power, not generally used, of being invulnerable to serpents, poisons, and fire), but also of making men saved or unsaved, and, above all, of transmitting this right to other men. And as soon as the idea of the Church was firmly established, then all the Gospel warnings for preventing the distortion of the religion became ineffectual. Reason was termed the source of error, and the Gospel was interpreted not as common sense demands, but as those who composed the Church desired.

And therefore all the three previous methods of distorting religions — Priesthood, Miracles, and the Infallibility of Writings — were also admitted into Christianity in their fullest power. The lawfulness of the existence of mediators between God and men was recognized, because the necessity and lawfulness of mediators was recognized by the Church; the reality of miracles was recognized because the Infallible Church witnessed to them; the Bible was recognized as sacred because the Church so recognized it.

And Christianity was distorted just as all the other religions were, but with this difference: that precisely because Christianity proclaimed with especial clearness its fundamental doctrine of the equality of men as the sons of God, it was necessary to distort the whole teaching with especial force in order to conceal this fundamental doctrine. And by the help of the idea of the Church, this was accomplished to an extent greater than in any other religion.

And as a result no religion ever proclaimed statements so obviously out of agreement with reason and contemporary human knowledge. Not to mention the absurdities of the Old Testament, such as the creation of light before the sun, the creation of the world six thousand years ago, the housing of all the species of animals in the ark, and various immoral abominations such as the direction to murder children and whole populations at the command of God; not to mention also that absurd sacrament, about which Voltaire even used to say that though many different religions had existed and still existed, never before had there been one the principal religious act of which consisted of eating one's God — to pass these things by, what can be more senseless than the assertions that the mother of God was both a mother and a virgin — that the sky opened and a voice was heard issuing from it — that Jesus flew away into the skies and is now sitting somewhere there on the right hand of the Father — or that God is One and Three, and not three Gods like Brahma, Vishnu, and Siva, but One, and at the same time Three? And what can be more immoral than that awful theology according to which God is cruel and revengeful, punishes all men for the sin of Adam, and to save them sends His Son to the earth knowing beforehand that men will kill him and will be cursed for doing so ; and that the salvation of men from sin consists in being christened, or in believing that all this is actually true, that the Son of God was killed by men for the salvation of men, and that those who do not believe this will be punished by God with eternal torments ? So that leaving aside the additions, as some regard them, to the chief dogmas of this religion, such as the beliefs in the various relics and *ikons*, of the Virgin Mary, of petitionary prayers directed to various saints according to their specialities, — leaving aside also the Protestant doctrine of predestination, — the foundations of this religion, established by the Nicene Creed, and recognized by every one, are so absurd and immoral, and are developed to such a degree of contradiction to normal human feeling and reason, that men cannot believe them. Men may with their lips repeat certain words, but they cannot believe that which has no sense. One may say with one's lips : "I believe that the world was created six thousand years ago ; " or, "I believe that Jesus flew away into the skies and is sitting on the right hand of the Father ; " or, "God is One, and also Three ; " — but no one can believe it, because the words have no sense. And therefore the men of our modern world who profess distorted Christianity, in reality believe in nothing.

And it is in this that the peculiarity of our time consists.

CHAPTER VII

In our time men believe in nothing, and yet, owing to
the false definition of faith which they have drawn
from the Epistle to the Hebrews, incorrectly attributed
to Paul, they imagine that they have a faith. Faith,
according to this definition, is ὑπόστασις (the realization)
of things hoped for, and ἔλευχος (the certainty) of things
not seen. But besides the impossibility of faith being
the realization of things hoped for, faith being a mental
state, and the realization of things hoped for an external
event, — faith also is not the certainty of things unseen,
for this certainty, as stated in the comment farther on,
is founded on confidence in the witness of the truth, and
confidence and faith are two different conceptions.

Faith is not hope, and not confidence, but a separate
mental state. Faith is man's consciousness of a certain
position in the world which imposes on him the obligation to fulfil certain actions. A man acts according to
his faith, not, as it is said in the Catechism, because he
believes in the Unseen as much as in the seen; and not
because he hopes to receive his expectation; but only
because having defined his position in the Universe he
naturally acts in conformity with this position. So that
an agriculturist cultivates the land, and a sailor undertakes a voyage, not because, as it is stated in the Catechism, they both believe in the Unseen, or hope to
receive a reward for their action (this hope does exist,
but it is not by it that they are directed), but because
they regard this activity as their calling. So also the
religious believer acts in a certain way, not because he
believes in the Unseen, or expects a reward for his activity, but because, having understood his position in
the Universe, he naturally acts in accordance with this
position. If a man has defined his position in society as
that of an unskilled or skilled laborer, or a government
official, or a merchant, he regards it as necessary to

work, and as an unskilled or skilled laborer, an official, or a merchant, he does his work. So also in general a man who defines his position in the Universe in one way or another, inevitably and naturally acts in accordance with this definition (sometimes even not a definition but only a vague consciousness). Thus, for example, a man who has defined his position as that of a member of a people chosen by God, who, in order to profit by God's protection, must obey the commands of this God, will so live as to obey these commands; and a second man who has defined his position as that of one who has passed and is passing through various forms of existence and from whose actions depend whether his future will be better or worse, will also be guided in life by this definition of his; and the conduct of a third man, who has defined his position as that of an accidental combination of atoms in which consciousness has become kindled for a time, but which will eventually perish forever, — will differ from the two former men.

The conduct of these men will be quite different because they have defined their position differently; that is, they have a different faith. Faith is the same as religion, only with this difference, that by the word *religion* we imply a certain phenomenon externally observed, whereas by *faith* we mean the same thing experienced by man within himself. Faith is man's conception of his relation to the Infinite Universe,[1] and the direction of his activity resulting from that conception. And therefore true faith is never irrational, or in disagreement with existing knowledge, and its feature cannot be supernaturalism and senselessness, as is supposed and has been expressed by a Father of the Church, who said, "*Credo quia absurdum.*" On the contrary, the assertions of true faith, although they cannot be proved, not only never contain anything contrary to the reason and the knowledge of man, but always explain that which in life without these conceptions of true faith appears irrational and contradictory.

[1] The Russian word, translated here as "Infinite Universe," embraces the whole spiritual and material existence. — *Trans.*

Thus, for instance, the ancient Hebrew who believed
in the existence of a Supreme, Eternal, Almighty Being,
who created the Universe, the Earth, the Animals, Man,
and so forth, and promised protection to His people if
this people obeyed His law, — this man believed in nothing irrational or opposed to his knowledge, but on the
contrary his faith explained to him many things in life
which otherwise were inexplicable.

So also the Hindoo who believes that our souls have
been in animals and that according to our good or bad
life they will pass into higher or lower animals, explains
to himself by this belief much which without it is incomprehensible.

So too with a man who regards life as an evil and the
object of life as the attainment of peace by the annihilation of desires. He believes not in something irrational,
but on the contrary in that which renders his life-conception more rational than it was without this belief.

So too with a true Christian, who believes that God is
the spiritual father of all men and that man's highest
welfare is attained when he recognizes his sonship to
God and the brotherhood of all men.

All these beliefs, even though they may not be prov-
able, are not irrational in themselves, but on the contrary
supply a more rational meaning to the phenomena of
life, which appear irrational and contradictory without
them. And besides this all these beliefs defining the
position of man in the universe necessarily demand
certain actions corresponding to this position. And
therefore if a religious teaching establishes senseless
ideas which explain nothing, but only still more confuse
the understanding of life, then this is not faith but a
distortion of faith, which has already lost the features of
true faith and which lays no obligations on men but
rather becomes their tool.

One of the chief distinctions between true faith and
its corruption, is that when it is corrupted man demands
of God that in return for his sacrifices and prayers God
should fulfil his desires, should be the servant of man.
Whereas according to true faith man feels that God

demands of him, a man, the fulfilment of *His* will, demands that man should serve Him.

And it is just this faith which is not only lacking in the men of our times, — they even do not know what it is, and imply by faith either the repetition with the lips of whatever is taught them as the essence of faith, or else the fulfilment of rites which according to the teaching of Church-Christianity contribute to their obtaining what they desire.

CHAPTER VIII

MEN to-day are without faith. One set, the educated well-to-do minority, have freed themselves from the influence of the Church and believe in nothing, regarding all faiths either as absurdities or as useful tools for keeping the masses under their power. Whereas the great destitute uneducated majority who with some few exceptions do indeed believe, being under hypnotic influence, imagine that what is suggested to them as faith is faith, but in reality it is not faith, as it not only fails to explain to man his position in the Universe but still more confuses him.

From this situation and from the mutual relation between the unbelieving and simulating minority and the hypnotized majority, is composed the life of our so-called Christian world.

And this life, both of the minority which holds in its hands the means of hypnotism, as well as of the majority which is hypnotized, is terrible, both because of the cruelty and immorality of the rulers and of the crushed and stupefied state of the great working masses. Never at any period of religious decline did the indifference to and forgetfulness of the principal feature of all religions, and especially of the Christian one, — the equality of man, — attain the degree it has reached in our day.

Besides the complete absence of religion, the main reason of the awful modern cruelty of man to man is also due to that refined complexity of life which conceals from men the effects of their actions. However cruel Attilas and Khenghiz Khans and their men may have been when they themselves killed face to face with their victims, the process of killing must have been much more unpleasant to them, and still more so the consequences of the killing, the cries of the relatives, the sight of the corpses; so that the consequences of their cruelty moderated it. But in our time we kill men through the medium of so complicated a transferring apparatus, and the consequences of our cruelty are so carefully removed and concealed from us, that there are no influences to moderate the cruelty, and the cruelty of one group of men toward others keeps increasing and increasing, and has at the present time attained limits which it never before reached.

If in our day any man — I do not say a Nero, a recognized villain, but any ordinary man — should wish to construct a pond of human blood for the purpose of enabling sick wealthy people under the advice of scientific medical men to bathe in, I think he would be able to arrange it without hindrance so long as he did so in the ordinary respectable way; that is, did not by force compel people to shed their blood, but placed them in a position where they could not live without shedding it; and, besides, if he invited the clergy, who would consecrate the new pond, just as they consecrate cannons, rifles, prisons, gallows, and men of science, who would invent the proofs of the necessity and lawfulness of such an institution, just as they have discovered the proofs of the necessity of wars and houses of ill-fame.

The essential principle of all religions, the equality of man, has been forgotten to such an extent, abandoned, and obstructed by various absurd dogmas, in the religion professed; whilst in science inequality in the form of the struggle of existence and the survival of the fittest has also been so completely recognized as the necessary phenomenon of life — that the destruction of millions of human lives for the convenience of those in power is regarded as a most ordinary and necessary phenomenon of life, and is continually being produced.

Men of our day cannot sufficiently plume themselves on those brilliant, unprecedented, colossal successes which have been won in the technical sphere during the nineteenth century.

There is no doubt that there has never been in history so great a material success — so great a control over the forces of nature — as that which has been attained in the nineteenth century. But there is also no doubt that never in history has there been such an example of immoral life, free from any forces that control the animal propensities of man, — as that lived by our Christian humanity, which is becoming more and more bestial.

The material success attained by the men of the nineteenth century is indeed great, but this success has been and is bought by an indifference to the most elementary demands of morality to which humanity has never before attained, even in the times of Khenghiz Khan, Attila, or Nero.

There is no dispute that ironclads, railways, book-printing, tunnels, photographs, Röntgen rays, and so forth, are all very fine. They are all very fine, but human lives are also fine, incomparably fine, as Ruskin used to say, those human lives which are pitilessly ruined by the million to purchase ironclads, railroads, tunnels, which not only do not adorn but disfigure life. To this it is generally replied that appliances are already being invented, and in the future will be invented still more, by means of which human lives will not be ruined as they are now; — but this is not true. If men do not regard themselves as all brothers, and human life is not considered the most sacred object, which not only cannot be violated, but the maintenance of which should be regarded as man's first and most urgent duty, — that is, if men do not regard each other religiously, they will always for their own personal advantages ruin each other's lives. Not even a fool will consent to spend thousands when he can attain the same end by spending a hundred, with the addition of a few human lives which are in his power. In

Chicago approximately the same number of men are killed by the railways every year. And the owners of the railways quite naturally do not adopt those appliances which would reduce the number, calculating that the annual payment to the injured or their families is less than the interest on the cost of the appliances.

It may well be that those who ruin human lives for their own advantages will be shamed by public opinion and compelled to adopt the necessary appliances; but if men are not religious and do their deeds to please men and not to please God, then, having adopted appliances to save human lives in one place, they will profit in some other way by human lives, as the most advantageous material for increasing their wealth.

It is easy to conquer nature, to construct railways, steamboats, museums, and so forth, if one is not sparing of human lives. The Egyptian kings were proud of their pyramids, and we admire them enthusiastically, forgetting those millions of lives of slaves which were destroyed during their construction. And so we admire also palaces, as we see them in exhibitions, our ironclads, our transoceanic cables, — forgetting what we pay for all this. We might be proud of these things if it were all done voluntarily by free men, and not by slaves.

The Christian nations have conquered and subdued the American Indians, Hindoos, Africans, are now conquering and subduing the Chinese, and they are proud of this. But these conquests and subjugations occur not because Christian nations are spiritually superior to those conquered, but on the contrary because spiritually they are incomparably inferior. Leaving Hindoos and Chinese aside, even the Zulus had and have obligatory religious rules of some kind which imposed certain actions and forbade others; whereas our Christian nations have none. Rome conquered the whole world just when it had become free from every religion. This, only in a still stronger degree, is now also taking place with the Christian nations. They are all in the same condition of the absence of religion, and therefore, notwithstanding their inner dissensions, they are all united as one federated band of robbers in which theft, loot, depravity, murder of individuals and masses are accomplished not only without the least tremor of conscience but with the greatest self-satisfaction, as in China the other day. Some believe in nothing, and are proud of it; others simulate belief in that which for their own advantage they instil into the people under the pretense of faith; others again — the great majority, the whole of the people — accept as faith that hypnotic suggestion to which they are subjected, and servilely submit to everything demanded of them by the ruling suggestors who themselves believe in nothing.

And these suggestors demand what was demanded by all the Neros who tried to fill up in some way their empty lives — the satisfaction of their insane luxury spreading out in all directions. And luxury is attained by naught else than the enslavery of man; the moment there is slavery luxury augments; the increase of luxury inevitably drags with it the increase of slavery, because only hungry, cold, want-driven people will all their lives do what is unnecessary for themselves but necessary for the amusement of their rulers.

CHAPTER IX

In the sixth chapter of the Book of Genesis there is a passage of deep meaning, in which the author says that God, before the Flood, having seen that that Spirit of His which He gave to men for His service was only used by them for the service of their flesh, — was so angry with them that He regretted their creation, and before their entire destruction decided to shorten the life of men to a hundred and twenty years. It is just this which according to the Biblical narrative angered God and caused Him to shorten the life of man, which has now occurred with the men of our Christian world.

Reason is that power in men which defines their relation to the Universe; and as the relation of all men to
the Universe is the same, the establishment of this relation, that is, religion, unites men. And the unity of
men affords them the highest physical and spiritual welfare accessible to them.

Complete unity in the most perfect, lofty reason, and
therefore complete welfare, is the ideal toward which
humanity is striving; and every religion which answers
the questions of the men of a given society both as to
what is the Universe, and what they are in this Universe,
unites men, and therefore brings them nearer to the
realization of complete welfare. But when reason,
abandoning its proper function of defining man's
relation to God and his corresponding activities, is
directed not only to the service of man's flesh, and not
only to cruel strife with men and other beings, but also
to the justification of their life, which is contrary both
to the nature and the destiny of man, then occur those
terrible calamities from which the majority of men are
now suffering and those conditions which appear to pre-
clude all possibility of a return to a rational and righteous
life.

Heathens mutually united by the crudest religious
teaching are much nearer the conception of the truth
than the pseudo-Christian nations of our time, who live
without religion, and amongst whom the foremost men
are persuaded and teach to others that religion is not
necessary, and that it is much better to live without any
religion.

Amongst heathens there may be found men who,
having become conscious of the contradictions between
their faith and their increasing knowledge and the demands of their reason, will work out or assimilate a new
religious teaching more in harmony with the new mental
state of their nation, — a religion which will be accepted
by their countrymen and fellow-believers. But the men
of our world, some of whom regard religion as an instrument for subjugation, others as nonsense, and others
again, — the great majority of the people, under the in-

fluence of a gross deceit, — believe they possess true religion, the men of our Christian world have become
impenetrable to the influence of any progressive movement toward truth.

Proud of their improvements for the life of the body,
and of their refined idle theories which not only justify
their life, but also demonstrate their superiority to all
nations of all past epochs, — they stagnate in their ignorance and immorality, in the full assurance that they stand
on a height to which humanity had never before attained, and that each step on the road of ignorance and
immorality lifts them up to a yet higher plane of enlightenment and progress.

CHAPTER X

It is natural to a man to establish conformity between his physical and his rational activities. A man can
have no peace until he has established this conformity
one way or another. But it can be established in two
ways. One way is when a man is persuaded by his
reason of the necessity or desirability of a certain action
or actions, and then acts according to this decision. The
other way is when a man acts under the influence of
his feelings, and then invents a mental explanation or
justification for his act.

The first method of conforming one's action with
one's reason is natural to those who profess some kind
of religion, and who know by its precepts what they
should and what they should not do. The second method
is natural chiefly to irreligious people, who do not possess any general principal for deciding the qualities of
their actions, and who therefore always establish the
harmony between reason and conduct, not by subordi-
nating conduct to reason, but, after having acted under
the influence of feeling, by using their reason to justify
their action.

A religious man, knowing what is good or bad in his
conduct, and that of other men, and why one thing is
good and another bad, will, if he sees a contradiction

between the demand of his reason and his actions, or
those of other men, use all the efforts of his reason to
discover a way to destroy these contradictions; that is,
to learn to harmonize his actions with the demands of
his reason in the best way   Whereas an irreligious
man, having no guide to decide the merits of his actions
other than the pleasure they afford him, surrendering to
the impulse of his numerous and often antagonistic
feelings, involuntarily falls into contradiction; and having so fallen endeavors to solve or conceal it by arguments more or less complicated and ingenious, but
always untruthful.   And therefore, while the reasoning
of religious people is always simple, uncomplicated, and
truthful, the mental activity of irreligious people becomes especially subtle, complicated, and untruthful.

I will take the commonest example.   A man is addicted to depravity; that is, is unchaste, unfaithful to his
wife, or else lives immorally being unmarried.   If he is
a religious man he knows this is wrong, and the whole
force of his reason is directed toward finding a way to
free himself from his vice: avoiding association with
adulterers, increasing his labors, arranging a rigorous
life, not allowing himself to look on women as objects
of lust, and so forth.   And this is all very simple and
can be understood by every one.   But if the depraved
man is irreligious, he immediately invents all sorts of
reasons why it is very good to love women.   And here
begin all kinds of most intricate, cunning, and refined
considerations, about the affinity of souls, about beauty,
about free love, etc., — which the more they are developed the more they obscure the question and conceal what is essential.

The same thing occurs with irreligious people in all
spheres of action and thought.   With the object of concealing their inherent contradictions, they accumulate all
sorts of elaborate and specious arguments, which by filling their minds with unnecessary frivolities divert their
attention from the important and essential, and give
them the possibility of becoming hardened in that deceit
in which the men of our world live without noticing it.

"Men loved the darkness rather than the light, for their works were evil," it is said in the Gospels. "For every one that doeth ill hateth the light, and cometh not to the light lest his works should be reproved."

And therefore the men of our civilized world, having organized the most cruel, animal, immoral life, owing to the absence of religion, have also brought their involved, elaborate, useless mental activities, concealing the evil of this life, to that degree of unnecessary complication and intricacy that the majority have entirely lost all capacity of recognizing the distinction between good and evil, falsehood and truth.

To the men of our civilized world not one question exists which they can approach directly and simply: every question, economical, civic, political, diplomatic, scientific, to say nothing of philosophic and religious questions, are presented so falsely and artificially, and are therefore enveloped in so dense a shroud of intricate, unnecessary arguments, of elaborate distortions of ideas and words, of sophisms and disputations, that all discussions of such questions move in circles, and, like wheels without a connecting strap, which propel nothing, lead to no results, except the one object for which they were produced: the concealment from oneself and others of the evil in which men live and which they commit.

CHAPTER XI

In all the spheres of the so-called science of to-day there is one feature which renders ineffective all the efforts directed to the investigation of the various departments of knowledge. This feature is that all the investigations of contemporary science avoid the essential problem to which an answer is required, and study secondary matters, the investigation of which leads to nothing and becomes the more confused the longer it is continued.

And indeed this cannot be otherwise with a science

which selects the objects of its investigations accidentally
and not according to the demands of a religious conception of life, which would define what should be studied
and why, what first and what after. Thus, for instance,
in the at present fashionable sciences of sociology or
political economy, one would think there could be but
one question : What is the cause and purpose of some
people doing nothing and others working for them?
(If there is another question : Why people work separately, hindering each other, and not together, in
common, which would be more advantageous?—this question is included in the other.   If there were no inequality
there would be no struggle.)   One would imagine there
was only this one question, but science does not even
think of putting it and answering it, but instead it raises
its own distant discussions and then leads them so that
in no way can their deductions either solve or contribute
to the solution of the fundamental question.   Arguments
are started about what was and is, and this past and present is considered as something as unalterable as the
movements of the stars.   Abstract theories are invented
about values, capital, profit, interest, — and a complex
mental play, a hundred years old, ensues between disputing men.   Whereas in reality the question is solved
very simple and easily.

The solution is in this : As all men are brothers and
equal, each should act with others as he desires that
others should act with him ; and therefore the whole
kernel of the matter lies in the destruction of the false
religious law and the reëstablishment of the true law.
But the leaders of our Christian world not only decline
to accept this solution, — on the contrary they endeavor
to conceal the possibility of such a solution, and for this
purpose lend themselves to those idle theorizings which
they call science.

The same thing occurs in the sphere of jurisprudence.
One would imagine that the one essential question is,
Why do people exist who allow themselves to exercise
violence toward other men, to rob, imprison, execute
them, send them to wars, and much else ?   The solution

is very simple if the question is considered from the only standpoint which is adequate — the religious standpoint. From the religious point of view man cannot and should not exercise violence toward his neighbor; and therefore to solve the question one thing is necessary: to destroy all the superstitions and sophisms which admit violence, and to instil into men the religious principles which clearly exclude the possibility of violence.

But the leaders not only refrain from this, but use all their mental subtlety to hide from men the possibility and necessity of this solution. They write a mountain of books about various rights — civil, criminal, police, ecclesiastical, financial, and so forth, and dilate and dispute on these themes, quite persuaded that they are doing not only a useful but a very important work. As to the question why amongst men who are in essence equal, some judge, coerce, plunder, and execute others, —to this they not only give no answer, they do not even recognize its existence. According to their doctrine it appears that these acts of violence are accomplished, not by men, but by some sort of abstraction called The State.

In the same way the scientists of our day avoid and pass by in silence all the essential questions and hide the inner contradictions in all spheres of knowledge.

In the sphere of historical knowledge there is only one question—How the workers, that is, 999 thousandths of all mankind, lived? To this question there is not even the semblance of an answer. The question does not even exist, but mountains of books are written by historians of one class about the stomach-aches of Louis XI., about the villainies of Elizabeth of England and Ivan the Terrible, and who were their ministers, and what verses and comedies were composed by the *litterateurs* for the amusement of these kings and their mistresses and ministers; while the historians of another class write about the importance of the land in which the peoples lived, what they ate, what they traded in, and what clothes they wore, — in general about everything which had no influence on the life of the people but was the result of their religion, which is regarded by

the historians of this category as itself the result of the
food and clothing used by the people.

And yet the answer to the question, how the workers
formerly lived, can be given only by recognizing religion
as the necessary condition of the life of the people.
And therefore the answer is to be found in the study of
the religions professed by the nations, which placed
them in their several positions.

In the sphere of natural sciences one would think
there was no particular necessity for obscuring the common sense of people, but here also, owing to the trend
of thought which the science of our day has taken, instead of the most natural answers to the question, What
is the description of this world of human beings, plants,
and animals, and how is it subdivided ? — only idle, obscure, and utterly useless chatter is circulated, chiefly
directed against the Biblical story of the creation of the
world, and about how organisms originated, which is
really of no use to any one, and besides cannot be ascertained, as this origin, however we explain it, will always
be concealed from us in the infinitude of time and space.
And on these themes theories, refutations, and supple-
mentary theories have been invented which form the
subject of millions of books, and the unexpected deduction from which is only one : That the law of life to
which man must submit is the struggle for existence.
More than this, practical sciences like technology and
medicine, in consequence of the absence of a leading
religious principle, involuntarily diverge from a rational
end and take a false direction.   Thus all technology is
directed, not to the end of alleviating the labor of the
people, but to improvements necessary only for the
wealthy classes, and which tend to separate still further
the rich from the poor, the masters from the slaves.
And if certain advantages from these inventions and
improvements, some crumbs, fall to the lot of the masses,
this is not at all because they have been apportioned, but
only because they are of such a character that they cannot be kept back.

And so with medical science, which has in its false

direction reached that stage where it is accessible only
to the wealthy classes, whereas the masses, owing to
their mode of life and their poverty, and to the neglect
of the chief problems of the amelioration of the life of
the poor, can only profit by it in such proportions and
under such conditions that its help only demonstrates
more clearly the deviation of medical science from its
proper end.

But these deviations from, and the distortion of, the
essential problems is most astounding in what is called
Philosophy. One would think there is one problem
which philosophy ought to solve: What am I to do?
And if in the philosophies of Christian nations the
answers to this question have been unnecessarily associated with the greatest confusion, yet there were answers, in the teaching of Spinoza, of Kant in his "Kritik
of Practical Reason," of Schopenhauer, and especially of
Rousseau. But in later days, since the time of Hegel,
who recognized everything that is as rational, the question "What am I to do?" recedes into the background,
and philosophy directs the whole of its attention to the
investigation of that which is, and to conforming it to
a previously prepared theory. This is the first step
in the descent. The next step, which reduces human
thought yet lower, is the recognition of "struggle for
existence" as the fundamental law, merely because this
struggle is observable in animals and plants. According to this theory it is claimed that the destruction of
the weaker is a law which should not be opposed. Finally comes the third step, the mischievous attempts at
originality of a half-mad Nietzsche, which do not even
represent anything whole and connected, — the random
jottings of immoral thoughts founded on nothing, — but
which are recognized by advanced people as the last
word of philosophical science; and in answer to the
question "What am I to do?" one is told directly,
"Live for your own pleasure without attending to the
life of others."

If any one were to doubt that terrible stupefaction
and bestiality which has been attained by modern Chris-

tian humanity, then, leaving out of account the latest
crimes, the Boer and Chinese wars, which are defended
by the clergy and recognized as heroic feats by all in
power, — this one extraordinary success of Nietzsche's
writings may serve as an irrefutable proof. The disconnected writings of an agile but unintelligent and
abnormal German, possessed of the mania of grandeur,
appear, aiming at effect in the most trivial way. Neither
in their ability nor their truth have these writings any
real claim to the attention of the public. Such writings,
not only in the time of Kant, Leibnitz, Hume, but even
fifty years ago, would not only have failed to attract
attention but could not even have appeared; whilst in
our time, all so-called educated humanity is enchanted
with the ravings of Mons. Nietzsche, refutes and inter-
prets him, and his works are published in every language in innumerable copies.

Turgenieff has humorously said that reversed plati-
tudes are often employed by incapable men to draw
attention to themselves. For instance, every one knows
that water is wet, but suddenly a man with a serious
mien says that water is dry, alluding to ice, and such a
statement, expressed with assurance, attracts attention.

Thus, also, the whole world knows that virtue consists
in the subjugation of one's passions — in self-sacrifice.
This is recognized not by Christianity alone, with which
Nietzsche imagines he is fighting, — it is the eternal
higher law which humanity has reached in Brahmanism,
Buddhism, Confucianism, in the ancient Persian religion.
And suddenly a man appears who declares that he has
become persuaded that self-sacrifice, meekness, humility,
love, are all vices which ruin mankind (he has in view
Christianity, forgetting all other religions). One can
understand that such an assertion staggers people at
first. But having reflected a little and failed to find in
the work any proof of this strange assertion, every
rational man must thrust aside such a book, and only
feel astonishment that in our time there is no absurdity
too great to find a publisher. But with Nietzsche's
books this is not the case. The majority of men, pseudo-

enlightened, examine the theory of the "Ober-Mensche"
seriously, and consider its author a great philosopher,
a successor to Descartes, Leibnitz, Kant.

And all this happens for this reason, that for the
majority of the pseudo-enlightened men of our day the
allusion to virtue and its principal basis, self-sacrifice,
love, which restrain and condemn their animal life, is
abhorrent, and it is pleasant to them to meet a doctrine
of cruelty asserting the justice of establishing one's
own happiness and greatness on the lives of the others
on whom we feed, even though expressed haphazardly,
illogically, disconnectedly.

CHAPTER XII

JESUS rebuked the Pharisees and Scribes for having
taken the keys of the Kingdom of Heaven, and neither
entered themselves nor allowed others to enter.

This is what is now being done by the scientific
Scribes of to-day : these men have taken the keys, not
of the Kingdom of Heaven, but of enlightenment, and
neither enter themselves nor admit others. The augurs
— the Priesthood — by the means of every kind of deceit and hypnotism have persuaded men that Christianity is not a doctrine which preaches the equality of all
men and so destroys the entire modern heathen organization of life, but on the contrary that it supports it,
and dictates to men that they must distinguish some
from others, as stars are distinguished ; that they must
recognize that all power is from God, and willingly submit to it ; and in general persuades the oppressed that
their position is from God, and that they must bear it in
meekness and humility, and submit to those oppressors
who not only may not be meek and humble themselves,
but must, while correcting others, teach and punish, —
like Emperors, Kings, Popes, Bishops, and every class
of secular and spiritual rulers, — living meanwhile in a
splendor and luxury which it is the duty of their infe-
riors to supply. It is, thanks to this false teaching,

which they support energetically, that those in power rule the people and force them to serve their idleness, luxury, and vices.

And the only men who are emancipated from the Church-hypnotism, and who alone might save the people from their oppression, and who say they do desire this, — the scientists, — instead of doing the things which might accomplish what they desire, do exactly the contrary, and imagine that they are thus serving the people.

One might think that the most superficial observation of that which above all preoccupies those who keep the people under their power would enable these men of science to understand what force moves and restrains nations in a certain position, and that they ought to direct all their attention to this force. But they not only fail to do this, — they regard it as utterly useless.

These men appear not to wish to see this, and they carefully, and often sincerely, do for the people the most varied things, but do not do that one thing which before all is necessary to the people. Their activity resembles that of a man who might endeavor to move a train by muscular efforts, — he need only mount the tender and do what he continually sees the engine driver do — turn the handle which admits the steam into the cylinder. This steam is the religious life-conception of men. And scientists need only observe with what jealousy all rulers reserve to themselves this motive force, through which they rule the nations, in order to understand to what their energies should be directed if they would liberate the people from their slavery.

What does the Turkish Sultan defend, and to what does he hold most closely? And why does the Russian Emperor, arriving at any town, go to kiss the local relics and *ikons* before he does anything else? And why, notwithstanding all the varnish of culture with which he covers himself, does the German Emperor, in all his speeches appropriately or inappropriately allude to God, to Christ, to the sanctity of religion and the oath, etc? Why, because they all know that their power is based

on the army, and the army, the possibility of the existence of the army, is based only on religion. And if the
wealthy are especially pious and pretend to be believers,
go to church and keep the Sabbath day, they do all this
chiefly because their instinct of self-preservation tells
them that their exceptionally advantageous position in
society is connected with the religion they profess.

These people often do not know in what way their
power is founded on the religious deceit, but through
the instinct of self-preservation they know where their
weak point lies, upon which their position is dependent,
and they protect this point before everything else.
These men will always permit, and have permitted within
certain limits, socialistic and even revolutionary propaganda, but the religious foundations they will never
allow to be touched.

And therefore if the leaders of to-day, the Scientists,
Liberals, Socialists, Revolutionists, Anarchists, cannot
understand from psychology or history what it is which
moves nations, they might at least through this obvious
experience become convinced that the motive power lies,
not in material conditions, but only in religion.

But, strange to say, the scientists, the leaders of
to-day, whilst very excellently analyzing and understanding the conditions of the life of the nations, do not see
what so obviously strikes one in the face.   If those who
act so leave the people in religious ignorance intentionally, in order to retain their advantageous position in
the minority, this is a terrible, an infamous deceit. Those
who so act are those very Pharisees whom more than
any one else, whom even alone amongst all men, Jesus
condemned — condemned because no monsters or mis-
creants have introduced and are introducing so much
evil into the life of mankind as they.

If, on the other hand, these men are sincere, then
the only explanation of this strange blindness is that,
as the masses are under the hypnotism of false religion,
so also these pseudo-enlightened people of to-day are
under the hypnotism of false science, which has decided
that the chief nerve by which humanity has always lived

and is living, is no longer necessary, and may be replaced by something else.

CHAPTER XIII

It is in this error or deceit of the Scribes — of educated men of our world — that the especial feature of our
period consists, and in this lies the cause of the calami-
tous state in which Christian humanity is living, and of
that animalism into which it is sinking deeper and
deeper.

Generally, the leading educated men of to-day assert
that those false religious beliefs which are held by the
masses are of no special importance, and that it is not
worth while to, nor is there any need of, contesting them
directly, as Hume, Voltaire, Rousseau, and others did.
Science, in their opinion, that is, that disconnected
casual information which they spread amongst the people, will attain this end by itself; that is, man, having
learnt how many millions of miles the earth is from the
sun, and what minerals the sun and stars contain, will
cease to believe in ecclesiastical doctrines.

In this sincere or insincere assertion or assumption
lies a great error or else a terrible piece of guile.
From earliest childhood, the age most receptive of
suggestion, at the very time when the educator cannot
be too careful about what he transmits, senseless and
immoral dogmas of so-called Christian religion, incompatible with reason or knowledge, are instilled into the
child. He is taught the dogma of the Trinity, un-
acceptable to common sense, the descent of one of
these three gods to earth to redeem the human race,
his resurrection and ascension to heaven; he is taught
to expect the second advent, and punishment with
eternal torments for unbelief in these dogmas; he is
taught to pray about his wants, and much else. And
when all these conceptions, opposed both to reason and
to modern knowledge, as well as to the human conscience, are ineffaceably printed on the receptive mind

of the child, he is left alone to discriminate as he can among all those contradictions which follow from the dogmas he has accepted and assimilated as the very truth. No one tells him how he can and should reconcile these contradictions, and if theologians endeavor to reconcile them, their efforts only still further confuse the matter. And so by degrees the man becomes accustomed (and in this the theologians vigorously support him) to the idea that one cannot trust in reason and that therefore everything is possible in the world, and that in man there is nothing by the aid of which he can distinguish for himself good from evil and falsehood from truth; and that in what is most important for him — his conduct — he must be guided, not by his reason, but by what other men tell him. One can understand what a terrible distortion must be produced in the spiritual part of man by such an education, maintained in maturity by all the means of hypnotic suggestion which are continually being applied to the people by the aid of the priesthood.

And if a man of strong spirit with great difficulty and sufferings frees himself from the hypnotic influence in which he was educated in childhood and confirmed in maturity, then the distortion of his mind produced by the persuasion that he must not trust his reason, cannot pass away without leaving traces, just as in the physical world the infection of an organism with a powerful poison cannot pass without traces. Having freed himself from the hypnotism of this deceit, such a man, hating the lie from which he has just escaped, will naturally adopt that theory of the leaders in which all religion is regarded as one of the principal obstacles to the advance of humanity along the way of progress. And having adopted this view, such a man will become, like his teachers, an unprincipled man; that is, without conscience, guided in life only by his lusts, and far from condemning himself for this, will regard himself as on the highest plane of mental development accessible to humanity.

So it will be with the strong man. Whereas the

weaker ones, although they may awake to doubt, will
never altogether liberate themselves from that deceit in
which they were educated, and accepting and inventing
various ingeniously woven cloudy theories intended to
justify the senselessness of the accepted dogmas, living in a region of doubts, mists, sophisms, and self-
deceit, will only contribute to the blinding of the masses
and to hindering their awakening.

And the masses, possessing neither the power nor the
possibility of struggling with the hypnotic influence they
are subjected to, will live and die, generation after generation, as they do now, bereft of the highest human
welfare, — of a true religious understanding of life, —
and will always be a passive tool in the hands of the
classes which rule and deceive them.

And it is this terrible deceit that the scientific leading
men say is not important and is not worth while fighting! The only explanation of such an assertion, if
those who make it are sincere, is, that they are themselves under the hypnotism of false science. And, if
they are not sincere, is, that to attack established beliefs
is disadvantageous and often dangerous. One way or
the other, at all events, the assertion that the profession
of a false religion is harmless or merely unimportant, and
that therefore one can spread enlightenment without
destroying the religious deceit, is utterly untrue.

The salvation of mankind from their calamities lies
only in their emancipation from that hypnotic influence
in which they are held by their priests, as well as from
that into which they are led by the scientists. Before
one can pour anything into a vessel one must first
empty it of what it already contains. So also it is necessary to free men from the deceit in which they are
held in order that they may accept true religion, that
is, a true relation to the source of all, — God, — corresponding to the development of humanity, and a
guide for their actions deduced from this relation.

CHAPTER XIV

"But does a true religion really exist? All religions are infinitely different, and one has no right to call any particular religion the true one merely because it corresponds most nearly to our tastes," those will say who examine religions in their externalities as some sort of disease, from which they feel themselves free, but from which others are still suffering. But this is untrue: Religions are different in their external forms, but they are all the same in their fundamental principles. And it is just these fundamental principles of all religions which represent that true religion which alone to-day is natural to all men, and the acceptation of which can alone save men from their calamities.

Humanity has existed for a long period, and just as it has from generation to generation elaborated its practical acquisitions, so also it could not help elaborating those spiritual principles which have formed the basis of its life, and the rules of conduct which follow from these principles. That blind men do not see them is no proof that they do not exist.

Such a modern religion, common to all men, — not some one particular religion with all its peculiarities and distortions, but a religion consisting of those principles which are the same in all the religions obtaining among men and known to us, professed by more than nine-tenths of the human race, — such a universal religion does exist, and men have not yet become finally brutalized only because the best men of all nations adhere to this religion and profess it, even though unconsciously, and it is only the inculcation of deceit which is practised on men by the aid of the priests and the scientists which hinders them from accepting it consciously.

The principles of this true religion are so natural to men that the moment they are communicated they are accepted as something long familiar and self-evident. For us this true religion is Christianity, in those of its

principles in which it coincides, not with the external
forms, but with the fundamental principles of Brahmanism, Confucianism, Taoism, Judaism, Buddhism, even
Mohammedanism.   In the same way, for those who
profess Brahmanism, Confucianism, and so on, the
true religion will be the one the fundamental principles
of which coincide with those of all the other great religions. And these principles are very simple, comprehensible, and not numerous.

They assert that there is a God, the source of all;
that in man there is a particle of this divine element
which he can either diminish or increase by his life;
that to increase this element man must suppress his
passions and increase love in himself; and that the
practical means to attain this is to act with others as
one wishes others to act toward oneself. All these
principles are common to Brahmanism and Judaism and
Confucianism and Taoism and Buddhism and Christianity and Mohammedanism. (If Buddhism gives no definition of God it nevertheless recognizes that with which
man unites and into which he is immersed when he
reaches Nirvana. So that what man is united with
when immersed in Nirvana is the same essence which
is recognized as God in Christianity, Judaism, and
Mohammedanism.)

" But this is not religion," the men of our times who
are accustomed to accept what is supernatural, that is,
senseless, as the chief feature of religion, will say;
"this is anything you may like: philosophy, ethics,
reason, but not religion."   Religion, according to their
conception, must be senseless and incomprehensible
(*credo quia absurdum*). And yet it was only out of
these very principles, or rather out of their being
taught as religious doctrine, that by a long process of
distortion all the absurdities about miracles and supernatural events which are regarded as the fundamental
features of religion were elaborated. To assert that
the supernatural and irrational elements represent the
essential features of religion, is like a man, while looking only at rotten apples, asserting that a repulsive

flavor and a pernicious effect on the digestion are the essential qualities of the apple as a fruit.

Religion must define the relation of man to the source of all, the destiny of man which follows from this relation, and the rules of conduct from this destiny. And the universal religion, the fundamental principles of which are identical in all faiths, entirely satisfies these demands. It defines the relation of man to God as that of a part to the whole; it deduces from this relation the function of man as the increase in himself of the divine element; and from this function it deduces practical rules from the principle of acting toward others as one wishes others to act toward oneself.

People often doubt, and I have myself at one time doubted, that such an abstract rule as the one that we should act toward others as we desire others to act toward oneself could be as obligatory a rule and guide in one's conduct as the more simple rules about fasting, prayer, communion, etc. But this doubt is irrefutably answered, if by nothing else, by the spiritual condition of the Russian peasant, who will rather die than spit the sacrament into the dust, although in obedience to the commands of men he is ready to kill his brothers.

Why should not the demands deduced from the rule of acting toward others as one wishes them to act toward oneself, — not to kill one's brothers, not to abuse men, not to commit adultery, not to revenge, not to profit by the need of one's brothers to satisfy one's fancies, and so on, — why should not these demands be instilled with the same strenuousness and become as obligatory and untransgressible as faith in the sanctity of the sacrament, *ikons*, and so on, for those whose faith is founded more on confidence than on a clear inner consciousness?

CHAPTER XV

THE truths of the universal religion of to-day are so simple, comprehensible, and near to the heart of every one that it would seem sufficient for all parents,

rulers, and teachers — instead of the outlived and senseless doctrines of Trinities, virgin mothers, redemptions,
Indras and Trimourtis, of Buddhas flying away into the
skies, of Mohammeds, in which they often do not themselves believe — to instil into children and adults those
clear, simple truths of the religion common to all men,
the metaphysical essence of which is that the Spirit of
God lives in man, and the practical rule of which is that
man should act toward others as he wishes others to act
toward himself, — for the whole life of mankind to
change of itself.

If instead of the faith that children are now taught
and adults are confirmed in, that God sent His Son
to redeem the sins of Adam, and to establish His Church
which must be obeyed, and the consequent rule that
one should pray and bring offerings at certain times
and at certain places, and refrain from a given food at
a given time and on certain days from work, — if
instead of this they were taught and confirmed in the
faith that God is a Spirit whose image lives in us, the
power of which we can increase by our conduct; — if
only they were taught this and all that naturally follows
from these principles, in the same way that they are
taught at present those unnecessary legends, about impossible events and the rules of the senseless rituals
which follow from such tales, — then, instead of irrational strife and separation, very soon, without the help
of diplomatists, international law, peace congresses, political economists, and socialists of all sections, a peaceful,
friendly, happy life would come about for humanity,
directed by this sole religion.

But nothing of the sort is attempted: not only is the
deceit of false religion not destroyed and the true religion not preached, but on the contrary more and more
men farther and farther recede from the possibility of
accepting the truth.

The chief reason why people do not do what is so
natural, necessary, and possible, is that men of to-day,
owing to a prolonged irreligious life, have become so
accustomed to organize and establish their mode of liv-

ing by violence, — bayonets, bullets, prisons, gallows, — that they imagine such an order of life is not only normal, but that no other is possible. Not only those to whom the existing order is advantageous think this, even those who suffer from it are so stupefied by the hypnotic influence practised upon them that they also regard violence as the only means of securing good order in human society. And yet more than anything else this organization and establishment of social life by violence removes men from the possibility of understanding the causes of their sufferings, and therefore from the possibility of true order; — like an incapable or ill-intentioned doctor when he drives inward a virulent eruption, thus not only deceiving the patient by his action, but increasing the disease itself and rendering a cure impossible.

To the rulers who have enslaved the masses and who think and say " After us, the Deluge," it appears very convenient, by the means of the army, the clergy, the police, and of the threats of bayonets, bullets, prisons, workhouses, gallows, to compel the enslaved people to continue to live in their stupefaction and slavery, and not to hinder the rulers from enjoying their position. And the rulers do this, and call it " right order," whereas nothing hinders true social order so much as this. In reality such an organization is not only not right order, but an organization of evil.

If the men of our world with the remnants of religious principles which still exist in the masses, had not continually before their eyes the crimes of those who had taken upon themselves the duty of conserving social order and social morality, — by wars, executions, prisons, taxation, the sale of intoxicants and opium, — they would never have dreamed of carrying out one hundredth part of those evil deeds, deceits, acts of violence, murders, which they now carry out in the full persuasion that such deeds are good and natural.

The law of human life is of such a nature that the improvement of life, of the individual as well of society, is possible only by inward moral perfecting. Whereas all the efforts of men to improve their life by external influence and coercion serve as the most effective propaganda and example of evil, and therefore fail not only to improve life, but on the contrary increase the evil, which, like a snowball, continually grows larger and larger, and more and more removes people from the only possibility of truly improving their life.

In proportion as the habit of violence and crimes practised under the guise of law by the custodians of order and morality themselves becomes more and more frequent and cruel, and is justified in greater measure by the inculcation of falsehood uttered as religion, people become more and more firmly established in the idea that the law of their life is not love and mutual service, but struggle and the devouring of each other.

And the more they become confirmed in this idea, which lowers them to the plane of animals, the more difficult is it for them to awaken from that hypnotic influence to which they are subjected, and to accept as the basis of life that true religion of our time common to all humanity.

A vicious circle is established. The absence of religion renders an animal life founded on violence possible, and this animal life founded on violence renders more and more impossible liberation from the hypnotic influence and the assimilation of true religion. And this is why people do not do what is natural, possible, and necessary in our time : do not destroy the deceit of the semblance of religion and do not accept and preach the true religion.

CHAPTER XVI

Is any issue out of this enchanted circle possible, and where is it ?

It seems at first that the Governments, having taken upon themselves the duty of guiding the life of nations for the welfare of the nations, ought to lead men out of the circle. So those who have endeavored to replace the

order of life founded on violence by a rational one
founded on mutual service and love have always thought.
So also thought Christian reformers, as well as the
founders of the various theories of European Com-
munism, and so also thought the famous Chinese reformer, Mi-Ti, who proposed to the Government to teach
children in the schools not military sciences and exercies,
and to give rewards to adults not for military exploits,
but to teach children and adults the rules of respect and
love, and to distribute prizes and encouragements for
exploits of love.

And thus also many Russian religious reformers
from the people have thought, whom I have known
and of whom I now know many, from Sutaief to the
old man who has already submitted a petition to the
Emperor five times, begging him to command the can-
celing of the false religion and the preaching of true
Christianity.

People naturally think that Governments who justify
their existence by their care of national welfare must,
in order to insure this welfare, desire to use that sole
means which cannot in any way harm the people, but
only produce the most fruitful results. But Governments
have not only never and nowhere taken this duty upon
themselves, but on the contrary have always and everywhere defended with the greatest jealousy the existing
false and outlived religious teaching, and persecuted by
every means those who have attempted to transmit to
the people the foundations of true religion. And
indeed it cannot be otherwise : for Governments to
reveal the falsehood of the existing religion and to
preach the true one would be like a man chopping the
branch on which he is sitting.

But if Governments do not do this, it would seem
that it certainly ought to be done by those men of
science who, having freed themselves from the deceit of
false religion, desire as they say to serve the people who
have reared them. But these men, like the Governments, do not do this. Firstly, because they regard it as
inexpedient to subject themselves to the unpleasant-

nesses and dangers of persecutions by the Governments
for revealing the deceit upheld by the Governments,
and which, according to the conviction of these men,
will disappear of itself; secondly, because, regarding all
religions as outlived errors, they have nothing to offer
the people in the place of the deceit which they might
overthrow.

There remain those great masses of unlearned people
under the hypnotic influence of the Church and Government deceit, and who therefore regard the semblance of religion instilled into them as the only true
religion, believing that there is not and cannot be any
other.   These masses are under the continual strenuous
influence of hypnotism; generation after generation is
born, lives, and dies in that stupefied state in which it is
held by the priesthood and Government; and if any
become freed from it, they inevitably drop into the
scientific school, which denies religion, and their influence becomes as useless and harmful as the influence
of their teachers.

So that for some it is disadvantageous, for others it is
impossible.

CHAPTER XVII

I⊤ looks as if there were no issue.

And indeed for irreligious people there is and can
be no issue from this position; people who belong
to the higher ruling classes, even if they pretend that
they are anxious about the welfare of the masses, will
never (nor can they, being guided by worldly motives)
seriously destroy that stupefaction and enslavement in
which these masses live, and which give the higher
classes the possibility of ruling over them.   In the
same way those also who belong to the enslaved, in
like manner being guided by worldly motives, cannot
desire to render worse their at present difficult position
by struggling with the higher classes for the purpose
of revealing the false teaching and preaching the true.

Neither have they any reason for doing so, and if they are intelligent men they never will do it.

But this is not so with religious people — those who, however depraved society may be, always by their lives preserve that sacred fire of religion without which human life could not exist. There are times (such is the present one) when these men are not seen, when, despised and humiliated by every one, they pass their lives obscurely, as with us in Russia, in exile, prisons, penal battalions, — but they exist, and on them depends the rational life of mankind. And it is these religious people, however few they may be, who alone can and will sever that enchanted circle in which men are riveted. These men can do this because all those disadvantages and dangers which prevent the worldly man from opposing the existing order of life, not only do not exist for the religious man, but increase his zeal in the struggle with falsehood, and in the profession by word and deed of that which he regards as divine truth. If he belongs to the ruling classes, he will not only not desire to conceal the truth out of regard to his advantageous position, but, on the contrary, having come to abhor these advantages, he will use all the powers of his soul to free himself from these advantages and to preach the truth, as he will no longer have any other object in life than that of serving God. If, on the other hand, he belongs to the enslaved, then, having likewise abandoned the desire common to people of his position, of bettering the conditions of his physical life, such a man will have no other object than the fulfilment of the will of God by revealing falsehood and professing the truth, and no sufferings or threats will any longer compel him to cease to live in accordance with that sole meaning which he has recognized in his life. Both the one and the other will act thus as naturally as the worldly man labors and undergoes privations for the possession of riches and for satisfying the ruler from whom he expects advantages. Every religious man acts thus because the human soul enlightened by religion no longer lives merely by the life of this world as irreligious people live, but lives by the eternal, infinite life, for which sufferings and death in this life are as insignificant as the corns on his hand and the fatigue of his limbs are insignificant to a laborer plowing a field.

It is these people who will sever the enchanted circle in which men are now riveted. However few they may be, however low their social position, however weak they may be in education and intellect, these men, as surely as fire ignites the dry prairie, will ignite the whole world, — all the hearts of men dried up from a long period of irreligious life and thirsting for renovation.

Religion is not a faith established once for all in supernatural events, supposed to have taken place at some time or other, or in the necessity of certain prayers and rites; neither is it, as the scientists think, the remains of the superstitions of ancient unenlightenment which in our time have no significance or adaptation to life: Religion is the relation of man to eternal life, to God, in accordance with reason and contemporary knowledge, which alone moves man forward toward the end for which he is intended.

"The human soul is a lamp of God," says a wise Hebrew proverb. Man is a weak, miserable animal until in his soul there burns the fire of God. But when this fire kindles (and it kindles only in a soul illumined by religion) man becomes the most powerful being in the world. And this cannot be otherwise, because then it is no longer *his* power which works in him, but the power of God.

So this is what religion is, and in what its essence consists.

THREE PARABLES

PARABLE THE FIRST

A WEED had spread over a beautiful meadow. And in order to get rid of it the tenants of the meadow mowed it, but the weed only increased in consequence. And now the kind, wise master came to visit the tenants of the meadow, and among the other good counsels which he gave them, he told them they ought not to mow the weed, since that only made it grow the more luxuriantly, but that they must pull it up by the roots.

But either because the tenants of the meadow did not, amongst the other prescriptions of the good master, take heed of his advice not to mow down the weed, but to pull it up, or because they did not understand him, or because, according to their calculations, it seemed foolish to obey, the result was that his advice not to mow the weed but to pull it up was not followed, just as if he had never proffered it, and the men went on mowing the weed and spreading it.

And although, during the succeeding years, there were men that reminded the tenants of the meadow of the advice of the kind, wise master, they did not heed them, and continued to do as before, so that mowing of the weed as soon as it began to appear became not only a custom but even a sacred tradition, and the meadow grew more and more infested. And the matter went so far that the meadow grew nothing but weeds, and men lamented this and invented all kinds of means to correct the evil; but the only one they did not use was that which had long ago been prescribed by their kind, wise master.

And now, as time went on, it occurred to one man who saw the wretched condition into which the meadow had fallen, and who found among the master's forgotten prescriptions the rule not to mow the weed, but to pull it up by the root — it occurred to the man, I say, to remind the tenants of the meadow that they were acting foolishly, and that their folly had long ago been pointed out by the kind, wise master.

But what do you think! instead of putting credence in the correctness of this man's recollections, and in case they proved to be reliable ceasing to mow the weed, and in case he were mistaken proving to him the incorrectness of his recollections, or stigmatizing the good, wise master's recommendations as impracticable and not obligatory upon them, the tenants of the meadow did nothing of the sort; but they took exception to this man's recollections and began to abuse him. Some called him a conceited fool who imagined that he was the only one to understand the master's regulations; others called him a malicious false interpreter and slanderer; still others, forgetting that he was not giving them his own opinions, but was only reminding them of the prescriptions of the wise master whom they all revered, called him a dangerous man because he wished to pull up the weed and deprive them of their meadow. "He says we ought not to mow the meadow," said they, purposely suppressing the fact that the man did not say that it was not necessary to destroy the weed, but said that they should pull it up by the roots instead of mowing it, "but if we do not destroy the weed, then it will spread and wholly ruin our meadow. And why was the meadow granted to us if we must train the weed in it?"

And the general impression that this man was either a fool or a false interpreter, or had the purpose of injuring the people, became so deeply grounded that every one cast reproaches and ridicule upon him. And however earnestly he asseverated that he not only did

not desire to spread the weed, but on the contrary considered that the destruction of the weed was one of the
chief duties of the agriculturist, just as it was meant by
the good, wise master whose words he merely repeated,
still they would not listen to him because they had
definitely made up their minds that he was either a
conceited fool misinterpreting the good, wise master's
words, or a villain trying to induce men not to destroy
the weeds but to protect and spread them more widely.

The same thing took place in my own case when I
pointed out the injunction of the evangelical teaching
about the non-resistance of evil by violence. This rule
was laid down by Christ and after Him in all times by
all His true disciples. But either because they did not
notice this rule, or because they did not understand it,
or because its fulfilment seemed to them too difficult,
as time went the more completely this rule was forgotten, the farther the manner of men's lives departed
from this rule; and finally it came to the pass to which
it has now come that this rule has already begun to
seem to people something new, strange, unheard-of, and
even foolish. And I, also, have the same experience as
the man had who reminded men of the good, wise master's prescription to refrain from mowing the weed, but
to pull it up by the roots.

As the tenants of the meadow purposely shut their
eyes to the fact that the counsel was not to give up
destroying the weed, but to destroy it by a different
method, and said, "We will not listen to this man, he is
a fool; he forbids us to mow down the weeds and tells
us to pull them up" — so in reply to my reminder that
according to Christ's teaching in order to annihilate evil
we must not employ violence against it, but must destroy it from the root with love, men said: "We will
not listen to him, he is a fool; he advises not to oppose
evil to evil so that evil may overwhelm us."

I said that, according to Christ's teaching, evil cannot
be eradicated by evil; that all resistance of evil by violence only intensifies the evil, that according to Christ's
teaching evil is eradicated by good. *Bless them that*

curse you, pray for them that abuse you, do good to them
that hate you, love your enemies, and you will have no
enemies ! [1]

I said that, according to Christ's teaching, the whole
life of man is a battle with evil, a resistance of evil by
reason and love, but that out of all the methods of resisting evil Christ excepted only the one unreasonable
method of resisting evil with violence, which is equivalent to fighting evil with evil.

And I was misunderstood as saying that Christ
taught that we must not resist evil.   And all those
whose lives were based on violence, and to whom in consequence violence was dear, were glad to take such a
misconstruction of my words, and at the same time of
Christ's words, and it was avowed that the teaching of
non-resistance of evil was incredible, stupid, godless, and
dangerous.   And men calmly continue under the guise
of destroying evil to make it more widely spread.

II

PARABLE THE SECOND

MEN were trafficking in flour, butter, milk, and all
kinds of food-stuffs.   And as each one was desirous of
receiving the greatest profit and becoming rich as soon
as possible, all these men got more and more into the
habit of adulterating their goods with cheap and injurious mixtures: with the flour they mixed bran and lime,
they put oleomargarin into their butter, they put water
and chalk into their milk.   And until these goods
reached the consumers all went well: the wholesale
traders sold them to the retailers, and the retailers dis-
tributed them in small quantities.

There were many stores and shops, and the wares,
it seemed, went off very rapidly.   And the tradesmen
were satisfied.   But the city consumers, those that did
not raise their own produce and were therefore obliged

1 " The Teaching of the Twelve Apostles."

to buy it, found it very harmful and disagreeable. The flour was bad, the butter and milk were bad, but as there were no other wares except those adulterated to be had in the city markets, the city consumers continued to buy them, and they complained because the food tasted bad and was unwholesome; they blamed themselves, and ascribed it to the wretched way in which the food was prepared. Meantime the tradespeople continued more and more flagrantly to adulterate their food-stuffs with cheap foreign ingredients. Thus passed a sufficiently long time. The city people were all suffering, and no one had the resolution to express his dissatisfaction.

And it happened that a housekeeper who had always given her family food and drink of her own make came to the city. This woman had spent her whole life in the preparation of food, and though she was not a famous cook, still she knew very well how to bake bread and to cook good dinners.

This woman bought various articles in the city and began to bake and cook. Her loaves did not rise, but fell. Her cakes, owing to the oleomargarin butter, seemed tasteless. She set her milk, but there was no cream. The housekeeper instantly came to the conclusion that her purchases were poor. She examined them, and her surmises were confirmed. She found lime in the flour, oleomargarin in the butter, chalk in the milk. Finding that all the materials she had bought were adulterated, the housekeeper went to the bazaars and began in a loud voice to accuse the tradesmen, and to demand that they should either stock their shops with good, nutritious, unadulterated articles, or else cease to trade, and shut up shop.

But the tradesmen paid no attention to the housekeeper, but told her that their goods were first class, that the whole city had been buying of them for so many years, and that they even had medals, and they showed her their medals on their signs. But the housekeeper did not give in.

" I don't need any medals," said she, " but wholesome

food, so that I and my children may not have stomach
troubles from it."

"Apparently, my good woman, you have never seen
genuine flour and butter," said the tradesmen, showing
her the white, pure-looking flour in varnished bins, the
wretched imitation of butter lying in neat dishes, and
the white fluid in glittering transparent jars.

"Of course I know them," replied the housekeeper,
"because all my life long I have had to do with them,
and I have cooked with them and have eaten them, I
and my children. Your goods are adulterated. Here
is the proof of it," said she, displaying the spoilt bread,
the oleomargarin in the cakes, and the sediment in the
milk. "You ought to throw all this stuff of yours into
the river or burn it, and get unadulterated goods instead."

And the woman, standing in front of the shops, kept
incessantly crying her one message to the purchasers
who came by, and the purchasers began to be troubled.

Then perceiving that this audacious housekeeper was
likely to injure their wares, the tradesmen said to the
purchasers : —

"Look here, gentlemen, what a lunatic this woman
is! She wants people to perish of starvation. She
insists on our burning up and destroying all our provisions. What would you have to eat if we should heed
her and refuse to sell you our goods? Do not listen to
her, she is a coarse countrywoman, and she is no judge of
provisions, and it is nothing but envy which makes her
attack us. She is poor, and wants every one else to be
as poor as she is."

Thus spoke the tradesmen to the gathering throng,
purposely blinking the fact that the woman wanted, not
that all provisions should be destroyed, but that good
ones should be substituted for bad.

And thereupon the throng fell upon the woman and
began to beat her. And though she assured them all
that she had no wish to destroy the food-stuffs, that, on
the contrary, she had all her life been occupied in feeding others and herself, but that she only wanted that
those men that took upon themselves the feeding of the

people should not poison them with deleterious adul-
terations pretending to be edible.   Though she pleaded
her cause eloquently, they refused to hear her because
their minds were made up that she wanted to deprive
people of the food which they needed.

The same thing has happened to me in regard to the
art and science of our day.

All my life long I have been fed on this food, and to
the best of my ability I have attempted to feed others
on it.   And as this for me is a food and not an object
of traffic or luxury, I know beyond a question when food
is food and when it is only a counterfeit.   And now
when I made trial of the food which in our time began
to be offered for sale in the intellectual bazaar under the
guise of art and science, and attempted to feed those
dear to me with it, I discovered that a large part of
this food was not genuine.   And when I declared that
the art and the science on sale in the intellectual bazaar
are *margarined* or at least contain great mixtures of
what is foreign to true art and true science, and that I
know this because the produce I have bought in the
intellectual bazaar has been proved to be, not merely
disadvantageous to me and those near and dear to me,
but positively deleterious, then I was hooted at and
abused, and it was insinuated that I did this because I
was untrained and could not properly treat of such
lofty objects.

When I began to show that the dealers themselves in
these intellectual wares were all the time charging one
another of cheating, when I called to mind that in all
times under the name of art and science much that was
bad and harmful was offered to men, and that consequently in our time also the same danger was threaten-
ing, that this was no joke, that the poison for the soul
was many times more dangerous than a poison for the
body, and that therefore these spiritual products ought
to be examined with the greatest attention when they
are offered to us in the form of food, and everything
counterfeit and deleterious ought to be rejected, — when
I began to say this, no one, no one, not a single man in

a single article or book made reply to these arguments, but from all the shops there was a chorus of cries against me as against the woman: "He is a fool! He wants to destroy art and science which we live by! Beware of him and do not heed him! Hear us, hear us! We have the very latest foreign wares!"

III

PARABLE THE THIRD

TRAVELERS were making a journey. And they happened to lose their way, so that they found themselves proceeding, not on a smooth road, but across a bog, among clumps of bushes, briers, and fallen trees, which blocked their progress, and even to move grew more and more difficult.

Then the travelers divided into two parties; one decided not to stop, but to keep going in the direction that they had been going, assuring themselves and the others that they had not wandered from the right road, and were sure to reach their journey's end.

The other party decided that, as the direction in which they were now going was evidently not the right one — otherwise they would long ago have reached the journey's end — it was necessary to find the road, and in order to find it, it was requisite that without delay they should move as rapidly as possible in all directions. All the travelers were divided between these two opinions: some decided to keep going straight ahead, the others decided to make trials in all directions; but there was one man who, without sharing either opinion, declared that before continuing in the direction in which they had been going, or beginning to move rapidly in all directions, hoping that by this means they might find the right way, it was necessary first of all to pause and deliberate on their situation, and then after due deliberation to decide on one thing or the other.

But the travelers were so excited by the disturbance,

were so alarmed at their situation, they were so desirous of flattering themselves with the hope that they had not lost their way, but had only temporarily wandered from the road, and would soon find it again, and, above all, they had such a desire to forget their terror by moving about, that this opinion was met with universal indignation, with reproaches, and with the ridicule of those of both parties.

"It is the advice of weakness, cowardice, sloth," they said.

"It is a fine way to reach the end of our journey, sitting down and not moving from the place!" cried others.

"For this are we men, and for this is strength given us, to struggle and labor, conquering obstacles, and not pusillanimously giving in to them," exclaimed still others.

And in spite of what was said by the man that differed from the rest, "how if we proceeded in a wrong direction without changing it, we should never attain our goal, but go farther from it, and how we should never attain it either if we kept flying from one direction to another, and how the only means of attaining our goal was by taking observation from the sun or the stars and thus finding what direction we must take to reach it, and having chosen it to stick to it — and how to do this it was necessary first of all to halt, and to halt not for the purpose of stopping, but to find the right way and then unfalteringly to go in it, and how for either case it was necessary to stop and consider" — in spite of all this argument, they refused to heed him.

And the first division of the travelers went off in the direction in which they had been going, and the second division kept changing their course; but neither division succeeded in attaining their journey's end, but up to the present time, moreover, they have not yet escaped from the bushes and the briers, but are still lost.

Exactly the same thing happened to me when I attempted to express my doubts as to whether the road which we have taken through the dark forest of the labor question and through the all-swallowing bog of the end-

less armament of the nations is exactly the right route
by which we ought to go, that it is very possible that
we have lost our way, and that, therefore, it might be
well for us for a time to stop moving in that direction
which is evidently wrong, and first of all to consider, by
means of the universal and eternal laws of truth revealed
to us, what the direction is by which we intend to go.

No one replied to this, not a person said, " We are not
mistaken in our direction and we are not gone astray;
we are sure of this for this reason and for that."

Not a person said, " Possibly we are mistaken, but
we have an infallible means of correcting our error without ceasing to move."

No one said either the one thing or the other. But
all were indignant, took offense, and hastened to quench
my solitary voice with a simultaneous outburst.

" We are so indolent and backward ! And this is the
advice of indolence, sluggishness, inefficiency ! "

Some even went so far as to add : —

" It 's all nonsense ! Don't listen to him. Follow us."

And they shouted like those that reckon that salvation is to be found in unchangedly traveling a once
selected road, whatever it may have been ; like those
also that expect to find salvation in flying about in all
directions.

"Why wait ? Why consider ? Push forward ! Everything will come out of itself ! "

Men have lost their way and are suffering in consequence. It would seem that the first main application
of energy which should be put forth ought to be directed, not to the confirmation of the movement that
has seduced us into the false position where we are, but
to the cessation of it. It would seem clear that as soon
as we stopped we might, in a measure, comprehend our
situation, and discover the direction in which we ought
to go in order to attain true happiness, not for one man,
not for one class of men, but that general good of humanity toward which all men are striving and every
human heart by itself. But how is it ? Men invent
everything possible, but do not hit upon the one thing

that might prove their salvation, or if it did not do that, might at least ameliorate their condition; I mean, that they should pause for a moment and not go on increasing their misfortunes by their fallacious activity. Men are conscious of the wretchedness of their condition, and are doing all they can to avoid it, but the one thing that would assuredly ameliorate it they are unwilling to do, and the advice given them to do it, more than anything else, rouses their indignation.

If there were any possibility of doubting the fact that we have gone astray, then this treatment of the advice to "think it over" proves more distinctly than anything else how hopelessly astray we have gone and how great is our despair.

1895.

INDUSTRY

" In the sweat of thy face shalt thou eat thy bread, till thou returnest unto the ground, for out of it wast thou taken." — GENESIS iii. 19.

SUCH is the title and such the epigraph to the work of Timofeï Mikhaïlovitch Bondaref. This work I read in manuscript.

Timofeï Mikhaïlovitch Bondaref's work seems to me very notable, as well for the force and clearness and beauty of the style in which it is written, as for the sincerity of his conviction manifest in every line, and especially for the importance, truth, and depth of the fundamental thought.

The fundamental thought of this work is as follows: In all terrestrial affairs the thing of importance is, not to know what is particularly fine and necessary, but out of all fine and necessary things or actions to know what is of first importance, what of second, what of third, and so on.

If this is important in terrestrial affairs, much so is it important in the matter of faith, which determines a man's obligations.

Tatian, a teacher in the early days of the Church, declares that the unhappiness of men comes not so much from the fact that they do not know God, as from the fact that they acknowledge a false God, they consider as God that which is not God. The same thing may be said also concerning the obligations of men. The unhappiness and wrong-doing of men come not so much from the fact that they do not know what their obligations are, as from the fact that they acknowledge

326

false obligations, that they consider as obligatory what is not obligatory, and they do not consider as obligatory what is their chief duty.

Bondaref declares that the unhappiness and wrong-doing of men come from the fact that they consider as religious duties many idle and injurious regulations, but forget and hide from themselves and others their first, chief, unquestionable duty, expressed in the first chapter of the Holy Scriptures: "*In the sweat of thy face shalt thou eat thy bread.*"

For men who believe in the sanctity and infallibility of the divine word expressed in the Bible, this command given by God himself and never repudiated is a sufficient proof of its truth. For men who do not accept the Holy Scriptures and the truth of this position, if we regard it merely without prejudice as a simple unsupernatural expression of human wisdom, it seems to be the fulfilment of the conditions of human life, just as Bondaref makes it in his work.

An obstacle to such a fulfilment, unfortunately, is found in the fact that many of us are so wonted to a perverted and senseless interpretation of the Holy Scriptures, that the mere mention of the fact that a certain position coincides with the Holy Scriptures is a sufficient ground for many to look with distrust on that position.

"What meaning have the Holy Scriptures for me? We know that we may build any argument we please on them."

But this is not just; the Holy Scriptures are not to blame because men interpret them falsely, and a man who speaks the truth is not to blame because he speaks the same truth as is spoken in the Holy Scriptures.

We must not forget that if it is admitted that the writings called the Holy Scriptures are the productions of God but of men, then it must be explained why these popular writings and not others are accepted by men as the work of God himself. There must be some cause for this.

And this cause is clear. These writings are called divine by superstitious people because they are higher than all the knowledge of men, and also because these writings, in spite of the fact that certain men have always denied them, have come down to us, and are still considered divine.   These writings are called divine and have come down to us simply because a lofty wisdom is embodied in them.   And such in many of their passages are the writings which we call the Bible.

And such especially is the forgotten text, neglected and incomprehensible in its actual sense — the text which Bondaref explains and makes the corner-stone of his work.

This text and the first events of life in Paradise are usually understood in the direct sense of the words, meaning that everything happened precisely as it is described; but meantime the sense of this whole passage is this also, that it presents in picturesque form the contradictory impulses which are found in human nature.

Man is afraid of death, and yet he must die; man, as long as he knows not good and evil, seems happier, but he irresistibly strives to attain knowledge.   Man loves idleness, and the gratification of his desires without suffering, and at the same time only labor and suffering give life to him and his race.

This text is important, not so much because it was spoken by God Himself to Adam, but because it is true: it utters one of the most undoubted laws of human life. The law of gravitation is not true because it was enunciated by Newton, but because I know Newton and am grateful to him for having discovered for me an eternal law which explains for me a whole series of phenomena.

The same thing also with the law, *"In the sweat of thy face thou shalt eat thy bread."*   This is a law which explains for me a whole series of phenomena.   And having once recognized it I can no longer forget it, and I am grateful to him who discovered it for me. This law seems very simple, and has been long known, but it only seems so, and to see that it is the opposite all you have to do is to look around about you.   Men not only do not acknowledge this law, but they acknowledge one precisely the opposite.   Men, by their faith,

— all, from the Tsar to the beggar, are striving not to
fulfil this law, but to avoid fulfilling it. The above mentioned work of Bondaref is consecrated to an explanation of the importance, of the unalterableness, of the law,
and the inevitability of the misfortunes arising from a
neglect of it. Bondaref calls this law primeval, and the
chief of all laws.

He shows that sin — in other words, the mistakes, the
false steps we make — results only from the neglect of
this law. Of all the obligations imposed on man, Bondaref considers the first, chief, and invariable duty of
every man to work with his hands for his daily bread,
meaning by bread all the heavy "black work" which is
necessary to save a man from death by cold and starvation — in other words, bread and drink and raiment
and shelter and warmth.

Bondaref's fundamental idea is that this law, — the
law that a man to eat must work, — which till now has
been considered as necessary, must be regarded as a
blessed law of life, an obligation for every one.

This law must be acknowledged as a religious law,
like the observance of the Sabbath, circumcision among
the Hebrews, like the observance of the sacraments and
Lent among Church Christians, like fivefold prayer
among the Mohammedans.

Bondaref says in one place that if only men will
recognize labor for their daily bread as a religious duty,
then no particular private occupations can prevent them
from doing this work, just as no special occupations can
prevent churchmen from participating in the inac-
tivity of their festivals. More than eighty days are
taken out for festivals, but according to Bondaref
only forty days are required to earn a man's daily bread.
Strange as it may seem at first that such a simple
method, comprehensible to all, free from anything
subtle or sophisticated, can serve as a salvation from
the actual numberless evils of humanity; it is still
stranger, when you come to think of it, how we, having
had such a simple and clear method, long known to all
men, have put it aside and sought relief from our ills in

various subtilities and philosophies. But if you consider this, you will see that it is so. Supposing a man
should make a tub without a bottom, and should then
devise all sorts of clever schemes to carry water in it!
This is what all our methods for curing existent evils
amount to!

In fact, whence arise the calamities of men, if you
exclude from the number the calamities that men
directly bring on one another by murders, capital
punishments, taxes, brawls, and all sorts of cruelties
in which they sin by not refraining from violence?

All the calamities of mankind, with the exceptions of
those caused by direct violence, proceed from hunger,
from all kinds of deprivation, from overwork, and at
the same time from superfluity, from sloth, and from
the vices growing out of them. Whatever may be the
holiest duty of man, is there any more so than that
of bringing about the destruction of this inequality, of
these calamities, of lack in some and of superfluity in
others? And how can a man coöperate in the destruction of these calamities otherwise than by taking part
in the labor which overcomes need, and by refraining
from the superfluities and the idleness which produce
vices and temptations; in other words, that every one
should labor for his daily bread, should provide himself
with food by the work of his hands, as Bondaref says?

We have so involved ourselves, laying down so many
laws, both religious and social and domestic, so many
precepts, — as Isaiah says, precept on precept, here a
precept, there a precept, — that we have entirely lost
the meaning of what is good and what is bad.

A man conducts a mass, another collects an army or
taxes for it, a third sits on the bench, a fourth studies
books, a fifth practises medicine, a sixth teaches men;
and under these pretexts, freeing themselves from
manual labor, they shirk it on others, and forget that
men are dying of overwork, toil, and starvation: and in
order that some one may sing at mass, some one may
be protected by an army, some one may sit in judgment, some one may practise medicine or teach, it is

necessary that first of all men may cease dying of starvation. We forget that there may be many duties, but that there is a first and a last, and that it is impossible to fulfil the last until the first is fulfilled, just as it is impossible to harrow before the plowing is done.

Here we are recalled to this first indubitable duty in the domain of practical activity by Bondaref's teaching. Bondaref shows that the fulfilment of this obligation does not interfere with any one, presents no difficulties, and at the same time saves people from the calamity of need and superfluity. The fulfilment of this duty especially annihilates the terrible division into two classes which hate each other, and by flattery palliate their mutual hatred. Manual labor, says Bondaref, equalizes all, and clips the wings of luxury and lust.

It is impossible to plow and dig wells in costly raiment and with clean hands and after feeding on delicate food. Occupation in one sacred labor common to all brings men close together. Labor for daily bread, says Bondaref, restores reason to those that have lost it by separation from the life natural to mankind, and gives happiness and contentment to men by occupying them in work, which is undoubtedly advantageous and cheery, assigned by God Himself or by the laws of nature.

Labor for daily bread, says Bondaref, is a remedy which saves humanity. Let men acknowledge this first law as the law of God and unchangeable, let each man acknowledge it as his infallible duty to labor for his daily bread, in other words, to earn his own living with his hands, and all men will be united in faith in one God, in love to one another, and the calamities which overwhelm mankind will be done away with.

We are so accustomed to an order of life which takes the opposite for granted, that is, that wealth, as a means of freeing men from the necessity of daily labor, is either the blessing of God or the highest social position, that, if we do not examine into this position, we prefer to call it narrow, one-sided, idle, and stupid. But we must seriously consider the matter, and judge whether this stand is not just.

As we test every kind of theory, religious and political, let us also test Bondaref's theory as a theory. Let us see what would result if, according to Bondaref's idea, the religious sermonizing were to direct its forces to the explanation of this law, and all men were to recognize this primary law of labor as obligatory.

All would work and eat the bread that resulted from their labors, and bread and objects of the first importance would no longer become objects of purchase and sale. Then what would result?

The result would be that there would be no more people perishing of want. If one man, in consequence of unfortunate circumstances, did not by his labor secure enough food for himself and his family, another, in consequence of fortunate circumstances having got more than he needed, would give to the one lacking, would give because, as he no longer sells, he would have nothing else to do with his superfluity. The result would be that a man would not be subjected to the temptation of acquiring bread by shrewdness, and not having this temptation, he would not use force or cunning, he would not need to do as he does at the present time.

If he employed cunning or violence, it would be only because he loved cunning and violence, and not because they are indispensable, as they are at the present time.

For the weak, for those that had not the strength for any reason to earn their own bread, or that had in some way lost it, there would be no necessity of selling themselves or their labor, or, as it sometimes happens, their very souls, to get their bread.

There would be none of our present universal striving to get rid of manual labor, and shirking it on others, — the striving to crush the weak with labor and to free the strong from all work.

There would be none of that disposition of the human mind whereby all the forces of the human intellect are directed, not to lightening the work of the workers, but to make the leisure of the leisure more light and attractive. The participation of all men in manual labor, and recognizing it as the chief of all human actions, would

do what a man would do with a cart which stupid people
would drag with the wheels in the air, while he would
turn it over and set on the wheels on the ground.   It
would not break the cart and it would go easily.

Now, our life with its scorn and dislike of manual
labor and our justification of this false life is the cart
which we drag with the wheels in the air.   And all our
justifications of this work do not profit us, since we do
not turn the cart over and set it where it should stand.

Such is Bondaref's idea, and I fully share it.   His
idea presents itself before me as follows : There was a
time when men ate one another.   The consciousness of
the unity of all men developed to such a degree that
cannibalism became impossible, and they ceased to eat
one another.   Then came the time when men by force
took away the labor of others and reduced them to
slavery.   The conscience of men developed to the point
that this became impossible.   Violence which still persisted in hidden forms was annihilated in its coarser
manifestation; man no longer openly took possession
of the labor of another.

In our time there exists the form of violence in so far
as men, profiting by the necessity of others, subject them
to themselves.   According to Bondaref's idea, the time
has now come for such recognition of the unity of man
that it is no longer possible for men to take advantage
of others' necessities — in other words, their hunger and
nakedness — to bring them into subjection, and for men,
acknowledging the law of manual labor as obligatory on
every one, to acknowledge their duty unconditionally, by
refraining from the sale of objects of the first importance in case of necessity to feed, clothe, and house one
another.

Again, on the other hand, I look on Bondaref's work
as follows : We often happen to hear criticisms on the
insufficiency of certain prohibitory laws or commands,
that is to say, regulations concerning what must not
be done.   They say : Positive laws or commands are
necessary, regulations are necessary as to what exactly

---

[1] *Golod i kholod.*

must be done.   They say the five commands of Christ:
(1) not to look down on any one, or call any one a fool,
or be angry with any one; (2) not to look on copula-
tion as a source of satisfaction, not to desert husband or
wife when once a union has been consummated; (3) not
to bind oneself with an oath to any one, not to fetter one's
free will; (4) to bear insults and violence and not to
resist; and (5) not to consider any men as enemies, but
to love your enemies as well as your neighbors — they
say that these five commands of Christ all prescribe
only what is necessary not to do, but that there are no
commands or laws prescribing exactly what must be
done; and indeed it may seem strange that in Christ's
teaching there are no definite commands as to what
must be done.   But this seems strange only to one who
does not believe in Christ's teaching itself, included, not
in the five commands, but in the teaching itself of truth.
    The teaching of truth expressed by Christ is not
found in laws and commands; it is found in one thing,
in the meaning that it gives to life.   The meaning of this
teaching is in this one thing, that life and the blessing of
life are not in personal happiness, as people suppose, but
in the service of God and man.   And this position is not
a prescription which should be carried out for the sake
of receiving a reward, is not a mystic expression of
something mysterious and incomprehensible, but is the
revelation of a hitherto hidden law of life, is an indication that life can be a blessing only when it is thus
understood.   And therefore all Christ's positive teaching of truth is expressed in one thing: *Love God, and
thy neighbor as thyself.*   And there can be no explanations of this position.   It is one thing because this one
thing is all.   Christ's laws and commands, like the Jewish
and Buddhist laws and commands, are only indications
of those conditions in which the temptations of the
world seduce men from the true understanding of life.
And therefore there may be many laws and commands,
but there can be only one positive teaching of life, of
what must be done.
    The life of every man is a movement in a certain di-

rection ; whether he wishes or not, he moves, he lives.
Christ shows a man his path, and moreover points out
the turns from the true path which may lead him into
falsehood, and there may be many such indications —
these are the commands.

Christ gives five such commands, and those He gives
are of such kind that up to the present time it is impossible to add one to them, or to take one away. But only
one single indication of the direction of the path was
given — since there cannot be more than one straight
line indicating any direction. Hence the idea that in
Christ's teaching there are only prohibitions, but no
positive commands, is right for those only that do not
know or believe in the teaching of the truth, in the direction of the true path of life, pointed out by Christ.
Men who do not believe in the truth of the way of life
pointed out by Christ cannot find positive commands in
Christ's teaching. All positive activity, even the most
varied, flowing from the teaching of the right way of
life, is clear and always undoubtedly definite for them.

Men who believe in the way of life are, according to
Christ's sentence, like a fountain of living water, that
is, like a fountain proceeding from the earth. All their
activity is like the flowing of water, which flows steadily
in all directions in spite of the obstacles blocking it. A
man who believes in Christ's teaching can just as little
ask what he must positively do, as the spring of water
flowing from the earth can ask such a question. It
flows, refreshing the soil, the turf, the trees, the birds,
the animals, and men. The same is true of the man
who believes in Christ's doctrine of life.

The man who believes in Christ's teaching will not
ask what he must do. The love which constitutes the
force of his life faithfully and undoubtedly shows him
where he must act and what he must do, both before
and after. To say nothing of those directions of which
Christ's teaching is full — as to what is the first and
most important act of love, as to feeding the hungry,
giving drink to the thirsty, clothing the naked, helping
the needy and imprisoned — both reason and conscience

and feeling, everything, lead us to this:—before all
other acts of love toward living men, to support this life
of our brethren, to deliver them from suffering and
death which overtakes them in their unequal struggle
with nature, in other words, lead us to the first act
necessary for the life of men — to primitive, coarse physical labor on the soil.

Just as a spring cannot ask where it is to send its
water, whether it shall spurt up on the grass and the
leaves of the trees, or trickle down to the roots of the
grass and the trees, so the man that believes in the
teaching of truth cannot ask what he must do first of
all; whether to teach them, defend them, amuse them,
give them the pleasures of life, or support them when
they are perishing from need.

And just as the spring of water flows down over levels
and fills the ponds, and quenches the thirst of animals
and men, only after it has soaked the soil, so also the man
that believes in the teaching of truth can help along the
less pressing demands of men, only after he has satisfied
the first demand, that is, when he has helped in the nourishment of men, in their salvation from destruction in
consequence of their struggle with need.

The man that follows, not in word, but in deed, the
teaching of truth and love, cannot be mistaken in the
direction in which first of all he must apply his activity. Never can a man who applies the meaning of
his life to the service of others, be so mistaken as to
begin to help cold and hungry humanity by founding
cannon, by the manufacture of elegant objects, or by
playing on the fiddle or on the pianoforte.

Love cannot be stupid. As love for one person does
not permit the reading of novels to him when he is hungry or putting on him costly earrings when he is cold,
so love for men does not allow it to be possible to serve
them by amusing the prosperous, while allowing the cold
and hungry to die of their necessities.

True love — expressed in deeds, not words — not only
cannot be stupid, but it is the only thing that gives true
sagacity and wisdom.

And therefore the man penetrated with love will make no mistake, and will always do first of all what love for men demands — that which supports the life of the cold, the hungry, and the despondent; — he does not support the life of the cold, the hungry, and the despondent, but the struggle, the out and out struggle with nature, does. Only the man that wishes to deceive himself and others can in the time of danger and men's battle with necessity turn aside from aiding them, augment the necessity of men, and persuade himself and those that are perishing before his eyes, that he is occupied in devising for them means of salvation.

No genuine man who applies his life to the service of others will say this. And if he says this, never will he find in his conscience any support for his mistake; he will find it only in the crafty doctrine of the division of labor.

In all expressions of genuine popular wisdom from Confucius to Mohammed he will find one thing, will find it with especial force in the Gospels, will find the demand for the service of men, not according to the theory of the subdivision of labor, but in the simplest, most natural, and only necessary way, will find the need of serving the sick, the imprisoned, the cold, and the starving. But to extend aid to the sick, the imprisoned, the cold, and the starving is impossible otherwise than by one's immediate instant labor, because the sick, the cold, and the hungry will not wait, but will die of cold and hunger. To the man who fulfils the teaching of the truth, his life, consisting in service of others, points to this fundamental law expressed in the first book of Genesis: *In the sweat of thy face shalt thou eat thy bread*, which Bondaref calls fundamental and makes mandatory.

This law is really such for men who do not acknowledge that significance of life which Christ made evident to men, and such it was for men before Christ's day, and such it remains for men who do not acknowledge Christ's teaching. It demands that every man, according to God's will, expressed both in the Bible and in

reason, should earn his own daily food. This law is
mandatory. Such was this law even before the meaning of life was made plain to men in the teaching of the
truth.

But in the loftiest consciousness of the meaning of
life discovered by Christ, the law of manual labor, still
remaining true, stands as a part of the only positive doctrine of Christ concerning the service of others, and
receives the significance, not of a positive, but of a prohibitory, law. This law, in the Christian conscience,
points only to an ancient temptation of men, to what a
man ought not to do if he would avoid departing from
the path of the true life.

For a man of the Old Testament, who did not acknowledge the teaching of the truth, this law has the
same significance : earn your bread with your own
hands. For the Christian its significance is negative.
This law says : Do not suppose it possible to serve men
while swallowing up the labor of others, and while you
do not earn your subsistence with your own hands. This
law, for the Christian, points to one of the oldest and
most terrible temptations that people suffer from.
Against this temptation, terrible in its consequences,
and so very ancient that we with difficulty may recognize
this temptation, not as a natural quality of a man, but
as a deception, this doctrine of Bondaref is directed, —
a doctrine obligatory on the Old Testament man who
believes in the Scriptures, and the Christian who believes in the Scriptures, and the man that does not
believe in the Scriptures, but follows his reason alone,
and for the man that recognizes the teaching of the
truth.

Reader and dear brother, whoever you are, I love you
and not only do not wish to offend or affront you, to
bring evil into your life, but I do wish one thing, and
that is to serve you.

I might write much, and I should like to write much,
in order to prove the truth of this position, and to refute
the various and complicated arguments against it, which
are on the lips of each one of us. We know that we are

to blame, and consequently we are always ready with a justification.

But, however much I wrote, however well I wrote, however correct I might be logically, I should not persuade a reader, if he used his reason to argue against me and his heart should remain cold. I fear this, I fear the pride of my own intellect, that my coldness may injure you.

And so I ask you, reader, even though for a time you set aside the activity of your mind, not to argue, nor to prove, but merely to question your heart. Who ever you are, however gifted, however kind to the men and women around you, in whatever condition you may be, can you be contented at your tea, your dinner, your work as a government employee, as an artist, a student, a physician, a teacher, if you hear or see at your doorstep a man cold, hungry, sick, or tormented?

No!

But here they are always with us — if not at our steps, then ten yards or ten miles away. They are here, and you know it!

And you cannot be satisfied, you cannot enjoy yourself, unless you rectify this state of things. In order that you may not see them at your door, you must shut yourself away from them, you must hold them at a distance by your coldness, or else go where they are not to be found. But they are everywhere.

And even if a place were found where you would not see them, you would not get away from your consciousness of the truth. How could you? You yourself know it, and the teaching of this book tells this to you : —

"Let yourself down to him who seems to you below but is really above ; stand in line with those that are feeding the hungry, clothing the cold ; fear nothing," there will be nothing worse, but much that is better in all directions. Stand in line, put your ignorant weak hands to the first task that will feed the hungry, clothe the cold ; undertake manual labor, the struggle with nature : and you will feel for the first time the firm soil underneath

your feet; you will feel that you are at home, that you
are free and strong; and you will experience the wholesome, unpoisoned pleasures which you will not find behind closed doors or drawn curtains.

You will recognize joys which you never have known
before. You will know for the first time those simple,
strong men and women, your brethren who far away
from you, have hitherto been supporting you; and to
your amazement you will see in them such virtues as
you had not suspected before, you will see in them such
modesty, such kindliness to you yourself, especially, as
you will feel you have not deserved.

Instead of the scorn, the ridicule, which you expected,
you will see such gentleness, such gratitude, such respect for you, because after you had lived all your days
and despised them, you suddenly woke up and with un-
accustomed hands wanted to help them.

You will see that what seemed to you an island on
which you were sitting, having been sand from the sea
that swallowed you up, is a swamp in which you were
sinking; and that the sea which you feared is dry land
on which you walk firmly, calmly, joyously, as could not
be otherwise, because from the deception into which you
did not go yourself, but were led into it, you have returned to the truth; from the deviation from God's will,
you have returned to its fulfilment.

1888.

STOP AND THINK

I

THE editor of a Paris review, thinking that the opinions of two celebrated writers on the state of mind of the present day would interest me, has sent me two extracts from French newspapers, one being a speech by M. Zola, delivered at the banquet of the General Students' Association, the other a letter from M. A. Dumas to the editor of the *Gaulois*.

These extracts did indeed interest me profoundly, both on account of their seasonableness and the renown of their authors, and because it would be difficult to find in current literature in a more succinct, vigorous, and brilliant form, an expression of the two fundamental forces, the resultant of which impels humanity along. I mean on the one hand the force of routine which tends to keep humanity in its present course, and on the other that of reason and love which impels it toward the light.

M. Zola disapproves of that faith in something vague and ill-defined which their new guides are recommending to the youth of France; and counsels them to believe in something which is neither clearer nor better defined, namely, science and work.

A little-known Chinese philosopher and founder of a religion, named Lao-Tze (the first and best translation of whose book, " The Way of Virtue," is that by Stanislas Julien), takes as the foundation of his doctrine the " tao," a word meaning " reason," " way," " virtue." If men follow the law of " tao," they will be happy. But the " tao," according to M. Julien's translation, is only attainable by " not-acting."

All the ills besetting mankind arise, according to Lao-
Tze, not from man's neglect to do what is necessary,
but because he does what is unnecessary, so that if men
would practise what he calls "not-acting," they would
be rid not only of their personal calamities, but also of
those inherent in every form of government, the latter
being the subject of which the Chinese philosopher particularly treats.

Lao-Tze's idea appears strange, but it is impossible
not to agree with him if one considers what are the
results from the activities of the great majority of the
men of our century.

Let all men apply themselves to work, says M. Zola,
and work will give them health and happiness, and will
free them from the torment of the Infinite. Work, yes;
but at what are we to work? Manufacturers and sellers
of opium, tobacco, and brandy, every gambler on the
Stock Exchange, all inventors and manufacturers of
engines of destruction, all the military, all jailers and
executioners, — all work, but it is evident that humanity
would be the gainer if all these workers ceased their
work.

But perhaps M. Zola's recommendation has reference
only to such work as is inspired by science? As a matter of fact the purpose of the greater part of M. Zola's
speech is to uphold science, which he thinks is being
attacked. Well! From various unappreciated authors
I am continually receiving pamphlets, treatises, and
printed books and manuscripts, the results of their
scientific work.

One has finally decided the question of the Christian
gnosiology, another has written a book on the cosmic
ether, a third has solved the social question, a fourth the
Eastern question, a fifth edits a Theosophical Review,
a sixth (in a thick volume) solves the knight's tour
problem in chess.

All these people work assiduously and in the name of
science, but I have no hesitation in saying that the time
and work of my correspondents have been spent in a
manner not only useless but even harmful, for they have

not been the only people whose labor has been spent
on this useless work; thousands of people have been
occupied in making the paper, the type, and machines
needed to print their works, and in feeding, clothing,
and housing these scientific laborers.

Work for science? But the word science is a term so
vague and ill-defined that what some people consider to
be science is considered by others to be utterly futile,
and this is the case not only with outsiders but even
with the priests of science themselves. While those
savants who favor a spiritual explanation of life, look
upon jurisprudence, philosophy, and even theology as
the most necessary and important of sciences, the Positivists consider these very sciences as childish twaddle
devoid of scientific value; and, *vice versa*, sociology,
which the Positivists look upon as the science of
sciences, is considered by the theologians, philosophers,
and spiritualists as an arbitrary and useless collection
of observations and assertions. But more than this,
even in one and the same branch of philosophy or
natural science, each system has ardent defenders and
equally ardent detractors, equally competent, yet holding diametrically opposite opinions.

Finally, does not each year witness fresh scientific
discoveries, which, after exciting the wonder of the
mediocrities of the whole world, and bringing fame and
fortune to their inventors, are eventually found to be
nothing but ridiculous errors even by those who pro-
mulgated them?

We all know that what the Romans looked upon as
science par excellence, as the most important of occupations, and one which showed how superior they were to
the barbarians, was rhetoric, that is to say, an exercise
which nowadays is regarded with derision, which with
us does not even rank as a science. It is equally
difficult for us to understand the state of mind of the
learned during the Middle Ages, who were quite convinced that all science was centered in scholasticism.

Unless, then, our century be quite an exception, —
which we have no right to suppose, — but little reflec-

tion is required to convince us that, among the subjects
principally engrossing the attention of our learned men
to-day, there are some which will be looked upon by our
descendants as we now look upon the rhetoric of the
ancients and the scholasticism of the Middle Ages.

II

M. ZOLA'S speech is chiefly directed against certain
leaders who are trying to direct the younger generation
back to religious beliefs; for M. Zola, as a champion of
science, looks upon himself as their opponent; but in
reality such is not the case, for his reasoning is based
upon the same foundation as that of his adversaries : on
faith, as he himself admits.

It is a generally received opinion that religion and
science are opposed to each other.   And such is really
the case,. but only with reference to any given time.
That is to say, what has been regarded by the people
of one time as science very often becomes religion for
their descendants.   What is usually connoted by the
term religion is generally the science of the past, while
that which is called science is to a large extent the
religion of the present.

We say that the statements of the Hebrews that the
world was created in six days, that children are punished
for the sins of their fathers, that certain maladies can be
cured by the sight of a serpent, are the data of religion ;
while we call data of science the statements of our contemporaries that the world created itself while turning
around a center which is everywhere, that all the various species arose from the struggle for existence, that
criminals are the product of heredity, that there exist
micro-organisms in the shape of commas which cause
certain diseases.   It is easy to see by reverting in imagination to the state of mind of an ancient Hebrew, that
for him the creation of the world in six days, the wound-
curing serpent, etc., served as the data of science at its
highest degree of development, just as for a man of our

time do the laws of Darwin, the commas of Koch, heredity, etc.

And just as it was not exactly in the creation of the world in six days, the wound-curing serpent, etc., that the Hebrew believed, but rather in the infallibility of his priests, and hence in the truth of their assertions; even so the great majority of the cultured people of our time believe neither in the formation of the world by rotation, nor in heredity, nor in comma-like bacilli, but in the infallibility of their lay priests who are called scientists, who affirm whatever they pretend to know, with the same assurance as did the Hebrew priests.

I will even say that if the priests of old, amenable to no control save that of their colleagues, permitted themselves sometimes to digress from the truth merely for the pleasure of astonishing and mystifying their public, the priests of modern science have done as much, with equal effrontery.

The greater part of what is called religion is but the superstition of the past; the greater part of what is called science is no more than the superstition of the present day. The proportion of error and of truth is, I suspect, about the same in the one as in the other. Hence to work in the name of any belief, be it religious or scientific, is not only a doubtful means of ameliorating the life of mankind, but it is a dangerous proceeding which may produce more harm than good.

To consecrate one's life to the fulfilment of the duties imposed by religion, — prayers, communion, almsgiving; or, following the advice of M. Zola, to devote it to some scientific work, — is to run too great a risk, for one may find on the eve of one's death that the religious or scientific principle, in whose service one has spent one's whole life, is nothing but an absurd mistake!

Even before reading the speech in which M. Zola holds up work, whatever kind it may be, as a kind of virtue, I had always been astonished at the strange opinion (current especially in Western Europe) in regard to work. I always felt that it was excusable only in an irrational creature, such as the ant in the fable, to elevate work

to the rank of a virtue and to make a boast of it.
M. Zola assures us that work makes men kind; the
contrary has always been true in my experience. Without considering selfish work, which is always bad, the
object of which is the well-being or aggrandizement of
the worker, even "work for its own sake," the pride of
the worker, renders both ants and men cruel. Which
of us does not know these men, untouched by considerations of truth and kindliness, who are always so busy
that they not only never have time to do good, but cannot even ask themselves whether their work is not harmful? You say to these people: "Your work is useless,
perhaps even pernicious, for the following reasons;
pause and consider them for a moment." They will
not listen to you, but scornfully reply: "You men have
leisure to reason about such matters, but what time have
I for discussions? I have worked all my life and work
does not wait; I have to edit a daily paper with a circulation of half a million; I have the army to organize, the
Eiffel Tower to build, the Chicago Exhibition to arrange,
to cut through the Isthmus of Panama, to make investigations on the subject of heredity, telepathy, or to find out
the number of times such and such a word occurs in the
works of such and such a classic author."

The most cruel of men, the Neros and the Peter the
Greats, have been constantly active, never pausing or
giving themselves a moment free from occupation or
distraction.

Even if work is not a vice, it can from no point of
view be looked upon as a merit.

Work can no more be considered a virtue than can
nutrition; work is a necessity of which one cannot be
deprived without suffering, and to elevate it to the rank
of a merit is as monstrous as it would be to do the like
for nutrition. The only explanation of this strange
value attributed to work in our society is that our
ancestors regarded laziness as an attribute of nobil-
ity, almost of merit, and that people of our time are
still somewhat influenced by the reaction from that
prejudice.

Work, the exercise of our organs, cannot be meritorious, for it is simply a physical necessity of man in common with all other animals, as is shown by a tethered calf galloping round and round, or, among ourselves, by the silly exercises to which rich and well-fed people of the leisured classes betake themselves, finding no better use for their mental faculties than reading novels and newspapers, or playing chess and cards, or for their muscles than gymnastics, fencing, lawn tennis, and horse-racing.

In my opinion, not only is work not a virtue, but in our defectively organized society it is more often a means of moral anæsthesia, just as are tobacco, wine, and other means of drowning thought and hiding from ourselves the disorder and emptiness of our lives; and it is precisely as such that M. Zola recommends work for young people.

III

THERE is a great difference between the letter of M. Dumas and the speech of M. Zola, without mentioning the external difference, namely, that the speech of M. Zola seems to court the approbation of the young men to whom it is addressed; whilst the letter of M. Dumas does not flatter young men, does not tell them that they are important persons and that everything depends on them (a notion which they ought never to cherish if they wish to be good for anything), but, on the contrary, points out to them their habitual faults, their presumption, and their levity. The principal difference between these two articles is that the speech of M. Zola aims at keeping men in the path they are in, by making them think that what they know is precisely what is necessary for them to know, and that what they are doing is exactly what they ought to do; whilst the letter of M. Dumas shows them that they are ignorant of the essentials of what they ought to know, and are not living as they should live.

The more men believe that they can be moved to a better state of things without effort of their own, by some external force acting of itself, whether religion or science, and that they have only to work on in the existing order, — with the more difficulty will this change be accomplished; and it is in this, above all, that the speech of M. Zola errs.

On the contrary, the more men believe that it only depends on themselves to modify their relations toward one another, and that they can do so when they will, by loving one another instead of tearing one another to pieces as they now do, the more will such change become possible. The more men allow themselves to follow this suggestion, the more will they be drawn to realize the prediction of M. Dumas. And in this lies the great merit of M. Dumas's letter.

M. Dumas does not belong to any party or to any religion; he has as little faith in the superstitions of the past as in those of the present, and it is just for this reason that he observes, that he thinks, and that he sees, not only the present but also the future, in the same way as those who in ancient times were called seers. It may appear strange to those who, when reading an author's works, see only the contents of his book and not the soul of the author, that M. Dumas — who wrote " La Dame aux Camélias " and " L'Affaire Clémenceau " — that this same Dumas sees into the future and prophesies. But, however strange it may seem, prophecy, though uttered not in the desert, nor by Jordan's banks, nor from the mouth of a hermit clothed in skins of beasts, but appearing in a daily paper on the banks of the Seine, — it is none the less prophecy.

The words of M. Dumas have all the characteristics of a prophecy : first, they are entirely opposed to the general ideas of the people in the midst of whom they are uttered; secondly, all who hear them feel their truth; and thirdly, above all, it urges men to realize what it foretells.

M. Dumas predicts that men, after having tried

everything, will begin seriously to apply to life the law of brotherly love, and that this change will come about sooner than one expects. The proximity of this change, even its possibility, may be disputed; but it is evident that, if it does come about, it will solve all contradictions, all difficulties, and will avert all the ills which the end of our century threatens.

The only objection, or rather the only question, that can be put to M. Dumas is : If love of our neighbor is possible to, and inherent in, human nature, why have so many thousand years passed (for the command to love God and one's neighbor is not a command of Christ, but dates back to Moses) during which men have known this means of happiness and yet have not practised it? What cause prevents the manifestation of a sentiment so natural and so beneficent to humanity?

It is evident that it is not enough to say : Love one another. That has been said for three thousand years; it has been continually repeated in all tones, from all platforms, religious and even secular, but men continue none the less to exterminate instead of love one another. In the present day no one can doubt that if men, instead of tearing one another to pieces, — each seeking his own happiness, that of his family, or that of his country, — would but help one another; if they would replace selfishness by love, and would organize their lives on the communistic instead of the individualistic principle (as the sociologists like to express it in their barbarous jargon); if they loved one another as each loves himself, if, at least, they did not do to others what they would not like done to them, as was said two thousand years ago, — the amount gained of that personal happiness which each man seeks would be greater, and human life in general would be reasonable and happy instead of being what it is now, a succession of contradictions and sufferings.

No one doubts but that if men continue to take away from one another the ownership of the land and the products of their labor, a retaliation by those who have been thus robbed must be expected, and that the op-

pressed will retake with violence and vengeance what
they have been deprived of. Every one knows also that
the preparations for war made by the different nations
lead on to terrible massacres, to the ruin and degenera-
tion of all the peoples who participate in this circle of
armaments. No one doubts but that if the present order
of things be prolonged for some dozens of years, the
result will be ruin, imminent and general. We have
only to open our eyes to see the abyss toward which
we are advancing. But it seems that Christ's prophecy
is fulfilled among the men of to-day; they have ears to
be deaf with, and eyes to be blind with, they have reason
to misunderstand with.

The men of to-day continue to live as they have always
lived, and do not leave off doing what must inevitably
lead to their ruin. Moreover, the men of our Christian
society acknowledge, if not the religious law of love, at
least the moral obligation of the Christian principle,
"not to do to others what they would not that others
do to them," but they do not act upon it. Evidently
some secret but overwhelming reason prevents them
from doing what is to their advantage — what would
save them from the dangers that menace them, and
what the law of their God and their conscience alike
dictate to them. Are we to conclude that love applied
to life is a chimera? If so, how is it that for so many
centuries men have allowed themselves to be deluded by
this unrealizable dream? It must be high time to recognize its futility. But mankind can neither resolve to follow the law of love in their lives nor to give up the idea.

Why is this? What is the reason of this contradiction, enduring so many centuries? It is not because men
of our day lack either the desire or the possibility to do
what is dictated to them, both by their common sense
and by the danger of their position, and above all, by the
law of that which they speak of as God and their conscience. But it is just because they are doing what M.
Zola advises them to do: they are so busy, they are all
so engrossed in work commenced long ago, and it is
impossible for them to pause to collect their thoughts

and consider what they ought to be. All great revolutions in the life of men commence in thought. Let but a change take place in men's thoughts, and action will follow the direction of the thought as certainly as the ship follows the direction of the rudder.

IV

In the words of His first sermon Christ did not tell men to love one another (He taught this to His disciples later on), but, like John the Baptist before Him, He preached repentance, μετάνοια, that is to say, a change of opinion with regard to life : μετανοεῖτε, change your conception of life, said He, or you will all perish. The meaning of your life cannot consist in the pursuit of your personal well-being, or in that of your family or your nation, because that well-being can be attained only by detriment of that of your neighbor. Know then that the meaning of your life can lie only in fulfilling the will of Him who sent you into this life, and who demands from you, not the pursuit of your personal interests, but the accomplishment of His own purpose : the establishment of the Kingdom of Heaven.

Μετανοεῖτε, change your conception of life, or you will all perish, said He, eighteen hundred years ago ; and, to-day, this is incessantly urged by all the contradictions and all the ills of our time, results of the fact that men have not heeded, and have not accepted the conception of life which he proposed to them. Μετανοεῖτε, said He, or you will all perish. And the alternative is still the same. The only difference is that now it is more pressing. If, two thousand years ago, at the time of the Roman Empire, even at the time of Charles V., or even before the Revolution and the Napoleonic wars, it was possible not to see the vanity, I will even say the absurdity, of attempting to insure personal happiness, the welfare of the family, the nation, or the State, by struggling against all who seek the same thing, — that illusion has now become absolutely impossible to any man who

will pause in his work, be it only for a moment, and
reflect upon what he is, upon the state of the world about
him, and upon what he ought to be. If, then, I were
asked for the most important advice I could give, that
which I considered to be the most useful to the men of
our century, I should simply say : In the name of God,
stop a moment, cease your work, look around you, consider what you are and what you ought to be, — think
of the ideal.

M. Zola says that people should not aspire, or believe
in a superior power, or trouble about the ideal. Perhaps M. Zola understands by the word "ideal," either
the supernatural, that is to say, the theological rubbish
about the Trinity, the Church, and the Pope, etc., or *the
unexplained*, as he calls the vast forces of the universe
into which we are plunged. And in this case men would
do well to follow M. Zola's advice. But, in reality, the
ideal is neither supernatural nor unexplained. On the
contrary, it is the most natural of things ; I will not say
it is the most thoroughly explained, but it appeals to
the human mind with more certainty than anything else.

The ideal in geometry is the perfectly straight line,
and the circle the radii of which are equal ; in science, it
is exact truths ; in morals, perfect virtue. Although all
these things, straight line, exact truth, and perfect virtue
alike, have never existed, not only are they more natural,
more known, and more *explicable* than all our other knowledge ; but they are the only things we truly and certainly
do know.

It is commonly said that reality is that which exists,
or in other words, only that which exists is real. The
contrary is, however, the case ; the true reality, that
which we truly know, is that which never existed. The
ideal is the only thing which we know with certainty,
and it has never existed. It is only thanks to the ideal
that we know anything at all, and that is why the ideal
alone can guide mankind in their lives, both individually
and collectively. The Christian ideal has been before
us for eighteen centuries ; it shines in our time with such
intensity that it is extremely difficult to avoid seeing that

all our ills proceed from the fact that we do not accept
its guidance; but the more difficult it becomes not to
see this, the greater are the efforts made by some people
to persuade us to do as they do, to close our eyes so as
not to see it. In order to be absolutely certain to arrive
safely in port, we ought, before all else, to throw over-
board the compass, say they, and forge ahead. Men of
our Christian society resemble people who, desiring to
pull down some object which annoys them, drag at it in
opposite directions, and have no time to agree as to the
direction in which they ought to pull. It is only necessary that a man of our day should cease his activity for
a moment and reflect, — comparing the demands of his
reason and of his heart with the actual conditions of his
life, — in order to perceive that his whole life and
his every action are in incessant and outrageous contradiction to his reason and his heart. If you were to
inquire separately of every civilized human being what
are the most moral bases of his conduct, nearly every
man would tell you that they are the Christian principles,
or at any rate those of justice. In saying this men are
sincere. If they acted according to their conscience,
men would live as Christians; but it is only necessary
to watch them to see that they live like wild beasts. So
that for the great majority of men in the Christian world,
the organization of their life is not the result of their
way of seeing and feeling, but of certain forms which
were once necessary, but which now only survive by
reason of the inertia of social life.

V

If in past times, — when the evils produced by the
pagan way of life were not so evident as now, and,
more important still, the Christian principles were not so
generally accepted, — men could consciously uphold the
bondage of the workers, the oppression of man by man,
penal law, and, above all, war, — it has become completely impossible at the present time to explain the
raison d'être of all these institutions.

In order that men should change their way of living
and feeling, they must first of all change their way of
thinking; and in order that such a change should come
about, men must stop and give their attention to what they
ought to understand.   To hear what those who wish to
save them are shouting, men who run singing toward
the precipice must cease their hubbub and stop short.

Let the people of our Christian society pause in their
work and reflect for a moment on the state of their
lives, and involuntarily they will be led to accept the
conception of life given by Christianity; a conception
so natural, so simple, and answering so completely the
needs of the heart and mind of humanity, that it would
arise almost spontaneously in the understanding of any
one willing to liberate himself, were it but for a moment,
from the entanglement in which he is held by the complications of his own work and the work of others.

For eighteen centuries the feast has been ready; but
one man does not come because he has bought a piece
of ground, another because he has married a wife, a
third because he must go and try his oxen, a fourth
because he is constructing a railway, a factory, doing
missionary work, working in Parliament, in a bank, or
at some scientific, artistic, or literary production.   For
two thousand years nobody has had the leisure to do
what Jesus advised at the beginning of His ministry:
to look around him, to consider the results of our work,
and to ask himself: *What* am I? *For* what?   Can it
be that this force, which has produced me with my reason
and my desire to love and be loved, has operated only
in order to deceive me; so that, having imagined the
aim of my life to be my personal well-being, — that my
life belongs to me and that I have the right to dispose
of it and the lives of other beings as I please, — I should
arrive at the conviction that this personal, family, or
national well-being cannot be attained; and that the
more I strive to attain it, the more I should find myself
in contradiction with my reason and the desire to love
and be loved, and the more I should experience disillu-
sionment and suffering?   Is it not more probable that,

not having come into the world spontaneously, but by the will of Him who sent me, my reason and my desire to love and be loved have been given to guide me in the accomplishment of that will?

Once that μετάνοια has taken place in the thought of man, — a pagan and egoistic conception of life replaced by the Christian conception, — the love of one's neighbor will become more natural than strife and egoism are at present. And when once the love of one's neighbor has become natural to man, the new conditions of the Christian life will come about spontaneously, just as in a liquid saturated with salt the crystals commence to form the moment one ceases to stir it.

And in order that such a result should come about and that men should organize in conformity with their conscience, no positive effort is necessary; on the contrary, we have only to stop in the efforts we are now making. If man only employed the hundredth part of his energy, now spent entirely contrary to his conscience in material occupations, to elucidate as much as possible the data of his conscience, to express these as clearly as possible, to make them known, and above all to practise them, the change foretold by M. Dumas and by all the prophets would be accomplished much more quickly and easily than we think, and man would acquire that good which Jesus proclaimed in His good news: " Seek the Kingdom of Heaven and all other things will be added unto you." [1]

[1] This essay was written by Tolstoï in 1893, first in Russian and then (after a mutilated version had appeared in France) again in French. From the latter this version is made. — TR.

MODERN SCIENCE

INTRODUCTION TO A RUSSIAN TRANSLATION OF EDWARD CARPENTER'S ESSAY, "MODERN SCIENCE"

I THINK that Carpenter's essay on Modern Science [1] may be especially useful to our Russian society, where, more than in any other in Europe, is spread the superstitious belief that, for the good of humanity, it is not at all necessary to propagate true religious and moral knowledge, but only to study the experimental sciences, and that a knowledge of these sciences will satisfy all the spiritual demands of humanity.

It is obvious what a pernicious influence (similar to that of religious superstitions) such a crude superstition must have on the moral life of men, and therefore the dissemination of the thoughts of writers who critically examine the results and methods of the experimental sciences is especially desirable in our society.

Carpenter proves that neither astronomy, nor physics, nor chemistry, nor biology, nor sociology gives us a true knowledge of actual facts, but that all the "laws" discovered by these sciences are only generalizations, which have but an approximate value as laws, and that only owing to ignorance or disregard of other factors. Further, that even these laws appear to be laws to us only because we discover them in a domain so distant from us in time and space that we cannot perceive their want of correspondence with actual fact.

Besides this, Carpenter also points out that the method of science, consisting in the explanation of phenomena

---

[1] "Modern Science: A Criticism. Civilization, its Cause and Cure, and other Essays." By Edward Carpenter.

356

near and important to us by phenomena more distant from and indifferent to us, is a false method which can never lead to the desired results.

"Each science," he says, "has been (as far as possible) reduced to its lowest terms. Ethics has been made a question of utility and inherited experience. Political economy has been exhausted of all conceptions of justice between man and man, of charity, affection, and the instinct of solidarity; and has been founded on its lowest discoverable factor, namely, self-interest. Biology has been denuded of the force of personality in plants, animals, and men; the "self" here has been set aside, and the attempt made to reduce the science to a question of chemical and cellular affinities, protoplasm, and the laws of osmose. Chemical affinities, again, and all the wonderful phenomena of physics are emptied down into a flight of atoms; and the flight of atoms (and of astronomic orbs as well) is reduced to the laws of dynamics. ....."

It is supposed that to reduce higher questions to terms of lower ones will explain the higher. But this explanation is never attained, and what happened is that, descending lower and lower in its investigations, from the most essential questions to those less essential, science at last reaches a domain quite foreign to man, and only adjacent to him, to which domain it confines its attention, leaving without any solution all questions most important for man.

What occurs is something similar to what the result would be if a man, desiring to understand the nature of an object before him, should, instead of approaching it, examining it on all sides, and handling it, remove farther and farther from it, finally removing to such a distance that all details of color and unevenness of surface should disappear, and there remained only the outline which detached it from the horizon. And from such a distance the man might begin to describe this object in detail, imagining that he has now a clear understanding of it, and that this idea, conceived at such a distance, would contribute to a complete understanding of the object. This self-delusion is partly exposed by Carpenter's criticism, which, in the first place points out that the knowledge science gives us in the sphere of natural science consists only of convenient modes of generalization, which by no means express actual facts; and secondly, that the method of science by which the phenomena of a higher order are reduced to the phenomena of a lower order, will never enable us to arrive at an explanation of the phenomena of the higher order.

But without settling beforehand the question whether the method of the experimental sciences can or cannot achieve a solution of the problems of life most important for humanity, the activity itself of the experimental sciences, considered in relation to the eternal and most legitimate demands of humanity, impresses one by its fallacy.

Men must live. And in order to live they must know how to live. All men always — well or ill — have learnt this, and in accordance with their knowledge, have lived and progressed. And this knowledge of how men should live has always, since the times of Moses, Solon, Confucius, been considered a science — the very science of sciences; and it is only in our time that it has begun to be considered that the science of how to live is not a science at all, but that true science is only experimental science, beginning with mathematics and ending with sociology.

And a strange misunderstanding ensues.

A simple and sensible working-man — according to the old sense and common sense as well — supposes that if there are men studying all their lives, and who think for him in return for being fed and provided for by him, then these men are probably engaged in studying what is needful for man, and he expects from science that it will solve for him those questions on which depend his welfare and that of all men. He expects that science will teach him how to live; how to act toward the members of his own family, his neighbors, and those of other countries; how to struggle with his passions;

in what he should and should not believe, and much besides. And what does our science reply?

It triumphantly announces how many millions of miles the sun is from the earth, with what rapidity light traverses space, how many millions of undulations of the ether a second are produced by light, and how many undulations of atmosphere by sound; it tells of the chemical composition of the Milky Way; it tells of a new element, helion, of micro-organisms and their excrements, of the points in the hand where electricity concentrates, of X-rays, and so on.

" But all this is not at all what I am in need of knowing," says the simple, sensible man. " I want to know how to live."

"I don't care what you are in need of knowing," replies science, " what you ask for refers to sociology. But before answering questions of sociology we must settle questions of zoölogy, botany, physiology — in short, biology. And in order to settle these questions it is first necessary to solve questions of physics, of chemistry; it is necessary also to agree as to the form of the infinitesimal atoms, and as to how it is that the ether with neither weight nor resistance transmits force."

And men, chiefly those who sit on the backs of others, and who can therefore conveniently wait, are satisfied by such answers, and continue sitting and yawning, awaiting what was promised. But the simple and sensible working-man, he on whose back the men studying science are sitting, the great mass of people, humanity at large, cannot be satisfied with such replies, and naturally ask in wonder, " But when will that be? We cannot wait. You yourselves say that you will find out all this after several generations. But we live, we are alive to-day and to-morrow we shall die, and therefore we must know how we are to live the life we are in now. Teach us, then."

"The stupid and ignorant man!" answers science; " he does not understand that what science serves is not utility but science. Science investigates that which is subject to investigation, and cannot choose the objects of its study. Science studies everything. Such is the nature of science."

Men of science are indeed convinced that the characteristic of attending to trifles and neglecting things more substantial and important is not their own characteristic, but that of science. But the simple, sensible man begins to suspect that this characteristic belongs, not to science, but to those who are inclined to occupy themselves with trifles, attaching to these trifles great importance.

"Science studies everything," say the men of science. But there is too much of everything. Everything means an infinite quantity of objects, and it is impossible to study all at once. As a lantern cannot light up everything but only the place it is directed toward, so also science cannot investigate everything, but inevitably investigates only that to which its attention is directed. And as the lantern throws the strongest light on the place nearest to it, weaker and weaker light on more remote objects, and does not light up at all those objects which its light cannot reach; so also human science, of whatever kind, has always investigated and is investigating in most detail that which appears to the investigators to be most important, studying in less detail what appears to them less important, and not at all concerning itself with all the remaining infinite quantity of objects.

The standard which has defined and defines for men the very important, the less important, and the unimportant is men's general understanding of the sense and object of life, *i.e.* religion.

But our modern men of science, not acknowledging any religion, — and therefore possessing no basis upon which they might select objects for study according to the degree of their importance, separating the most important from the less important, and from that vast number of objects which will always remain uninvestigated because of the limitations of the human mind and their infinite quantity, — have invented for themselves a theory of "science for science's sake," according to which science studies, not what is necessary to men, but everything.

Indeed, experimental science does study everything, only not in the sense of the totality of objects, but in the sense of disorder and chaos in the distribution of the investigated subjects, *i.e.* science does not most investigate what is most needed by men, less what is less needed, and not at all what is not needed, but investigates, haphazard, anything it comes across. Although there do exist classifications of the sciences by Comte and others, these classifications do not direct the choice of subjects for investigation, this being directed by human weaknesses inherent in men of science as in all men.

So that in reality experimental scientists do not, as they imagine and assert, study everything, but that which is more advantageous and easier for them to study. It is more advantageous to study what may contribute to the welfare of those higher classes to which the men occupied with science themselves belong, and it is easier to study things devoid of life. And this is what the investigators of experimental science do: they study books, monuments, and dead bodies, and this study they regard as the most real science.

So that what in our time is regarded as the true and only "science" (in the sense that the "Bible" was once called the only book worthy of the name) is not the investigation of how to make the life of men better and happier, but consists in collecting and copying out of many books into one what was written concerning a certain subject by former men, or in pouring liquids from one vial into another, in skilfully dissecting microscopic preparations, in cultivating bacteria, in cutting up frogs and dogs, in investigating the X-rays, the chemical composition of the stars, and so forth.

And all those sciences the object of which is to make human life better and happier — religious, moral, and social sciences — are not regarded as sciences by the reigning science, and are relegated to the theologians, philosophers, jurists, historians, and political economists, who are occupied, under the pretense of scientific investigation, only in proving that the existing order of life, which puts them in an advantageous position, is precisely the one which should exist, and should, therefore, not only not be reformed, but be maintained by all means.

Not to speak of theology, philosophy, and jurisprudence, very noticeable in this respect is the most fashionable of this kind of science — political economy. The political economy most widely spread (that of Marx), acknowledging the existing order of life to be normal, not only does not now require of men the reformation of this order, *i.e.* does not point out how men should live in order that their condition might be improved, but, on the contrary, demands the continuation of the cruelty of the present state of things in order that the more than doubtful prophecies of what will happen if men continue to live as badly as they do at present, should be realized.

And, as always happens, the lower a human activity descends, the farther it recedes from what it should be, the more its self-assertion increases. This has happened with the science of our time. True science has never been appreciated by its contemporaries, but, on the contrary, has for the most part been persecuted. And it could not be otherwise. True science indicates to men their errors, and points to new, unusual ways of life, both of which services are obnoxious to the ruling part of society. Whereas the present science not only refrains from counteracting the tastes and demands of the ruling part of society, but completely coincides with them; it satisfies idle curiosity, astonishes people, and promises them increase of pleasure. And so, whereas all that is truly great is quiet, modest, imperceptible, the science of our time knows no limits to its self-glorification.

"All former methods were erroneous, and thus all that was formerly regarded as science is fraudulent, fallacious, frivolous. Our method is the only true one, ours the only true science. The progress of our science is such that thousands of years have not attained what we have achieved in the last century. In the future, by following in the same path, our science will solve all questions, and give happiness to all humanity. Our science is the most important activity in the world, and we men of science the most important and necessary men on earth."

So think and say the men of science of our time, and yet, seen in its full significance, no science in any age or nation has stood on so low a plane as the present one. One part of it, that which should study the means of making human life good and happy, is occupied in justifying the existing bad order of life, and the other is absorbed with the solution of questions of idle curiosity.

"How idle curiosity?" I hear exclaimed by voices indignant at such blasphemy. "How about steam, electricity, telephones, and all our technical improvements? Not to speak of their scientific importance, observe the practical results they have achieved. Man has conquered nature, subjected its forces to himself".... and so on.

"But," replies the simple and sensible man, "all the practical results of man's victory over nature from long ago up to the present, are applied to manufactures injurious to the people; to means for exterminating men, to increasing luxury, dissoluteness; and therefore, man's victory over nature has not increased the welfare of men, but, on the contrary, made their condition worse."

If the organization of a society is bad, as ours is, where a small number of men dominate the majority and oppress them, then every victory over nature will inevitably only serve to increase this power and this oppression. And so it happens.

With a science taking as its subject, not the investigation of how people should live, but of what exists, and therefore occupied chiefly in investigating inanimate objects, and meanwhile leaving the organization of human society as it is, — with such science no improvements, no victories over nature, can improve the condition of men.

"And medical science? You forget its beneficial achievements. And inoculation with bacteria! And modern surgical operations!" generally exclaim the defenders of science, who, as their last resort, bring forward the successes of medicine in proof of the fruitfulness of all science.

"We can by inoculation prevent disease and cure it, we can perform painless operations, we can cut open and treat the vital organs of the body, we can straighten deformity," generally say the advocates of science, thinking somehow, that a child cured of diphtheria (one out of thousands of children who, in Russia, independently of diphtheria, average a death rate of 50 per cent and in foundling asylums 80 per cent) must convince people of the usefulness of science in general.

The order of our life is such that not only children, but the majority of adults, through bad food, heavy, injurious work, bad dwellings, bad clothes, and many hardships, do not live half so long as they should ; it is such that children's diseases, syphilis, consumption, and alcoholism are getting a firmer and firmer hold of men, that a great part of the results of men's labor is taken from them for preparations for war, and that every ten or twenty years millions of men are exterminated by war. And all this occurs because science, instead of spreading amongst men correct religious, moral, and social ideas which would cause all these calamities to disappear of themselves, is occupied on the one hand with the justification of the existing order, and on the other hand with playthings. And in proof of the fruitfulness of science we are reminded that it cures one out of a thousand of those invalids who in reality become ill precisely because science does not fulfil its natural function.

If even a small portion of its efforts, of that attention and toil which science devotes to the trifles it is occupied with, had been directed toward the development amongst men of correct religious, moral, social, and even hygienic notions, there would not have occurred a hundredth part of those diphtherias, women's diseases, and deformities upon the curing of which science so prides itself, effecting these cures in hospitals, the luxurious appointments of which cannot be accessible to all.

It is just as if men who had badly ploughed a field and badly sown it with bad seed should walk on this field and treat some broken ears of corn, meanwhile trampling on the rest ; and should then exhibit this art of treating the broken ears as a proof of their knowledge of agriculture.

Our science, in order to become a science and to be really useful instead of harmful to humanity, must first of all renounce its experimental method, which causes it to consider as its business merely the study of what exists, and return to the only wise and fruitful understanding of science, according to which its subject is the investigation of how men must live. In this is the object and meaning of science, whereas, the investigation of what exists can be the subject of science only to the extent to which this investigation contributes to the knowledge of how men should live.

It is precisely this acknowledgment of the incompetency of experimental science and of the necessity of adopting another method that is expressed in Carpenter's essay.

1898.

PREFACE TO AMIEL'S JOURNAL

A YEAR and a half ago, I had the privilege of reading Amiel's book — "Fragments d'un journal intime." I was struck by the significance and depth of the subject, the beauty of the thought, and, above all, the sincerity of the book. In reading it I made note of those passages that especially struck me. My daughter undertook to translate these passages, and thus arose these extracts from Amiel's Private Journal; that is, extracts from extracts of Amiel's very voluminous, unprinted journal kept by him from day to day in the course of thirty years.

Henri Amiel was born in 1821, in Geneva, and was early left an orphan. Having completed a course of higher education in Geneva, Amiel went abroad and then spent some years in the universities of Heidelberg and Berlin. After his return to his own country in 1849, though only twenty-eight years old, he received the appointment in the Geneva Academy, first as Professor of Æsthetics and then of Philosophy, and there he remained until his death.

Amiel's whole life was spent in Geneva, where he died in 1881, in no wise distinguished from the great number of those very ordinary professors who, mechanically compiling their lectures from the latest books in their specialty, likewise mechanically repeat them to their hearers, and from the still larger number of unrestrained versifiers who offer their unnecessary but still salable wares to journals having a circulation of tens of thousands. Amiel had not the slightest success either in teaching or in the domain of literature. He was nearing old age when he wrote the following about himself : —

"What have I been able to extract from the talents which were given to me, from the peculiar conditions of my half-century life? Are all my scribblings, collected together, my correspondence, *these thousands of sincere pages*, my lectures, my articles, my verses, my various memoranda, anything else than dry leaves? To whom and to what have I ever been of any use? Will my name last one day longer than I, and will it mean anything to any one? — An empty life." [1]

After Amiel's death two well-known French authors wrote about him and his diary: his friend, the well-known critic, Edmond Schérer, and the philosopher Caro. Curious was the sympathetic but somewhat condescending tone with which these two writers treated Amiel, and they regretted that he lacked the qualities necessary for a perfectly genuine work. But meantime the genuine labors of these two writers — E. Schérer's critical works and Caro's philosophical writings — have barely outlived their authors; while Amiel's unexpected non-genuine work, his diary, remains a book forever alive, necessary for men, fruitfully affecting their lives.

A writer is dear and necessary to us only in proportion as he opens to us the inner laboratory of his soul, if being taken for granted, of course, that his work is new, and not something done before. Whatever he may have written, — a drama, a text-book, a story, a philosophical treatise, a lyrical poem, a criticism, a satire, — we care only for the inner work of his soul as displayed in the production, and not for the architectural construction according to which he arranges his thoughts and feelings, while largely, and I think always, maiming them.

---

[1] " *Est-ce que toutes mes paperasses réunies, ma correspondance, ces milliers de pages intimes, mes cours, mes articles, mes rimes, mes notes diverses sont autre chose que des feuilles sèches ? A qui et à quoi aurai-je été utile? Est-ce que mon nom durera un jour et signifier a-t-il quelque chose pour quelqu'un ? — Vie nulle.* Vol. II., p. 190, 191.

Everything Amiel molded in ready form — his lectures, treatises, verses — is dead; his diary, where, without thinking of form, he spoke with himself, is full of life, vigor, instruction, consolation, and will always remain one of the best books, such as have been unwittingly left to us by men like Marcus Aurelius, Pascal, and Epictetus.

Pascal said : —

" There are only three kinds of men : first, those who, finding God, serve Him; secondly, those who, not finding Him, are occupied in the search for Him; and thirdly, those who neither find Him nor seek for Him.

" The first are reasonable and happy; the last are unreasonable and unhappy; those between are unhappy but reasonable."

I think that the distinction established by Pascal between the first and the second classes, — between those who, as he says, finding God, serve Him with all their hearts, and those who, not finding Him, seek Him with all their hearts, — is not only not so great as he imagined, but does not even exist at all. I think that those who with all their hearts and with agony, — *en gémissant*, as Pascal says, — seek God, are already serving Him. They are serving Him by the fact that by these sufferings their searchings "trace out and open the way for others to reach God," as Pascal himself did in his "Thoughts," and as Amiel did all his life in his journal.

All Amiel's life, as it is presented to us in this journal, was full of this passionate, painful search for God; and the contemplation of this search is the more instructive that it never ceases to be a search, never pauses, never passes over into a consciousness of having discovered the truth, never into preaching.

Amiel never says to himself or to others, "I know the truth now; hear me!" On the contrary, it seems to him, as is characteristic of one who honestly seeks the truth, that the more he knows the more he needs to know, and he unceasingly does all he can to discover more and more of it, and then he is constantly conscious of his ignorance. He keeps conjecturing what Christianity and the condition of the Christian should be, never for a minute pausing on the thought that Christianity is the thing which he professes, and that he himself realizes in his own case the condition of a Christian.

And meantime his whole journal is full of expressions of the deepest Christian understanding and feeling. And these expressions affect the reader with especial force, owing to their very unconsciousness and sincerity. He talks to himself, not thinking of any one hearing him, not striving to seem to believe in what he does not believe, not concealing his sufferings and his searchings.

It is as if you were present without the knowledge of the master at the most mysterious and the profoundest and the most passionate inner work of the soul, ordinarily concealed from the sight of strangers.

And so you may find many far more artistic and eloquent expressions of religious feeling than Amiel's, but it would be difficult to find any more sincere or soul-affecting.

Not long before his death, knowing that his illness might at any moment end with suffocation, he wrote : —

" When one does not dream of having before one a decade, a year, a month of reprieve, when one cannot reckon on more than a dozen hours, and the next night brings the threat of the unknown, it is evident that one must renounce art, science, politics, and be content to commune with oneself, and this is possible even to the very end. This interior soliloquy is the sole resource of the man condemned to death when the execution of the sentence is delayed. He collects himself in his inmost tribunal. He no longer radiates, he psychologizes. He no longer acts, he contemplates. .... Like the hare he returns to his ' form ' to die, and this ' form ' is his conscience, his thought. It is also his *journal intime.* As long as he can hold his pen, and while he has a moment of solitude, he collects himself before this echo of himself, and converses with his God.

" Nevertheless there is not here a moral examination, an act of contrition, a cry of help. It is only an Amen of submission. .... ' My child, give me thy heart.'

" Renunciation and acquiescence are less difficult to me than to others, for I wish nothing. I should wish only not to suffer, but Jesus at Gethsemane believed that he might offer the same prayer : let us join as he did these words, *Nevertheless not my will but Thine be done*, and let us wait." [1]

Such he was on the eve of his death. He was not any the less frank and grave all through his journal, notwithstanding its beauty, and the refinement of his language, shown in many places and grown to be habitual with him. In the course of the whole thirty years of his journal he feels what we are all so apt to forget, that we are all condemned to death and our execution is only postponed. And this is what causes this book to be so frank, serious, and useful.

1893.

[1] Vol. II., pp. 318, 319.

THOUGHTS ON GOD [1]

I

GOD is for me what I strive for — what as I strive for it constitutes my life, and therefore for me He *is*; but He is necessarily such that I cannot comprehend or name Him.

If I understood Him, I should have reached Him, and there would be nothing to strive after and there would be no life. But, and this seems a contradiction, though I cannot understand or name Him, yet at the same time I know Him and the direction toward Him, and even of all my knowledge this is the most certain.

I do not comprehend Him, yet at the same time I am always anxious when I am without Him, and only when I am with Him am I not anxious. What is stranger still is that to know Him more and better than I do at present is not my desire now in this present life, neither is it necessary. I can draw nearer to Him, and I wish

---

[1] The first six sections of this article are taken from the work published in Geneva under the title *Ponyatiye o Boge* — "The Conception of God." The rest is a collection of extracts from his diaries, private letters, note-book jottings, draught manuscripts of unfinished papers, and various writings of the same kind.

Mr. V. Tchertkof, Tolstoï's former secretary, who has put them together, says : —

"The reader is requested to bear in mind that the thoughts here presented, not being originally intended by the author for publication, are not expressed as precisely and carefully as they would have been had he been preparing them for the general public ; and also that the translation of writings of this character affords special difficulties, owing to their rough and unfinished form.

"In order, therefore, that the reader may both do justice to these expressions of thought and himself fully profit by them, it is desirable that he should endeavor to understand any verbal imperfections according to the spirit of the whole paper, and to fill up, in the sense most advantageous for the thought expressed, any omission he may remark."

to do so — in that is my life; but such drawing nearer in no way increases, and cannot increase, my knowledge.

Every endeavor of the imagination to know Him more definitely (for instance, as my Creator, or as a Merciful Being) removes me farther from Him, and prevents me drawing nearer to Him.

Stranger still, I can love truly — that is, more than myself or anything else — Him alone. This love only knows no check, no decrease (on the contrary, all is increase), no sensuality, no insincerity, no subserviency, no fear, no self-satisfaction. Only through this love does one love all that is good; so that one loves and lives only through Him and by Him.

This is how I think, or rather feel. I have only to add that the pronoun "He" somewhat destroys my idea of God: the word "He" somewhat diminishes Him.

To the definition of God I find it necessary to add Matthew Arnold's, which I have always kept in mind as expressing one aspect, and that the chief, in which God presents Himself to us. (Matthew Arnold deduces his definition from the Old Testament prophets, and, indeed, for the time previous to Christ, it is sufficiently complete.) According to Matthew Arnold God is that eternal, infinite "not ourselves" which "makes for righteousness." One may call it the law of human life, the will of God in relation to that part of men's life which is in their power. I say that this definition was sufficient up to the time of Christ, but by Christ it has been revealed to us that the fulfilment of this law, besides its external obligation to human reason, has also another and more simple inner motive which penetrates all man's being, namely, love: love, not of wife, or child, or country, but love of God — *God is Love*, — love of love — that very feeling of kindness, sympathy, and joy of life which constitutes man's natural, blissful, true life which knows no death.

II

I UNDERSTAND by the word "God" that whereby the knowledge of something higher — of righteousness, goodness, gentleness to another being, truth — came into my soul. Having realized this higher idea in my mind, I find in myself the life of God, and am satisfied with it. This higher idea is spirit; when my life is the movement and life of the spirit, then am I filled with something beautiful and joyous, and I do not seek the limits of my life, but I seek only union with that spirit which dwells as well in others as in me. Having realized in myself this higher thing — spirit, I make it manifest surrounding me, I diffuse *Him!* When I find in myself the spirit the highest thing, then I thereby recognize God.

By fulfilling God's will I realize God in myself, what He is. To behold Him, in other words to define Him completely and clearly to apprehend Him, is impossible for me. For me He is the Father of what I call the highest in me. Of course He requires that my life should be the realization of what is highest in the flesh, of what He produces in me.

III

IT may seem strange, but I must confess that I use the term "God" in different significations, depending on whom I am talking with, and what I am talking about. This is so if I employ it consciously. It often falls from my lips unconsciously, for example in the commonly used expressions: *Slava Bohu*; "Glory to God"; *S Bogom*, "Good-by," and the like.

In the first case, that is, when I use the term "God" consciously, it seems to me I very rarely use it separately. In connection with other expressions, it appears in such words as *zhit' po Bozhyi*, "to live in a godly manner." When I say this I really mean "to live righteously, lovingly, reasonably."

Hence, God is righteousness, love, the reason, all the higher limited significations.

I use the expression *Bog* — "God" — as synonymous with Creator with less clearness in my own mind. The Biblical despotic conception of God the Creator is not suited to my mind. The scientific conceptions in part merely complicate the Biblical conception, in part entirely destroy it, substituting for it the conception *chance* or *self-created force ;* this also does not satisfy me. When I analyze my mental concept, I find only a commensurable cause which had no beginning. Here are the two principal meanings that I attribute to the word "God." The first I can call *practical* — reason, righteousness, love ; the second, *theoretical* — final, endless cause.

Generally speaking, it is impossible to give an accurate definition to the word " God " and still more difficult to pass it by. The most veritable will be : *God is God*, as it is self-defining. Additional concepts will depend on what side you approach him from. Their infinite number is like an endless number of radii to the same center, or like a quantity of paths leading to one and the same mountain-top. And all these radii or paths are subjective.

IV

BESIDES the activities peculiar to man as an animal, he is conscious in himself of a still higher law of life, which in the first place subjects to him the whole domain of animal inclinations and repulsions ; in the second place gives a man the only joyous possibility of perceiving life and the indestructibility of this life ; in the third place, animates for him the whole world, even to the tiniest grain of sand, spiritualizes this life; and all the work of the world is for him a movement toward this one only higher law of life. Here is the foundation of the gospel. The gospel teaching takes a trait, an atom, of a man, torn by desire to live, leads him into the house of his parents and friends, and gives him the joy of nearness and union with his parents. The man then feels, "His own has come to his own."

This is something vital which a man is conscious of in himself; this something vital gives him life, and the joy of life is the "Son of God" in man. And the work of a man exalts this Son of God, lives by it, is united with it. The material for this work is the very native environment in which a man lives, including his own body. You cannot get rid of this work, and a hundred lives like yours would not suffice to accomplish it; but nevertheless work on, and know that this work is the only thing needful, immortal. And whatever you do, you will do all, if only you really do all that you can do.

V

You wish to know how I understand God. Well, here is my answer : —

I believe in Christ and I understand with perfect clearness what He says about the Father, and I acknowledge His Sonship to the Father. I know that you understand it the same way, and that you ask me about something else : that is, What significance has the Father to the whole world and not to man only? This is what I think : I know that God the Father is the beginning, spirit, consciousness, love, thought, life — what is eternal, what is for the whole universe, as consciousness for man. If there is a bond connecting me with all the whole universe of animals and plants, that is the reason why. And everything fulfils His will and receives a blessing; man when he does not fulfil His will is conscious of it, and perishes in accordance with a law unalterable for the whole world, and knows this even while he perishes. This is all I can say hastily in regard to this. As one time I was thinking how painful it is that men do not live in accordance with God's will, suddenly it became clear to me that however a man lives he will always live so that the law will not be broken, and the loss will be man's. He has not fulfilled the law as a

man — he has fulfilled it as an animal, or lower still,
as a mass of decomposing flesh. For me this became
clear and consoling.   In my mind the ordinary mistake
is also clear : it is often thought that God exists only
for Nature and not for me, or that God exists for me
and not for the whole universe at the same time.   I
clearly understand the unity, the universal cause, for if
I do not know it, I cannot think otherwise.   My consciousness is the consciousness of the whole universe —
in other words, is homogeneous.

VI

LIFE in me is consciousness.   Consciousness is not
mine — it does not depend on my will; it comes and
goes as it wishes, but when it is in me then I am not
less than it.   I am perfectly conscious of my consciousness.   Consciousness is the most unquestionable of all
things that exist.   Consciousness has no time or space ;
it has nothing personal, is not good or evil.   I am alive
while I am conscious, and when it is in me, I cannot be
unconscious of it.   This consciousness is also God.   I cannot know what God is outside of me, just as I cannot
know whence arises the consciousness in me — I know
it when it is in me.   I know at the same time that I
and consciousness are not one, but two things, because
consciousness may be for me a pain and a happiness,
according as I treat it.

I remember the time when my consciousness poisoned
my life.   I remember how at that time I adapted myself
to it ; and now I know that it is the only thing that gives
me happiness, and that outside of judgment, by it there
is no true or inviolable happiness.

What adapted this consciousness to me was reason.
Reason is the light that shines upon me through consciousness (the abode of life in me).   I put it to myself
thus : The temporary abode of life in me is a tunnel.
Consciousness is a light.   Reason is a lamp adapted to
the tunnel.   When I have come out of the tunnel, I

no longer need the lamp, but while I am in the tunnel the lamp is precious, as the light adapted to the tunnel. The adaptation of consciousness to me is to love, to serve my fellow-men, not to consider the mandates of consciousness, though they poison my comfort, as an unhappiness, but on the contrary as a salvation — in a word, this adaptation is also reason.

When I live in accordance with reason, then I am well off, that is, I am happy; when I live without reason, then I am in an evil state, in other words, I suffer from want of reason and melancholy, from the contrariety of consciousness and my passions.

In God there is neither good nor evil — that is to say, in the consciousness outside of me there is no good or evil. Good and evil exist only for me, and I can do either only for myself. Good is the service of consciousness, evil is the revolt against consciousness; but since consciousness is the life in me, so good is life and the service of life, while evil is the failure to comprehend life in oneself.

God, that is consciousness, is no respecter of persons; consciousness does not love and does not hate. Love is my sustenance, so that consciousness might become my delight. Consciousness in me has neither past nor present, and for that reason is eternal, and will not die. Here I am conscious, here I am eternal, because when I am conscious, I am no longer *I*, but consciousness only, eternal, not in the future, not at any past time, but now, at the present, because the present is eternal and endless. There is nothing eternal in the past, as in the future, because there is no future and no past — they only are presentations, they are only forms of actual thoughts — there is only the present and that is endless.

If a man rebels against consciousness, then for him immediately and forever the present perishes — he is in death; in other words, he is deprived of consciousness, and this death is absolute, without the slightest relief, since this death from a quarrel with consciousness means deprivation of all life. If a man, however, serves consciousness with his reason, then he is in complete life, and for him there is no trace of death, nothing terrible and unknown — he is then endlessly alive, as alive as consciousness itself.

VII

ONE knows God, not so much through reason, nor even through the heart, but through one's feeling of complete dependence on Him, akin to the feeling experienced by an unweaned child in the arms of its mother. It does not know who holds it, warms it, feeds it ; but it knows that there is this someone; and more than merely knows — it loves that being.

Formerly I witnessed the phenomena of life without thinking whence they came, or why I witnessed them.

Subsequently I realized that all I see is the outcome of light, which is understanding.   And I was so glad to have brought everything into harmony, that I was quite satisfied in acknowledging the understanding alone to be the source of everything.

But after that I saw that the understanding is a light which reaches me through a kind of dim glass.   I see the light, but its source I do not know.   Yet I know that the source exists.

This same source of the light that enlightens me — a source I do not know, but the existence of which I do know — is God.

VIII

YES, love is God.

Love — love him who has caused thee pain, whom thou hast blamed, disliked ; and then all that which had concealed his soul from thee will disappear, and thou wilt, as through clear water, see at the bottom of his soul the divine essence of his love ; and thou wilt not have to, thou wilt not be able to, pardon him ; thou

wilt only have to pardon thyself for not having loved
God in him in whom He was, and for not having seen
Him through the absence of thy love.

Love is the manifestation within oneself (the consciousness) of God, and therefore the propensity to get
out of oneself, to liberate oneself, to live a godly life.
And this propensity calls forth God, *i.e.* love, in others.
   This is not expressed clearly.
   My chief idea is that love evokes love in others. God,
having awakened in me, produces the awakening of the
same God in others also.

To love means to desire that which the one we love
desires.   But men desire opposite things, whereas that
only can be loved which desires one and the same thing.
One and the same thing is desired only by God.

To love God means to desire that which He desires.
And He desires universal welfare.
   " Brethren, let us love one another.   He that loveth
is born of God and knoweth God, because (it is written
' God is Love,' but we ought to say) Love is God."   But
also God is love, *i.e.* we know God only in the form of
love; and love is. God, *i.e.* if we love, we are not God's,
but God.

IX

It is astonishing how I could formerly fail to see the
indubitable truth, that behind this world and our life in
it, is some one, something, that knows why this world
exists, and why we in it, like bubbles in boiling water,
rise, burst, and disappear.
   It is certain that something is being done in this world,
and that by all living beings; being done by me, by my
life.   Otherwise, wherefore this sun, these seasons, and
above all, wherefore this three-year-old child, frenzied
with superabundance of life; that old woman who has
outlived her reason, or yonder lunatic ?   These separate

beings, which in my eyes evidently have no meaning, and which are yet living so vigorously, are so tenacious of life, and in whom life is so firmly planted, those beings more than anything convince me that they are wanted for some purpose that is wise and good, and inaccessible to me.

X

SOMEHOW, while praying to God, it became clear to me that God is indeed a real Being, Love — is that All which I just touch, and which I experience in the form of love.   And this is not a feeling, not an abstraction, but a real Being ; and I have felt Him.

All that I know, I know because there is a God, and because I know Him.   Only upon this can one firmly base one's relations with other men and with oneself, as well as with life outside space and time.   Not only do I regard this as not mystical, but I hold the opposite view to be mystical, whereas this is the most intelligible and accessible reality.

XI

WHY are you downcast?   You are waiting for something too great — waiting, it seems to me, for God in thunder and storm, and not in stillness.   The best of it is that, as you say, you cannot "get away anywhere." In this the hand of God is most visible and palpable.

You say that I do not seem to acknowledge God.   This is a misunderstanding.   I acknowledge nothing but God.

I think I wrote and spoke to you about my definition of God, which I would now give in answer to the question, What is God ?   *God is that All, that infinite All, of which I am conscious of being a part, and therefore all in me is encompassed by God, and I feel Him in everything.*

And this is not at all a play of words; it is that by which I live.

What is God? Wherefore God?
God is that *un*limited *all* which I know within myself in a limited form. I am limited, God is infinite; I am a being which has lived sixty-three years, God lives eternally; I am a being which reasons within the limits of its understanding, God reasons without limit; I am a being which loves sometimes a little, God loves always infinitely. I am a part, He is all. I cannot understand myself otherwise than as a part of Him.

When an unsolved question torments one, then one feels oneself to be a diseased member of some whole, healthy body; one feels oneself to be an unsound tooth in a sound body, and asks the whole body to help the one member.
The whole body is God; the member is myself.

XII

ONE of the superstitions that most confuse our metaphysical conceptions, is the superstition that the world was created, that it arose out of nothing, and that there is a God-Creator.
In reality we have no ground for imagining a God-Creator, nor any necessity. The Chinese and Indians have no such conception, and moreover a Creator, a Providence, is incompatible with the Christian God-Father, God-Spirit, — the God who is Love, a particle of whom lives in me and constitutes my life, the manifestation and avocation of which particle constitutes the meaning of my life.
God the Creator is indifferent, and allows suffering and evil. God the Spirit delivers from suffering and evil, and is always perfect welfare. A God-Creator there is not. There is *myself* acknowledging the universe through the faculties given me, and inwardly

recognizing my Father-God. He is the origin of my spiritual self — the external world is only my limit.

People often speak of the evil which God causes to men (for instance, when they are overcome with grief at the loss of one they love), and while so saying and thinking, they imagine that they believe in God, and they pray to Him.

God does evil! And, if God does evil, He is not good, not Love; and, if He is not good, then He does not exist.

This comes of people being so certain that what they do wrongly is not only good but excellent — as when they affirm that to give all one's love to one's children is very good — so that when they experience the evil which is only the result of their own mistakes, their own sins, they blame, not themselves, but God. And they therefore, in the depth of their soul, acknowledge God to be evil, *i.e.* deny Him, and therefore do not receive consolation from Him.

One should do as do the Spirit-Wrestlers — bow down to the ground before every man, remembering that in him is God. If to bow physically is impracticable, we should at least do so spiritually.

XIII

THE consciousness, the sensation of God who is living in me and acting through me, cannot be felt always.

There are activities to which one has got to give oneself up altogether, unlimitedly, without thinking of anything save that one thing. In these cases it is impossible to think of God; it would distract, and is unnecessary.

One should live simply, without exertion, giving oneself up to one's tendencies; but the moment there arise inward doubt, struggle, despondency, fear, ill-will, then immediately, recognizing in oneself one's spiritual being,

recognizing one's connection with God, one should trans-
port oneself from the material into the spiritual region;
and that not in order to escape the work of life, but,
on the contrary, to gather strength for its accomplishment, for the victory over, the mastering of, the obstacle.
Like a bird — to advance on one's legs with folded wings,
but the moment an obstacle is encountered, then to
unfold one's wings and fly up . . . and one finds relief,
and one's burden disappears.

This is what has happened to me: I began to think
more and more abstractedly about the problems of life
— In what does life consist? What is its aim? What
is love? — and I got farther and farther away, not only
from the Old Testament conception of God the Creator,
but also from the conception of Him as a Father, the
righteous source of all life, and of my own being. And
the devil ensnared me, and it began to enter my mind
that it is possible, and especially desirable for union
with the Chinese Confucians, with the Buddhists, and
our own atheists and agnostics, altogether to avoid this
conception. I thought it was possible to restrict oneself to the conception and acknowledgment of that God
only which is in me, without acknowledging any God
apart from that — without acknowledging the One
who has implanted in me a particle of Himself. And,
strange to say, I suddenly began to feel dull, depressed,
and alarmed. I did not know the cause of this, but I
felt that I had suddenly undergone a dreadful spiritual
fall, had lost all spiritual joy and energy.

And then only did I comprehend that this had happened because I had deserted God. And I began to
think, and, strange to say, to guess whether there be a
God or not; and I found Him, as it were, afresh. And
I was filled with such joy, and such a firm assurance did
I gain of Him, and of the possibility and duty of communion with Him, and of His hearing me; and my joy
grew so great that all these last days I have been experiencing the feeling that something very good has
come to me, and I keep asking myself, " Why do I feel

so happy? Yes! God! There *is* a God, and I need be neither anxious nor afraid, but can only rejoice."

I am afraid that this feeling will pass away, will grow dull; but for the present it is very joyous. It is as if I had been within a hair's-breadth of losing, nay, had thought that I had actually lost, the Being dearest to me; and yet had not so lost Him, but had only realized His priceless worth. I hope, if it does pass away, that it will only be the ecstatic feeling, but that there will remain much of what I have newly gained.

Perhaps this is what some call the "living God"; if that be so, then I did very wrong toward them in contradicting them instead of agreeing with them.

The chief thing in this feeling is a consciousness of entire security, a consciousness that He *is*, that He is good, that He knows me, and that I am entirely surrounded by Him, that I have come from Him, and am going to Him, form a part of Him, am His child. All that seems bad, seems so only because I trust to myself and not in Him, and from this life, in which it is so easy to do His will (this will at the same time being mine), I cannot fall anywhere, except only into Him; and in Him is perfect joy and welfare.

All that I might write would not express what I have felt. Whether I am suffering physical or moral pain, whether my son is dying, or that which I love is perishing and I cannot help it, or sufferings are awaiting me,— suddenly the thought recurs to me: "And how about God?" and all becomes good and joyous and clear.

XIV

THERE is not one believing man to whom moments of doubt do not come — doubt in the existence of God. And these doubts are not harmful; on the contrary, they lead to a higher understanding of God.

That God, whom one knew, has become familiar, and one no more believes in Him. We entirely believe in God only when He discloses Himself afresh to us.

And he discloses Himself to us from a new side when we seek Him with all our soul.

I have been thinking much about God, about the essence of my life, and, as it seemed, only to feel doubtful as to both the one and the other; and I questioned the evidence of His existence. And then, not long ago, I simply felt the desire to lean myself upon faith in God, and in the imperishableness of my soul; and to my astonishment I felt such a firm, quiet assurance as I had never felt before. So that all the doubts and testings evidently not only did not weaken, but to an enormous extent confirmed, my faith.

One should never go to God, as it were "on purpose." " Now let me just go to God. I will begin to live according to God. I have been living according to the devil; let me now try to live according to God; who knows — perhaps no harm will come of it ...."

There *is* harm in this, and great harm. Coming to God is something like getting married: one should do it only when one would be glad not to come to Him, or not to get married, but cannot help doing so. And therefore it is not that I would tell a man: "Go purposely into temptations"; but to him who formulates the question thus: "Well, and is it certain that I will not lose by going to God instead of to the devil?" — I would cry out as loud as I can: "Go, go to the devil, by all means to the devil!"

It is a hundred times better to get well scalded against the devil than to continually stand at the cross-roads, or insincerely go to God.

XV

I HAVE read Herbert Spencer's reply to Balfour,[1] the profession of agnosticism, as they now call atheism.

I mean that agnosticism, although it wishes to be something different from atheism by setting up the supposed impossibility of knowing, yet is, in reality, the

---

[1] From an article by Herbert Spencer on "Mr. Balfour's Dialectics."

same as atheism, because their common root is the non-
acceptance of a God.

And so I read Herbert Spencer, who says that he
does not *desire* to throw off belief in God, but that he is
obliged to do so ; self-deception is the only other alternative. "There is no pleasure," he says, "in the consciousness of being an infinitesimal bubble on a globe
that is itself infinitesimal compared with the totality of
things." (I should like to ask him what he understands
by "the totality of things.") "Those on whom the
unpitying rush of changes inflicts sufferings which are
often without remedy, find no consolation in the thought
that they are at the mercy of blind forces, which cause,
indifferently, now the destruction of a sun, and now the
death of an animalcule. Contemplation of a universe
which is without intelligible purpose yields no satisfaction. The desire to know what it all means is no less
strong in the agnostic than in others, and raises sympathy with them. Failing utterly to find any interpretation himself, he feels a regretful inability to accept
the interpretations they offer."

Some one else was saying exactly the same thing to
me the other day. "A sort of circumrotation takes
place, and in the center of this vortex, endless in time
and space, *I* appear, live, and disappear. This is certain. All the rest — *i.e.* the conception of some intelligent being, from which I have proceeded, and for the
attainment of whose object I exist in common with all
that exists — such a conception is a self-deception."

There are two distinct and mutually contradictory
theories of the universe, which may be represented
thus : —

The agnostic says, "Myself, a being born of my
parents, I observe in the same way as all other living
beings which surround me, and which exist under certain conditions subject to my examination and study ;
and I study myself and other objects, both animate and
inanimate, and the conditions in which they exist. And
in accordance with this study I order my life. Questions as to origin I investigate in the same way, both by

observation and by experiment, and I attain a greater
and greater knowledge of them. As to the question
whence all this universe has proceeded, why it exists,
and why I exist in it, I leave it unanswered, as I do not
see the possibility of answering it as definitely, clearly,
and convincingly as I answer questions concerning the
conditions of things *in* the universe. And therefore the
answer to this question which consists in saying that
there exists a supposed rational Being, a God, from
whom I have proceeded (it is generally said, 'from
whom the world proceeds,' by which is meant the creation of the world, which the Christian teaching does not
affirm), which Being, for some reason known to itself,
has determined the law of my life — this answer to the
question I do not accept, as it does not contain the clearness and demonstrability possessed by the scientific
answers to the questions concerning the causes and
conditions of various natural phenomena."

So says the agnostic, and in not admitting the possibility of any other knowledge but what is acquired by
observation and the analysis of observation, he is, if not
right, at least quite logical and consequent.

The Christian, on the other hand, acknowledging God,
says, "I am conscious that I exist only because I feel
myself to be a rational being. And in feeling myself to
be so, I cannot but recognize that my life and that of
all that exists must be equally rational. And in order
to be so it must have an object. The object of my life
must be outside myself, in that Being for which both I
and all that exists serve as instruments for the attainment of the object of life. This Being does exist, and
I must, in my life, fulfil its law or will. Questions as
to the nature of this Being which demands of me the
fulfilment of its law, and as to when and how, in time
and space, this rational life originated in me and originates in other beings — *i.e.* 'What is God?' 'Is He personal or impersonal?' 'Did He create the world, and
how?' 'When did a soul awake in me?' 'At what
time, and how, did it originate in others?' 'Whence
has it come and whither will it go?' 'In what part of

the body does it reside?' — all these questions I must leave unanswered, because I know beforehand that in the region of their observation and analysis I shall never come to a definite answer, as all will disappear into the infinitude of time and space. For this reason I do not accept the answers given by science as to how the universe (the suns and worlds) has originated, how the soul originates, and in what part of the brain it is located."

In the first instance the agnostic, acknowledging himself to be a mere animal, and therefore admitting that he is subject only to external sensations, does not admit a spiritual origin, and resigns himself to that senselessness of existence which violates the demands of reason.

In the second instance the Christian, acknowledging himself to be only a rational being, and therefore accepting only that which corresponds to the demands of reason, does not acknowledge the adequacy of the data of external experience, and considers those data fantastic and erroneous.

Both are equally right. But the difference between them, and an essential one, lies in the fact that, according to the former conception, everything in the universe is strictly scientific, logical, and rational, except the meaning of the life itself of man and the whole universe; and they have no meaning, and consequently, from such a conception, there may proceed very many interesting and amusing considerations, but, notwithstanding all efforts to the contrary, nothing necessary for guidance in life. Whereas, according to the latter conception, the life of man and of the whole universe acquires a definite, rational meaning, which has the most direct, simple, and universally accessible adaptability to life, at the same time not excluding the possibility of scientific investigations which, in this case, are put in their proper place.

XVI

NOTHING better proves the existence of God than the attempts of the evolutionists to accept morality and deduce it from the struggle for existence.

It is obvious that morality cannot emanate from struggle; and yet they feel that we cannot do without it, acknowledge its existence, and endeavor to deduce it from their own propositions; though to deduce it from the theory of evolution is as strange and illogical (or even more so) as to deduce it from the ordinances given by the Hebrew God on Sinai. Their mistake, which consists in denying the consciousness of one's spiritual self as a product of God, a particle of Him, without which there can be no rational view of life, — this mistake forces them to admit an unjustifiable and even contradictory mystery, *i.e.* to admit in the form of morality that same God whom they have excluded from their view of life.

XVII

THE other day a Frenchman asked me, "Would it not be sufficient to base morality upon righteousness and beauty?" *i.e.* again that same God whom they are afraid to name.

Let us endeavor to express that which we know, that which is necessary to us, joyful and certain; and God (the same whom you think it necessary to evade) will help us. By naming Him I acknowledge my incompleteness, I, His weak, small vessel, endeavor to open myself — that part of me which can receive Him — in order that He may enter into me, in so far as I am able and worthy to receive Him.

Above all, He is necessary to me in order that I may express whither I am tending and to whom I go. In this monotonous earthly life I may not feel Him, I may do without this form of thought and expression; but in

relation to this passage from the past life into this one,
and from this one into another, I cannot avoid expressing by Him that from whence I come and whither I am
going, this being the form of expression nearest to the
true character of the case ; from God to God, *i.e.* from
that which is outside of time and space to the same
again.

XVIII

It is not that I altogether agree with what you
say about the understanding and about God, but my
thoughts are in conformity with yours. I do not say
that I agree, because in speaking about these matters it
is often difficult to express accurately what one thinks,
and words may say too much or too little, and therefore
it is never possible to admit that a certain way of formu-
lating completely corresponds to one's conception. But
I see that we think and feel in the same direction, and
this gives me great pleasure. It is impossible not to
think about these matters, but each of us involuntarily
thinks in his own way. To formulate one's thoughts in
the way it has been done in various creeds is not only
useless, but may be dangerous. It is possible and necessary to formulate deductions which are applicable to
life, as did Moses : " Thou shalt not kill! " or Christ :
" Resist not evil! " I repeat, however, that I think in
the same direction, and quite agree with you that the
understanding is attainable in proportion to one's purity,
humility, and love.

XIX

What am I here, abandoned in the midst of this
world ? To whom shall I turn ? From whom shall I
seek an answer ? — From men ?

They do not know ; they laugh ; they do not wish to
know. They say, " That is nonsense. Do not think
about it. Here is the world and its attractions — live ! "

But they shall not deceive me. I know that they do

not believe what they say. They too, like me, are tormented and suffer from the fear of death, of themselves, and of Thee, Lord, whom they do not wish to name.

I too, for long did not name Thee, and I too did the same that they do. I know this deception, and how it oppresses the heart, and how terrible is the fire of despair which is concealed in the heart of him who does not name Thee. However much they strive to quench it, it will burn up their heart as it used to burn mine.

But, Lord, I named Thee, and my sufferings ceased. My despair has passed.

I cursed my weakness, but I seek Thy way and do not despair. I feel Thy nearness, feel Tny help when I walk in Thy ways, and Thy pardon when I stray from thee.

Thy way is clear and plain. Thy yoke is easy and Thy burden light, but I have long wandered outside Thy ways, long in the abominations of my youth have I proudly flung off every burden, freed myself from every yoke, and untaught myself to walk in Thy ways; and both Thy yoke and Thy burden have become heavy for me, though I know they are good and light.

Lord, pardon the errors of my youth, and help me to bear Thy yoke as joyfully as I accept it.

ON REASON, FAITH AND PRAYER

(January, 1901*)*

I. — REASON

You ask me what my Christian creed is. You have read my "Short Exposition of the Gospels," and you know, therefore, how I understand the teaching of Jesus.

If, however, you wish to know what I consider the essential meaning of the teaching: in my opinion the essential meaning, which I should like to transmit to all mankind, and in which I wish all children could be educated, consists in this, that *man has come into the world not by his own will but by the will of Him that sent him.* And that man should know what He who sent him into this world requires, reason has been bestowed on him, by the help of which, if he truly desire it, he can always know the will of God — he can always know what He who sent him into the world requires of him.

The Pharisees and Scribes of our time always say that one should not believe in reason, because it will deceive, but that one should believe them and they will not deceive. But what they say is untrue. If one believes in men, and, as the Gospels say, "in the traditions of men," then we shall all crawl astray from each other like blind puppies, and hate each other, as we do now : the Christian Churchman hates the Mohammedan, the Mohammedan hates the Christian, and the Christians themselves hate each other ; the (Greek) Orthodox hates the Catholic, the Old Believer [1] hates the Orthodox, and so on ; but if we adhere to the voice of our reason, we shall all unite, because reason is one and the same for all, and reason alone unites men and does not hinder the manifestation of the mutual love natural to them.

Reason unites us, not only with our contemporaries, but with men who lived two thousand years before us, and with those who will live after us. Thus we profit by all that has been produced by the reason of Isaiah, and Jesus, and Buddha, and Socrates, and Confucius, and of all the men who lived before us and believed in reason and served it. "Act toward others as thou wouldst wish them to act toward thee ; do not revenge thyself against those who do evil unto thee, but return good for evil ; be abstinent, chaste ; not only refrain from killing people, but be not angry against them ; keep peace with all," and much else. All this is the product of reason, and all this has been preached equally

---

[1] An ancient Russian sect. — TR.

by Buddhists, Confucianists, Christians, Taoists, and the
Greek and the Egyptian sages.   It is also preached by
all good people of our time, and all agree with it.

And, therefore, I repeat, the chief meaning of the
Christian teaching consists, in my opinion, in what is
expressed in the Gospels, in the parable of the Work-
men in the Vineyard, for whose use a garden had been
given under condition of a payment to the owner, but
who imagined it their own; and in the parable of the
Talents, where the meaning is that men must fulfil the
will of Him who sent them into life, which will consists
in men becoming perfect, "as their Heavenly Father,"
as it is said in another place; *i.e.*, in approaching as
near as they can to supreme perfection.

That the will of God consists only in this is also
demonstrated to us by reason, and so clearly that there
can be no dissension nor doubt.   Every man who has
thought of it cannot but see that in all the undertakings
of life man does and will meet obstacles, and that only
in this work (perfection) need man meet no obstacle;
that is, in perfecting himself, clearing his soul from
evil, and doing good to all that lives.   Neither is this
work arrested, destroyed, nor hindered by death, which
stops, destroys, and renders meaningless all other
worldly undertakings.   Death neither arrests nor destroys this work, because the man who fulfils the will
of Him who sent him, knowing that what he does is
necessary to the Master, peacefully performs it here as
long as he has the power, and knows that death destroys
neither himself nor his relation to the Master, but that
"there" also, although in quite different form, he will
be in the same dependence on the Master, and have the
same joy of a continually growing participation in the
life and the work of the Master, *i.e.*, God.

It is thus I understand the teaching of Jesus; thus
would I wish it to be understood by all; and in this I
wish all children could be educated.   Not to blindly
believe the things told them about God and life; and to
believe the things they do believe, not because they are
told they are the utterances of prophets, or Christ, but

because their reason tells them they are true. Reason is older and more reliable than all the writings and all the traditions. It existed even when there were no traditions and no writings, and it is given to each of us direct from God.

The Gospel statement that all sins shall be pardoned except the sin against the Holy Ghost, in my opinion refers directly to the assertion that one should not believe in reason. Indeed, if we do not believe in the reason given us from God, in what shall we believe? Are we to believe those very men who wish to compel us to accept what is inconsistent with the reason given us by God?

II.—FAITH

You ask, what will give a weak, degenerated, depraved man (as we all are), amidst the snares surrounding him on all sides — what will give such a man the power to live a Christian life?

Instead of answering, and before answering, this question, I will ask you, What does it really mean?

We have become so accustomed to the question that it appears quite natural and intelligible, whereas it is not only not natural and not intelligible, but exceedingly strange and curious for every rational man not educated in the superstitions of the Church faith.

Why doesn't the smith hammering iron, or the peasant plowing the field, ask where he will obtain the strength to do the work he has undertaken, but instead does it to the best of his strength, makes mistakes, tries to correct them, becomes tired, halts, leaves his work for a time, rests, and again betakes himself to it? Is not every servant of God in the same position, when trying to live the Christian life, to fulfil the will of God he has become conscious of? Just in the same way such a man, if he be sincere, will live a Christian life to the best of his strength — obey the will of God, and if he makes mistakes will correct himself, will become tired, and rest, and again betake himself to the

same life-work — that of approaching to the best of his
strength that perfection of the Heavenly Father indicated to him.

The question as to where one should get the strength
for the Christian life only shows that some one has persuaded men that certain means exist, by whose aid
men, without their own incessant efforts, strife, without
falls, repentance, upheavals, again falls, and again
upheavals, can obtain the necessary strength for a
good, saintly life. It is this very superstition, that
man does not approach perfection by his own slow
efforts, but can purify himself all at once and become
a saint, which is one of the most terrible and pernicious
errors, — and it is this which is strenuously preached
by all the Churches. Some assure their disciples that
through the sacraments of baptism, confession, communion, man is freed from sin ; others affirm that one
is freed from sin by faith in the redemption, because
the Christ-God has purified us with his blood. Both the
one and the other teach that besides this we are purified
by petitionary prayer to God that He should pardon our
sins and make us good — and not that we should ourselves strive to become better.

This superstition is very pernicious because it contains
a deceit.

The deceit consists, firstly, in the supposition that
man can become quite pure and saintly ; whereas for a
living man this is impossible. Man cannot be perfect
and sinless ; he can only more or less *approach* perfection, regarding this approach as the sole meaning of his
life. I even think that life after death will again consist
only in advance toward perfection, although in a completely different form. In this personal effort toward
perfection lies the whole meaning and joy of life. And
therefore if perfection were attainable by external means
we should be deprived of the very essence of life.

A deceit, secondly, because through it man's efforts
are withdrawn from the thing he has to do — from
improving himself — and are directed toward something unnecessary. To rely on sacraments, or belief in

the redemption, or prayer, contributing to the perfecting of oneself, is like a smith, while holding in his hands the iron and the hammer, and possessing an anvil and a well-lighted fire, trying to devise some other means of forging the iron besides striking it with a hammer, or praying to God to give him the strength to do the work.

One might pray to God, and devise other means for perfecting oneself, in the event of obstacles being put before us in this work and if we ourselves had not the strength for it. But in this work of perfecting oneself, or the Christian life, or the fulfilment of the will of God, God does not demand of us something we cannot do, — on the contrary He has taken care to give us all we are in need of for fulfilling His will.

We are here in this world as in a wayside inn in which the master has arranged everything really needful to us travelers, and has gone away himself leaving instructions how we should behave in this temporary shelter. All that we require is within our reach! Then what other means should we devise, and for what should we pray? We have only *to obey our instructions!* So also in our spiritual life: all that we require is given us, and the rest is in our own hands.

It is clear that if we wish to become saints all of a sudden, or to feel ourselves justified, and desire besides this to be rich — if we desire that our friends and ourselves shall not be subject to disease or to death, and that we shall always have good harvests, and that our foes shall be destroyed — then we, too, must ask all this of God as it is done in our churches.

But God has not destined us to anything of this kind. He not only has not ordained us to be perfectly righteous and sinless, but on the contrary He has given us a life the meaning of which consists only in our liberating ourselves from our sins, and so *approaching* toward Him. And He has not destined us to be rich, disease-less, and deathless, but has given us trials, in the form of poverty, disease, the death of our friends and of ourselves — for the very purpose of teaching us to center our lives not in wealth, health, and this temporary exist-

ence, but in serving Him. And He has given us foes
not in order that we should desire their ruin, but that
we should learn to overcome them by love. He has
given us a law of such a nature that it is always well
with us if we fulfil it.

So that we have no need to invent any special means
of salvation, nor to ask God for anything. All that we
require is given us, if only we follow the instructions
both of our conscience, and of God as expressed in the
Gospels.

The third deceit, an especially pernicious one, consists in this, that the people who have come to believe
that they cannot fulfil the will of God and live well by
their own efforts, cease to labor at self-improvement;
and not only this, but they lose the possibility of self-
perfection. A man need only persuade himself that he
cannot do something he has to do, and his hands become
helpless, and he will indeed be unable to do what is necessary. A man need only become persuaded that he is
ill, and he will be ill. Hysterical subjects feel impelled
to scream because they believe they are forced to scream.
Habitual drunkards do not recover, because they are
persuaded they cannot abstain. There is no more immoral and pernicious teaching than that man cannot
perfect himself by his own efforts.

This argument, that for a good Christian life one's
own efforts are insufficient, and that some kind of external power is necessary, is like the assertion that reason
is not sufficient to obtain knowledge of the truth, but
that external indubitable proofs are necessary, which I
mentioned in my first letter. In the former case, it is
supposed beforehand that something or other exists
which will give man the power to live a Christian life
and to fulfil the will of God. In the latter case, it is
supposed that something exists by which a man can
ascertain positively that that which he is told is the
absolute truth. It is supposed that some kind of means
exists for ascertaining truth, independently of one's personal exertions of reason, and that, complete and absolute truth. But this is as impossible as it is to see the

light without eyes. Truth is ascertained by effort, and cannot be ascertained by any other means. And truth ascertained by man's reason can never be perfect, but only more or less approximate to absolute truth. So that "truth" may be the highest truth accessible to man at a given time, but it can never be absolute and positive truth for all times. No proposition can be an absolute truth for all time, were it only for this, that the life of all mankind, as well as that of individual man, is engaged in, and even consists of, the attainment of more and more perfect truth.

The erroneous and absurd idea that human reason cannot by its own efforts *approach* the Truth, proceeds from the same kind of terrible superstition as the one which asserts that man cannot approach the fulfilment of the will of God without external help. The essence of this superstition consists in the supposition that the complete, perfect truth has presumably been revealed by God Himself : to the Jews it was revealed on Mount Sinai, and then by various prophets ; to Christians — by Christ, the Apostles, the Councils, the Church ; to the Brahmans, in the Vedas ; to the Buddhists, in the Tripitaka ; to the Mohammedans, in the Koran.

This superstition is evil, firstly, because it distorts the very idea of truth ; secondly, because once one has admitted as positive truth all the absurdities and horrors which are accepted as the revelation of God in the Scriptures, one has to keep on distorting common sense more and more in order to justify all these horrors and absurdities ; and thirdly, because having accepted an infallible, external revelation as the source of truth, man ceases to believe in the only means to the knowledge of truth — the exertions of his reason. The man who acts thus is like one who, in search of a road, shuts his eyes and surrenders to the guidance of the first stranger who offers to show him the way, instead of exerting himself to the utmost to find it.

It is said, " How can one believe in reason when we see that people who are guided by it fall into error ? Protestants, guided by reason, split up into numberless

faiths, and even one and the same man, trusting himself
to reason, passes from one teaching to another.   Therefore," it is said, "reason may be mistaken, and one cannot trust it."

But why so ?   When man believed in one Something,
and his reason pointed out nothing more true, he was
conscious of the highest truth accessible to him, and was
right.   Then he became conscious of a higher truth, and
was right in acknowledging IT.   So also was he right
when he became conscious of a yet higher and purer
truth.   The highest, clearest, truest, which man can see
and contemplate, that is for him the Truth.

It may be well and desirable, very possibly, that all
men should suddenly recognize one and the same Perfect
Truth (although if this were so life would cease), but
even were we to admit that this might be desirable, —
things do not occur as we would like.   It might be very
desirable (to unreasonable people) that man should not
suffer sicknesses, or that some means should exist which
should cure him from all diseases ; or that all men should
speak the same tongue.   But this will not take place
merely because we imagine that all men can be cured by
our remedy, or that all men can speak and understand
Russian.   If we do imagine this we only make things
worse for ourselves, just as we only make it worse for
ourselves when we imagine that the complete and eternal
Truth is revealed to us in the Scriptures, in tradition, or
in the Church.

This might have been imagined at the beginning of
Christianity, when one faith appeared possible ; but in
our time, when by our sides we can see people of the
most various religions all imagining that the complete
and eternal Truth is revealed to them and not to us
— to imagine that precisely we, who have been born in
our faith, possess the complete Truth, as the Buddhists,
Mohammedans, Catholics, Taoists, and others imagine —
is especially foolish.

So mistaken an idea is especially harmful, because it
disunites men more than anything else.   Men ought to
go on uniting closer and closer, as Jesus teaches, and as

our reason and heart indicate. But dogmas about "revelations" *disunite* men more and more.

Besides this, one should understand also that if man believes in revelation he believes so only because reason has told him that he should believe in such or such a revelation — the Mohammedan, Buddhist, or Christian. Whether we desire it or not, no truth can enter man's mind independently of his reason. Reason is like the sieves attached to the threshing machines, so that one cannot get the grain otherwise than through the sieve. It may be that chaff has passed and still passes through the sieve, but there is no other way of getting the grain. And if we imagine that we can have pure grain without sifting, then we deceive ourselves, and fill ourselves with chaff instead of bread, as Churchmen do.

So that we should not imagine everything is happening as we would like, but remember that everything follows laws established by God. And human life has been so ordained by God that men cannot grasp the whole truth, but are continually approaching it; and by comprehending it more and more clearly they are mutually more and more being drawn together.

You ask my opinion about the person of Jesus; whether I regard him as God; about his birth; about future life; about whom I understand by Scribes and Pharisees; and about the holy communion.

I regard Jesus as the same kind of man we all are, and I believe it to be the greatest sacrilege and an evident proof of heathenism, to regard him as God. To consider Jesus as God is to renounce God.

Jesus I regard as man, but his teaching I regard as Divine, in so far as it expresses Divine truths. I know no higher teaching. It has given me life, and I try as far as I can to follow it.

About the birth of Jesus I know nothing, nor do I need to know.

About future life we know that it does exist, that life does not end with death. As to what that life will be it is not given us to know, because it is not necessary to us.

By Pharisees I mean principally the priesthood.   By Scribes I mean men of science who do not believe in God.

Concerning the eating of the body and the drinking of the blood, I think this passage in the Gospel the least important, and that it signifies either imbibing the teaching, or a commemoration, but that neither in the one case nor the other has it any importance; nor does it signify what the Church fanatics understand by it.   I have expressed my understanding of this passage as well as I could in the " Short Exposition of the Gospels " (*Gospel in Brief*).

III. — PRAYER

In my last letter I wrote about the futility of prayer, in respect both to the realization of our desires concerning events of the external world, and also to the inner world, for perfecting oneself.

I am afraid that owing to my own fault you will not understand me as I would wish, and I will add here, therefore, some thoughts on the subject of prayer.

One cannot pray for external events, such as that it might rain, or that an individual loved by me might remain alive, or that I should keep healthy and not die, for these events occur according to laws established by God once for all, and so established that if we act as we should they are always beneficial.   It is just the same as if a good man has built a house with substantial walls and roof, which shelter me, and I capriciously desire to enlarge or alter the position of the walls, and ask for this.

As to one's inner perfection, one cannot pray for this, because everything necessary for it has been given us and it is neither possible nor needful to add anything more.

But because petitionary prayer has no meaning, it does not follow that one cannot or should not pray. On the contrary, I believe it is impossible to live well without prayer, and that prayer is the necessary condition of a good, peaceful, and happy life. The Gospels indicate how one should pray, and what prayer should consist of.

In every man there is the divine spark, the Spirit of God. Every man is the son of God. Prayer consists in calling forth in oneself the divine element while renouncing all that is of this world, all which can distract one's feelings. (Mohammedans do very well when they shut their eyes and ears with their fingers on entering their mosques or beginning to pray.) The best method is the one Jesus teaches: to enter alone into one's chamber and lock the door; *i.e.*, to pray in complete solitude, whether in a room, a wood, or a field.

Prayer consists in renouncing all that is of this world, external, and evoking in oneself the divine part of one's soul by throwing oneself into it, entering by it communion with Him of whom It is a part; recognizing oneself as the slave of God; and testing oneself, one's actions, one's desires, according to the demands not of the external circumstances of the world but of this divine part of one's soul.

And such prayer is not an idle sentimentality and excitement, such as is produced by public prayer with its accompaniments of singing, images, illuminations, and exhortations — but is always a help to life, reforming and directing it.

Such a prayer is a confession, a test of one's past actions, and an indication of the direction of one's future actions. Suppose I have been insulted and have an ill-feeling toward the man, and desire evil to him, or do not wish to do him the good I could; or else suppose I have lost my property, or a dear one; or am living and acting not in accordance with my faith. If I do not pray in the right way, but continue to live superficially, I shall not be delivered from the painful feeling of ill-will to the one who has insulted me. So also the loss of property or of the dear one will poison my life. And preparing to act contrary to the demands of my conscience, I shall

feel uneasy. But if I test myself before my soul and
before God, all will change. I shall condemn *myself*,
not my enemy, and shall search for an opportunity
of doing good to him; my losses I shall accept as
a trial, and try to bear submissively. And thus I
shall find consolation, and shall see my way clearer for
my actions; shall not, as before, conceal from myself the inconsistency between my life and my faith,
but shall endeavor with repentance to bring them
into harmony; and in this effort I shall find peace and
joy.

But, you ask, in what should prayer consist? Jesus
has given us a model prayer in " Our Father," and
this prayer, reminding us of the essence of our life
(which consists in being in accordance with the will
of the Father and obeying it), and of our most usual
sins : condemnation, or not forgiving one's brothers;
and above all, of the dangers or snares of our lives
— this remains until the present time the best prayer,
and the most complete, of all which I know.

But besides this prayer, true solitary prayer also consists of all which in the words of other wise and righteous
men, or in one's own, brings the soul back to the consciousness of its divine source, to a more vivid and clear
expression of the demands of one's conscience, *i.e.*, of
one's divine nature. Prayer is a test of one's present
and past actions according to the highest demands of
the soul.

So that I not only do not reject solitary prayer, which
reëstablishes the divinity of the soul, but I regard it on
the contrary as a necessary condition of spiritual (true)
life. I reject petitionary prayer and public prayer with
its singing, images, candles, and even theatricalities, as
sacrilegious. I often wonder how this public and petitionary prayer can exist among men calling themselves Christians, when Jesus clearly and definitely said
that one should pray in solitude, and that you should
not ask for anything, because before you open your
mouth " Your Father in heaven knoweth what ye
need."

As to myself I will say — without at all thinking that
this is good for all, and that all ought to do so — that I
have long ago contracted the habit of praying in solitude
every morning, and that this my daily prayer is as
follows : —

*Our Father who art in Heaven, hallowed be Thy
name.* And after this I add, from the Gospel of
John : Thy name is love, God is love. He who abides
in love abides in God, and God in him. No man hath
seen God anywhere, but if we love one another then
He abides in us, and His love is fulfilled in us. If any
man say " I love God " but hateth his brother, he is a
liar, for he that loveth not his brother whom he sees, how
can he love God whom he hath not seen ? Brothers, let
us love one another ; love is from God, and every man
that loveth is from God and knoweth God, because God
is love.

Thy Kingdom Come. And I add : Seek ye the kingdom of God and His righteousness and all the rest will
be added unto you. The Kingdom of God is within
you.

Thy will be done on earth as it is in Heaven. And
here I ask myself whether I really believe that I am in
God and God in me ? And do I believe that my life
consists in increasing love in myself ? I ask, do I remember that to-day I am alive, and to-morrow dead ?
Is it true that I do not wish to live for personal desires
and human glory, but only for the fulfilment of the will
of God ? And I add the words of Jesus from the three
Gospels : Not my will, but Thine ; and not what I
desire but what Thou desirest. And not as I desire
but as Thou desirest.

Give us this day our daily bread. I add : My food
consists in doing the will of Him that sent me, and completing it. Deny thyself, take up thy cross for each
day, and follow me. Take my yoke upon you and learn
of me, for I am meek and humble in heart, and you will
find peace for your soul. For my yoke is easy, and my
burden is light.

And forgive us our sins as we forgive those who sin

against us. I add: And your Father will not forgive
you your sins unless each one of you forgive his brother
who has sinned against him.

And lead us not into temptation. I add: Beware of
the temptations of the flesh, of ambition, of ill-will, of
gluttony, adultery, human glory. Do not give your
alms before men, but so that your right hand does not
know what your left is doing. And he is not meet for
the kingdom of God who having taken the plow looks
back. Rejoice when thou art abused and humiliated.

But deliver us from evil. I add: Beware of what
issues from the heart: evil thoughts, murders (every
ill-will toward men), thefts (profiting by what one has
not earned), adultery (even in thought), false witness,
slander.

I conclude the prayer again with the words of the
Gospel of John: "And we know that we have passed
from death into life if we love our brother. He that
loveth not his brother has not eternal life abiding in
him."

So do I daily pray, adapting the words of this prayer
to my actions and my spiritual state.

But besides this prayer I pray when I am alone with
myself. I read the thoughts of wise and righteous men,
not only Christian and not only ancient; and reflect,
searching out before God the evil in my heart, and trying to extract it. I also endeavor to pray during the
daily round of my life when I am with men, and passions are getting hold of me. It is in these cases I try
to recall to mind all that took place in my soul during
my solitary prayer; and the more sincere that prayer
was, the easier it is to refrain from evil.

This is all I wished to tell you about prayer, in order
that you should not think I reject it.

THE GOSPELS IN BRIEF

AUTHOR'S PREFACE

THIS present book is extracted from a larger work, which exists in manuscript, and cannot be published in Russia.

That work consists of four parts, namely : —

1. An account of that course of my personal life, and of my thoughts, which led me to the conviction that in the Christian teaching lies the truth.

2. An investigation of the Christian teaching — first, according to the interpretation of the Greek Church solely ; then, according to the interpretation of the Churches generally, and the interpretation of the apostles, councils, and so-called " Fathers." Also, an exposition of the falsity in these interpretations.

3. An investigation of the Christian teaching, based, not upon the above interpretations, but solely upon the words and deeds ascribed to Christ by the four Gospels.

4. An exposition of the real meaning of the Christian teaching, of the motives for its perversions, and of the consequences to which it should lead.

From the third of these parts this present volume is condensed. I have there effected the fusion of the four Gospels into one, according to the real sense of the teaching. I had no need to digress from the order in which each Gospel is written, so that in my harmonisation the transpositions of verses, rather than being more, are less numerous than in the greater part of those known to me, and in our Grechoulevitch's version of the four Gospels. In my treatment of the Gospel of John there is no transposition, but all stands in the same order as in the original.

My division of the Gospel into twelve chapters (or six, since each pair of the twelve may be taken as one) came about spontaneously from the nature of the teaching. The following is the purport of the chapters: —

1. Man is the son of the Infinite Source of Being; he is the son of this Father, not by the flesh but by the spirit.

2. And therefore, man must serve the Source of his being, in the spirit.

3. The life of all men has a divine Origin. This Origin only is sacred.

4. And therefore, man must serve this Source of all human life. This is the will of the Father.

5. Service of the Will of the Father of Life is life-giving.

6. And therefore, it is not necessary to life that each man should satisfy his own will.

7. This present life in time is the food of the true life.

8. And therefore, the true life is outside time; it is in the present.

9. Time is an illusion in life; the life of the past and the future clouds men from the true life of the present.

10. And therefore, one must aim to destroy the deception arising from the past and future, the life in time.

11. The true life is that now present to us, common to all, and manifesting itself in love.

12. And therefore, he who lives by love now, in this present, becomes, through the common life of all men, at one with the Father, the source, the foundation of life.

So that the chapters, in pairs, are related as cause and effect.

Besides these twelve chapters, this exposition includes — (*a*) The introduction of the first chapter of the Gospel of John, where the writer of the Gospel speaks, in his own name, as to the purport of the whole teaching: and (*b*) a portion of the same writer's Epistle (written probably before the Gospel); this containing the general sense to be derived from the preceding exposition.

These two parts are not essential to the teaching
Although the former, as well as the latter of them,
might be omitted without loss (the more so as they come
in the name of John, and not of Christ), I have, nevertheless, kept them, because, to a straightforward understanding of the whole teaching, these parts, confirming
each other and the whole, as against the strange commentaries of the Churches, yield the plainest evidence
of the meaning to be put upon the teaching.

At the beginning of each chapter, besides a brief indication of the subject, I had put words from the prayer
taught by Jesus to His disciples, such as corresponded
with the contents of the chapter.

At the conclusion of my work I found, to my astonishment and joy, that the Lord's Prayer is nothing less
than Christ's whole teaching, stated in most concise form,
and in that same order in which I had already arranged
the chapters, each phrase of the prayer corresponding to
the purport and sequence of the chapters, as follows:—

1. Our Father,	Man is the son of the Father.
2. Which art in heaven,	God is the infinite spiritual source of life.
3. Hallowed be Thy name,	May the Source of Life be held holy.
4. Thy kingdom come,	May His power be established over all men.
5. Thy will be done, as in heaven,	May His will be fulfilled, as it is in Himself,
6. So also on earth.	So also in the bodily life.
7. Give us our daily bread	The temporal life is the food of the true life.
8. This day.	The true life is in the present.
9. And forgive us our debts as we forgive our debtors,	May the faults and errors of the past not hide this true life from us,
10. And lead us not into temp-tation,	And may they not lead us into delusion,
11. But deliver us from evil,	So that no evil may come to us,
12. For Thine is the kingdom, the power, and the glory.	And there shall be order, and strength, and reason.

In that large third part from which this work is condensed, the Gospel according to the four Evangelists

is presented in full. But in the rendering now given,
all passages are omitted which treat of the following
matters, namely, — John the Baptist's conception and
birth, his imprisonment and death; Christ's birth, and
his genealogy; his mother's flight with him into Egypt;
his miracles at Cana and Capernaum; the casting out
of devils; the walking on the sea; the cursing of the
fig-tree; the healing of sick, and the raising of dead
people; the resurrection of Christ Himself; and, finally,
the reference to prophecies fulfilled in His life.

These passages are omitted in this abridgment, because, containing nothing of the teaching, and describing only events which passed before, during, or after
the period in which Jesus taught, they complicate the
exposition. However one takes them, under any circumstance, they bring to the teaching of Jesus neither
contradiction nor confirmation of its truth. Their sole
significance for Christianity was that they proved the
divinity of Jesus Christ for him who was not persuaded
of this divinity beforehand. But they are useless to
one whom stories of miracles are powerless to convince,
and who, besides, doubts the divinity of Jesus as evi-
denced in His teaching.

In the large work, every departure from the ordinary
version, as well as every comment added to the text,
and every omission, is made clear, and proved by the
comparison of the various versions of the Gospels, from
the examination of contexts, and finally, by considerations, philological and other. But in the present
abridged rendering, all these arguments and refutations
of the false understanding of the Churches, as well as
the minute notes and quotations, are omitted; because,
however true and exact they may be in their places,
they cannot carry conviction as to the true understanding of the teaching. The justness of a conception
of this kind is better proved, not by arguing particular
points, but by its own unity, clearness, simplicity, full-
ness, as well as by its harmony with the inner feelings
of all who seek truth. Speaking generally, in regard
to what divergence there is between my rendering and

the Church's authorized text, the reader must not for
get that it is a gross error to represent the four Gospels,
as is often done, to be books sacred in every verse and
in every syllable. The reader must not forget that
Jesus never Himself wrote a book, as did, for instance,
Plato, Philo, or Marcus Aurelius ; that He, moreover,
did not, as Socrates did, transmit His teaching to informed and literate men, but spoke to a crowd of illiter-
ate men ; and that only a long time after His death men
began to write down what they had heard from Him.

The reader must not forget that a great number of
such accounts have been written, from which, at first,
the Churches selected three, and then another. Moreover, in selecting those which seemed to them the best
according to the proverb, " No stick without knots," the
Churches, out of the enormous heap of the Christian literature, have been forced to take in with their bargain a
great many knots ; so that the canonical Gospels contain
nearly as many faulty passages as those Gospels rejected as apocryphal.

The reader must not forget that it is the teaching of
Christ which may be sacred, but in no way can a certain
measure of verses and syllables be so ; and that certain
verses, from here to here, say, cannot be sacred merely
because men say they are so.

Moreover, the reader must not forget that these selected Gospels are, at any rate, the work of thousands of
various brains and hands of men ; that during centuries
the Gospels have been selected, enlarged, and com-
mented upon ; that the most ancient copies which have
come down to us, from the fourth century, are written
straight on without punctuation, so that, even after the
fourth and fifth centuries, they have been the subject
of the most diverse readings; and that such variations
in the Gospels may be counted up to fifty thousand.
The reader must have all this present in mind in order
to disengage himself from the opinion, so common
among us, that the Gospels, in their present shape, have
come to us directly from the Holy Spirit. The reader
must not forget that, far from it being blamable to dis

encumber the Gospels of useless passages, and to illumi
nate passages the one by the other, it is, on the contrary,
unreasonable not to do this, and to hold a certain number
of verses and syllables as sacred.

On the other hand, I pray my readers to remember
that, if I do not hold the Gospels to be sacred books
emanating from the Holy Spirit, I yet less regard the
Gospels as mere historical monuments of religious literature.   I understand the theological as well as the historical standpoint on the Gospels, but regard the books
myself from quite another.   I pray the readers of my
rendering not to be misled, either by the theological
view, or by that other, so usual in our day among educated men, the historical view, neither of which I hold
with.   I consider Christianity to be neither a pure revelation nor a phase of history, but I consider it as the
only doctrine which gives a meaning to life.

And it is neither theology nor history which has won
me to Christianity; but just this, that, when fifty years
old, having questioned myself, and having questioned
the reputed philosophers whom I knew, as to what I
am, and as to the purport of my life, and after getting
the reply that I was a fortuitous concatenation of atoms,
and that my life was void of purport, and that life itself
is evil, I became desperate, and wished to put an end
to my life.   But after recalling to myself how formerly, in
childhood, while I still had religious faith, life possessed
meaning for me; and that the great mass of men about
me, who hold to faith and are uncorrupted by wealth,
possess the meaning of life : after all this, I was brought
into doubt as to the justness of the reply given to me by
the wisdom of men of my own station, and I tried once
more to understand what answer it is that Christianity
gives to those men who live a life with meaning.   And
I embarked upon the study of Christianity, as to what
in this teaching guides the lives of men.   I began to
study that Christianity which I saw applied in life, and
to make the comparison of this applied Christianity with
the sources whence it percolates.   The source of the
Christian teaching is the Gospels, and there I found the

explanation of the spirit which animates the life of all
who really live. But along with the flow of that pure,
life-giving water I perceived much mire and slime un-
rightfully mingled therewith ; and this had prevented
me, so far, from seeing the real, pure water. I found
that, along with the lofty Christian teaching, are bound
up the teachings of Hebraism and the Church, both of
which are repugnant and foreign to the former. I thus
felt myself in the position of a man to whom is given a
sack of refuse, who, after long struggle and wearisome
labor, discovers among the refuse a number of infinitely
precious pearls. This man then knows that he is not
blameworthy in his distaste for the dirt, and also that
those who have gathered these pearls at the same time
with the rest of the sackful, and who have preserved
them, are no more to blame than himself, but, on the
contrary, deserve love and respect.

I knew not the light, and I thought there was no
sure truth in life ; but when I perceived that only light
enables men to live, I sought to find the sources of the
light. And I found them in the Gospels, despite the
false commentaries of the Churches. And when I
reached this source of light I was dazzled with its
splendor, and I found there full answers to my questions as to the purport of the lives of myself and others,
— answers which I recognized as wholly harmonious
with all the known answers gained among other nations,
and, to my mind, surpassing all other answers.

I sought a solution of the problem of life, and not of
a theological or historical question ; and that is why I
was indifferent to know whether Jesus Christ is or is
not God, and from whom proceeds the Holy Spirit, etc.
And it is just as unimportant and unnecessary to know
when and by whom such and such a Gospel was written,
and whether such and such a parable came from Jesus
Himself or not. For me, the only important concern
was this light, which, for eighteen hundred years, has
shone upon mankind ; which has shone upon me likewise, and which shines upon me still. But to know,
more than this, how I ought to name the source of this

light, what elements compose it, and what kindled it, 1 in no way concerned myself.

I might end this preface here if the Gospels were newly discovered books, and if the teaching of Jesus had not been, these eighteen hundred years, the subject of a continuous series of false interpretations. But to-day, to rightly understand the teaching of Jesus as He must needs have understood it Himself, it is indispensable to know the chief causes of these false interpretations. The prime cause of such false interpretations, which make it now so difficult for us to recover the true teaching of Jesus, is the fact that, under the cover of the Christian teaching, have been preached the teachings of the Church, which are made up from explanations of most contradictory writings, in which only a small part of the true teaching enters; even that being distorted, and adapted to the commentaries. The teaching of Christ, according to this misinterpretation, is simply one link in the great chain of revelation which began with the world's beginning, and stretches into the Church of our own time.

These misinterpreters call Jesus God; but the recognition of His divinity does not make them recognize a greater importance in His words and teaching than in the words of the Pentateuch, the Psalms, the Acts, the Epistles, the Apocalypse, or even the decisions of the Councils and the writings of the Fathers.

And this false understanding allows no presentment of the teaching of Jesus which does not accord with the revelations which have preceded and followed Him; doing this with the purpose, not to make clear the meaning of the teaching of Jesus, but to harmonize, as far as possible, various writings which contradict each other; such as the Pentateuch, the Psalms, the Gospels, Epistles, Acts, and, generally, all those which pass for sacred.

It is possible, indeed, to make a limitless number of such interpretations, having for object, not truth, but the reconcilement of those two irreconcilables, the Old and the New Testaments. And, in fact, the number of these is unlimited. This is the case with the Epistles of Paul, and with the decisions of the Councils (which last begin with the formula: "It is the will of us and the Holy Spirit"); and such, also, is the case with the decrees of popes and synods, with the teachings of the Khlysty,[1] and with all false interpreters of the thought of Jesus. All recur to the same gross sanctions of the truth of their reconcilements, affirming that these reconcilements are not the result of their personal thought, but a direct witness from the Holy Spirit.

Without entering upon an analysis of these different dogmatic systems, each of which pretends to be the only true one, we may, nevertheless, well see that all of them, beginning by holding sacred the multitude of writings which make up the Old and New Testaments, thereby impose upon themselves an insurmountable barrier to the understanding of the real teaching of Jesus; and out of this confusion necessarily results the possibility, and even the necessity, of an infinite variety of opposed sects.

The reconcilement of all the revelations can be infinitely varied, but the explanation of the teaching of one person, and one looked upon as a God, should, on the contrary, not give rise to any difference of sect. It is impossible there should be conflicting ways of interpreting the teaching of a God come down to earth. If God had so come down to reveal unfailing truth to men, at least He would have revealed it in such a way that all might understand; if, then, this has not been done, that is because it was not God who came; or if, indeed, the truths of God are such that God Himself cannot make them plain to mankind, how can men do so?

If, on the other hand, Jesus was not God, but only a great man, His teaching can still less engender sects. For the teaching of a great man is only great because it explains in a clear, understandable way that which others have set out obscurely, incomprehensibly. That which is incomprehensible in the teaching of a great man is not great. The teaching of a great man can, there

---

[1] A Russian sect.

fore, engender no sects. Only, then, this interpretation, which pretends to be a revelation from the Holy Spirit, and to contain the sole truth, raises up antagonisms and gives birth to sects. However much the sects of various religions may assure us that they do not condemn those of other sects, that they pray for union with them, and have no hate to them, it is not true. Never, since the time of Arius, has a single dogma arisen from other cause than the desire to contradict an opposing dogma.

To maintain that a particular dogma is a divine revelation, inspired by the Holy Spirit, is in the highest degree presumption and folly. The highest presumption, because there is nothing more arrogant than for a man to say, "What I tell you, God Himself says through my mouth." And the highest folly, because there is nothing more stupid than to reply to one who says that God speaks by his mouth, "God says quite the opposite, and by mine own mouth." But in this way reason all the Churches; and hence have been born, and are now being born, all the sects and all the evil brought, and being brought, into the world in the name of religion.

And yet deeper than this surface evil, all the sects cherish a second internal vice, which destroys in them any character of clearness, certainty, and honesty. It is this. While these sects present us with their false interpretations, as the last revelation from the Holy Spirit, they are careful never to precisely and decisively determine what is the very essence and purport of this revelation, which they profess is continued through them, and which they call "the Christian teaching."

All the sectarians who accept the revelation from the Holy Spirit, along with the Mohammedans, recognize Moses, Jesus, and Mohammed. The Churchmen accept Moses, Jesus, and the Holy Spirit. But to Mohammedanism, Mohammed is the last prophet, who alone has given the definite explanation of the two preceding revelations, —this is the last revelation, which explains all the preceding; and this one every true believer has before him.

With the religion of the Churches it is quite otherwise. That also, like the Mohammedan, accepts three revelations, but in place of calling their religion by the name of their last revealer, that is, the " religion of the Holy Spirit," they maintain their religion to be that of Jesus, and refer themselves to His teaching. So that, in giving to us what are really their own doctrines, they pretend to rest them upon the authority of Jesus.

Those religions of the Holy Spirit which offer to us the last and most decisive of revelations, whether it be in the writings of the Apostle Paul or the decisions of such and such Councils, or the decrees of popes or patriarchs, ought to say so, and call their faith by the name of him who had the last revelation. And if the last revelation is by the Fathers of the Church, or a decree of the Patriarch of the East, or a papal encyclical, or the syllabus or the catechism of Luther or Philaretus, people should say so, and call their faith by this name ; because the last revelation, which explains all the preceding, is always the most important one. But they decline to adorn their dogmatic systems with the names of these authorities, and, continuing to preach quite against Christ's own teaching, they persist in maintaining that Jesus has revealed their doctrine to them. So that, according to their teaching, Jesus declared that He, by His blood, redeemed our humanity, ruined through Adam's sin ; that there are three Persons in God ; that the Holy Spirit came down upon the apostles, and was transmitted to the priesthood by the laying on of hands ; that seven sacraments are necessary to salvation ; that communion must be in two kinds ; and so on. They would have us believe that all this is part of the teaching of Jesus ; whereas we shall there seek in vain even the least allusion to any such matters. The Churches which so pretend would do well in concluding to give all this to us at once as the doctrine of the Holy Spirit, not of Jesus ; for, in short, only those are Christians who hold the revelation of Jesus Himself as the decisive one, in virtue of His own saying, that His followers must own no other master than Himself.

It would seem that the matter is so plain that it is not worth thinking about; but however strange it seems to say so, it is none the less true that up till now the teaching of Jesus is not separated, on the one hand, from artificial and unwarrantable connection with the Old Testament, and, on the other hand, from the superadded fantastic notions which have been imposed upon it under cover of the name of the Holy Spirit. Up to now, there are some who, in calling Jesus the second Person of the Trinity, will not conceive of His teaching otherwise than as in accordance with the so-called revelations of the third Person, as these are found in the Old Testament, the decrees of Councils, and the conclusions of the Fathers of the Church; and in preaching the most extravagant things, they affirm these extravagances to be the religion of Christ. Others there are who, in refusing to regard Jesus as a God, similarly conceive of His teaching, not at all as He Himself declared it, but as what Paul and the other interpreters have made of it. Whilst considering Jesus as a man, and not as a God, these learned men deprive Him of a common natural right: the right of being held responsible for His own words only, and not for the words of His misinterpreters. In their endeavors to elucidate the teaching of Jesus, they attribute to Him ideas which He never thought of uttering. The representatives of this school, to begin with Renan, the most popular of them, do not see it their duty to take the trouble of distinguishing between that which bears the stamp of Jesus Himself and that which His interpreters have wrongly ascribed to Him. And, instead of thus troubling to search out the teaching of Jesus Himself a little more deeply than the Churches have done, they have been led to seek in the events of His life, and in the facts of history contemporary with Him, the explanation of His influence and of the diffusion of His ideas.

The problem they are called upon to solve is, in effect, this —

Eighteen hundred years ago a poor wanderer appeared on earth who taught certain things. He was flogged and executed. And since then, although many and many just men have suffered for the belief, millions of people, wise and foolish, learned and ignorant, cannot shake off the conviction that this man, alone among men, was God. Here is a strange phenomenon; how is it to be explained? The Churches explain it by saying that this man, Jesus, was really God, by which everything is explained. But if this man was not God, how are we to explain why this mere man, in particular, has been acknowledged as God?

On this point the learned people of our schools of history gather with extreme care every detail of the life of this man, without noticing that, even though they should succeed in gathering a great number of these details (in truth, they have gathered none); and even though they should succeed in entirely reconstructing the life of Jesus in the smallest details, the supreme question remains unanswered, — the question as to why Jesus, and no one else, exercised such an influence over men. The answer to this is not found in knowledge of the society in which Jesus was born, brought up, and so on; still less is it found in knowledge of the happenings in the Roman world at about this time, or in the fact that the people were inclined to superstitious beliefs. To gain this answer, it is only needful to find what precisely was the especial mark of Jesus which has led so many people to raise Him above the rest of men, and, for eighteen hundred years, to hold Him as a God.

He who would solve this problem, it would seem, must, before all, bring himself to understand the teaching of Jesus: His true teaching, clearly seen, and not the crude interpretations which have been put upon it. But this is just what is neglected. The learned historians of Christianity are so satisfied to think that Jesus was no God, they are so keen to prove that His teaching holds nothing divine, and is, therefore, not binding, that they are not alive to a very plain fact: they do not see that, the more they prove Jesus to have been simply a man, and in nothing divine, the darker and more insoluble they make the problem they have in hand. They are

making their full efforts to prove that He was simply a
man, that, therefore, His teaching is not obligatory.   To
see clearly this astonishing error, one has only to remember the last writings of Renan's follower, M. Havet, who
remarks, with much simplicity, "Christ was never, in
anything, a Christian."   And M. Soury, for his part, is
altogether ravished with the idea that Jesus was a cul-
tureless man, a simple soul.

The essential thing is : not to prove that Jesus was no
God, and His doctrine not divine, any more than to prove
He was not a Catholic : but to know what His teaching
essentially is ; that teaching which has seemed to men
so lofty and so precious, that they have again and again
owned Him for God who gave it to them.

If the reader belongs to that vast body of educated
men who have been brought up in the beliefs of a Church,
and who have not renounced its absurdities ; if he be a
man of reason and conscience (whether retaining love
and respect for the Christian teaching, or whether, following the proverb, "Burn the coat now the vermin
have got in," he thinks the whole of Christianity a pernicious superstition), I pray him to reflect that that which
shocks him, and seems to him a superstition, is not the
real teaching of Jesus ; and that it were unjust to make
Jesus responsible for the follies which have, since His
time, incrusted His teaching.   It is only necessary to
study the teaching of Jesus in its proper form, as it has
come down to us in the words and deeds which are
recorded as His own.   With readers of the kind I have
addressed, my book will go to show that Christianity is
not only a mixture of things sublime and things base ;
that it is not only not a superstition, but that, on the
contrary, it is the most convincing presentment of metaphysics and morals, the purest and most complete doctrine of life, and the highest light which the human
mind has ever reached ; a doctrine from which all the
noblest activities of humanity in politics, science, poetry,
and philosophy instinctively derive themselves.

If, on the other hand, my reader belongs to that small
minority of educated men who remain attached to Church

doctrines, and who accept religion, not for an outward end, but to gain inward quietude, then I ask such a reader to remember that the teaching of Christ, as set forth herein, is quite other than that teaching as he has been given to understand it; and that, therefore, the question for him is, not as to whether the doctrine here put before him agrees with his beliefs, but, as to which is more in harmony with his reason and his heart — the teaching of his Church composed of reconcilements of many scriptures, or the pure teaching of Jesus. It concerns him only to decide whether he will accept the new teaching, or whether he prefers to retain the teaching of his Church.

If, finally, my reader belongs to the category of men who value and accept outwardly the belief of some Church, not at all for truth's sake, but for the outward consideration of gains that come therefrom, such an one should inform himself that, whatever be the number of his coreligionists, whatever their power, whatever their station, even though monarchs, and whatever lofty personages they can reckon among them, he himself forms one of a party, not of the accusers, but of the accused. Such readers should inform themselves that they are not asked to furnish arguments for their case, because, this long while, all such arguments have been given which can be given; and even should they cite their proofs, they would only prove that which every one of the hundreds of opposing sects proves in its own case.

And, in truth, such people need not to prove anything, but to clear themselves, first, ôf the sacrilege they commit in putting the teaching of Jesus, whom they hold to be God, upon the same footing as the teachings of Ezra, of the Councils, of Theophylact; and in allowing themselves to distort the sayings of God into agreement with the sayings of men. Again, they must clear themselves of blasphemy in ascribing to God-Jesus all the zealotry which abides in their own hearts, and declaring it to be teaching of Christ. And finally, they must clear themselves of the treason they commit in hiding from men the teaching of God, who has come down to earth to bring us salvation; and by sliding in, to displace this teaching, the tradition of the Holy Spirit, thus depriving thousands of millions of that salvation which Jesus brought for men; and thus, instead of peace and love, bringing in all the diversity of sects, and all the recriminations, murders, and all sorts of misdeeds which follow.

For these readers there are only two issues: either to make humble submission, and renounce their deceits; or, to persecute those who arise to accuse them of the evil they have done and are doing.

If they will not renounce their deceits, it remains for them to take the only other part, that is, to persecute me. For which, in now completing my writing, I am prepared, with joy, and with fear for my own human weakness.

THE GOSPELS IN BRIEF

CHAPTER I

THE SON OF GOD

Man, the son of God, is powerless in the flesh, and free in the spirit

("𝕺ur 𝕱ather")

Mt. i. 18. THE birth of Jesus Christ was thus:—
His mother Mary was betrothed to Jo
seph. But, before they began to live as man
19. and wife, Mary proved with child. But Joseph
was a good man, and did not wish to disgrace
24. her; he took her as his wife, and had nothing
25. to do with her until she had borne her first son,
and called him Jesus.

Lk. ii. 40. And the boy grew and matured, and was
intelligent beyond his years.
41. Jesus was twelve years old; and it happened
42. that Mary and Joseph went to the feast at
43. Jerusalem, and took the boy with them. The
44. feast was over, and they went homeward, and
forgot about the boy. Afterward they recol-
lected, and thought that he had gone off with
45. the children, and they inquired about him along
the road. He was nowhere to be found, and
46. they went back to Jerusalem after him. And
it was the third day before they found the boy
in the temple, sitting with the teachers, ques-
47. tioning them, and listening. And every one
48. wondered at his intelligence. His mother
caught sight of him, and said: "Why have

you done this way with us ?   Your father and
I have been grieving, and looking for you."
And he said to them: "But where did you   Lk.   ii. 49
look for me ?   Surely you ought to know that
the son must be looked for in his Father's
house?"   And they did not understand his   50.
words; they did not understand whom it was
he called his Father.

And after this, Jesus lived at his mother's,   51.
and obeyed her in everything.   And he ad-   52.
vanced in age and intelligence.   And every   iii. 23.
one thought that Jesus was the son of Joseph;
and so he lived to the age of thirty.

At that time the prophet John appeared in   Mt.   iii. 1.
Judea.   He lived in the desert of Judea, on   Mk.   i. 4.
the Jordan.   John's clothes were of camel's   Mt.   iii. 4.
hair, girt round the waist with a strap; and
he fed on bark and herbs.

He summoned the people to a change of   Mk.   i. 4.
life, in order to get rid of wickedness; and,
as a sign of the change of life, he bathed people in the Jordan.   He said: "A voice calls   Lk.   iii. 4.
to you: Open a way for God through the wild
places, clear the way for Him.   Make it so   5.
that all may be level, that there may be neither
hollows nor hills, neither high nor low.   Then   6.
God will be among you, and all will find their
salvation."

And the people asked him, "What are we   10.
to do ? "   He answered: "Let him who has two   11.
suits of clothes give one to him who has none.
Let him who has food give to him who has
none."   And tax-collectors came to him, and   12.
asked: "What are we to do?"   He said to   13.
them: "Extort nothing beyond what is or-
dered."   And soldiers asked: "How are we   14.
to live?"   He said: "Do no one any harm,
do not deal falsely; be content with what is
served out to you."

And inhabitants of Jerusalem came to him,   Mt.   iii. 5

and all the Jews in the neighborhood of the

Jordan. And they acknowledged their wickedness to him; and, in sign of the change of life, he bathed them in the Jordan.

7. And many of the orthodox and conventional religionists also came to John, but secretly. He recognized them, and said : "You race of vipers! Have you, also, got wind of it, that you cannot

8. escape the will of God? Then bethink yourselves, and change your faith! And if you wish to change your faith, let it be seen by your fruits that you have bethought yourselves.

10. The ax is already laid to the tree. If the tree produces bad fruit, it will be cut down

11. and cast into the fire. In sign of your change I cleanse you in water; but, along with this bathing, you must be cleansed with the spirit.

12. The spirit will cleanse you, as a master cleanses his threshing-floor; when he gathers the wheat, but burns the chaff."

13. Jesus came from Galilee to the Jordan to be bathed by John; and he bathed, and heard John's preaching.

iv. 1. And from the Jordan he went into the wild

2. places, and there he strove in the spirit. Jesus passed forty days and nights in the desert, without food or drink.

And the voice of his flesh said to him : "If you were Son of the Almighty God, you might of your own will make loaves out of stones; but you cannot do this, therefore you are not

4. Son of God." But Jesus said to himself : "If I cannot make bread out of stones, this means that I am not Son of a God of the flesh, but Son of the God of the spirit. I am alive, not by bread, but by the spirit. And my spirit is able to disregard the flesh."

But hunger, nevertheless, tormented him; and the voice of the flesh again said to him : "If you live only by the spirit, and can disre gard the flesh, then you can throw off the flesh, and your spirit will remain alive." And it Lk. iv. 9. seemed to him that he was standing on the roof of the temple, and the voice of the flesh said to him : " If you are Son of the God of the spirit, throw yourself off the temple. You will not be killed. But an unforeseen force will 10. keep you, support you, and save you from all harm." But Jesus said to himself : " I can 11. 12. disregard the flesh, but may not throw it off, because I was born by the spirit into the flesh. This was the will of the Father of my spirit, and I cannot oppose Him."

Then the voice of the flesh said to him : " If you cannot oppose your Father by throwing yourself off the temple and discarding life, then you also cannot oppose your Father by hungering when you need to eat. You must not make light of the desires of the flesh; they were placed in you, and you must serve them." Then Jesus seemed to see all the kingdoms of 5. the earth, and all mankind, just as they live and labor for the flesh, expecting gain therefrom. And the voice of the flesh said to him : 6. " Well, you see, these work for me, and I give them all they wish for. If you will work for 7. me you will have the same." But Jesus said 8. to himself : " My Father is not flesh, but spirit. I live by Him ; I always know that He is in me. Him alone I honor, and for Him alone I work, expecting reward from Him alone."

Then the temptation ceased, and Jesus knew 13. the power of the spirit.

And when he had known the power of the 14. spirit, Jesus went out of the wild places, and Jn. i. 35. went again to John, and stayed with him.

And when Jesus was leaving John, John said 36. of him : " This is the saviour of men."

On account of these words of John, two of 37. John's disciples left their former teacher and

Jn. i. 38. went after Jesus. Jesus, seeing them following him, stopped and said: "What do you
want?" They said to him: "Teacher! we
wish to be with you, and to know your teach-
39. ing." He said: "Come with me, and I will
tell you everything." They went with him,
and stayed with him, listening to him until the
tenth hour.

40. One of these disciples was called Andrew.
41. Andrew had a brother Simon. Having heard
Jesus, Andrew went to his brother Simon, and
said to him: "We have found him of whom
the prophets wrote, the Messiah; we have
found him who has announced to us our sal-
42. vation." Andrew took Simon with him, and
brought him also to Jesus. Jesus called this
brother of Andrew, Peter, which means a
stone. And both these brothers became disciples of Jesus.

43. Afterward, before entering Galilee, Jesus
met Philip, and called him to go with him.
44. Philip was from Bethsaida, and a fellow-vil-
45. lager of Peter and Andrew. When Philip
knew Jesus, he went and found his brother
Nathanael, and said to him: "We have found
the chosen of God, of whom the prophets and
Moses wrote. This is Jesus, the son of Joseph,
46. from Nazareth." Nathanael was astonished
that he of whom the prophets wrote should be
from the neighboring village, and said: "It
is most unlikely that the messenger of God
47. should be from Nazareth." Philip said: "Come
with me, you shall see and hear for yourself."
48. Nathanael agreed, and went with his brother,
and met Jesus; and, when he had heard him,
49. he said to Jesus: "Yes, now I see that this is
true, that you are the Son of God and the king
51. of Israel." Jesus said to him: "Learn something more important than that. Henceforth
heaven is opened, and people may be in com·

munion with the forces of heaven. Henceforth
God will be no longer separate from men."

And Jesus came home to Nazareth ; and on   Lk. iv. 16
the Sabbath he went as usual into the synagogue, and began to read. They gave him the   17.
book of the prophet Isaiah, and, unrolling it,
he began to read. In the book was written : —

"The spirit of the Lord is in me. He has   18.
chosen me to announce happiness to the unfortunate and the broken-hearted, to announce
freedom to those who are bound, light to the
blind, and salvation and rest to the weary.   To   19.
announce to all men the time of God's mercy."

He folded the book, gave it to the attendant,   20.
and sat down. And all waited to hear what
he should say. And he said: "This writing
has now been fulfilled before your eyes."

CHAPTER II

LIFE IN THE SPIRIT

Therefore man must work, not for the flesh, but for the spirit

("𝔚hich art in heaven")

It happened once that Jesus, with his dis-   Mt. xii. 1.
ciples, went through a field on the Sabbath.   Mk. ii. 23,
                                               Lk. vi. 1
His disciples were hungry, and on the way
plucked ears of corn, bruised them in their
hands, and ate the grain. But, according to
the teaching of the orthodox, God had made
an agreement with Moses, that all should observe the Sabbath, and do nothing on that day.
According to this teaching of the orthodox, God
commanded that he who worked on the Sab-
bath should be stoned to death. The orthodox   Mt. xii. 2
saw that the disciples were bruising ears of
corn on the Sabbath, and said; "It is not

right to do so on the Sabbath. One must not work on the Sabbath, and you are bruising ears of corn. God ordained the Sabbath, and commanded the breaking of it should be punished with death." Jesus heard this, and said:

Mt. xii. 7. "If you understand what is the meaning of God's words, 'I desire love, and not sacrifice,' you would not attach blame to that which is 8. not blameworthy. Man is more important than the Sabbath."

Lk. xiii. 10. It happened another time, on a Sabbath, that 11. when Jesus was teaching in the synagogue, a sick woman came up to him and asked him to 12-14. help her. And Jesus began to cure her. Then the orthodox church-elder was angry with Jesus for this, and said to the people: "It is said in the law of God: There are six days in the week xiv. 3. on which to work." But Jesus, in reply, asked the orthodox professors of the law: "Well, then, in your opinion, may not one help a man 6. on the Sabbath?" And they did not know 5. what to answer. Then Jesus said: "Deceiv-Lk. xiii. 15. ers! Does not each of you untie his beast from the manger and lead him to water on the Mt. xii. 11. Sabbath? And if his sheep falls into a well, any one will run and drag it out, although even 12. on the Sabbath. And a man is much better than a sheep. But you say that one must not Mk. iii. 4. help a man. What, then, in your opinion, must one do on the Sabbath, good or evil: save a soul or destroy it? Good must be done always, on the Sabbath too."

Mt. ix. 9. Jesus once saw a tax-gatherer receiving taxes. The tax-gatherer was called Matthew. Jesus began to speak with him, and Matthew understood him, liked his teaching, and invited him to his house, and showed him hospitality. 10. When Jesus came to Matthew, there came also Matthew's friends, tax-gatherers and unbelievers, and Jesus did not disdain them, and sat

down, he and his disciples. And the orthodox Mt.   ix. 11.
saw this, and said to Jesus' disciples : " How
is it that your teacher eats with tax-gatherers
and unbelievers?"   According to the teaching
of the orthodox, God forbade communion with
unbelievers.   Jesus heard, and said : " He who 12.
is satisfied with his health does not need a doctor, but he who is ill, does.   Understand what 13.
is the meaning of God's words : 'I desire love
and not sacrifice.'   I cannot teach a change of
faith to those who consider themselves orthodox, but I teach those who consider themselves
unbelievers."

There came to Jesus orthodox professors of xv. 1.
Mk. vii. 1.
the law from Jerusalem.   And they saw that Mt. xv. 2.
Mk. vii. 2.
his disciples and Jesus himself ate bread with
unwashed hands ; and these orthodox began to
condemn him for this, because they themselves 3.
strictly observed, according to church tradition,
how plates and dishes should be washed, and
would not eat unless they had been so washed.
Also, they would eat nothing from the market 4.
unless they had washed it.

And the orthodox professors of the law asked 5.
him : "Why do you live not according to church
tradition, but take and eat bread with unwashed
hands?"   And he answered them : "But in Mt. xv. 3.
what way do you break God's commandment,
following your church tradition?   God said to Mk. vii. 10,
11.
you : 'Honor your father and mother.'   But
you have twisted it so that every one can say :
'I give to God what I used to give my parents.'
And he who so says need not support his father 12.
and mother.   Thus, then, you break God's com- 13.
mandment by church tradition.   Deceivers !
The prophet Isaiah spoke the truth about you : Mt. xv. 7.
'Because this people only fall down before me 8.
in words, and honor me with their tongue,
while their heart is far from me ; and because 9.
their fear of me is only a human law which

they have learnt by heart; therefore I will perform a wonderful, an extraordinary thing upon this people: The wisdom of its wise men shall be lost, and the reason of its thinkers shall be dimmed. Woe to them who take thought to hide their desires from the Eternal, and who

Mk. vii. 8. do their deeds in darkness.' And so it is with you: You leave that which is important in the law, that which is God's commandment, and observe your human tradition as to the washing of cups!"

14. And Jesus called the people to him, and
15. said: "Hearken all, and understand: There is nothing in the world that, entering a man, could defile him; but that which goes forth from him, this defiles a man. Let love and mercy be in your soul, and then all will be
16. clean. Try to understand this."
17. And when he returned home, his disciples
18. asked him: "What do these words mean?" And he said: "Do you also not understand this? Do you not understand that everything external, that which is of the flesh, cannot de-
19. file a man? The reason is, it enters not his soul, but his body. It enters the body, and
20. afterward goes out from it. Only that can defile a man which goes out from the man
21. himself, from his soul. Because from the soul of man proceed evil, fornication, impurity, murder, theft, covetousness, wrath, deceit, insolence, envy, calumny, pride, and every kind of folly.
23. All this evil is out of the soul of man and it alone can defile a man."

Jn. ii. 13. After this, the Passover came, and Jesus went to Jerusalem, and entered the temple.
14. In the inclosure of the temple stood cattle, cows, bulls, rams; and there were cotes full of pigeons, and money-changers behind their counters. All this was necessary in order to make offerings to God. The animals were

slaughtered and offered in the temple. This
was the method of prayer among the Jews, as
taught by the orthodox professors of the law.
Jesus went into the temple, twisted a whip, Jn.   ii. 15
drove all the cattle out of the inclosure, and
set free all the doves. And he scattered all   16.
the money, and bade that none of this should
be brought into the temple. He said : " The Mt. xxi. 13.
prophet Isáiah said to you : The house of God Mk. xi. 17.
is not the temple in Jerusalem, but the whole (Isa. lvi. 7.
world of God's people. And the prophet Jere- Jer. vii. 4,
miah also told you : Do not believe the false-   11.)
hoods that here is the house of the Eternal.
Do not believe this, but change your life ; do not
judge falsely ; do not oppress the stranger, the
widow, and the orphan ; do not shed innocent
blood, and do not come into the house of God,
and say : Now we may quietly do foul deeds.
Do not make my house a den of robbers."

And the Jews began to dispute, and said to   18.
him : " You say that our piety is wrong. By
what proofs will you show this ? " And, turn-   19.
ing to them, Jesus said : " Destroy this temple
and I will in three days awaken a new, living
temple." And the Jews said : " But how will   20.
you at once make a new temple, when this was
forty-six years in building ? " And Jesus said Mt. xii. 6.
to them : " I speak to you of that which is
more important than the temple. You would   7.
not say this if you understood the meaning of
the words of the prophet : I, God, do not rejoice
at your offerings, but rejoice at your love to each
other. The living temple is the whole world
of men, when they love each other."

And then in Jerusalem many people believed Jn. ii. 23.
in what he said. But he himself believed in   24.
nothing external, because he knew that everything is within man. He had no need that any   25.
one should give witness of man, because he
knew that in man is the spirit.

Jn. iv. 4. And Jesus happened once to be passing
5. through Samaria. He passed by the Samaritan
village of Sychar, near the place which Jacob
6. gave to his son Joseph. There was Jacob's
well. Jesus was tired, and sat beside the well.
8. His disciples went into the town to fetch bread.
7. And a woman came from Sychar to draw water,
9. and Jesus asked her to give him to drink. And
she said to him : " How is it that you ask me to
give you to drink ? For you Jews have no intercourse with us Samaritans."
10. But he said to her : " If you knew me, and
knew what I teach, you would not say this, and
you would give me to drink, and I would give
13. you the water of life. Whoever drinks of the
14. water you have will thirst again. But whoever
shall drink of the water I have shall always be
satisfied, and this water shall bring him ever-
19. lasting life." The woman understood that he
was speaking of things divine, and said to him :
" I see that you are a prophet, and wish to teach
20. me. But how are you to teach me divine things,
when you are a Jew and I a Samaritan? Our
people worship God upon this hill, but you Jews
say that the house of God is only in Jerusalem.
You cannot teach me divine things, because you
have one belief, and we another." And Jesus
21. said to her : " Believe me, woman, the time is
already here, when people, to pray to the Father,
23. will come neither to this hill nor to Jerusalem.
The time has come when the real worshipers
of God will worship the Heavenly Father in
24. spirit and with works. Such are the worshipers the Father needs. God is a spirit, and He
must be worshiped in the spirit and with
25. works." The woman did not understand what
he told her, and said : I have heard that the
messenger of God will come, he whom they call
the anointed. He will then declare every-
26. thing." And Jesus said to her : " It is I, the

same who has spoken with you.   Expect nothing more."

After this, Jesus came into the land of Judea,   Jn.   iii. 22
and there lived with his disciples, and taught.
At that time John taught the people near Salim,   23.
and bathed them in the river Enon.   For John   24.
was not yet put in prison.

And a dispute arose between the disciples of   25.
John and the hearers of Jesus, as to which was
better, John's cleansing in water or Jesus' teaching.   And they came to John, and said to him :   26.
"You cleanse with water, but Jesus only teaches,
and all go to him.   What have you to say of   27.
him?"   John said: "A man of himself can
teach nothing, unless God teach him.   Who   31.
speaks of the earth, is of the earth; but who-
soever speaks of God, is from God.   It is no-   32–34.
wise possible to prove whether the words that
are spoken are from God or not from God.   God
is a spirit; He cannot be measured, and He
cannot be proved.   He who shall understand
the word of the spirit, by this very thing proves
that he is of the spirit.   The Father, loving His   35.
Son, has intrusted all to him.   Whoever be-   36.
lieves in the Son has life, and whoever does not
believe in the Son has not life.   God is the
spirit in man."

After this there came to Jesus one of the or-   Lk.   xi. 37.
thodox, and invited him to dinner.   Jesus went
in and sat down at table.   The host noticed that   38.
he did not wash before dinner, and wondered
thereat.   And Jesus said to him : "You ortho-   39 41.
dox wash everything outside ; but are you clean
inside ?   Be well-disposed to men, and all will
be clean."

And while he sat in the house of the orthodox,   vii. 37.
there came a woman of the town, who was an
unbeliever.   She had learnt that Jesus was in
the house of the orthodox man, and she came
there too, bringing a bottle of scent.   And she   38.

knelt at his feet, wept, and washed his feet with
her tears, wiped them with her hair, and poured

Lk. vii. 39. scent over them.   The orthodox man saw this,
and thought to himself : " He is hardly a pro-
phet.   If he were really a prophet, he would
know what kind of a woman it is that is washing his feet.   He would know that this is a
wrong-doer, and would not allow her to touch

40. him."   Jesus guessed his thought, and, turning
to him, said : " Shall I tell you what I think ? "

41. The host assented.   And Jesus said : " Well, it
is this.   Two men held themselves debtors to a
certain man of property, one for five hundred

42. pence, the other for fifty.   And neither the one
nor the other had anything to pay with.   The
creditor pardoned both.   Now, in your opinion,
which will love the creditor more, and show him

43. greater attention ?   And he said : " Of course,

44. he that owed more."   Jesus pointed to the
woman, and said : " So it is with you and this
woman.   You consider yourself orthodox, and
therefore a small debtor ; she considers herself
an unbeliever, and therefore a great debtor.   I
came to your house ; you did not give me water
to wash my feet.   She washed my feet with her

45. tears, and wiped them with her hair.   You did

46. not kiss me, but she kissed my feet.   You did
not give me oil to anoint my head, but she

47. anoints my feet with precious scent.   He who
rests in orthodoxy will not do works of love, but
he who considers himself an unbeliever will do
works of love.   And for works of love, all is

48-50. forgiven."   And he said to her : " All your
wickedness is forgiven you."   And Jesus said :
" All depends upon what each man considers
himself.   Whoever considers himself good will
not be good ; but whoever considers himself bad
will become good."

xviii. 10. And Jesus said further : " Two men once
came into a temple to pray ; one orthodox, and

the other a tax-gatherer. The orthodox man Lk xviii 11
prayed thus : ' I thank Thee, God, that I am not
as other men, I am not a miser, nor a libertine ;
I am not a rogue, not such a worthless fellow as
that tax-gatherer. I fast twice weekly, and give   12.
away a tithe of my property.' But the tax-   13.
gatherer stood afar off, and dared not look up
at the sky, but merely beat his breast, and said :
' Lord, look down upon me, worthless as I am.'
Well, and this man was better than the ortho-   14.
dox, for the reason that whoever exalts him-
self shall be humbled, and whoever humbles
himself shall be exalted."

After this, disciples of John came to Jesus,   v. 33
and said : "Why do we and the orthodox fast
much, while your disciples do not fast ? For,
according to the law, God commanded people
to fast." And Jesus said to them : "While   34
the bridegroom is at the wedding, no one
grieves. Only when the bridegroom is away,   35.
do people grieve. Having life, one must not   36.
grieve. The external worship of God cannot
be combined with works of love. The old
teaching of the external worship of God cannot be combined with my teaching of works
of love to one's neighbor. To combine my
teaching with the old, is the same as to tear
off a shred from a new garment and sew it on
an old one. You will tear the new and not
mend the old. Either all my teaching must
be accepted, or all the old. And having once
accepted my teaching, it is impossible to keep
the old teaching, of purification, fasting, and
the Sabbath. Just as new wine cannot be   37
poured into old skins, or the old skins will
burst and the wine run out. But new wine   38
must be poured into new skins, and both the
one and the other will remain whole."

CHAPTER III

THE SOURCE OF LIFE

The life of all men has proceeded from the spirit of the Father

("𝔥allotoed be 𝔗𝔥𝔶 𝔑ame")

M . xi. 2,   AFTER this, John's disciples came to ask
3. Jesus whether it was he of whom John spoke;
whether he was revealing the kingdom of God,
4. and renewing men by the spirit? Jesus answered and said: "Look, listen,—and tell
John, whether the kingdom of God has begun,
and whether people are being renewed by the
spirit. Tell him of what kingdom of God I
5. am preaching. It is said in the prophecies
that, when the kingdom of God shall come,
all men will be blessed. Well, tell him that
6. my kingdom of God is such that the poor are
blessed, and that every one who understands
me becomes blessed."

7.   And, having dismissed John's disciples, Jesus
began to speak to the people as to the kingdom of God John announced. He said:
"When you went to John in the wilderness
to be baptized, what did you go to see? The
orthodox teachers of the law also went, but
did not understand that which John announced.
16. And they thought him nothing worth. This
breed of orthodox teachers of the law only
consider that as truth which they themselves
invent and hear from each other, and that as
law which they themselves have devised. But
18. that which John said, that which I say, they
do not hearken to, and do not understand.
Of that which John says, they have understood only that he fasts in the wild places, and
19. they say: 'In him is an evil spirit.' Of that
which I say, they have understood only that

I do not fast, and they say : 'He eats and
drinks with tax-gatherers and sinners — he is
a friend of theirs.' They chatter with each   17
other like children in the street, and wonder
that no one listens to them. And their wis-   19
dom is seen by their works. If you went to   8
John to look at a man attired in rich clothes,
why, such dwell here in palaces. Then, what   9
did you go to seek in the desert? Did you go
because you think John was the same as other
prophets? Do not think this. John was not
a prophet like others. He was greater than
all prophets. They foretold that which might
be. He has announced to men that which
is, namely, that the kingdom of God was,
and is, on earth. Verily, I tell you, a man has   10
not been born greater than John. He has
declared the kingdom of God on earth, and
therefore he is higher than all. The law and   Lk. xvi. 16
the prophets, — all this was needful before
John. But, from John and to the present
time, it is announced that the kingdom of God
is on earth, and that he who makes an effort
enters into it."

And the orthodox came to Jesus, and began   xvii 20
asking him : " How, then, and when, will the
kingdom of God come ? " And he answered
them : " The kingdom of God which I preach
is not such as former prophets preached.
They said that God would come with divers
visible signs, but I speak of a kingdom of
God, the coming of which may not be seen
with the eyes. And if any one shall say to
you, 'See, it is come, or it shall come,' or,
' See, it is here or there,' do not believe them.
The kingdom of God is not in time, or in
place, of any kind. It is like lightning, seen   24
here, there, and everywhere. And it has   21
neither time nor place, because the kingdom of
God, the one which I preach, is within you."

ᴵⁿ iii. 1,
2. After this, an orthodox believer, one of the Jewish authorities, named Nicodemus, came to Jesus at night, and said : " You do not bid us keep the Sabbath, do not bid us observe cleanliness, do not bid us make offerings, nor fast ; you would destroy the temple. You say of God, He is a spirit, and you say of the kingdom of God, that it is within us. Then, what kind of a kingdom of God is this ? "

3. And Jesus answered him : " Understand that, if man is conceived from heaven, then in him there must be that which is of heaven."

Nicodemus did not understand this, and said : " How can a man, if he is conceived of the flesh of his father, and has grown old, again enter the womb of his mother and be conceived anew ? "

5. And Jesus answered him : "Understand what I say. I say that man, besides the flesh, is also conceived of the spirit, and therefore every man is conceived of flesh and spirit, and therefore may the kingdom of heaven be in

6. him. From flesh comes flesh. From flesh, spirit cannot be born ; spirit can come only

8. from spirit. The spirit is that which lives in you, and lives in freedom and reason ; it is that of which you know neither the beginning nor the end, and which every man feels in him.

7. And, therefore, why do you wonder that I told you we must be conceived from heaven ? "

9. Nicodemus said : " Still I do not believe that this can be so."

10. Then Jesus said to him : "What kind of a teacher are you, if you do not comprehend

11. this ? Understand that I am not interpreting some learned points ; I am interpreting that which we all know, I am averring that which

12. we all see. How will you believe in that which is in heaven if you do not believe in that which is on earth, which is in you yourself ?

"For, no man has ever gone up to heaven, Jn. iii. 13
but there is only man on earth, come down
from heaven, and himself of heaven. Now,   14.
this same heavenly Son in man it is that must
be lifted up, that every one may believe in him   15.
and not perish, but may have heavenly life.
For God gave His Son, of the same essence   16.
as Himself, not for men's destruction, but for
their happiness. He gave him in order that
every one might believe in him, and might not
perish, but have life without end. For He did   17.
not bring forth His Son, this life, into the world
of men in order to destroy the world of men;
but He brought forth His Son, this life, in order
that the world of men might be made alive
through him.

"Whoever commits his life to him does not   18.
die; but he who does not commit his life to
him destroys himself thereby, in that he has
not trusted to that which is life. Death con-   19.
sists in this, that life is come into the world,
but men themselves go away from life.

"Light is the life of men; light came into
the world, but men prefer the darkness to
light, and do not go to the light. He who   20.
does wrong does not go to the light, so that
his deeds may not be seen, and such a one
bereaves himself of life. Whereas he who   21.
lives in truth goes to the light, so that his
deeds are seen; and he has life, and is united
with God.

"The kingdom of God must be understood,
not, as you think, in the sense that it will come
for all men at some time or other, and in some
place or other, but thus, — In the whole world
always, some people, those who trust in the
heavenly Son of man, become sons of the kingdom, but others who do not trust in him are destroyed. The Father of that spirit which is in
man is the Father of those only who acknowl-

edge themselves to be His sons. And, therefore, only those exist to Him who have kept in
themselves that which He gave them."

Mt xiii. 3. And, after this, Jesus began to explain to the
people what the kingdom of God is, and he
made this clear by means of parables.

He said: "The Father,—who is spirit,—
sows in the world the life of understanding,
4. as the husbandman sows seed in his field. He
sows over the whole field, without remarking
where any particular seed falls. Some seeds
fall upon the road, and the birds fly down and
5. peck them up. And others fall among stones;
and although among these stones they come
up, they wither, because there is no room for
7. the roots. And others, again, fall among wormwood, so that the wormwood chokes the corn,
8. and the ear springs up, but does not fill. And
others fall on good soil; they spring up, and
make return for the lost corn, and bear ears,
and fill, and one ear will give a hundredfold,
another sixtyfold, and another thirtyfold. Thus,
then, God also sowed broadcast the spirit in
men; in some it is lost, but in others it yields
a hundredfold: these last are they who form
Mk. iv. 26. the kingdom of God. Thus the kingdom is not
such as you think, that God will come to reign
over you. God has only sown the spirit, and
the kingdom of God will be in those who preserve it.

27. "God does not force men. It is as when the
sower casts the seeds in the earth, and himself
28. thinks no more of them; but the seeds of themselves swell, sprout up, put forth leaf, sheath,
29. and ear, and fill with grain. Only when it is
ripened, the master sends sickles to reap the
cornfield. So also God gave His Son, the
spirit, to the world; and the spirit of itself
grows in the world, and the sons of the spirit
make up the kingdom of God.

A woman puts yeast in the kneading trough   Mt. xiii. 33
and mixes it with the flour; she then stirs it
no more, but lets it ferment and rise. As long
as men live, God does not interpose in their
life. He gave the spirit to the world, and the
spirit itself lives in men, and men who live by
the spirit make up the kingdom of God. For
the spirit there is neither death nor evil. Death
and evil are for the flesh, but not for the spirit.

The kingdom of God comes in this way.   24.
A farmer sowed good seed in his field. The
farmer is the Spirit, the Father; the field is
the world; the good seeds are the sons of the
kingdom of God. And the farmer lay down   25
to sleep, and an enemy came and sowed darnel
in the field. The enemy is temptation; the
darnel is the sons of temptation. And his   27.
laborers came to the farmer and said: "Can
you have sown bad seed?" Much darnel has
come up in your field. Send us, we will weed   28.
it out." And the farmer said: "You must   29.
not do that, for in weeding the darnel you will
trample the wheat. Let them grow together.
The harvest will come, when I shall bid the   30.
reapers take away the darnel and burn it; and
the wheat I shall store in the barn."

Now, the harvest is the end of man's life,
and the harvesters are the power of heaven.
And the darnel shall be burnt, but the wheat
shall be cleaned and gathered. Thus also, at
life's end, all shall vanish which was a guile of
time, and the true life in the spirit shall alone
be left. For the Spirit, the Father, there is no
evil. The spirit keeps that which it needs, and
that which is not of it does not exist for it.

The kingdom of God is like a net. The net   47.
will be spread in the sea, and will catch all
kinds of fish. And afterward, when it is   48.
drawn out, the worthless will be set aside and
thrown into the sea. So will it be at the end

of the age; the powers of heaven will take the good, and the evil will be cast away.

Mt. xiii. 10.   And when he finished speaking, the disciples asked him how to understand these parables?

11. And he said to them: "These parables must be understood in two ways. I speak all these parables because there are some like you, my disciples, who understand wherein is the kingdom of God, who understand that the kingdom of God is within every man, who understand how to go into it; while others do not under-

14. stand this. Others look, but see not; they hearken, and do not understand, because their

15. heart has become gross. Therefore I speak these parables with two meanings, for both classes of hearers. To the others I speak of God, of what God's kingdom is to them, and they may understand this; while to you I speak of what the kingdom of God is for you — that kingdom which is within you.

18.   "And see that you understand as you ought

19. the parable of the sower. For you the parable is this: Every one who has understood the meaning of the kingdom of God, but has not accepted it in his heart, to him temptation comes and robs him of that which has been

20. sown: this is the seed on the wayside. That which was sown on stones, is he who at once

21. accepts with joy. But there is no root in him, and he only accepts for a time; but let straits and persecution befall him, because of the meaning of the kingdom, and he straightway

22. denies it. That which was sown among the wormwood is he who understood the meaning of the kingdom, but worldly cares and the seductions of wealth strangle the meaning

23. in him, and he yields no fruit. But that which was sown on good soil is he who understood the meaning of the kingdom, and accepted it into his heart; such yield fruit, one a hundred-

fold, another sixtyfold, another thirtyfold. For   Mt xiii. 12
he who retains, to him much is given ; while
from him who does not retain, the whole will
be taken.

"And, therefore, take care how you under-   Lk. viii. 18
stand these parables.   Understand them so as
not to give way to deceit, wrong, and care;
but so as to yield thirtyfold, or sixtyfold, or a
hundredfold.

"The kingdom of heaven grows and spreads   Mt. xiii. 31.
in the soul out of nothing, providing everything.   It is like a birch seed, the very smallest of seeds, which, when it grows up, becomes
greater than all other trees, and the birds of
heaven build their nests in it."

CHAPTER IV

GOD'S KINGDOM

Therefore the will of the Father is the life and welfare of
all men

("𝕿𝖍𝖞 𝖐𝖎𝖓𝖌𝖉𝖔𝖒 𝖈𝖔𝖒𝖊")

AND Jesus went among the towns and vil-   Mt. ix. 35.
lages, and taught all men the happiness of fulfilling the Father's will.   Jesus was sorry for   36.
men, that they perish without knowing wherein
is the true life, and are driven about and suffer,
without knowing why, like sheep left without
a shepherd.

Once a crowd of people gathered to Jesus,   v. 1.
to hear his teaching ; and he went up on a hill
and sat down.   His disciples surrounded him.

And Jesus began to teach the people as to   2.
what is the Father's will.   He said : —

Blessed are the poor and homeless, for they   Lk. vi. 20,
are in the will of the Father.   Even if they   21.
hunger for a time, they shall be satisfied ; and

if they grieve and weep, they shall be comforted. If people look down upon them, and
thrust them aside and everywhere drive them
away, let them be glad at this; for the people
of God have ever been persecuted thus, and
they receive a heavenly reward.

But woe to the rich, for they have already
got everything they wish, and will get nothing more. They are now satisfied; but they
shall be hungry. Now they are merry; but
they shall be sad. If all praise them, woe to
them, because only deceivers get everybody's
praise.

Blessed are the poor and homeless, but
blessed only then, when they are poor, not
merely externally, but in spirit; as salt is good
only when it is true salt; not externally only,
but when it has the savor of salt.

So, you also, the poor and homeless, are the
teachers of the world; you are blessed, if you
know that true happiness is in being homeless
and poor. But if you are poor only externally,
then you, like salt without savor, are good for
nothing. You must be a light to the world;
therefore do not hide your light, but show it to
men. For when one lights a candle, one does
not put it under a bench, but upon the table,
that it may light all in the room. So, you also,
do not hide your light, but show it by your
works, so that men may see that you know the
truth, and, looking at your good works, may
understand your Heavenly Father.

And do not think that I free you from the law.
I teach not release from the law, but I teach
the fulfilment of the eternal law. As long as
there are men under heaven, there is an everlasting law. There will be no law, only when
men shall of themselves act wholly according
to the eternal law. And now I am giving you
the commandments of the eternal law. And

if any one shall release himself, if only from one
of these short commandments, and shall teach
others that they may so release themselves, he
shall be least in the kingdom of heaven ; while
he who shall fulfil them, and shall thereby teach
others, shall be the greatest in the kingdom of
heaven.　Because if your virtue be not greater　Mt.　v. 20
than the virtue of the orthodox leaders, you
will in no way be in the kingdom of heaven.

These are the commandments : —

I

In the former law it was said : " Do not　21
kill." But if any one shall kill another, he
must be judged.

But I tell you, that every one is worthy of　22
judgment who gets angry with his brother.
And still more to blame is he who abuses his
brother.

So that, if you wish to pray to God, re-　23
member, first, whether there is no man who
may have something against you. If you remember that but one man considers you have
offended him, leave your prayer, and go first　24
and make peace with your brother ; and then
you may pray. Know that God wants neither
sacrifice nor prayer, but peace, concord, and
love among you. And you may neither pray,
nor think of God, if there is but one man to
whom you do not bear love.

And so this is the first commandment : Do
not be angry, do not abuse ; but having
quarreled, make peace in such a way that
no one may have cause for offense against
you.

II

Mt **v. 31.** In the former law it was said : "Do not commit adultery; and if you wish to put away your wife, give her a bill of divorce."

28. But I tell you, if you are drawn by the beauty of a woman, you are already commit-

29. ting adultery. All sensuality destroys the soul, and therefore it is better for you to renounce the pleasure of the flesh than to destroy your life.

32. And if you put away your wife, then, besides being vicious yourself, you drive her also into vice, and him who shall have to do with her.

And therefore, this is the second commandment: Do not think that love toward woman is good ; do not admire the beauty of women, but live with the one to whom you have become united, and do not leave her.

III

33. In the former law it was said : "Do not utter the name of the Lord your God in vain, do not call upon your God when lying, and do not dishonor the name of your God. Do not swear by Me in untruth, so as to profane your

34. God." But I tell you that every oath is a profanation of God.

35. Therefore, swear not at all. Man cannot promise anything, because he is wholly in the

36. power of the Father. A man cannot turn one hair from gray to black; how then shall he swear beforehand, that he will do this and that, and swear by God? Every oath is a profanation of God, for, if a man shall have to fulfil an oath which is against the will of God, it must follow that he has sworn to go against

God's will; so that every oath is evil. But Mt.　v 37
when men question you about anything, say:
" Yes," if yes, — " No," if no. Everything
added to this is evil.

Therefore, the third commandment is:
Swear nothing, to any one; say "Yes," when
it is yes, — " No," when it is no; and understand that every oath is evil.

IV

In the former law it was said: " He who de- 38
stroys life, shall give a life for a life; an eye
for an eye, a tooth for a tooth, a hand for a
hand, an ox for an ox, a slave for a slave,"
and so on.

But I tell you: Do not wrestle with evil by 39.
evil. Not only do not take by law an ox for
an ox, a slave for a slave, a life for a life, but
do not resist evil at all. If any one wishes to 40.
take an ox from you by law, give him another;
if any one wishes to get your coat by law, give
him your shirt also; if any one strikes out your
tooth on one side, turn to him the other side.
If you are made to do one piece of work, do 41.
two. If men wish to take your property, vi 30.
give it to them. If they do not return your
money, do not ask for it.

And therefore: Do not judge, do not go to 37.
law, do not punish, and you yourself shall not
be judged, nor punished. Forgive all, and you
shall be forgiven, because if you shall judge
people, they will judge you also.

You cannot judge, because you, all men, are Mt. vii. 1.
blind, and do not see the truth. How, with 3
obstructed eyes, will you discern the mote in
your brother's eye? You must first clear your
own eye. But whose eyes are clear? Can a Lk. vi 39
blind man lead a blind man? Both will fall

into the pit. Thus, also, they who judge and punish, like the blind, are leading the blind.

Lk. vi. 40. They who judge and condemn people to violent treatment, wounds, maiming, death, wish to teach people. But what else can come from their teaching, than that the pupil will learn his lesson, and will become quite like the teacher? What, then, will he do, when he has learnt his lesson? The same that the teacher does : violence, murder.

Mt. vii. 6. And do not think to find justice in the courts. To seek legal justice, to hand matters over to human courts, is the same as to cast precious pearls before swine ; they will trample upon it, and tear you to pieces.

And, therefore, the fourth commandment is : However men may wrong you, do not resist evil, do not judge and do not go to law, do not complain and do not punish.

V

v. 43. In the former law it was said : "Do good to men of your own nation, and do evil to strangers."

44. But I tell you, love not only your own countrymen, but people of other nations. Let strangers hate you, let them fall upon you, wrong you ; but you speak well of them, and

46. do them good. If you are only attached to your countrymen, why, all men are thus attached to their own countrymen, and hence

45. wars arise. Behave equally well toward men of all nations, and you will be the sons of the Father. All men are His children, and therefore all are brothers to you.

And, therefore, this is the fifth commandment : Behave equally well toward foreigners, as I told you to behave among yourselves

then all your soul will be in darkness. You Mt. vi. 24
cannot serve at one time two masters. You
will please one, and offend the other. You cannot serve God and the flesh. You will either
work for the earthly life or for God. There- 25.
fore, do not be anxious for what you shall eat
and drink, and wherewith you shall be clothed.
Life is more wonderful than food and clothing,
and God gave it you.

Look at God's creatures, the birds. They do 26.
not sow, reap, or harvest, but God feeds them.
In God's sight, man is not worse than the bird.
If God gave man life, He will be able to feed
him too. But you yourselves know that, how- 27.
ever much you strive, you can do nothing for
yourselves. You cannot lengthen your life by
an hour. And why should you care about 28.
clothing? The flowers of the field do not 29.
work and do not spin, but are dressed as Solomon in all his glory never was. Well, then, if 30.
God has so adorned the grass, which to-day
grows and to-morrow is mown, will he not
clothe you?

Do not trouble and worry yourselves; do 31.
not say that you must think of what you will
eat and how you will be clothed. This every 32.
one needs, and God knows this need of yours.
And so, do not care about the future. Live 33.
in the present day. Take care to be in the
will of the Father. Wish for that which alone
is important, and the rest will all come of itself.
Strive only to be in the will of the Father. 34.
And so, do not trouble about the future.
When the future comes, then it will be time to
do so. There is enough evil in the present.

Ask and it shall be given you, seek and you Lk. xi. 9
shall find, knock and it shall be opened to you.
Is there a father who would give his son a Mt. vii. 9,
stone instead of bread, or a snake instead of a 10.
fish? Then, how is it that we, wicked men, 11.

are able to give our children that which they
need, while your Father in heaven shall not
give you that which you truly need, if you ask
Him? Ask, and the Heavenly Father will
give the life of the spirit to them who ask Him.

Mt. vii. 13.   The way to life is narrow, but enter by the
narrow way. The way into life is one only.
It is narrow and strait. About it the plain
lies great and wide, but it is the way of de-

14. struction. The narrow way alone leads to

Lk. xii. 32. life; and few find it. But do not quail, little
flock! The Father has promised you the
kingdom.

Mt. vii. 15.   Only, beware of false prophets and teachers;
they approach you in sheepskins, but within
they are ravening wolves.

16.   By their fruits will you know them; by that
which they yield. Figs are not gathered from

17. thistles, nor grapes from thorns. But a good
tree brings forth good fruit. And a bad tree

20. brings forth bad fruit. And so you will know

Lk. vi. 45. them by the fruits of their teaching. A good
man, from his good heart, brings forth everything that is good; but a wicked man, from
his evil heart, brings forth everything evil; for
the lips speak from the overflow of the heart.
And therefore, if teachers teach you to do
to others that which is bad for yourselves, —
teach violence, executions, wars, — know that
they are false teachers.

Mt. vii. 21.   For it is not he that says: Lord, Lord!
who shall enter the kingdom of heaven, but he
who fulfils the word of the Heavenly Father.

22. The false teachers will say: "Lord, Lord! we
have taught your teaching, and we have driven

23. away evil according to your teaching." But I
will disown them, and say to them: No, I never
acknowledged you, and do not acknowledge
you. Go out of my sight, you are doing that
which is unlawful.

And so, every one who has heard these words   Mt. vii. 24.
of mine, and fulfils them, he, like a reasonable
man, builds his house upon a rock. And his   25.
house will stand against all storms. But he   26.
who hears these words of mine, and does not
fulfil them, he, like a foolish man, builds his
house upon sand. When the storm comes,   27.
it will overthrow the house, and all will perish.

And all the people wondered at such teaching;   Lk. iv. 32.
because the teaching of Jesus was quite other
than that of the orthodox teachers of the law.
These taught a law which must be obeyed, but
Jesus taught that all men are free. And in   Mt. iv. 14.
Jesus Christ were fulfilled the prophecies of
Isaiah : " The people living in darkness, in the   16.
shadow of death, saw the light of life, and he
who furnished this light of truth does no violence nor harm to men, but he is meek and
gentle. He, in order to bring truth into the   xii. 19.
world, neither disputes nor shouts ; his voice
is never heard raised. He will not break a   20.
straw, and will not blow out the smallest light.
And all the hope of men is in his teaching.   21.

CHAPTER V

THE TRUE LIFE

*The fulfilment of the personal will leads to death; the fulfil-
ment of the Father's will gives true life*

(" Thy will be done ")

AND Jesus rejoiced at the strength of the   Mt. xi. 25.
spirit, and said : —

" I acknowledge the spirit of the Father, the
source of everything in heaven and earth, Who
has revealed that which was hidden from the
wise and learned, to the simple, solely through

their acknowledging themselves Sons of the
Father.

Mt. xi. 28. "All take care for fleshly happiness, and
have put themselves to a load which they cannot draw; they have put a yoke upon themselves which was not made for them.

"Understand my teaching and follow it;
and you shall know rest and joy in life. I
give you another yoke, and another load;

29. namely, the spiritual life. Put yourselves to
that, and you shall learn from me peace and
happiness. Be calm and meek in heart, and

30. you will find blessedness in your life. Because
my teaching is a yoke made for you, and the
fulfilment of my teaching is a light load, with
a yoke made for you."

Jn. iv. 31. The disciples of Jesus once asked him
32. whether he wished to eat. He said: "I
33. have food of which you do not know." They
thought that some one had brought him some-
34. thing to eat. But he said: —

"My food is to do the will of Him who gave
me life, and to fulfil that which He intrusted
35, to me. Do not say 'There is still time,' as the
36. plowman said, waiting for the harvest. He
who fulfils the will of the Father is always satisfied, and knows neither hunger nor thirst.
The fulfilment of the will of God always satisfies, bearing its reward within itself. You
must not say, 'I will afterward fulfil the will
of the Father.' While there is life, you always
can, and must, fulfil the will of the Father.

37. Our life is the field which God has sown, and
38. our business is to gather its fruits. And if
we gather the fruits, we get the reward, life
beyond time. True it is, that we do not give
ourselves life; some one else does. And if we
labor to gather in life, then we, like reapers,
get our reward. I teach you to gather in this
life, which the Father has given you."

Once, Jesus came to Jerusalem. And there ^{Jn.} ^{v.} ^{1,}
was then a bathing-place there. And men said ^{2,} ^{4.}
of this bathing-place, that an angel came down
into it, and through this the water in the bath
would begin to move, and he who first plunged
into the water after it was moved got well from
whatever he was ailing. And sheds were made ^{2.}
around the bath, and under these sheds sick
men lay, waiting for the water in the bath to ^{3.}
be moved, in order to plunge into it.

And a man was there who had been infirm ^{5.}
thirty-eight years. Jesus asked who he was.

And the man told how he had been ailing so
long, and was still waiting to get into the bath
first, upon the water being moved, in order to
be healed; but for these thirty-eight years he
had been unable to get in first, others always
getting into the bath before him.

And Jesus saw that he was old, and said to ^{6.}
him: "Do you wish to get well?"

He said: "I wish to, but I have no one to ^{7.}
carry me into the water in time. Some one
always will get in before me."

And Jesus said to him: "Awake, take up ^{8.}
your bed and walk."

And the sick man took up his bed and ^{9.}
walked.

And it was the Sabbath. And the orthodox ^{10.}
said: "You must not take up the bed, for to-
day is the Sabbath." He said: "He who ^{11.}
raised me, bade me also take up the bed."
And the infirm man said to the orthodox, that ^{15.}
it was Jesus who had healed him. And they ^{16.}
became angry, and accused Jesus, because he
did such things on the Sabbath.

And Jesus said: "That which the Father ^{17.}
always does, I also do. In truth, I say to you, ^{19.}
the Son of himself can do nothing. He does
only that which he has understood from the
Father. What the Father does, he also does. ^{20.}

The Father loves the Son, and by this very fact has taught him everything which the Son should know.

Jn.   v. 21. "The Father gives life to the dead, and thus the Son gives life to him who desires it; because, as the business of the Father is life,

22. so the business of the Son must be life. The Father has not condemned men to death, but has given men power, at will, to die or live.

23. And they will live, if they shall honor the Son as the Father.

24. "I tell you truly, that he who has understood the meaning of my teaching, and has believed in the common Father of all men, already has life, and is delivered from death.

25. They who have understood the meaning of human life, have already escaped from death

26. and shall live forever. Because, as the Father lives of Himself, so also has He given

27. the Son life within himself. And He has given him freedom. It is by this, that he is the Son of Man.

28. "Henceforth all mortals shall be divided

29. into two kinds. They alone, who do good, shall find life; but they who do evil shall be

30. destroyed. And this is not my decision, but it is what I have understood from the Father. And my decision is true, because I thus decide, not in order to do that which I wish, but in order that all may do that which the Father of all wishes.

31. "If I were to assure all that my teaching is true, this would not establish my teaching.

36. But there is that which establishes my teaching; namely, the conduct which I teach. That shows that I do not teach of myself, but in the

37. name of the Father of all men. And my Father, He who has taught me, confirms the truth of my commandments in the souls of all.

"But you do not wish to understand and to
know His voice. And you do not accept the   Jn.   v. 38
meaning this voice speaks. That that which
is in you, is spirit descended from heaven, —
this, you do not believe.

"Enter into the meaning of your writings.   39.
You will find in them the same as in my teaching, commandments to live, not for yourself
alone, but for the good of men. Why, then, do 40.
you not wish to believe in my commandments,
which are those that give life to all men? I   43.
teach you in the name of the common Father
of all men, and you do not accept my teaching; but if any one shall teach you in his own
name, him will you believe.

"One cannot believe that which people say   44.
to each other, but one can only believe that in
every man there is a Son like the Father."

And that men may not think that the king-   Lk. xix. 11.
dom of heaven is established by anything
visible; but that they may understand that
the kingdom of God consists in the fulfilment
of the Father's will; and understand that the
fulfilment of the Father's will depends on
each man's effort and striving to make people
see that life is given, not for oneself personally, but for the fulfilment of the Father's
will, which alone saves from death and gives
life, — Jesus told a parable. He said: —   12.

"There was a rich man, who had to go
away from his home. Before he went, he   13.
called his slaves, and gave among them ten talents, one to each, and said: 'While I am away,
labor each of you upon what I have given.'
But it happened that, when he was gone, cer-   14
tain inhabitants of that town said: 'We do not 15.
wish to serve him any more.' When the rich
man came back, he called the slaves to whom
he had given the money, and bade each say
what he had done with his money. The first   16.

came, and said : ' See, master, for your one I
Lk. xix. 17. have earned ten.' And the master said to
him : 'Well done, good servant; you have
been trustworthy in a little, I will place you
over much; be one with me in all my wealth.'
18. Another slave came, and said : 'See, master,
19. for your talent I have earned five.' And the
master said to him : 'Well done, good slave,
20. be one with me in all my estate.' And yet
another came, and said : 'Here is your talent,
I hid it in a cloth and buried it; because I was
21. afraid of you. You are a hard man, you take
where you did not store, and gather where
22. you did not sow.' And the master said to
him : 'Foolish slave ! I will judge you by your
own words. You say that, from fear of me,
you hid your talent in the earth, and did not
work upon it. If you knew that I was severe,
and take where I did not give, then why did
Mt. xxv. 26, you not do that which I bade you do? If you
Lk. xix. 23. had worked upon my talent, the estate would
have been added to, and you would have fulfilled that which I bade you. But you have
not done that for which the talent was given
you, and, therefore, you must not own it.'
24. And the master bade the talent be taken from
him who had not worked upon it, and given to
25. him who had worked most. And then the
servants said to him : 'Sir, he already has
26. much.' But the master said : 'Give to them
who have worked much, because he who looks
after that which he has, shall receive an in-
Mt. xxv. 30. crease. As to them who did not wish to be in
my power, drive them forth, so that they may
be here no more.' "

Now this master is the source of life, the
spirit, the Father. His slaves are men. The
talents are the life of the spirit. As the master does not himself work upon his estate, but
bids the slaves to work, each by himself, so

the spirit of life in men has given them the
command to work for the life of men, and
then left them alone.   They who sent to say
that they did not acknowledge the authority
of the master, are they who do not acknowledge the spirit of life.   The return of the
master, and the demand for an account, is the
destruction of fleshly life, and the decision of
the fate of men as to whether they have yet
life beyond that which was given them. Some,
the slaves who fulfil the will of the master,
work upon that which was given them, and
make gain on gain ; they are those men who,
having received life, understand that life is the
will of the Father, and is given to serve the
life of others.   The foolish and wicked slave,
who hid his talent and did not work upon it,
represents those men who fulfil only their
own will, and not the will of the Father; who
do not serve the life of others.   The slaves
who have fulfilled the master's will, and worked
for the increase of his estate, become sharers
of the whole estate of the master, while the
slaves who have not fulfilled the master's will,
and have not worked for him, are bereft of
that which was given them.   People who have
fulfilled the will of the Father, and have served
life, becomes sharers in the life of the Father,
and receive life, notwithstanding the destruction of the fleshly life.   They who have not
fulfilled the will, and have not served life, are
bereft of that life which they had, and are
destroyed. They who did not wish to acknowledge the authority of the master, such do not
exist for the master; he drives them forth.
People who do not acknowledge within themselves the life of the spirit, the life of the Son
of man, such do not exist for the Father.

After this, Jesus went into a desert place. Jn.   vi. 1,
And many people followed him.   And he   2.
                                                        3.

climbed a mountain, and sat there with his
Jn. vi. 5. followers. And he saw that there was a great
throng, and said : " Whence shall we get bread
7. to feed all these people ? " Philip said : " Even
two hundred pence will not suffice, if to each
Mt. xiv. 17. be given but a little. We have only a little
Jn. vi. 9. bread and fish." And another disciple said :
" They have bread ; I have seen it. There is
a boy who has five loaves and two small fishes."
10. And Jesus said : " Bid them all lie down on
the grass."

11. And Jesus took the loaves which he had,
and gave them to his disciples, and bade them
give them to others ; and so all began to hand
from one to another what there was, and all
were satisfied, yet much was left over.

26. The next day, the people came again to
Jesus. And he said to them : " See, you come
to me, not because you have seen wonders,
but because you have eaten bread and were
27. satisfied." And he said to them : " Work not
for perishable food, but for everlasting food,
such as only the spirit of the Son of Man gives,
sealed by God."

28. The Jews said : " But what must we do, in
order to do the works of God ? "

29. And Jesus said : " The work of God is in
this, to believe in that life which He has given
you."

30. They said : " Give us a sign that we may
believe. What are your deeds which can serve
31. as a proof ? Our fathers ate manna in the wilderness. God gave them bread from heaven
to eat ; and so it is written."

32. Jesus answered them : " The true heavenly
bread is the spirit of the Son of Man, that
33. which the Father gives. Because the nourishment of man is the spirit descended from
heaven. This it is which gives life to the
35. world. My teaching gives true nourishment

to man. He who follows me shall not hunger, and he who believes in my teaching will
never know thirst.

"But I have already told you that you have Jn. vi. 36.
seen this, yet do not believe.

"All that life which the Father gave the Son   37.
will be realized through my teaching; and every one who believes will be a sharer in it.   I   38.
came down from heaven, not to do that which
I wish, but to do the will of the Father, of Him
who gave me life.   But the will of the Father   39.
who sent me is this, that I should keep all that
life which He gave, and should not destroy anything of it.   And therefore, herein is the will of   40.
the Father who sent me, that every one who
sees the Son, and believes in him, should have
everlasting life.   And my teaching gives life
at the last day of the body."

The Jews were shocked at his saying that his   41.
teaching was come down from heaven.   They   42.
said: "Why, this is Jesus, the son of Joseph;
we know his father and mother.   How, then,
can he say that his teaching has descended from
heaven?"

"Do not debate as to who I am, and whence   43.
I am come," said Jesus.   "My teaching is true,   44.
not because I declare, like Moses, that God
spoke with me on Sinai; but it is true because
it is in you also.   Every one who believes my
commandments, believes, not because it is I who
speak, but because our common Father draws
him to Himself; and my teaching will give
him life at the last day.   And it is written in   45.
the prophets, that all shall be taught by God.
Every one who shall understand the Father,
and shall learn to understand His will, thereby
yields himself to my teaching.

"That any man has seen the Father, this has   46.
never been, except he who is from God; he has
seen, and sees, the Father.

Jn. vi. 47. " He who believes in me (in my teaching) has everlasting life.

48, " My teaching is the nourishment of life.
49. Your fathers ate manna, food straight from
50. heaven, and yet they died. But the true nourishment of life, which descends from heaven, is such, that he who is fed with it will not die.

51. My teaching is this nourishment of life descended from heaven. He who is fed with it lives forever. And this nourishment which I teach is my flesh, which I give for the life of all men."

52. The Jews did not understand what he said, and began to dispute as to how it was possible to give one's flesh for the nourishment of men, and why.

53. And Jesus said to them: " If you shall not give up your flesh for the life of the spirit,
54. there will be no life in you. He who does not give up his flesh for the life of the spirit, has
55. not real life. That in me which gives up the flesh for the spirit, that alone lives.

" And therefore, our flesh is the true food
56. for the real life. That only which in me consumes my body, that which gives up the fleshly
57. life for the true life, that only is I. It is in me, and I am in it. And as I live in the flesh by the will of the Father, similarly, that which lives in me lives by my will."

60. And some of his disciples, when they heard this, said: " These are hard words, and it is difficult to understand them."

61. And Jesus said to them: " Your ideas are so confused, that my sayings as to what man was, is, and always will be, seem difficult to
63. you. Man is the spirit in the flesh, and the spirit alone gives life, but the flesh does not give life. In the words which seem so difficult to you, I have really said nothing more than that the spirit is life."

Afterward, Jesus chose seventy men out of Lk.   x.   1.
his near friends, and sent them into those places
where he himself wished to go.   He said to 2.
them :—

" Many people do not know the blessing of
real life.   I am sorry for all ; and wish to teach
all.   But as the master is not enough for the
reaping of his field, so also I shall not suffice.
Go you, then, through the various cities, and 3.
everywhere proclaim the fulfilment of the will
of the Father.

" Say, The will of the Father is in this : Not
to be angered, not to be sensual, not to swear,
not to resist evil, and not to make any distinction between people.   And accordingly, do ye
in everything fulfil these commandments.

"I send you like sheep among wolves.   Be Mt.   x. 16.
wise as snakes, and pure as doves.

" Before everything, have nothing of your Lk.   x.   4.
own ; take nothing with you, neither wallet, nor
bread, nor money ; only clothes upon your body,
and shoes.   Further, make no distinction be- 5.
tween people ; do not choose your hosts, where
you shall put up.   But in whichever house you Mt.   x. 12.
shall come first, stay there.   When you come
into the house, greet the master.   If he welcome you, stay ; if not, go into another house.

" For that which you shall say, they will hate 22.
you, and fall upon, and persecute you.   And 23.
when they shall drive you out, go into another
village ; and if they all drive you out of that,
go yet into another.   They will persecute you
as wolves hunt sheep ; but do not quail, suffer
to the last hour.   And they will take you into
the courts, and will try you, and will flog you,
and will take you before the authorities, that
you may justify yourselves before them.   And 19.
when you shall be taken into the courts, be
not afraid ; and do not bethink yourselves
what you shall say.   The spirit of the Father

will speak through you, what is needful to be said.

Mt. x. 23. "You will not have passed through all the towns, before people will have understood your teachings, and will turn to it.

27. "And so, be not afraid. That which is hidden in the souls of men will come forth.

26. That which you shall say to two or three will
28. spread among thousands. But chiefly, be not afraid of those who may kill your body. To your souls, they can do nothing. And so, do not fear them. But be afraid lest both your bodies and souls be destroyed, by your abstaining from the fulfilment of the will of the
29. Father. That is what you have to fear. Five sparrows are sold for a farthing, but even they
30. shall not die without the Father's will. And a hair shall not fall from the head without the
31. Father's will. So then, what need you be afraid of, seeing you are in the Father's will?

34. "Not all will believe in my teaching. And they who will not believe, will hate it ; because it bereaves them of that which they love, and
Lk. xii. 49. strife will come of it. My teaching, like fire,
51. will kindle the world. And from it strife must
52, arise in the world. Strife will arise in every
53. house. Father against son, mother against daughter ; and their kin will become haters of them who understand my teaching, and
xiv. 26. they will be killed. Because, for him who shall understand my teaching, neither his father, nor his mother, nor wife, nor children, nor all his property, will have any weight."

Mk. iii. 22. Then the learned orthodox gathered at Jerusalem, and went to Jesus. Jesus was in
20. a village, and a crowd of people thronged into the place, and stood around.

Mt. xii. 24. The orthodox began to speak to the people, in order that they might not believe in the teaching of Jesus. They said that Jesus was

possessed; that if they should live by his commandments, there would then be yet more
evil among the people than now. They said,
that he drove out evil with evil.

Jesus called them to him, and said : " You   Mt. xii. 25.
say that I drive out evil with evil. But no   26.
power destroys itself. If it destroys itself,
then it would not be. You would drive out   27.
evil with threats, executions, murders; but
evil, nevertheless, is not destroyed, precisely
because evil cannot make head against itself.
But I drive out evil by other means than you
do ; that is to say, not with evil.

" I drive out evil by summoning people to   28.
fulfil the will of the Spirit, the Father, who
gives life to all. Five commandments express
the will of the Spirit which gives happiness
and life. And these commandments destroy   29.
evil. By their doing so, you have a proof
that they are true.

" If men were not sons of one spirit, it would
not be possible to overcome evil; as it is not
possible to go into the house of a strong man,
and rob it. In order to rob the house of a
strong man, it is necessary first to bind the
strong man. And men are bound thus in the
unity of the spirit of life.

"And therefore I tell you, that every mis-   31.
take of men, and every wrong interpretation,
shall escape punishment; but false representation about the Holy Spirit, which gives life to
all, shall not be forgiven to men. Should any   32.
one say a word against man, that is not important ; but should any one say a word against
that which is holy in man, against the spirit,
this cannot pass unpunished. Gird at me as
much as you like, but do not call evil the commandments of life which I have disclosed to
you. It cannot pass unpunished, if a man
shall call that good which is evil.

Mt. xii. 30.　" It is necessary to be at one with the spirit
of life.　He who is not at one with it, is against
it.　It is necessary to serve the spirit of life
and of good in all men, and not in oneself
　　33.　alone.　You must either hold that life and
happiness is good for the whole world, then
love life and happiness for all men, or else
hold life and happiness an evil, and then not
love life and happiness for yourself.　You
must either hold a tree good, and its fruit good
or else hold a tree bad, and its fruit bad.
Because a tree is valued by its fruit."

CHAPTER VI

THE FALSE LIFE

*Therefore, in order to receive the true life, man must on earth
resign the false life of the flesh, and live by the spirit*

("𝔒n 𝔈art𝔥, a𝔰 in 𝔥ea𝔳en")

Lk. viii. 19.　AND there came once to Jesus his mother
Mt. xii. 46.　and brothers, who could in no way get to see
him, because there was a great crowd around
　　47.　him.　And a man saw them, and went up to
Jesus, and said: " Your family, your mother
and brothers, are standing without, and wish to
see you."

Lk. viii. 21.　And Jesus said: " My mother and my
brothers are they who have understood the
will of the Father, and fulfil it."

xi. 27.　And a woman said : " Blessed is the womb
that has brought you forth, and the breasts
that you have sucked."

28.　Jesus said to this : " Blessed only are they
who have understood the spirit of the Father,
and keep it."

ix. 57.　And a man said to Jesus : " I will follow
you whithersoever you may go."

And Jesus said to him, in answer: "You   Lk.   ix. 58
cannot follow me ; I have neither house nor
place to live in.   Wild beasts have their lairs
and burrows, but man is everywhere at home,
if he lives by the spirit."

And it happened once that Jesus was, with   Mk.   iv. 35.
his followers, sailing a boat.   He said : "Let
us pass over to the other side."   A storm arose   37.
upon the lake, and the boat began to fill, so
that it nearly sank.   And Jesus lay in the   38.
stern, and slept.   They woke him, and said :
"Teacher, is it really all the same to you that
we are perishing ?"   And, when the storm had   40.
fallen, he said : "Why are you so timid ?   You
do not believe in the life of the spirit."

Jesus said to a man : "Follow me."   Lk.   ix. 59.

And the man said : "I have an aged father,
let me first bury him, and then I will follow
you."

And Jesus said to him : "Let the dead bury   60.
the dead, but do you, if you wish to truly live,
fulfil the will of the Father, and make that will
known everywhere."

And again, another man said : "I wish to be   61.
your disciple, and will fulfil the will of the
Father, as you command, but let me first settle
my family."

And Jesus said to him : "If the plowman look   62.
behind, he cannot plow.   However strong the
reasons you have to look behind, so long as you
look behind, you cannot plow.   You must forget
everything except the furrow you are driving ;
then only can you plow.   If you consider as
to what will be the outcome for the life of the
body, then you have not understood the real
life, and cannot live by it."

After this, it happened once that Jesus went   x. 38
with his disciples into a village.   And a woman
named Martha invited him into her house.
Martha had a sister named Mary, who sat at   39.

the feet of Jesus, and listened to his teaching.
𝕃𝕜. x. 40. But Martha was busy getting ready the meal.

And Martha went up to Jesus, and said : " Do you not see that my sister has left me alone to serve ? Tell her to help me in the work."

41. And Jesus said to her in answer : " Martha, Martha ! you trouble and busy yourself with many things, but only one thing is needful.

42. And Mary has chosen that one thing which is needful, and which none shall take from her. For true life the food of the spirit alone is needful."

ix. 23. And Jesus said to all : " Whoever wishes to follow me, let him forsake his own will, and let him be ready for all hardships and sufferings of the flesh at every hour ; then only can

24. he follow me. Because he who wishes to take heed for his fleshly life will destroy the true life. And he who fulfils the will of the Father, even if he destroy the fleshly life, shall save the true

25. life. For, what advantage is it to a man if he should gain the whole world, but destroy or harm his own life ? "

xii. 15. And Jesus said : " Beware of wealth, because your life does not depend upon your having more than others.

16. " There was a rich man, who had a great harvest of corn. And he thought to himself :

17, 18. Let me rebuild my barns. I will erect larger

19. ones, and gather there all my wealth. And I will say to my soul : ' There, my soul, you have everything after your desire ; rest, eat,

20. drink, and live for your pleasure.' But God said to him : ' Fool, this very night your soul shall be taken ; and all that you have stored up shall go to others.'

21. " And thus it happens with every one who provides for the bodily life, and does not live in God."

xiii. 2. And Jesus said to them : " Now, you say

that Pilate killed the Galileans. But were
these Galileans any worse than other people,
that this happened to them ? In no way. We
are all such, and we shall all perish likewise,
unless we find salvation from death.

Lk. xiii. 3

"Or of those eighteen men, whom the tower
crushed in falling, were they particularly worse
than all the other dwellers in Jerusalem? In
no wise. If we do not find salvation, sooner
or later we shall perish in the same way. If
we have not yet perished as they, we must
think of our position, thus : —

4.

5.
6.

"A man had an apple tree growing in his
garden. The master came into the garden,
and saw there was no fruit on the tree. And
the master said to his gardener : 'It is now
three years since I have watched this apple
tree, and it is still barren. It must be cut
down, for as it is, it only spoils the place.
And the gardener answered : 'Let us wait yet
a little, master; let me dig it round. I will
dung it, and let us see what it will be next
summer. Maybe it will yield fruit. But if it
yields nothing by the summer, well then, we
will cut it down.'

7.

8.

"Likewise we, as long as we live by the
flesh, and yield no fruit to the life of the spirit,
are barren apple trees. Only by the mercy of
some power are we yet left for a summer.
And if we do not yield fruit we shall also
perish, even like him who built the barn, like
the Galileans, like the eighteen men crushed
by the tower, and like all who yield no fruit;
perishing, dying forever, by death.

"In order to understand this, there is no
need of special wisdom; each one sees this for
himself. For not only in domestic affairs, but
in that also which happens in the whole world,
are we able to reason and to foresee. If the
wind is in the west, we say there will be rain,

Lk. xii. 54

Lk. xii. 55. and so it happens. But if the wind is from the south, we say there will be fair weather,

56. and so it is. How, then, is it that we are able to foresee the weather, and yet we cannot foresee that we shall all die and perish, and that the only salvation for us is in the life of the spirit, in the fulfilment of its will?"

xiv. 25. And a great multitude went with Jesus, and he once more said to all : —

26. "He who wishes to be my disciple, let him count for nothing father and mother, and wife and children, and brothers and sisters, and all his goods, and let him at every hour be ready

27. for anything. And only he who does as I do, only he follows my teaching, and only he is saved from death.

28. "Because every one, before beginning anything, will reckon whether that which he does is profitable, and if it is profitable, will do it, but if unprofitable, will abandon it. Every one who builds a house will first sit down and reckon how much money is wanted, how much he has, and whether that will suffice to finish

29. it. He will do this, so that it may not happen that he should begin to build, and not finish, for people to laugh at him.

30. "Likewise also, he who wishes to live the fleshly life must first reckon whether he can finish that with which he is busy.

31. "Every king, if he wishes to make war, will first think whether he can go to war with ten

32. thousand against twenty thousand. If he concludes that he cannot, then he will send ambassadors, and make peace, and will not make war. So also, let every man, before giving himself over to the fleshly life, bethink him whether he can wage war against death, or whether death is stronger than he; and whether it is not then better for him to make peace beforehand.

"And so, each of you should first examine Lk. xiv. 33
what he considers his own family, money, or
estate. And, when he has reckoned what all
this avails him, and understands that it avails
him nothing, then only can he be my disciple."

And upon hearing this, a man said: "That   15
is very well, if there be indeed a life of the
spirit. But what if one abandons all, and
there be no such life?"

To this Jesus said: "Not so; every one knows
the life of the spirit. You all know it; but you
do not do that which you know. Not because
you doubt, but because you are drawn away
from the true life by false cares, and excuse
yourselves from it.

"This is like your conduct, like your deeds: 16
A master got ready a dinner, and sent to invite guests, but the guests began to decline.
One said: 'I have bought land, and I must   18
go and look after it.' Another said: 'I have   19
bought oxen, and I must try them.' A third   20
said: 'I have taken a wife, and am going to
celebrate the wedding.' And the messengers   21
came and told the master that no one was
coming. The master then sent the messengers to invite the beggars. The beggars did   22
not refuse, but came. And when they were
come, there was still room left. And the mas-   23
ter sent to call in still more, and said: 'Go and
persuade all to come to my dinner, in order
that I may have more people.' And they who
had refused, from want of leisure, found no
place at the dinner.

"All know that the fulfilment of the will of
the Father gives life, but do not go because
the guile of wealth draws them away.

"He who resigns false temporary wealth for
the true life in the will of the Father, does as
did a certain clever steward. There was a man   vi. 1

who was steward to a rich master. This steward saw that, sooner or later, the master would drive him away, and that he would remain Lk. xvi. 3. without food, and without shelter. And the steward thought to himself: 'This is what I will do: I will privately distribute the master's goods to the laborers; I will reduce their debts, and then, if the master drives me out, the laborers will remember my kindness, and will 5. not abandon me.' And so the steward did. He called the laborers, his master's debtors, 6. and rewrote their documents. For him who owed a hundred he wrote fifty; for him who owed sixty, he wrote twenty, and similarly for 8. the rest. And the master learned this, and said to himself: 'Well, he has done wisely; otherwise he would have had to beg his bread. To me he has caused a loss, but his own reckoning was wise.'

"For, in the fleshly life, we all understand wherein is the true reckoning, but in the life of the spirit, we do not wish to understand. 9. Thus must we do with unjust, false wealth, — give it up, in order to receive the life of the 10. spirit. And if we regret to give up such trifles as wealth for the life of the spirit, then this 11. life will not be given us. If we do not give up false wealth, then our own true life will not be given us.

12. "It is impossible to serve two masters at one time; to serve God and Wealth, the will of the Father, and one's own will. Either one or the other."

14. And the orthodox heard this. But loving wealth, they jeered at him.

15. And he said to them: "You think that, because men honor you on account of wealth, you are really honorable. It is not so. God does not look at the exterior, but looks at the heart. That which stands high among men, is

abomination in the eyes of God. Now the
kingdom of heaven is attainable on earth,
and great are they who enter it. But there
enter it, not the rich, but those who have nothing. And this has always been so, both according to your law, and according to Moses,
and according to the prophets also. Listen.   17
How does it stand with rich and poor in your
way of thinking?

"There was a rich man. He dressed well,   19
led an idle and amusing life every day. And   20.
there was a vagrant, Lazarus, covered with
sores. And Lazarus came to the yard of the   21.
rich man, and thought there would be leavings
from the rich man's table, but Lazarus did not
get even the leavings, the rich man's dogs ate
up everything, and even licked Lazarus' sores.
And both these died, Lazarus and the rich   22.
man. And in Hades, the rich man saw, far   23.
off, Abraham; and behold, Lazarus, the beggar, was sitting with him. And the rich man   ·4.
said: 'Father Abraham, see, Lazarus the beggar is sitting with you. He used to wallow
under my fence. I dare not trouble you, but
send Lazarus the beggar to me; let him but
wet his finger in water, to cool my throat, because I am burning in the fire.' But Abraham   25.
said: 'But why should I send Lazarus into
the fire to you? You, in that other world, had
what you wished, but Lazarus only saw grief;
so that he ought now to be happy. Yes, and   26.
though I should like to help you, I cannot,
because between us and you there is a great
pit, and it is impossible to cross it. We are
living, but you are dead.' Then the rich man   27.
said: 'Well, Father Abraham, send Lazarus
the beggar to my home. I have five brothers;   28.
I am sorry for them. Let him tell everything
to them, and show how harmful wealth is; so
that they may not fall into this torture.' But   29

Abraham said: 'As it is, they know the harm. They were told of it by Moses, and by all the prophets.' But the rich man said: 'Still, it would be better if some one should rise from the dead, and go to them; they would the sooner bethink themselves.' But Abraham said: 'But if they do not listen to Moses and the prophets, then, even if a dead man came to life, they would not listen, even to him.'"

"That one should share all with one's brother, and do good to everybody; this all men know. And the whole law of Moses, and all the prophets, said only this: 'You know this truth, but cannot do it, because you love wealth.'"

And a rich official among the orthodox went up to Jesus, and said to him: "You are a good teacher, what shall I do to receive everlasting life?"

Jesus said: "Why do you call me good? Only the Father is good. But, if you wish to have life, fulfil the commandments."

The official said: "There are many commandments; which do you mean?"

And Jesus said: "Do not kill, Do not commit adultery, Do not lie, Do not steal. Further, honor your Father, and fulfil His will; and love your neighbor as yourself."

But the orthodox official said: "All these commandments I have fulfilled from my childhood; but I ask, what else must one do, according to your teaching?"

Jesus looked at him, at his rich dress, and smiled, and said: "One small thing you have left undone. You have not fulfilled that which you say. If you wish to fulfil these commandments: Do not kill, Do not commit adultery, Do not steal, Do not lie, and, above all, the commandment: Love your neighbour as your-

Lk. xvi. 30.

31.

Mk. x. 17.

18.

19.

20.

21.

self, — then, at once sell all your goods, and
give them to the poor. Then you will have
fulfilled the Father's will."

Having heard this, the official frowned, and   Mk.   x 22
went away, because he was loath to part with
his estates.

And Jesus said to his disciples: "As you   23.
see, it is in no wise possible to be rich, and to
fulfil the Father's will."

The disciples were horrified at these words,   24.
so Jesus once more repeated them, and said:
"Yes, children, he who has his own property,   25.
cannot be in the will of the Father. Sooner   Lk. xviii. 25.
may a camel pass through a needle's eye than
he who trusts in wealth fulfil the will of the
Father." And they were still more horrified,   26.
and said: "But, in that case, is it at all possible
to keep one's life?"

He said: "To man it seems impossible to   27.
support one's life without property; but God,
even without property, can support a man's
life."

Once, Jesus was going through the town of   xix. 1.
Jericho. And in this town was the chief of   2
the tax-gatherers, a rich man named Zaccheus.
This Zaccheus had heard of the teaching of   3.
Jesus, and believed in it. And when he knew
that Jesus was in Jericho, he wished to see
him. But there were so many people around,
that it was impossible to push through to him.
Zaccheus was short of stature. So he ran   4.
ahead and climbed a tree, in order to see Jesus
as he was going past. And thus, in passing   5.
by, Jesus saw him, and having learnt that he
believed his teaching, said: "Come down from
the tree, and go home; I will come to your
house." Zaccheus climbed down, ran home,   6.
made ready to meet Jesus, and joyfully welcomed him.

The people began to criticize, and to say of   7

Jesus: "See, he has gone into the tax-gatherer's house, — the house of a rogue."

Lk. xix. 8.   Meanwhile, Zaccheus said to Jesus: "See, sir, this is what I will do. I will give away half of my goods to the poor, and out of what is left I will repay fourfold those whom I have wronged."

9.   And Jesus said: "Now you have saved yourself. You were dead, and are alive; you were lost, and are found; because you have done as Abraham did, when he wished to slay his son;

10.   you have shown your faith. Therein is the whole business of man's life; to seek out and save in his soul that which is perishing. But such sacrifice as yours must not be measured by its amount."

Mk. xii. 41.   It happened once that Jesus and his disciples were sitting opposite a collecting-box. People were placing their contributions in the box, for God's service. Rich people went up to the box,

42.   and put in much. And a poor woman, a widow, came and put in two farthings.

43.   And Jesus pointed her out, and said: "See, now, this poor widow has put two farthings in

44.   the box. She has put in more than all. Because they put in that which they did not need for their own livelihood; while this woman has put all that she had; she has put in her whole life."

Mt. xxvi. 6.   It happened that Jesus was in the house of

7.   Simon the leper. And a woman came into the house. And the woman had a vase of precious oil worth fifteen pounds. Jesus said to his disciples, that his death was near. The woman heard this, and pitied Jesus, and, to show him her love, wished to anoint his head with the oil. And she forgot everything, and broke the vase, and anointed his head and feet, and poured out all the oil.

8.   And the disciples began to discuss among

themselves, thinking that she had done wrong.
And Judas, he who afterward betrayed Jesus,
said: "See how much good stuff has gone for
nothing.   This oil might have been sold for fif-   Mt. xxvi 9
teen pounds, with which, how many poor might
have been helped!"   And the disciples began
blaming the woman; who was troubled, and did
not know whether she had done well or ill.

Then Jesus said: "You are troubling the   10.
woman without cause.   She has, indeed, done a
good work, and you mistakenly think of the poor.
If you wish to do good to the poor, do so; they   11.
are always with you.   But why call them to mind
now?   If you pity the poor, go with your pity,
do them good.   But she has pitied me, and done
real good, because she has given away all that
she had.   Who of you can know what is useful,
and what is not necessary?   How do you know
that there was no need to pour the oil over me?
She has thus anointed me with oil, and if it
were but to get ready my body for burial, this
was needful.   She truly fulfilled the will of the   13
Father, in forgetting herself and pitying another.
She forgot the reckonings of the flesh and gave
away all that she had."

And Jesus said: "My teaching is the fulfilment of the Father's will; and the Father's
will can be fulfilled by deeds only; not by
mere words.   If a man's son, in answer to his   xxi. 28
father's bidding, keeps saying, 'I obey, I
obey,' but does nothing which his father bids,
he then does not fulfil the will of his father.
But if another son keeps saying, 'I do not wish   29
to obey,' and then goes and does his father's
bidding, he indeed fulfils the father's will.
And so with men: Not he is in the Father's
will who says: 'I am in the Father's will,' —
but he who does that which the Father
wishes."

CHAPTER VII

I AND THE FATHER ARE ONE

The true food of everlasting life is the fulfilment of the Father's will

("Give us our daily bread")

Jn. vii. 1.   AFTER this the Jews tried to condemn Jesus to death, and Jesus went away into Galilee, and lived with his relations.

The Jewish feast of tabernacles was come.
2, And the brothers of Jesus got ready to go to
3. the feast, and invited him to go with them.
5. They did not believe in his teaching, and said
3. to him : —

"Now, you say that the Jewish service of God is wrong, that you know the real service of God by deeds. If you really think that no one but yourself knows the true service of God, then come with us to the feast. Many people will be there, and you can declare before them all that the teaching of Moses is wrong. If all believe you, then it will be clear to your disciples also, that you are right. Why
4. make a secret of it? You say that our service is wrong, that you know the true service of God ; well then, show it to all."

6. And Jesus said : " For you, there is a special time and place in which to serve God ; but for me, there is none. I always and everywhere
7. work for God. This is just what I show to people. I show to them that their service of God is wrong, and therefore do they hate me.
8. Go you to the feast, and I will go when I think fit."

9, And the brothers went, but he remained
10. behind, and only came up at the middle of
11. the feast. And the Jews were shocked at

his not honoring their feast, and delaying to
come.   And they discussed his teaching much.   Jn vii. 12
Some said that he spoke the truth, while
others said that he only disturbed the people.

At the middle of the feast, Jesus entered   14
the temple, and began to teach the people
that their service of God was wrong; that
God should be served not in the temple and
by sacrifices, but in the spirit, and by deeds.
All listened to him and wondered that he   15
knew the whole of wisdom without having
learnt.   And Jesus, having heard that all   16.
wondered at his wisdom, said to them : —

" My teaching is not my own, but His who
sent me.   If any one wishes to fulfill the will   17.
of the Spirit which sent us into life, he will
know that I have not invented this teaching,
but that it is of God.   Because he who invents   18.
from himself, follows his own mere imagina-
tions ; but he who seeks the mind of Him
who sent him, he is right, and there is no
wrong in him.

"Your law of Moses is not the Father's law,   19.
and, therefore, they who follow it do not fulfil
the Father's law, but work evil and falsehood.
I teach you the fulfilment of the will of the   21.
Father alone, and in my teaching there cannot   22.
be contradiction.   But your written law of   23.
Moses is all full of contradictions.   Do not   24.
judge by outside appearance, but judge by the
spirit."

And some said : " While he has been called   25.
a false prophet, see, he condemns the law, and
no one makes a charge against him.   Maybe   26
in very deed he is a true prophet; maybe even
the authorities have acknowledged him.   Only   27
one reason makes it impossible to believe
him, namely, that it is said, when he who is
sent from God shall come, no one will know

whence he is come; but we know this man's birth and all his family."

The people still did not understand his teaching, and still sought proofs.

Jn. v i. 28. Then Jesus said to them : "You know me, and whence I am, after the flesh. But you do not know whence I am, after the spirit. You do not know Him, from whom I am according to the spirit; and that is the only needful

29. knowledge. If I had said that I am Christ, you would have believed me, the Man, but you would not have believed the Father who is in me, and in you. But it is necessary to believe the Father only.

33. "I am here among you for the short space of my life. I point out to you the way to that source of life, from which I have come forth.

34. And you ask of me proofs, and wish to condemn me. If you do not know the way, then, when I shall be no more, you will in nowise find it. You must not discuss me, but must follow me. Whoever shall do that which I say, he shall know whether what I say is true. He for whom the fleshly life has not become the food of the spirit, he who follows not the truth, thirsting for it as for water, cannot

37. understand me. But he who thirsts for the

38. truth, let him come to me to drink. And he who shall believe in my teaching shall receive the

39. true life. He shall receive the life of the spirit."

40. And many believed in his teaching, and said : "That which he says is the truth and is of God."

42. Others did not understand him, and still sought in prophecies for proofs that he was sent from

43. God. And many disputed with him, but none

44. could controvert him. The learned orthodox

45. sent their assistants to contend with him, but their assistants returned to the orthodox priests and said : "We can do nothing with him."

And the high priests said to them : "But why

have you not convicted him?" And they an-   Jn. vii. 46
swered: "Never did any man speak as he."

Then the orthodox said: "It signifies noth-   47.
ing that it is impossible to controvert him, and
that the people believe in his teaching. We do   48.
not believe, and none of the authorities believe.
But the people is cursed, they were always stu-   49.
pid and unlearned; they believe every one."

And Nicodemus, the man to whom Jesus ex-   50.
plained his teaching, said to the high priests:
"It is impossible to condemn a man without   51.
having heard him to the end, without understanding whither he is leading." But they said   52.
to him: "It is useless to discuss, or pay any attention to this affair. We know that a prophet
cannot come from Galilee."

At another time, Jesus was speaking with the   viii. 12
orthodox, and said to them: "There can be no
proofs of the truth of my teaching, as there cannot be of the illumination of light. My teaching is the real light, by which people tell what
is good and what is bad, and therefore it is impossible to prove my teaching; which itself
proves everything. Whoever shall follow me
shall not be in darkness, but shall have life.
Life and enlightenment, which are one and the
same."

But the orthodox said: "You alone say this."   13.

And he answered them and said: "And if I   14.
alone say this, yet I am right; because I know
whence I came, and whither I go. According
to my teaching, there is reason in life; whereas,
according to yours, there is none. Besides this,   18.
not I alone teach, but my Father, the Spirit,
teaches the same."

They said: "Where is your Father?"   19.

He said: "You do not understand my teaching, and therefore you do not know my Father.
You do not know whence you are and whither   21.
you go. I lead you, but you, instead of follow-

ing me, discuss who I am.   Therefore you cannot come to that salvation of life to which I

Jn. viii. 24. lead you.   And you will perish, if you remain
in this error, and do not follow me."

And the Jews asked : " Who are you ? "

26.   He said : " From the very beginning, I tell
you, I am the Son of Man, acknowledging the

27.   Spirit as my Father.   That which I have understood of the Father, the same I tell to the

28.   world.   And when you shall exalt in yourselves the Son of Man, then you shall know
what I am ; because I do and speak, not of
myself, as a man, but I do and speak that
which the Father has taught me.   This I say,
this I teach.

29.   " And he who sent me is always with me ;
and the Father has not left me, because I do

31.   His will.   Whoever will keep to my understanding of life, whoever will fulfil the will of the
Father, he will be truly taught by me.   In
order to know the truth, it is necessary to do
good to men.   He who does evil to men, loves
darkness, and goes into it ; he who does good
to men, goes to the light ; so that, in order to
understand my teaching, it is necessary to do

32.   good deeds.   He who shall do good, shall know
the truth ; he shall be free from evil and death.

34.   Because every one who errs becomes the slave
of his error.

35.   " And as the slave does not always live in
the house of the master, while the son of the
master is always in the house, so also a man,
if he errs in his life and becomes a slave
through his errors, does not live always, but
dies.   Only he who is in the truth remains
always living.   The truth is in this, to be not
a slave, but a son.   So that, if you err, you will

36.   be slaves and die.   But if you are in the truth,
then you shall be free sons, and shall be living.

37.   " You say of yourselves that you are sons of

Abraham, that you know the truth.   But see, you wish to kill me, because you do not understand my teaching.   It comes to this, that I Jn. viii. 38 speak that which I have understood from my Father, and you wish to do that which you have understood from your father."

They said : " Our father is Abraham."   39

Jesus said to them : " If you were the sons of Abraham you would do his deeds.   But see, 40 you wish to kill me because I told you that which I had learnt from God.   Abraham did not do in that way ; therefore you do not serve God, but serve your father, another one."

They said to him : " We are not bastards, 41. but we are all children of our Father, all sons of God."

And Jesus said to them : " If your father 42. were one with me, you would love me, because I came forth from that Father.   For I was not born of myself.   You are not children of 43. the one Father with me, therefore you do not understand my word ; my understanding of life does not find place in you.   If I am of the Father, and you of the same Father, then you cannot wish to kill me.   But if you wish to kill me, then we are not of one Father.

" I am from the Father of good, from God ; 44 but you are from the devil, from the father of evil.   You wish to do the lusts of your father the devil, who is always a murderer, and a liar, with no truth in him.   If he, the devil, says anything, he says what is of himself, and not common to all, and he is the father of lying. Therefore you are the servants of the devil and his children.   Now you see how plainly 46. you are convicted of error.   If I err, then convict me ; but if there is no error in me, then why do you not believe in me ? "

And the Jews began to revile him, and to 48 say he was possessed.

Jn. viii 49. He said: " I am not possessed ; but I honor
the Father, and you wish to kill me ; therefore
you are not brothers of mine, but children of
50. another father.   It is not I that affirm that I
51. am right, but the truth speaks for me.   Therefore I repeat to you : he who shall comprehend
my teaching and perform it, shall not see death."

52. And the Jews said : " Well, do not we speak
the truth in saying that you are a Samaritan
possessed, and that you convict yourself ?   The
prophets died, Abraham died ; but you say that
he who performs your teaching shall not see
53. death.   Abraham died, and shall you not die ?
Or are you greater than Abraham ? "

54. The Jews were still discussing as to whether
he, Jesus of Galilee, was an important prophet,
or unimportant, and forgot that he had told them
that he said nothing of himself as a man, but
spoke of the spirit that was within him.

And Jesus said : " I do not make myself to
be anything.   If I spoke of myself, of that
which only seems to me, then all that I should
say would mean nothing.   But there is that
source of everything which you call God ; well,
55. it is of Him that I speak.   But you have not
known, and do not know the true God.   But
I know Him, and I cannot say that I do not
know Him ; I should be a liar like you, if I
said that I do not know Him.   I know Him,
56. and know His will, and fulfil it.   Abraham,
your father, saw and rejoiced over my understanding."

57. The Jews said : " You are only thirty years
old, how were you living at the same time as
Abraham ? "

58. He said : " Before Abraham was, there was
the understanding of good, there was that which
I tell you."

59. Then the Jews picked up stones in order to
kill him, but he went away from them.

Jesus said: "My teaching is the awakening   Jn. xi. 25
of life.   He who believes in my teaching, notwithstanding that he dies in the flesh, remains
living, and every one who lives and believes in   26.
me shall not die."

And yet a third time Jesus taught the peo-   x. 1.
ple ; he said: " Men surrender themselves to
my teaching, not because I myself prove it.
It is impossible to prove the truth.   The truth
itself proves all the rest.   But men surrender
to my teaching, because there is no other than
it ; it is known to men, and promises life.

" My teaching is to men as the shepherd's   2.
familiar voice is to the sheep, when he comes   3.
among them through the door, and gathers
them, to lead them to the pasture.   But your   5.
teaching, no one believes ; because it is foreign
to them, and because they see in it your own
lusts.   It is with men as with sheep, at the
sight of a man who does not enter by the door,
but climbs over the fence.   The sheep do not
know him, but feel that he is a robber.   My   7.
teaching is the only true teaching ; like the one
door for the sheep.   All your teachings of the   8.
law of Moses are lies, they are all like thieves
and robbers to the sheep.   He who shall give   9.
himself up to my teaching shall find true life ;
just as the sheep go forth and find food, if they
follow the shepherd.

" A thief only comes to steal, rob, and de-   10.
stroy, but the shepherd comes to give life.
And my teaching alone promises, and gives
the true life.

" There are shepherds to whom the sheep   11.
are the chief interest in life, and who give up
their lives for the sheep.   These are true   12
shepherds.   And there are hirelings who do
not care about the sheep, because they are hirelings, and the sheep are not theirs ; so that if
a wolf comes they abandon their charge and

flee from them, and the wolf devours the sheep.

Jn. x. 13. These are false shepherds. And so there are false teachers, such as have no concern with the life of people; while true teachers give up their lives for the life of men.

14, 17. "I am such a teacher. My teaching is this, —to give up one's life for the life of men.

18. No one shall take my life from me, but I myself freely give it up for men, in order to receive true life. The commandment to do this I re-

15. ceived from my Father. And as my Father knows me, so I also know Him; and therefore

17. I lay down my life for men. Therefore the Father loves me, because I fulfil His commandments.

16. "And all men, not only those here now, but all men, shall understand my voice; and all shall come together into one, and all men shall be one, and their teaching one."

24. And the Jews surrounded him, and said: "All that you say is difficult to understand, and does not agree with our writings. Do not torment us, but simply and straightforwardly tell us, whether you are that Messiah who, according to our writings, should come into the world."

25. And Jesus answered them: "I have already told you who I am, but you do not believe. If you do not believe my word, then believe my works; by them understand who I am, and wherefore I am come.

26. "But you do not believe me because you do

27. not follow me. He who follows me, and does

28. that which I say, he understands me. And he who understands my teaching and fulfils it, re-

29. ceives the true life. My Father has united

30. them with me, and no one can disunite us. I and the Father are one."

31. And the Jews were offended at this, and took up stones to kill him.

But he said to them: "I have shown you   Jn x. 32
many good works, and have disclosed the
teaching of my Father. For which, then, of
these good works do you wish to stone me?"

They said: "Not for the good do we wish   33
to stone you; but because you, a man, make
yourself God."

And Jesus answered them: "Why, this is   34
just what is written in your writings, where
it says that God Himself said to the wicked
rulers: 'You are gods.' If He called even   35.
vicious men gods, then why do you consider   36.
it sacrilege to call that the son of God, which
God in His love sent into the world? Every
man in the spirit is the son of God. If I do   37.
not live in God's way, then do not believe that
I am a son of God. But if I live after God's   38.
way, then believe from my life that I am in
the Father, and then you will understand that
the Father is in me and I in Him."

And the Jews began to dispute. Some said   20.
that he was possessed, and others said: "A   21.
man who is possessed cannot enlighten men."
And they did not know what to do with him,   39.
and could not condemn him. And he went   40.
again across the Jordan, and remained there.
And many believed in his teaching, and said   41.
that it was true, as the teaching of John was.
Therefore many believed in it.   42.

And Jesus once said to his disciples: "Tell   Mt. xvi. 13.
me how the people understand my teaching
about the son of God and the son of man."

They said: "Some understand it like the   14.
teaching of John, others like the prophecies of
Isaiah; others, again, say that it is like the
teaching of Jeremiah. They understand that
you are a prophet."

"And how do you understand my teaching?"   15.

And Simon Peter said to him: "In my   16.
opinion, your teaching consists in this, that

you are the chosen Son of the God of Life. You teach that God is the life in man."

Mt. xvi. 17. And Jesus said to him: "Happy are you, Simon, that you have understood this. No man could disclose this to you; but you have understood this, because God in you has disclosed it to you. Not fleshly understanding, and not I, my words, have disclosed this to you; but God my Father has directly disclosed

18. it. And upon this is founded that society of men for whom there is no death."

CHAPTER VIII

LIFE IS NOT TEMPORAL

Therefore true life is to be lived in the present

(" This day ")

Mt. x. 38. JESUS said: "He who is not ready for all fleshly sufferings and bereavements, has not

39. understood me. He who shall obtain all that is best for the fleshly life, shall destroy the true life; he who shall destroy his fleshly life in fulfilling my teaching, shall receive the true life."

xix. 27. And in answer to these words, Peter said to him: "See, we have listened to you, have thrown off all cares and property, and have followed you. What reward shall we have for this?"

Mk. x. 29, 30. And Jesus said to him: "Every one who has abandoned home, sisters, brothers, father, mother, wife, children, and his fields, for my teaching, shall receive a hundredfold more than sisters and brothers and fields, and all that is needful in this life; and besides this, he re-

31. ceives life beyond the power of time. There are no rewards in the kingdom of heaven, the kingdom of heaven is its own aim and reward.

In the kingdom of God all are equal, there is
neither first nor last.

"Because the kingdom of heaven is like this. Mt xx. 1.
The master of a house went in the early morning to hire laborers for his grounds.   He   2.
hired laborers at a penny a day, and set them
to work in the garden.   And he again went at   3.
mid-day and hired more, and sent them into
the garden to work; and at evening he hired
still more, and sent them to work.   And with
them all he agreed at a penny.   The time   8.
came for the reckoning.   And the master
ordered all to be paid alike.   First, those who 9.
came last; and afterward, the first.   And the
first saw that the last received each a penny.
And they thought that they would receive   10.
more; but the first were also given each a
penny.   They took it and said: 'But how is   11.
this?   They only worked one shift, and we all 12.
four; why, then, do we receive alike?   This   13.
is unjust.'   But the master came up, and said:
'What are you complaining about?   Have I
offended you?   The amount I hired you for, I
have given you.   Our agreement was for a   14.
penny, take it and go.   If I wish to give to
the last the same as to you, am I not master
of my own will?   Or because you see that I   15.
am good, is that the cause of your grudging?'"

In the kingdom of God there is neither first   16.
nor last, for all there are as one.

There came to Jesus two of his disciples,   20.
James and John, and said: "Promise us that Mk x. 35.
you will do that for us which we shall ask of
you."

He said: "What do you wish?"   Mt. xx. 21.

They said: "That we may be equal with
you."

Jesus said to them: "You yourselves do not   22.
know what you ask.   You may live just as I
do, and be cleansed from fleshly life like me,

but to make you like myself is not in my

Mt. xx. 23. power. Every man may, by his own effort, enter the kingdom of his Father, having submitted to His power, and fulfilling His will."

24. When they heard of this, the other disciples grew angry with the two brothers, because these wished to be equal to their teacher, and the first among his disciples.

25. But Jesus called them, and said: "If you brothers, James and John, asked me to make you such as I am in order to be first among my disciples, then you were mistaken; but if you, my other disciples, are angry with them because they wish to be your elders, then you also are mistaken. Only in the world are kings and officials reckoned by seniority for governing the people. But among you, there

26. cannot be either elder or younger. Among you, for one to be greater than another, it is

27. necessary to be the servant of all. Among you, let him who wishes to be first, consider

28. himself last. Because therein is the will of the Father as to the Son of Man; who does not live to be served, but to himself serve all, and to give up his fleshly life, as a ransom for the life of the spirit."

xviii. 11. And Jesus said to the people: "The Father

12. seeks to save that which perishes. He rejoices over it, as a shepherd rejoices when he has found one sheep that was lost. When one is lost, he leaves the ninety-nine, and goes

Lk. xv. 8. to save the lost one. And if a woman lose a farthing, she will sweep out the whole hut and

10. seek until she find it. The Father loves the Son, and calls him to Himself."

xiv. 8. And he told them yet another parable, to the effect that they who live in the will of God ought not to exalt themselves. He said: "If you are invited to dinner, do not seat yourself in the front corner; some one will

come of more consideration than yourself, and
the master will say: 'Leave your place, and   Lk. xiv. 9.
allow him who is better than you to be seated.'
Then you will be put to shame. But do better,   10.
take your seat in the very last place, then the
master will find you, and call you to a place
of honor, and you will be honored.

"So also in the kingdom of God there is no   11.
room for pride. He who exalts himself, by so
doing lowers himself; but he who humbles
himself, and considers himself unworthy, by
this same means raises himself in the kingdom
of God.

"A man had two sons. And the younger   xv. 11.
said to his father: 'Father, give me my prop-   12.
erty.' And the father gave him his share.
The younger son took his share, went abroad,   13.
squandered all his property, and began to
suffer want. And abroad, he became a swine-   15.
herd. And he so hungered, that he ate acorns   16.
with the swine. And he bethought himself of   17.
his life, and said: 'Why did I take my share
and leave my father? My father had plenty
of everything; at my father's, even laborers
ate their fill. But I here am eating the same
food as the swine. I will go to my father, fall   18.
at his feet, and say: I am to blame, father,
before you, and am not worthy to be your
son. Take me back even as a laborer.'
So he thought, and he went to his father.   20.
And when he was still far off, his father at
once recognized him, and himself ran to meet
him, embraced him, and began to kiss him.
And the son said: 'Father, I am to blame   21.
before you, I am not worthy to be your son.'
But the father would not even listen, and said   22.
to the laborers: 'Bring quickly the best
clothes and the best boots, to clothe him and
shoe him. And go and bring a fatted calf and   23.
kill it, and we will rejoice that this my son was   24.

dead and is now alive, was lost and is now
Lk. xv. 25. found.' And the elder brother came from
the field, and as he approached he heard the
26. sounds of music in the house. He called a
servant to him, and said : ' Why is there this
merry-making here?' And the boy said :
27. ' Have you not heard that your brother is
returned, and your father is full of joy, and
has ordered a fatted calf to be killed, for joy
28. that his son has returned?' The elder brother
was offended, and did not go into the house.
29. And the father came out and called him. And
he said to his father: ' See, father, how many
years I have worked for you, and have not
disobeyed your command, while you never
30. killed a fatted calf for me. But my younger
brother left the house and squandered all his
property with drunkards, and you have now
killed the calf for him.' And the father said :
31. ' You are always with me, and all mine is
32. yours ; and you should not be offended, but
should be glad that your brother was dead and
has become alive, was lost and is found.'

Mk. xii. 1. " A master planted a garden, cultivated it,
arranged it, did everything so that the garden
might yield as much fruit as possible. And
he sent laborers into the garden, that they
might work there, and gather the fruit, and
pay him according to the agreement for the garden. (The master is the Father ; the garden,
the world ; the laborers, men. The Father
does no more than send His Son, the Son of
Man, into the world, that men may yield fruit
to the Father from the understanding of life
2. which He placed in them.) The time came
when the master sent a servant for the rents.
(The Father, without ceasing, tells men that
3. they must fulfil His will.) The laborers drove
away the messenger of the master with nothing,
and continued to live, imagining that the gar-

den was their own, and that they themselves,
of their own will, were settled on it. (Men
drive away from themselves the declaration of
the will of the Father, and continue to live,
each one for himself, imagining that they live
for the joys of the fleshly life.) Then the   Mk.   xii   4.
master sent one after another his chosen ones,   6.
then his son, to remind the laborers of their
debt. But the laborers quite lost their reason,   7.
and imagined that if they killed this son of the
master, who reminded them that the garden
was not theirs, they would be left quite in
peace. So they killed him.   8.

"Thus men do not love even a reminder of
the spirit which lives in them, and declares to
them that it is eternal and they are not eternal;
and they have killed, as far as they could, the
consciousness of the spirit; they have wrapped
in a cloth and buried in the ground the talent
that was given them.

"What, then, is the master to do? Nothing   Mt.   xxi. 40,
else than drive forth those laborers, and send   41.
others.

"What is the Father to do? Sow until there
shall be fruit. And this He does.

"People have not understood and do not   42.
understand that the consciousness of the spirit
which is in them, and which they hide because
it troubles them, brings life to them through
understanding it. They reject that stone upon   43.
which everything rests. And they who do not
take as foundation the life of the spirit, do
not enter into the kingdom of heaven, and do
not receive life. In order to have faith, and to
receive life, it is necessary to understand one's
position, and not to expect rewards."

Then the disciples said to Jesus: "Increase   Lk.   xvii. 5
in us our faith. Tell us that which will make
us more strongly believe in the life of the spirit,
that we may not regret the life of the flesh,

which must be given up wholly for the life of the spirit. For reward, you yourself say there is none."

Lk. xvii. 6. And in answer to this, Jesus said to them : " If you had such a faith as the faith that from a birch seed there springs up a great tree ; if, also, you believed that in you there is the germ, the only germ, of the spirit whence springs up the true life, you would not ask me to increase in you your faith.

"Faith does not consist in believing something wonderful, but faith consists in understanding one's position, and wherein lies salvation. If you understand your position, you will not expect rewards, but will believe in that which is intrusted to you.

7. " When the master returns with the laborers from the field, he does not seat the laborer at 8. his table. But he bids him see to the cattle, and prepare his supper, and after this only 9. says to the laborer : 'Sit down, drink and eat.' The master will not thank the laborer for having done what he ought to do. And the laborer, if he understands that he is a laborer, is not offended, but works, believing that he will receive his due.

10. " And so you, also, must fulfil the will of the Father, and think that we are worthless laborers, having only done what we ought to do, and not expect a reward, but be content with receiving that which is due to you.

" There is no need to take care to believe that there will be a reward, and life ; this cannot be otherwise ; but there is need to take care not to destroy this life, not to forget that it is given us that we may bring forth its fruits, and fulfil the will of the Father.

xii. 35, 36. " And therefore always be ready, like servants awaiting a master, to answer him im-
37. 38. mediately when he comes. The servants do

not know when he will return, either early or late, and they must always be ready. And when they meet the master, they have fulfilled his will, and it is well for them.

" So in life also. Always, every minute of the present, you must live the life of the spirit, not thinking of the past or the future, and not saying to yourself : then or there I will do this or that.

" If the master knew when the thief would come, he would not sleep ; and so do you also never sleep ; because, to the life of the son of man time is nothing ; he lives only in the present, and does not know when is the beginning or end of life. Lk. xii. 39.

" Our life is the same as that of a slave whom the master has left as chief in his household. And well it is for that slave if he does the will of the master always ! But if he shall say, 'The master will not soon return,' and shall forget the master's business, then the master will return unexpectedly, and will drive him out. Mt. xxiv. 45, 46.

48.

50,

51.

" And so, be not downcast, but always live in the present by the spirit. For the life of the spirit there is no time. Mk. xiii. 33.

" Look to yourselves, so as not to weigh yourselves down, and not to blind yourselves with drunkenness, gluttony, and cares ; so as not to let the time of salvation pass. The time of salvation, like a web, is cast over all; it is there always. And therefore always live the life of the Son of Man. Lk. xxi. 34.

" The kingdom of heaven is like this. Ten maidens went with lamps to meet the bridegroom. Five were wise and five foolish. The foolish ones took lamps but did not take oil ; but the wise took lamps and a store of oil. While they waited for the bridegroom, they went to sleep. When the bridegroom was approaching, the foolish maidens saw that they had little oil, and went to buy some ; and while they were gone, Mt. xxv. 1.

2, 3.

4.

5.

6.

7.

10.

the bridegroom came. And the wise maidens
who had oil went in with him, and the doors
were shut. Their business was only this, to
meet the bridegroom with lights; and the five
foolish ones forgot that it was important, not
only that the lights should burn, but that they
should burn in time. And in order that they
might be burning when the bridegroom came,
they must burn without stopping.

"Life is only for this, to exalt the Son of
Man, and the Son of Man exists always. He
is not in time; and therefore, in serving him,
one must live without time, in the present
alone.

Lk. xiii. 24. "Therefore make efforts in the present to
 25. enter into the life of the spirit. If you do not
make these efforts you shall not enter. You
will say: 'We said so and so.' But there will
be no good works to show, and there will not
Mt. xvi. 27. be life. Because the Son of Man, the one true
spirit of life, will appear in each man, as such
man has acted for the Son of Man.

Mt. xxv. 32. "Mankind is divided according to the way
in which men serve the Son of Man. And
by their works men shall be divided into two
classes, as sheep are divided from goats in
the flock. The one shall live, the other perish.

 34. "They who have served the Son of Man,
they shall receive that which belonged to them
from the beginning of the world, that life
which they have kept. They have kept life
by the fact that they have served the Son of
Man. They have fed the hungry, clothed the
naked, welcomed the stranger, visited the pris-
oner. They have lived in the Son of Man,
felt that he only is in all men, and therefore
they have loved their neighbors.

"Whereas they who have not lived in the
Son of Man, they have not served him, have

not understood that he alone is in all, and
therefore have not joined in him and have lost
life in him, and have perished."

CHAPTER IX

TEMPTATIONS

*The illusions of temporal life conceal from men the true life
in the present*

("ꜰꝋꝛgíbe us our debts as we forgibe our debtors")

ONCE, children were brought to Jesus. His disciples began to drive the children away. Jesus saw this being done, and was grieved, and said:— Mt. xix. 13.
14.

"You drive the children away without reason. They are better than any, because children all live after the Father's will. They are, indeed, already in the kingdom of heaven. You should not drive them away, but learn from them; because, in order to live in the Father's will, you must live as children live. Children do not abuse one another, do not bear ill-will to people, do not commit adultery, do not swear by anything, do not resist evil, do not go to law with any one, acknowledge no difference between their own people and foreigners. Therefore are they better than grown people, and are in the kingdom of heaven. If you do not refrain from all the temptations of the flesh, and become as children, you will not be in the kingdom of heaven. Lk. xviii. 17.
Mt. xviii. 3.

"Only he who understands that children are better than we, because they do not break the Father's will, only he understands my teaching. And he who understands my teaching, he alone understands the Father's will. We cannot despise children, because they are bet- 5.
Lk. ix. 48.
Mt. xviii. 10.

ter than we, and their hearts are pure in the sight of the Father, and are always with Him.

Mt. xviii. 14 "And not one child perishes by the Father's will. They perish only as men entice them from the truth. And therefore it behooves us to take care of them, and not to entice them from the Father, and from true life.

"That man does ill who entices them from purity. To entice a child from good, to lead it into temptation, is as bad as to hang a millstone on its neck and throw it into the water. It is hard for it to swim to the surface; it is more likely to drown. It is as hard for a child to get out of temptation into which a grown-up man leads it.

7. "The world of men is unhappy only on account of temptations. Temptations are everywhere in the world, they always were and always will be; and man perishes from temptations.

8. "Therefore give up everything, sacrifice everything, if only you may not fall into temptation. A fox, if it fall into a trap, will wrench off its paw and go away, and the paw will heal and it will remain alive. Do you likewise. Give up everything, if only not to sink into temptation.

Lk. xvii. 3. "Beware of temptation under that first commandment; do not bear ill-will against men, when people offend you, and you would wish to be avenged on them.

Mt. xviii. 15. "If a man offend you, remember that he is the son of the same Father, and your brother. If he has offended you, go and persuade him of it face to face. If he listen to you, then you have the advantage, you will have found a new 16. brother. If he do not listen to you, then call to your aid two or three others who may per- Lk. xvii. 4. suade him. And if he repent, forgive him. And if he offend you seven times, and seven

times says, 'Forgive me,' then forgive him.
But if he does not listen, then tell the society Mt. xviii. 17
of believers in my teaching, and if he listens
not to them, then forgive him, and have nothing to do with him.

"Because the kingdom of God is like this. 23.
A king began to settle with his tenants. And 24.
there was a man brought to him who owed him
a million, and had nothing to pay him with.
Then the king commanded to sell the man's 25.
estate, his wife, his children, and the man
himself. But the tenant began to beg mercy 26.
of the king. And the king was gracious to 27.
him, and pardoned all his debt. And now, 28.
this same tenant went home, and saw a peasant. This peasant owed him fifty shillings.
The king's tenant seized him, began to strangle
him, and said: 'Give me what you owe me.'
And the peasant fell at his feet, and said: 29.
'Have patience with me, I will pay you all.'
But the tenant showed him no mercy, and put 30.
the peasant into prison, to stay there until he
paid everything. Other peasants saw this, 31.
and went to the king, and told what the tenant had done. Then the king called the 32.
tenant, and said to him: 'Wicked creature,
I pardoned you all your debt, because you
prayed me. And you, also, should have shown 33.
mercy to your debtor, because I showed mercy
to you.' And the king became angry, and gave 34.
the tenant to be made to suffer, until he should
pay all his rent.

"Just so, the Father will do with you, if 35.
you do not forgive, from the bottom of your
heart, all those who are to blame in your sight.

"You know that if a quarrel arise with a v. 25
man, it is better to make it up with him without going to the court. You know this, and
you act so because you know, should it go to
the court, you will lose more. Now, it is the

same with all malice. If you know that malice is a bad thing, and removes you from the Father, then get clear of malice as soon as possible, and make your peace.

Mt. xviii. 18. "You yourselves know that as you become bound on earth, so you will be before the Father. And as you free yourselves on earth, so you will be also free before the Father.

19. Understand that if two or three on earth are united in my teaching, everything they may desire they already have from my Father.

20. Because where two or three are joined in the name of the spirit in man, the spirit of man is living in them.

Mk. x. 2. "Beware also of temptation under the second commandment; the temptation for men to change their wives."

Mt. xix. 3. There once came to Jesus orthodox teachers, who, trying him, said: "May a man leave his wife?"

4. He said to them: "From the very beginning man was created male and female. This was

5. the will of the Father. And therefore a man leaves father and mother and cleaves to his wife. And husband and wife unite in one

6. body. So that the wife is the same for a man as his own flesh. Therefore man must not break the natural law of God, and separate

8. that which is united. According to your law of Moses, it is said that you may abandon a wife and take another; but this is untrue. According to the Father's will, this is not so,

9. and I tell you that he who casts off his wife drives into immorality both her, and him who shall have to do with her. And casting off his wife, a man breeds immorality in the world."

20. And the disciples said to Jesus: "It is too hard to be tied for life, whatever happens, to one wife. If that must be, it were better not to marry."

He said to them: "You may refrain from Mt. xix. 11
marriage, but you must understand what you
are about. If any one wishes to live without 12
wife, let him be quite pure, and not approach
women; but he who loves women, let him
unite with one wife and not cast her off, and
not gaze upon others.

"Beware of temptation against the third
commandment; the temptation to force people
to fulfil obligations and to take oaths."

Once, tax-gatherers came to Peter, and asked xvii. 24.
him: "How about your teacher, does he pay
taxes?" Peter said: "No, he does not." 25.
And he went and told Jesus that he had been
stopped, and told that all were bound to pay
taxes.

Then Jesus said to him: "The king does
not take taxes of his sons; and moreover, men
are not bound to pay any one but the king. Is
this not so? Well, so it is with us. If we are
sons of God, then we are bound to no one but
God, and free from all obligations. And if they 27
demand taxes of you, then pay. But do so,
not because it is your duty, but because you
may not resist evil. Otherwise resistance to
evil will cause a greater evil."

Another time, the orthodox joined with xxii. 16.
Cæsar's officials, and went to Jesus, to entrap
him in his words. They said to him: "You
teach every one according to the truth. Tell 17.
us, are we bound to pay taxes to Cæsar or
not?" Jesus understood that they wished to 18.
convict him of not acknowledging duty to
Cæsar. And he said to them: "Show me 19.
that with which you pay taxes to Cæsar."
They handed him a coin. He looked at the 20.
coin, and said: "What is this here? Whose
effigy and whose signature are these?" They
said: "Cæsar's." And he said: "Well then, 21.
pay Cæsar that which is Cæsar's, but that

which is God's, your soul, give to no one but to God." Money, goods, your labor, give everything to him who shall ask it of you. But your soul, give to none but God.

"Your orthodox teachers go about every-
Mt. xxiii. 15. where, and compel people to swear and vow that they will fulfil the law. But by this they only pervert people, and make them worse than before. It is impossible to promise with one's
16- body for one's soul. In your soul, God is;
22. therefore people cannot promise for God to men.

"Beware. Temptation under the fourth commandment is the temptation for men to judge and execute people, and call upon others to take part in these judgments and executions."
Lk. ix. 52. The disciples of Jesus once went into a village, and asked for a night's lodging; but they
53. were not admitted. Then the disciples went
54. to Jesus to complain, and said: "Let these
55. people be struck with lightning." Jesus said: "You still do not understand of what spirit you
56. are. I am teaching, not how to destroy, but how to save people."
xii. 13. Once a man came to Jesus, and said: "Bid my
14. brother give me my inheritance." Jesus said to him: "No one has made me judge over you, and I judge no one. And neither may you judge any one."
Jn. viii. 3. The orthodox once brought a woman to
4. Jesus, and said: "See, this woman was taken
5. in adultery. Now, by the law she should be stoned to death. What do you say?"
6. Jesus answered nothing, and waited for them
7. to bethink themselves. But they pressed him, and asked what he would adjudge to this woman. Then he said: "He among you who is without fault, let him be the first to cast a
8. stone at her." He said nothing more.
9. Then the orthodox looked within themselves,

and their consciences smote them; and they
who were in front sought to get behind the
others, and all went away. And Jesus re-   Jn. viii. 10
mained alone with the woman. He looked
round, and saw that there was none else.
"Well," said he to the woman, "has no one
condemned you?" She said: "No one." Then   11.
he said: "And I do not condemn you. Go,
and henceforth sin no more."

Beware. Temptation against the fifth commandment is the temptation for men to consider themselves bound to do good only to
their countrymen, and to consider foreigners
as enemies.

A teacher of the law wished to try Jesus,   Lk.   x. 25.
and said: "What am I to do in order to receive
the true life?" Jesus said: "You know, — love   27.
your Father, God, and him who is your brother
through your Father, God; of whatever country
he may be." And the teacher of the law said: 29.
"This would be well, if there were not different nations; but as it is, how am I to love the
enemies of my own people?"

And Jesus said: "There was a Jew who fell   30.
into misfortune. He was beaten, robbed, and
abandoned on the road. A Jewish priest went   31.
by, glanced at the wounded man, and went on.
A Jewish Levite passed, looked at the wounded   32.
man, and also went by. But there came a man   33.
of a foreign, hostile nation, a Samaritan. This
Samaritan saw the Jew, and did not think of
the fact that Jews have no esteem for the
Samaritans, but pitied the poor Jew. He   34.
washed and bound his wounds, and carried
him on his ass to an inn, paid money for him   35.
to the innkeeper, and promised to come again
to pay for him. Thus shall you also behave
toward foreign nations, toward those who
hold you of no account and ruin you. Then
you will receive true life."

Mt. xvi. 21. Jesus said: "The world loves its own, and hates God's people. Therefore men of the world — priests, preachers, officials — will harass those who shall fulfil the will of the Father. And I am going to Jerusalem, and shall be persecuted and killed. But my spirit cannot be killed, but will remain alive."

Mk viii. 32. Having heard that Jesus would be tortured and killed in Jerusalem, Peter was sad, and took Jesus by the hand, and said to him: "If so,

33. then you had better not go to Jerusalem." Then Jesus said to Peter: "Do not say this. What you say is temptation. If you fear tortures and death for me, this means that you are not thinking of that which is godly, of the spirit, but are thinking of what is worldly."

34. And having called the people and his disciples, Jesus said: "He who wishes to live according to my teaching, let him forsake his fleshly life, and let him be ready for all fleshly suffering; because he who fears for his fleshly life, shall destroy the true life; he who despises the fleshly life, shall save the true life."

Mt. xxii. 23. And they did not understand this, and certain materialists coming, he explained to all what is the meaning of the true life and the awakening from death.

The materialists said that after the fleshly

24. death there is no longer any life. They asked: "How can all rise from the dead? If all were to rise, then in rising they could in no way have

25. life together. For instance, there were seven brothers among us. The first married and died. The wife was taken by the second brother and

28. he died, and she was taken by the third, who also died, and so on unto the seventh. Well now, how shall these seven brothers live with one wife if all arise from the dead?"

Lk. xx. 34. Jesus said to them: "You either purposely confuse things, or you do not understand what

the awakening to life is.   Men in this present
life marry.   But they who shall earn everlast-   Lk. xx. 35
ing life, and the awakening from death, do not
marry.   And that because they can no longer   36
die, but are united with the Father.   In your   Mt. xxii. 31.
writings, it is said that God said : ' I am the God   32.
of Abraham, Isaac, and Jacob.'   And this was
said when Abraham, Isaac, and Jacob had died
from among men.   It follows, that they who
have died from among men are alive to God.
If God is, and God does not die, then they who
are with God are always alive.   The awakening
from death is, to live in the will of the Father.
For the Father, there is no time ; therefore in
fulfilling the will of the Father, in joining Him,
man departs from time and death."

When they heard this, the orthodox no longer   34.
knew what to devise to compel Jesus to hold
his tongue ; and together they began to question Jesus.   And one of the orthodox said :   35.
" Teacher, what, in your opinion, is the chief   36.
commandment in the whole law ? "

The orthodox thought that Jesus would get
confused in the answer about the law.   But   37
Jesus said : " It is, to love the Lord with all
one's soul, in whose power we are.   From it the
second commandment follows, which is, to love
one's neighbor.   Because the same Lord is in   39.
him.   And this is the substance of all that is   40.
written in all your books."

And Jesus said further : " In your opinion,   42
what is Christ?   Is he some one's son ? "   They
said : " In our opinion, Christ is the son of
David."   Then he said to them : " How, then,   43
does David call Christ his Lord?   Christ is
neither son of David, nor any one's son after
the flesh ; but Christ is that same Lord, our
Ruler, whom we know in ourselves as our life.
Christ is that understanding which is in us."

And Jesus said : " See, beware of the leaven   Lk. xii. 1.

of orthodox teachers. And beware of the leaven
of the materialists and of the leaven of the gov-
Lk. xii. 5 ernment. But most of all, beware of the leaven
of the self-styled 'orthodox,' because in them
is the chief stumbling-block."

xx. 45. And when the people understood of what he
46. was speaking, he repeated: "Most of all, beware of the teaching of the scholars, of the
Mt. xxiii. 2. self-called 'orthodox.' Beware of them, because they have taken the place of the prophets
who declared the will of God to the people.
They have perversely assumed authority to
preach to the people the will of God. They
preach words, and do nothing. And the result
3. is that they no more than say: 'Do this and
that.' And there is no further result, because
4. they do nothing good, but only talk. And they
tell people to do what is impossible to be done,
5. and they themselves do nothing. They only
labor to keep the teaching in their own hands;
and with this aim they strive to appear imposing; they dress themselves up and exalt them-
8. selves. Know, therefore, that no one should
13. call himself teacher and leader. But the self-
styled orthodox are called teachers, and by this
very thing they hinder you from entering into
the kingdom of heaven, where they themselves
15. do not enter. These orthodox think that people may be brought to God by exterior rites
16. and pledges. Like blind men, they do not see
that the outside show means nothing; that all
23. depends upon the soul of man. They do the
easiest thing, the external thing; that which is
needful and difficult— love, compassion, truth
28. —they leave undone. It suffices them to be
only outwardly in the law, and to bring others
27. outwardly to the law. And therefore they, like
painted coffins, outwardly look clean, but are
30. an abomination within. They outwardly honor
31. the holy martyrs. But in very deed they are the

same as those who torture and kill the saints.
They were before, and are now, the enemies
of all good.   From them comes all the evil
in the world; because they hide the good,
and instead of it uphold evil.   Most of all to   Mk   iii. 28
be feared, therefore, are self-called teachers.
Because you yourselves know every mistake
may be made good.   But if people are mis-   29
taken as to what good is, this mistake can
never be set right.   And this is precisely the
condition of self-called leaders."

And Jesus said: "I wished, here in Jeru-   Mt. xxiii. 37.
salem, to join all men in one understanding
of true happiness; but the people here are
only capable of putting to death the teachers
of good.   And therefore they will remain the   38.
same godless people as they were, and will not
know the true God; until they shall lovingly   39.
welcome the understanding of God."   And   xxiv. 1.
Jesus went away from the temple.

Then his disciples said to him: "But what
will happen to this temple of God, with all its
embellishments which people have brought
into it, to give to God."   And Jesus said: "I   2.
tell you truly, the whole of this temple, with
all its embellishments, shall be destroyed, and
nothing shall remain of it.   There is one temple of God; that is, the hearts of men when
they love each other."

And they asked him: "When shall there be   3.
such a temple?"   And Jesus said to them: 4.
"That will not be soon.   People will yet long
be deceived in the name of my teaching, and
wars and rebellions will be the result.   And   12.
there will be great lawlessness, and little love.
But when the true teaching shall spread among   14
all men, then will be the end of evil and temptations."

CHAPTER X

THE WARFARE WITH TEMPTATION

Therefore, not to fall by temptation, we must, at every moment of life, be at one with the Father

("Lead us not into temptation")

Lk. xi. 53. AFTER this, the orthodox chief priests began to do all they could to lay traps for Jesus, in
Jn. xi. 47. some way or other to destroy him. They gath-
48. ered in council, and began to consider. They said: "This man must somehow or other be put an end to. He so proves his teaching that, if he be left alone, all will believe in him, and cast off our belief. Already half of the people believe in him. But if the Jews believe in his teaching, that all men are sons of one Father, and brothers, and that there is nothing in our Hebrew people different from other peoples, then the Romans will completely overwhelm us, and the Hebrew kingdom will be no more."

Lk. xix. 47. And the orthodox high priest and learned men for long counseled together, and could
48. not think what to do with Jesus. They could not make up their minds to kill him.

Jn. xi. 49. Then one of them, Caiaphas, the chief priest of that year, thought of the following device.
50. He said to the others: "You must remember this: it is expedient to kill one man, that the whole people may not perish. If we leave this man alone, the people will perish; this I declare to you. Therefore it is better to kill
52. Jesus. Even if the people do not perish, they will nevertheless go astray, departing from the one belief, if we do not kill Jesus. Therefore it is better to kill Jesus."

53. And when Caiaphas said this, they resolved

that there was no need to discuss, but that
Jesus must be killed without fail.

They would have taken Jesus at once and   Jn. xi. 54
killed him, but he withdrew from them into
the desert. But at this time the feast of the   55
Passover was approaching, when a great multitude always gathered in Jerusalem. And the   56
orthodox high priests reckoned upon Jesus
coming with the people to the feast. And   57.
they made known to the people that if any one
should see Jesus he should bring him to them.

And it so happened that, six days before the   xii. 1.
Passover, Jesus said to his disciples : "Let us   xi. 7.
go to Jerusalem." And he went with them.

And the disciples said to him : "Do not go   8
into Jerusalem. The high priests have resolved
now to stone you to death. If you come they
will kill you."

Jesus said to them : "I can fear nothing,   9.
because I live in the light of understanding.
And as every man, that he may not stumble,
walks by day and not by night, so every man,
that he may doubt nothing and fear nothing,
must live by this understanding. Only he   10
doubts and fears who lives by the flesh ; but
he who lives by understanding, for him there
is nothing doubtful or fearful."

And Jesus came to the village of Bethany,   xii. 1.
near Jerusalem, and to the house of Martha
and Mary which was there.

Early in the morning Jesus went into Jeru-   12
salem. There was a great crowd for the feast.
And when they recognized Jesus, they sur-   13
rounded him, tore branches from the trees,
and threw their clothes before him on the
road, and all shouted : "Here is our true king,
he who has taught us the true God."

Jesus sat upon an ass's foal, riding, and the   14
people ran before him and shouted ; thus he
rode into Jerusalem. And when he had thus   Mt. xxi. 10

ridden into the town, the whole people were
Mt. xxi. 11. excited, and asked : "Who is he?" They who
knew him answered : "Jesus, the prophet of
Nazareth, in Galilee."

Mk. xi. 15. And Jesus went into the temple, and again
drove out thence all the buyers and sellers.

Jn. xii. 19. And the orthodox high priests saw all this,
and said to each other : "See what this man
is doing. The whole people are following
him."

Mk. xi. 18. But they did not dare to take him straight
from among the people, because they saw that
the people were gathering round him, and they
bethought them how to take him by cunning.

Jn. xii. 20. Meanwhile Jesus was in the temple, and
taught the people. Among the people, besides Jews, there were Greeks and heathen.
The Greeks heard of the teaching of Jesus, and
understood his teaching in this way, namely,
that he taught the truth, not only to Hebrews
21. but to all men. Therefore they wished to be
also his disciples, and spoke about this to
22. Philip. And Philip told this to Andrew.

These two disciples feared to bring Jesus
together with the Greeks. They were afraid
lest the people should be angry with Jesus,
because he did not recognize any difference
between Hebrews and other nations, and they
long wavered about telling this to Jesus ; but
afterward both together told him, and hearing
that the Greeks wished to be his followers,
Jesus was troubled. He knew that the people
hated him because he made no difference
between the Hebrews and the heathen, but
acknowledged himself to be the same as the
heathen.

23. He said : "The hour is come to explain
what I understand by the Son of Man, though
I perish because, in explaining this, I destroy
distinction between Jews and heathen. I must

speak the truth. A grain of wheat will only Jn. xii. 24
bring forth fruit when it itself perishes. He 25.
who loves his fleshly life loses the true life, and
he who despises the fleshly life keeps it for the
everlasting life. He who wishes to follow my
teaching, let him do as I do. And he who 26
does as I do shall be rewarded by my Father.
My soul is now wrestling. Shall I surrender 27.
myself to the compromises of temporary life,
or fulfil the will of the Father, now, at this
hour? And what then? Surely now, when
this hour is come in which I am living, I shall
not say: 'Father, save me from that which I
should do.' I cannot say this for the sake of
my life. And therefore I say: 'Father, show 28.
yourself in me.'"

And Jesus said: "Henceforth the present 31.
society of men is condemned to destruction.
From now that which rules this world shall be
destroyed. And when the Son of Man shall 32
be exalted above the earthly life, then shall
he unite all in one."

Then the Jews said to him: "We under- 34
stand from the law what the everlasting Christ
is; but why do you say that the Son of Man
shall be exalted? What is the meaning of
exalting the Son of Man?"

To this Jesus answered: "To exalt the 35.
Son of Man, means to live by the life of understanding that is in you. To exalt the Son 36
of Man above that which is earthly, means to
believe in the light while there is light, in
order to be a son of understanding.

"He who believes in my teaching believes 44
not in me, but in that spirit which gave life
to the world. And he who understands my 45
teaching, understands that spirit which gave
life to the world. But if any one hears my 47
words and does not fulfil them, it is not I who
blame him, seeing that I came, not to accuse,

Jn. xii. 48. but to save. He who does not accept my
words is accused, not by my teaching, but by
the understanding which is in himself. This
49. it is which accuses him. I did not speak of
myself, but said what my Father, the living
50. spirit in me, suggested to me. That which I
say, the spirit of understanding has told me,
and that which I teach is the true life."

36. And having said this, Jesus went away, and
again hid from the chief priests.

42. And of those who heard these words of
Jesus, many of the powerful and wealthy
people believed, but were afraid to acknowledge it to the chief priests, because not one
of these priests believed and acknowledged it.
43. They were accustomed to judge according to
man, and not according to God.

Mt. xxvi. 3. After Jesus had hidden, the high priests and
the elders again met in the court of Caiaphas.
4. And they began to plan how to take Jesus
5. unknown to the people, for they were afraid
14. to seize him openly. And there came to their
council one of the first twelve disciples of
15. Jesus, Judas Iscariot, who said : "If you wish
to take Jesus secretly, so that the people may
not see, I will find a time when there will be
few people with him, and will show you where
he is ; and then take him. But what will you
give me for this?" They promised him for
16. this thirty silver coins. He agreed ; and from
that time began to seek an opportunity to bring
the chief priests upon Jesus, in order to take
him.

17. Meanwhile Jesus withdrew from the people,
and with him were only his disciples. When
the first feast of unleavened bread approached,
the disciples said to Jesus : "Where, then, shall
18. we keep the Passover?" And Jesus said : "Go
into some village, and enter some one's house,
and say that we have not time to prepare the

feast, and ask him to admit us to celebrate the
Passover." And the disciples did so; they   Mt. xxvi 19
asked a man in the village, and he invited them
in. And they came and sat down to the table,   20
Jesus and the twelve disciples, Judas among
them.

Jesus knew that Judas Iscariot had already   Jn. xiii. 11
promised to betray him to death, but he did
not accuse Judas for this, or show him ill-will,
but as in all his life he taught his disciples
love, so even now he only reproached Judas
lovingly. When they all twelve were seated   Mt. xxvi. 21.
at table, he looked at them, and said: "Among   Mk. xiv. 18.
you sits he who has betrayed me. Yes, he who   Mt. xxvi. 23.
eats and drinks with me shall also destroy me."
And he said nothing more, so that they did not
know of whom he spoke, and they began to sup.

When they began to eat, Jesus took a loaf   26.
and broke it into twelve parts, and gave each
of the disciples a piece, and said: "Take and
eat, this is my body." And he then filled a   27.
cup with wine, handed it to the disciples, and
said: "Drink, all of you, of this cup." And
when they had all drunk, he said: "This is
my blood. I shed it that people may know   28.
my will, to forgive others their sins. For I   Lk. xxii. 18
shall soon die, and be no more with you in this
world, but shall join you only in the kingdom
of heaven."

After this, Jesus got up from the table, girt   Jn. xiii. 4
himself with a towel, took a ewer of water,   5
and began to wash the feet of all the disciples.
And he came to Peter; and Peter said: "But   6.
why will you wash my feet?" Jesus said to   7.
him: "It seems strange to you that I should
wash your feet; but you will know soon why I
do this. Though you are clean, yet not all of   10
you are so, but among you is my betrayer, to
whom I gave, with my own hand, bread and
wine, and whose feet I wish to wash."

Jn. xiii. 12.   When Jesus had washed all their feet, he again sat down, and said : " Do you understand
14. why I did this ? It was so that you always may do the same for each other. I, your teacher, do this, that you may know how to
17. behave toward those who do you evil. If you have understood this, and will do it, then you will
18. be happy. When I said that one of you will betray me, I did not speak of all of you, because only a single one of you, whose feet I washed, and who ate bread with me, will betray me."

21. And having said this, Jesus was troubled in spirit, and yet again said : " Yes, yes, one of you will betray me."

22. And again the disciples began to look round at each other, not knowing of whom he spoke.
23. One disciple sat near to Jesus, and Simon
24. Peter signed to him in a way to ask who
25. the betrayer was. The disciple asked. And
26. Jesus said : " I will soak a piece of bread, and give it to him : and he to whom I shall give it
27. is my betrayer." And he gave the bread to Judas Iscariot, and said to him : "What you
30. wish to do, do quickly." Then Judas understood that he must go out, and as soon as he had taken the bread he forthwith went out. And it was impossible to follow him, as it was night.

31. And when Judas was gone out, Jesus said : " It is now clear to you what the Son of Man is. It is now clear to you that in him God is, to make him as blessed as God Himself.

33. "Children ! I have not long now to be with you. Do not equivocate over my teaching, as I said to the orthodox, but do that which I do.
34. I give you this, a new commandment. As I always, and to the end, have loved you all, do you always, and to the end, love each other.
35. By this only will you be distinguished. Seek to be only thus distinguished from other people. Love one another."

And after this, they went to the Mount of   Mt. xxvi. 30
Olives.

And on the way Jesus said to them: "See,   31.
the time is coming when that shall happen
which is written, the shepherd shall be killed,
and all the sheep shall be scattered. And
to-night this shall happen. I shall be taken,
and you will all abandon me, and scatter."

Peter said to him in answer: "Even if all   33.
shall be frightened, and scatter, I will not deny
you. I am ready for prison and for death with
you."

And Jesus said to him: "But I tell you that   34.
this very night, before cock-crow, after I have
been taken, you will deny me, not once, but
thrice."

But Peter said that he would not deny him;   35.
and the other disciples averred the same.

Then Jesus said to the disciples: "Before,   Lk. xxii. 35.
neither I nor you had need of anything. You
went without wallet and without change of
shoes, and I so bade you do. But now, if I   36.
am accounted an outlaw, we can no longer do
so, but we must be furnished with everything,
and with swords, that we may not perish in
vain."

And the disciples said: "See, we have two   38.
swords."

Jesus said: "It is well."

And having said this, Jesus went with the fol-   Mt. xxvi. 36.
lowers into the garden of Gethsemane. Com-   Jn. xviii. 1.
ing into the garden, he said: "Wait you here,
but I wish to pray."

And while near to Peter and the two brothers,   Mt. xxvi. 37.
sons of Zebedee, he began to feel weary and sad,
and he said to them: "I feel very sad and my   38.
soul is full of the anguish before death. Wait
here, and be not cast down as I am."

And he went off a little way, lay on the ground   39.
on his face, and began to pray, and said: "My

Father, the Spirit! Let it be not as I will, which is that I should not die, but let it be as Thou wilt. Let me die, but for Thee, as a spirit, all is possible; let it be that I may not fear death, that I may escape the temptation of the flesh."

Mt. xxvi. 40. And then he arose, went up to the disciples, and saw that they were cast down. And he said to them: "How is it you have not strength for one hour to keep up your spirit even as I! 41. Keep up your spirit, so as not to fall into the temptation of the flesh. The spirit is strong, the flesh is weak."

42. And again Jesus went away from them, and again began to pray, and said: "Father, if I must suffer, must die, and am about to die, then 43. so let it be. Let Thy will be done." And having said this, he again went up to the disciples, and saw that they were still more cast down, and ready to weep.

44. And he again went away from them, and the third time said: "Father, let Thy will be done." 45. Then he returned to the disciples, and said to them : "Now be easy, and be calm, because it is now decided that I shall give myself into the hands of worldly men."

CHAPTER XI

THE FAREWELL DISCOURSE

The self-life is an illusion which comes through the flesh, an evil. The true life is the life common to all men

("Deliver us from evil")

Jn. xiii. 36. AND Peter said to Jesus: "Whither are you going?"

Jesus answered: "You will not have the strength now to go whither I am going; but afterward you will go the same way."

And Peter said : " Why do you think that I Jn. xiii. 37.
have not the strength now to follow whither you
go ? I will give up my life for you."

And Jesus said : " You say that you will give   38.
up your life for me, and yet even before cock-
crow you shall deny me thrice."   And Jesus   xiv. 1.
said to the disciples : " Be not troubled and be
not afraid, but believe in the true God of life,
and in my teaching.

"The life of the Father is not only that which   2.
is on earth, but there is another life also.   If   3.
there were only such a life as the life here, I
would say to you, that when I die I shall go
into Abraham's bosom, and make ready a place
there for you, and I shall come and take you,
and we shall together live happily in Abraham's
bosom.   But I point out to you only the direc-   4.
tion to life."

Thomas said : " But we do not know whither   5.
you go, and therefore we cannot know the way.
We want to know what there will be after death."

Jesus said : " I cannot show you what will be   6.
there ; my teaching is the way, and the truth,
and the life.   And it is impossible to be joined
with the Father of life otherwise than through
my teaching.   If you fulfil my teaching, you   7.
shall know the Father."

Philip said : "But who is the Father ? "   8.

And Jesus said : "The Father is He who gives   9.
life.   I have fulfilled the will of the Father, and
therefore by my life you may know wherein is
the will of the Father.   I live by the Father,   10.
and the Father lives in me.   All that I say and   11.
do, I do by the will of the Father.   My teaching
is, that I am in the Father and the Father is in
me.   If you do not understand my teaching, yet
you see me and my works.   And therefore you
may understand what the Father is.   And you   12.
know that he who shall follow my teaching may
do the same as I ; and yet more, because I shall

Jn xiv. 13. die, but he will still live. He who shall live according to my teaching, shall have all that he wishes, because then the Son will be one with
14. the Father. Whatever you may wish that accords with my teaching, all that you shall
15. have. But for this you must love my teaching.
16. My teaching will give you, in my place, an in-
17. tercessor and comforter. This comforter will be the consciousness of truth, which worldly men do not understand; but you will know it in your-
18. selves. You never will be alone, if the spirit of
19. my teaching is with you. I shall die, and worldly men will not see me; but you will see me because my teaching lives and you will live
20. by it. And then, if my teaching shall be in you, you will understand that I am in the Father and
21. the Father in me. He who shall fulfil my teach- ing, shall feel in himself the Father; and in him my spirit shall live."

22. And Judas, not Iscariot, but another, said to him: "But why, then, may not all live by the spirit of truth?"

23. Jesus said in answer: "Only he who fulfils my teaching, only him the Father loves, and in
24. him only can my spirit abide. He who does not fulfil my teaching, him my Father cannot love, because this teaching is not mine, but the
25. Father's. This is all that I can tell you now.
26. But my spirit, the spirit of truth, which shall take up its abode in you after I am gone, shall reveal to you all, and you shall recall and understand much of that which I have told
27. you. So that you may always be calm in spirit, not with that worldly calm which men of the world seek, but with that calm of spirit in
28. which we no longer fear anything. On this account, if you fulfil my teaching, you have no reason to grieve over my death. I, as the spirit of truth, will come to you, and, together with the knowledge of the Father, will take up

my abode in your heart. If you fulfil my
teaching, then you must rejoice, because instead of me you will have the Father with you
in your heart, and this is better for you.

" My teaching is the tree of life. The Father   Jn. xv. 1.
is He who tends the tree. He prunes and   2.
cherishes those branches upon which there is
fruit, that they may yield more. Keep my   4.
teaching of life, and life will be in you. And
as a shoot lives not of itself, but out of the
tree, so do you live by my teaching. My   5.
teaching is the tree, you are the shoots. He
who lives by my teaching of life yields much
fruit; and without my teaching there is no
life. He who does not live by my teaching   6.
withers and dies; and the dry branches are cut
off and burnt.

" If you will live by my teaching, and fulfil it, 7.
then you shall have all that you desire. Be-   8.
cause the will of the Father is, that you may
live the true life and have that which you desire. As the Father gave me happiness, so I   9.
give you happiness. Hold to this happiness.
I am living, because the Father loves me and   10.
I love the Father; do you also live by the
same love. If you will live by this, you shall   11.
be blessed.

" My commandment is, that you love one   12.
another as I have loved you. There is no   13.
greater love than to sacrifice one's life for the
love of one's own, as I have done.

" You are my equals, if you do that which I   14.
have taught you. I do not hold you as slaves,   15.
to whom orders are given, but as equals; because I have made clear to you all that I have
known of the Father. You do not, of your   16
own will, choose my teaching; but because I
have pointed out to you that only truth by which
you will live, and from which you will have all
that you wish.

Jn. xv. 17. "The teaching is summed up in this — Love one another.

18. "If the world should hate you, then do not
19. wonder; it hates my teaching. If you were at one with the world, it would love you. But I have severed you from the world, and for
20. that it will hate you. If they persecuted me,
21. they will persecute you also. They will do all this, because they do not know the true
22. God. I explained to them, but they did not
23. wish to hear me. They did not understand my teaching, because they did not under-
24. stand the Father. They saw my life, and my
25. life showed them their error. And for this
26. they still more hated me. The spirit of truth which shall come to you will confirm this
27. to you. And you will accept it. I tell you
xvi. 1. this beforehand, so that you may not be deceived when persecutions shall be upon
2. you. You shall be made outcasts; men shall think that in killing you they do God's pleas-
3. ure. All this they cannot help doing, be-cause they understand neither my teaching
4. nor the true God. All this I tell you before-hand, so that you may not wonder when it comes about.

5. "Well then, I now go away to that Spirit which sent me; and now you understand, you
6. need not ask me whither I go. But before, you were grieved that I did not tell you whither, to what place, I depart.

7. "But I tell you truly that it is well for you that I am going. If I do not die, the spirit of truth will not appear to you, but if I die, it
8. will take up its abode in you. It will take up its abode in you, and it will be clear to you where untruth is, where truth is,
9. and how to make decision. Untruth, in that people do not believe in the life of the
10. spirit. Truth, in that I am one with the

Father.   Decision, in that the power of Jn. xvi. 11.
the fleshly life is at an end.

"I would say yet much more to you, but it   12.
is difficult for you to understand.   But when   13.
the spirit of truth dwells in you, it will show
you the whole truth, because it will tell you,
not a new thing of its own, but that which is
of God; and it will show you the way in all
concerns of life.   It also will be from the   15.
Father, as I am from the Father; therefore it
also will tell you the same as I tell you.

"But when I, the spirit of truth, shall be in   16.
you, you will not always see me.   Sometimes
you will, and sometimes you will not, hear
me."

And the disciples said one to another: 17.
"What does he mean when he says: 'Sometimes you will see me, sometimes you will not
see me.'   What means this, 'Sometimes you   18.
will, sometimes you will not'?"

Jesus said to them: "Do you not under-   19.
stand what this means, 'Sometimes you will,
sometimes you will not, see me'?   You know   20.
how it always is in the world, that some are
sad and grieved, while others rejoice.   And
you will grieve, but your grief will pass into
joy.   A woman, when she bears, grieves while   21.
she is in the pangs of childbirth; but when
that is ended, she does not remember the pangs,
for joy that a man is born into the world.   And   22.
so you will grieve; anon you will see me, the
spirit of truth will enter into you, and your
grief will be turned into joy.   Then you will   23.
no longer ask anything of me, because you will
have all that you wish.   Then all which one of
you desires in the spirit, all that he will have
from his Father.

"You formerly asked for nothing for the   24.
spirit; but now ask what you will for the
spirit, and you will have all; so that your

Jn. xvi. 25. bliss will be full.   Now I, as a man, cannot
tell you this clearly in words, but when I, as
the spirit of truth, shall live in you, I will
proclaim to you clearly about the Father.

26. Then it will not be I who will give you all you
ask of the Father in the name of the spirit.

27. But the Father will Himself give, because He
loves you for having received my teaching.

28. You have understood that understanding proceeds from the Father into the world and returns from the world to the Father."

29. Then the disciples said to Jesus: "Now
we have understood everything, and have

30. nothing more to ask, we believe that you are
from God."

33. And Jesus said: "All that I have said to
you is in order that you may have confidence
and rest in my teaching.   Whatever ills may
befall you in the world, fear nothing: my
teaching will conquer the world."

xvii. 1. After this, Jesus raised his eyes to heaven,
and said:
"My Father! Thou hast given Thy Son
the freedom of life in order that he may re-

3. ceive the true life.   Life is the knowledge of
the true God of the understanding, Who is

6. discovered to me.   I have discovered Thee to

4. men on earth; I have done that work which
Thou hast bidden me do.   I have shown Thy

6. being to men on earth.   They were Thine
before, but by Thy will I have discovered to

7. them the truth, and they know Thee.   They
8. have understood that all they have, their life,
is from Thee only, and that I have taught
them, not of myself, but as proceeding, I with

9. them, from Thee.   But I pray to Thee for

10, those who acknowledge Thee.   They have

11. understood that all that I have is Thine, and
all that is Thine is mine.   I am no longer in the
world, for I return to Thee; but they are in

the world, and therefore I pray Thee, Father,
to preserve in them Thy understanding.   I do   Jn. xvii. 15
not pray Thee to remove them from the world,
but to free them from evil; to confirm them   17,
in Thy truth.   Thy understanding is the truth.   18.
My Father! I wish them to be as I am; to   21.
understand as I do, that the true life began
before the beginning of the world.   That they
should all be one; as Thou, Father, art in me,
and I in Thee, so they may also be one in me.
I in them, Thou in me, so that all may be one;   23.
so that all men may understand they are not
self-created, but that Thou, in love, hast sent
them into the world as Thou didst send me.
Father of truth! the world did not know Thee,   25.
but I knew Thee, and they have known Thee
through me.   And I have made plain to them   26.
what Thou art.   Thou art in me, that the
love with which Thou hast loved me may be
in them also.   Thou gavest them life, and
therefore didst love them.   I have taught them
to know this, and to love Thee; so that Thy
love might be returned from them to Thee."

CHAPTER XII

THE VICTORY OF THE SPIRIT OVER THE FLESH

*Therefore, for him who lives, not the self-life, but a common
life in the will of the Father, there is no death.   Bodily
death is for him union with the Father*

("𝕿𝖍𝖎𝖓𝖊 𝖎𝖘 𝖙𝖍𝖊 𝖐𝖎𝖓𝖌𝖉𝖔𝖒, 𝖕𝖔𝖜𝖊𝖗, 𝖆𝖓𝖉 𝖌𝖑𝖔𝖗𝖞")

AFTER this, Jesus said: "Now arise, and   Mt. xxvi. 46
let us go; already he is coming who will betray me."
    And he had hardly said this, when suddenly   47
Judas, one of the twelve disciples, appeared,
and with him a great throng of people with

Mt. xxvi. 48. sticks and swords. Judas said to them : " I will bring you where he and his followers are. and so that you may know him among them all, he whom I shall first kiss, that is he."

49. And he straightway went up to Jesus, and said : " Hail, teacher ! " and kissed him.

50. And Jesus said to him : " Friend, why are you here ? "

Then the guard surrounded Jesus, and wished to take him.

51. And Peter snatched the sword from the high priest's servant, and slashed the man's ear.

52. But Jesus said : " You must not oppose evil. Cease." And he said to Peter : " Return the sword to him from whom you took it ; he who shall draw the sword, shall perish with the sword."

55. And after this, Jesus turned to the crowd, and said : " Why have you come out against me, as against a robber, with arms ? I was every day among you in the temple, and taught

Lk. xxii. 53. you, and you did not take me. But now is your hour, and the power of darkness."

Mt. xxvi. 56. Then, having seen that he was taken, all the disciples ran away.

Jn. xviii. 12. And the officer ordered the soldiers to take Jesus, and bind him. The soldiers bound him,

13. and took him first to Annas. This was the father-in-law of Caiaphas, and Caiaphas was the high priest for that year, and lived in the

14. same house with Annas. This was the same Caiaphas who planned how to destroy Jesus. He held that it was good for the sake of the people to destroy Jesus, because, if that were not done, it would be worse for the whole peo-

Mk. xiv. 53. ple. And they took Jesus to the house where this high priest lived.

Mt. xxvi. 58. When they had brought Jesus thither, one of his disciples, Peter, followed him from afar,

and watched where they were taking him.
When they brought Jesus into the court of the
high priest, Peter went in also, to see how all
would end.   And a girl in the yard saw Peter,   Mt. xxvi. 69
and said to him: "You, also, were with Jesus
of Galilee."   Then Peter was afraid that they   70.
would accuse him also, and he said aloud before all the people: "I do not know what you
are talking about."   Afterward, when they   71.
had taken Jesus into the house, Peter also
entered thc hall, with the people.   In the hall,
a woman was warming herself at the fire, and
Peter approached.   The woman looked at Peter,
and said to the people: "See, this man is likely
to have been with Jesus of Nazareth."   Peter   72.
was still more frightened, and swore that he
never was with him, and did not even know
what kind of a man Jesus was.   A little while   73.
after, the people came up to Peter, and said:
"It is quite clear that you also were among the
disturbers.   By your speech one may know that
you are from Galilee."   Then Peter began to   74.
swear, and aver that he had never known or
seen Jesus.

And he had hardly said this, when the cock   75.
crew.   And Peter remembered those words
which Jesus had said to him, when Peter swore
that if all denied Jesus, he would not deny him:
"Before the cock crow this night, you will deny
me thrice."   And Peter went out, and cried
bitterly.   Jesus had prayed that he might not
thus fall into temptation.   He had fallen into
one temptation, that of strife, when he began
to defend Jesus; and into another temptation,
the fear of death, when he denied Jesus.

And there gathered to the high priest, the   Mk xiv. 53.
orthodox chief priests, assistants, and officials.
And when all were assembled, they brought in   Jn. xviii. 19
Jesus; and the chief priests asked him, what
was his teaching, and who were his followers.

Jn. xviii. 20.   And Jesus answered: "I always said all I
had to say before everybody openly, and so
I speak now; I concealed nothing from any
21. one, and I conceal nothing now.   But about
what do you question me?   Question those
who heard and understood my teaching.   They
will tell you."

22. When Jesus had said this, one of the high
priest's servants struck him in the face, and
said: "To whom are you speaking?   Is this
the way to answer the high priest?"

23. Jesus said: "If I spoke ill, say what I spoke
ill.   But if I said nothing ill, then there is no
cause to beat me."

Mt. xxvi. 59.   The orthodox chief priests strove to accuse
Jesus, and at first did not find any proofs against
him for which it was possible to condemn him.
60, Afterward they found two witnesses.   These
61. said about Jesus: "We ourselves heard how
this man said: 'I will destroy this temple of
yours made with hands, and in three days will
build up another temple to God, not made with
59. hands.'"   But this evidence, also, was not
62. enough to condemn him.   And therefore the
high priest called up Jesus, and said: "Why
do you not answer their evidence?"

63. Jesus held his tongue, saying nothing.   Then
the high priest said to him: "Well, say then,
Are you the Christ, and of God?"

64. Jesus answered him, and said: "Yes, I am
the Christ, and of God.   You yourselves will
now see that the Son of Man is made like God."

65. Then the high priest cried out: "You blas-
pheme!   Now we do not want any evidence.
We all hear, now, that you are a blasphemer."

66. And the high priest turned to the assembly,
and said: "You have yourselves heard that
he blasphemes God.   To what do you sentence
him for this?"

And all said: "We sentence him to death."

Then all the people, and the guards, fell Mt. xxvi. 67
upon Jesus, and began to spit in his face, to
strike him on the cheeks, and to tear at him.
They covered his eyes, hit him in the face,
and asked : " Now, prophet, guess who it was   68.
that hit you ? "

But Jesus held his peace.

Having abused him, they took him, bound, xxvii. 2.
to Pontius Pilate.   And they brought him into Jn. xviii. 28.
the court.

Pilate, the governor, came out to them and   29.
asked : " Of what do you accuse this man ? "

They said : " This man is doing wrong ; so   30.
we have brought him to you."

And Pilate said to them : " But if he does   31.
wrong, then judge him yourselves according
to your law."

And they said : " We have brought him to
you that you might execute him, for we are
not allowed to kill any one."

And so that happened which Jesus expected.   32.
He said that one must be ready to die on the
cross at the hands of the Romans, more likely
than at the hands of the Jews.

And when Pilate asked, whereof they accused Lk. xxiii. 2.
him, they said, that he was guilty of stirring up
the people, and that he forbade the payment
of taxes to Cæsar, and that he set up himself
as Christ and king.

Pilate listened to them, and bade Jesus be Jn. xviii. 33.
brought to him in the court.   When Jesus
came in, Pilate said to him : " So you are king
of the Jews ? "

Jesus said to him : " Do you really suppose   34.
that I am a king, or are you repeating only
that which others have told you ? "

Pilate said : " I am not a Jew, therefore you   35
cannot be my king, but your people have
brought you to me.   What kind of a man are
you ? "

Jn. xviii 36.   Jesus answered: "I am a king; but my kingdom is not an earthly one. If I were an earthly king, my subjects would fight for me, and would not yield to the high priests. But as it is, you see that my kingdom is not an earthly one."

37.   Pilate said to this: "But yet, do you not consider yourself a king?" Jesus said: "Not only I, but you also, cannot but consider me a king. For I only teach, in order to discover to all the truth of the kingdom of heaven. And every one who lives by the truth, is a king."

38.   Pilate said: "You spoke of truth. What is truth?"

And having said this, he turned, and went to the chief priests. He went out and said to them: "In my opinion, this man has done no wrong."

Mk. xv. 3.   But the chief priests insisted upon their opinion, and said that he was doing much evil, and stirring up the people, and had raised the whole of Judea right from Galilee.

4.   Then Pilate, in the presence of the chief priests, began to question Jesus. But Jesus did not answer. Pilate then said to him: "Do you hear of what they accuse you? Why do you not justify yourself?"

5.   But Jesus still held his tongue, and said not another word, so that Pilate wondered at him.

Lk. xxiii. 6.   Pilate remembered that Galilee was in the power of King Herod, and asked: "Ah! he is from Galilee?" They answered: "Yes."

7.   Then he said: "If he is from Galilee, then he is under the authority of Herod, and I will send him to him." Herod was then in Jerusalem, and Pilate, in order to rid himself, sent Jesus to Herod.

8.   When they brought Jesus to Herod, Herod was very glad to see him. He had heard much

of him, and wished to know what kind of man
he was.   So he called Jesus to him, and began   Lk. xxiii. 9
to question him about all he wished to know.
.But Jesus answered him nothing.   And the   10
chief priests and teachers, just as with Pilate,
so before Herod, vehemently accused Jesus,
and said that he was a rioter.   And Herod   11
deemed ·Jesus an empty fellow, and to mock
him, bade them clothe him in red, and send
him back to Pilate.   Herod was pleased at   12
Pilate's showing respect to him, by sending
Jesus for his judgment, and on this account
they became friends, whereas formerly they
had been at variance.

Now, when they brought Jesus again to   13.
Pilate, Pilate called back the chief priests
and Jewish authorities, and said to them:
"You brought this man to me for stirring   14.
up the people, and I have examined him
before you, and do not see that he is a rioter.
I sent him with you to Herod, and now, see,   15.
— nothing wrong is found in him.   And, in
my opinion, there is no cause to punish him
with death.   Had you not better punish him
and let him go?"

But when the chief priests heard this, all   Mt. xxvii. 23.
cried out: "No, punish him in the Roman
fashion!   Stretch him on the cross!"   Pilate   21.
heard them out, and said to the chief priests:
"Well, as you will!   But you have a custom
at the feast of the Passover to pardon one
condemned malefactor.   Well, I have lying
in prison, Barabbas, a murderer and rioter.
Which one of the two must be let free:
Jesus or Barabbas?"

Pilate thus wished to save Jesus; but the
chief priests had so worked upon the people,
that all cried out: "Barabbas, Barabbas!"

And Pilate said: "And what shall be done   22
with Jesus?"

They again cried out: " Roman fashion, —
to the cross, to the cross with him."

Mt.xxvii. 23.   And Pilate tried to talk them over. He said :
" Why do you press so hardly on him? He
has done nothing that he should be punished
Jn. xix. 4. with death, and he has done you no harm. I
will set him free, because I find no fault in him."

6.   The chief priests and their servants cried
out : " Crucify, crucify him ! "

And Pilate said to them : " If so, then take
him and crucify him yourselves. But I see no
fault in him."

7.   The chief priests answered : " We ask only
that which our law demands. By our law, he
must be executed for having made himself out
to be Son of God."

8.   When Pilate heard this word, he was
troubled, because he did not know what this
9. term " Son of God " meant.   And having
returned into the court, Pilate called up Jesus
again, and asked him : " Who are you, and
whence are you? "

But Jesus did not answer.

10.   Then Pilate said : " But why do you not
answer me? You surely see that you are in
my power, and that I can crucify you, or set
you free."

11.   Jesus answered him : " You have no power.
There is power only from above."

12.   Pilate, nevertheless, wished to set Jesus free,
15. and he said to them : " How is it you wish to
crucify your king? "

12.   But the Jews said to him : " If you set Jesus
free, you will thereby show that you are a dis-
loyal servant to Cæsar, because he who sets
himself up as king is an enemy to Cæsar.

15. Our king is Cæsar; but crucify this man."

13.   And when Pilate heard these words, he
understood that he could now no longer
refuse to execute Jesus.

Then Pilate went out before the Jews, took Mt.xxvii. 24
some water, washed his hands, and said: "I
am not guilty of the blood of this just man."
And the whole people cried out: "Let his 25.
blood be upon us and all our children."

So that the chief priests gained the upper Lk. xxiii. 23.
hand. And Pilate sat in his place of judgment, Jn. xix. 13.
and ordered Jesus to be first flogged. Mt. xxvii. 26.

When they had flogged him, the soldiers, 28,
who had done this, put a crown upon his head 29.
and a rod in his hand, and threw a red cloak
over his back, and fell to reviling him; in
mockery, they bowed down to his feet, and
said: "Hail, king of the Jews!" And others
struck him on the cheeks, over the face, and
spat in his face.

But the chief priests cried: "Crucify him! Jn. xix. 15.
Our king is Cæsar! Crucify him!"

And Pilate bade him be crucified. 16.

Then they stripped Jesus of the red dress, Mt. xxvii. 31.
put on him his own clothing, and bade him
bear the cross to a place called Golgotha, there
to be crucified at once. And he carried his Jn. xix. 18.
cross, and so came to Golgotha. And there
they stretched Jesus on the cross, beside two
other men. These two were at the sides, and
Jesus was in the middle.

When they had crucified Jesus, he said: Lk. xxiii. 34.
"Father! forgive them; they do not know what
they are doing."

And when Jesus was hung on the cross, the 35.
people thronged round him and railed at him.
They came up, wagged their heads at him, and Mk. xv. 29.
said: "So, you wish to destroy the temple of
Jerusalem, and to build it up again in three
days. Well now, save yourself, come down from 30.
the cross!" And the chief priests and leaders 31.
stood there also, and mocked at him, and said:
"He thought to save others, but cannot save
himself. Now show that you are Christ; come 32.

down from the cross, and then we will believe you. He said that he was the Son of God, and that God would not forsake him. But how is it that God has now forsaken him?" And the people, and the chief priests, and the soldiers, railed at him, and even one of the robbers crucified with him, he too railed at him.

Lk. xxiii. 39. One of the robbers, reviling him, said: "If you are Christ, save yourself and us."

40. But the other robber heard this and said: "Do you not fear God? You who are yourself on the cross, do you even rail at the inno-

41. cent? You and I are executed for our deserts, but this man has done no harm."

42. And, turning to Jesus, this robber said to him: "Lord, remember me in your kingdom."

43. And Jesus said to him: "Even now you are blessed with me!"

Mt.xxvii.46. But at the ninth hour, Jesus, worn out, cried aloud: "Eloi, Eloi, lama sabachthani!" This means: "My God, my God! why hast Thou forsaken me?"

47. And when the people heard this, they began to say jeeringly: "He is calling the prophet Elias! Let us see whether Elias will come!"

Jn. xix. 28. Afterward, Jesus cried out: "Let me drink!"

And a man took a sponge, soaked it in vinegar, that stood by, and gave it to Jesus on a reed.

30. Jesus sucked the sponge, and cried out in a loud voice: "It is finished! Father, I give up

Lk. xxiii. 46. my spirit into your hands!" And, letting his head fall, he gave up the ghost.

A PROLOGUE

THE UNDERSTANDING OF LIFE

*The proclamation of Christ has replaced the belief in an
external God by the understanding of life*

THE Gospel is the revelation of this truth,
that the first source of everything is the understanding of life itself.   This being so, the
Gospel puts in the place of what men call
"God" a right understanding of life.   With
out this understanding there is no life ; men
only live in so far as they understand life.

Those who do not grasp this, and who deem
that the body is the source of life, shut themselves out from true life ; but those who comprehend that they live, not through the body,
but through the spirit, possess true life.   This
is that true life which Jesus Christ came to
teach to men.   Having conceived that man's
life flows from the understanding, he gave to
men the teaching and example of a life of the
understanding in the body.

Earlier religions were the announcements of
law as to what men ought to do, and not to
do, for the service of God.   The teaching of
Jesus, on the other hand, deals only with the
understanding of life.   No man has ever seen,
and no man can see or know, an external God ;
therefore our life cannot take for its aim the
service of such a God.   Only by adopting for
his supreme principle the inner understanding

of life, having for its source the acknowledgment of God, can man surely travel the way of life.

<table>
<tr><td>Mk.</td><td>i. 1.</td></tr>
</table>

The announcement of salvation of Jesus Christ, the Son of God. This is the announcement of salvation ; all men who come to know they are sons of God receive true life. The foundation and beginning of all things is the understanding of life. Understanding of life is God. This the announcement of Jesus Christ reveals as the foundation and beginning of everything. All is built upon the understanding of life, without which there can be no living. In this is true life.

This understanding is the light of truth. But this light shines amid the darkness, and the darkness is not able to overcome it. The true light has always been in the world, and shines upon all men who come into the world. It has been in the world, and the world existed only because it contained this light; but the world has not adhered to it. This light has appeared in its place, but its place has not retained it.

All those who have grasped the understanding of life have received the opportunity of becoming like it through belief in it. Those who have believed that life is in the understanding have become the sons, not of the flesh, but of the understanding.

And the understanding of life was united with the flesh in the person of Jesus Christ, and so we were given to know that the offspring of understanding, man in the flesh, is of the same nature as his Father, the original source of life.

The teaching of Jesus is the perfect and true faith. In fulfilling the teaching of Jesus, we have understood the new faith which re-

places the old.   It was law that Moses gave, Jn.   i. 17.
but we come to understand the true faith
through Jesus Christ.

No man has ever seen God; the Son only,   18.
who is in the Father, has shown us the way
of life.

A SUMMARY

THE UNDERSTANDING OF LIFE IS TO DO GOOD

The announcement of blessedness made by Jesus Christ is an announcement of understanding of life

THE understanding of life is this : The source of life is perfect goodness, and therefore human life is perfectly good in its nature. To understand the source of life, it is necessary to believe that our spirit, the life in man, came from this source. The man, formerly not living, is summoned into life by this, his origin. This source of life appoints blessedness for man, because its own being is blessedness.

To keep in harmony with the source of his life, a man must fix himself upon the one characteristic of this source which is comprehensible to him, and which finds blessedness in doing good. Therefore man's life must be devoted to this blessedness; that is, to doing good from love. But we can find no objects of goodness other than men. All our own bodily desires are out of harmony with this principle of blessedness ; and therefore they, with all the life of the body, must be surrendered to the principle of blessedness, to active love to mankind.

Love to our fellow-men follows from the understanding of life revealed by Jesus Christ. The confirmations of this understanding of life are twofold. One is, that when not accepted, the source of life seems to be an impostor, who gives to men an unsatisfied craving for life and blessedness. The other is, that man feels in his soul that love and goodness toward his fellow-men is the only true, free, eternal life.

The First Epistle of John the Divine

This is the announcement of the understanding of life through which men have fellowship with the Father of life, and therefore have eternal life. *1 Jn. i. 1–3*

This is an announcement of blessedness. *4.*

The understanding of life is, that God is life and blessedness, and that in life and blessedness death and evil do not exist. *5.*

If we say that we are at one with God, while we feel we are living in evil and death, then either we are imposing upon ourselves, or we are not doing what we ought to do. *6.*

Only by living the same life as His, do we become at one with Him. *7.*

As a teacher of this life, we have Jesus Christ, the right-living. He freed us and all who will, from wrong-living. *ii. 1.* *2.*

The proof that we know the teaching of Jesus Christ is, that we carry out his commandments. Any one who says he knows the teaching of Jesus Christ, and does not keep his commandments, is a liar, and there is no truth in him. But the man who carries out his commandments has the love of God in him. Only through love can we know that we are at one with God. *3.* *4.* *5.*

He who says he is at one with Jesus Christ, must also live as Jesus lived. *6.*

He who says of himself that he is in life and blessedness, but hates his living brother-man, is not in life and blessedness, but in *9–11.*

death and evil; and he does not know what he is doing; he is blind, hating the life which is in himself also.

1 Jn. ii. 15. To escape this blindness, a man must remember that everything in the world, in the earthly life, is the desire of the flesh, or vanity, and that all this is not from God. And that

16. all this passes away, perishes. And that only

17. he who does the will of God, which is love, endures for ever.

23. Only he who recognizes that his spirit is the offspring of the Father, is united with the

24. Father. Therefore remain in the knowledge that you are, in the spirit, sons of the Father, God, and you will have eternal life.

iii. 1. God gives us the opportunity of being His sons, and like Himself. So that, in this present

2. life, we become His sons. We do not know what we are to be, but we know that we are like Him, and that we are united with Him.

3. Confidence in this eternal life rids us of our mistakes, and purifies us to the Father's purity.

4. For whoever commits sin, violates the will of God.

5. Jesus Christ came to teach us the way to deliverance from sin, and unity with God.

6. Therefore those who become united with Him can no longer sin. Only that man will

7. sin who does not know Him. But he who

8. lives in God, acts righteously; and only he

9. who is not united with God, does unrighteously. He who owns his origin from God, cannot do any falsehood.

10. Therefore men are of two classes — men of God, and men who are not of God; men who know the right and love the brethren, and men who do not know the right and do not love the brethren.

11. For, following the teaching of Jesus Christ,

we cannot refrain from loving one another.
Through the teaching of Jesus Christ, we   1 Jn. iii 14
know that we have passed from death to life,
because we love the brethren, and that he who
does not love his brother is in death.   We   15.
know that one who does not love his living
brother does not love life.   And he who does
not love life cannot himself possess life.

By this teaching we recognize love, in the   16.
fact that life is given to us; and we know,
therefore, that we also must give up our life
for our brother.   So that he who, himself   17.
having the means of life, sees his brother in
need, and does not yield his own life for his
brother's sake, — in him there is no divine
love.

We must love, not by words, but by deeds,   18.
in truth.   And he who so loves has a quiet   19.
heart, because he is at one with God.

If our heart is at strife in us, we subduc it   20.
to God.   For God is higher than the wishes   21.
of our hearts.   But if there is no strife in our
hearts, then we are blessed, and that because   22.
we do all we can, the best deeds, and fulfil all
that is ordained for us.

And this is ordained for us — to believe that   23.
man is the son of God, and to love our brother.
Those who do this are united with God, and   iv. 4.
are risen above the world, because that which
is in us is greater, of more consequence, than
all the world.

Therefore let us love one another.   Love is   7.
from God, and every one who loves is the son
of God, and knows God.   And he who does   8.
not love, does not know God.   Because God
is love.

That God is love, we know because He sent   9
into the world this Spirit, such as He Himself is, and thereby gave us life.   We did not   10
exist, and God was under no compulsion, but

He gave us life and blessedness; therefore He must love us.

¶ Jn. iv. 11-13. No man can perfectly know God. All we can know of Him is, that He had love toward us, and because of this love gave us life. And to be in fellowship with God, we must be like Him, and do as He does; we must love one another. If we love one another, God dwells in us, and we dwell in Him.

16. Having understood the love of God toward us, we believe that God is love, and that he 17. who loves is united with God. And having understood this, we do not fear death, because in this world we become such as God Himself 18. is. Our life becomes love, and is thus freed from fear and all sufferings.

19. We love, because He loves. And we love not a God whom no one can love, because no one sees Him, but our brother-man, whom it is 20. possible to love. He who says he loves God, and yet hates his brother, is deceiving himself. Because, if he does not love the brother whom he sees, how, then, can he love God whom he 21. does not see? For it is ordained to us to love God in our brother.

v. 3. To love God, is to fulfil His commandments. And these commandments are not hard for 4. him who, recognizing that his origin is from 5. God, rises above the world. Our faith lifts us above the world. And our faith in that which Jesus, the Son of God, taught us, is true. He has taught us that he lived in the world, not merely in the way of truth, but by the power 6. of the spirit. And that spirit is in us, and makes us strong in truth, following out the teaching.

9. If we believe in what men affirm, why, then, should we not believe in the spirit that is in 10. ourselves? He who believes in that spirit of life which is in us, has assurance within him-

self.   And he who does not believe that there
is a spirit from above us, from the Father,
makes God a deceiver.

The spirit in us affirms that our life is eter-   1 Jn. v. 11.
nal.   He who knows that this spirit is the off-   12.
spring of the Infinite Spirit, and becomes like
Him, has eternal life.   And for him who so   14.
believes, there is no difficulty left in his life,
but everything he desires in the will of the
Father will come to him.

Therefore he who believes himself to be a   18.
son of God, will not live in any deception, but
is free from evil.   Because he knows that this   19.
material world is an illusion, and that in man   20.
himself there is the capacity to know that which
has real existence.   And only the Spirit, the
Son, the offspring of the Father, really exists.

A RECAPITULATION

CHAPTER I

THE SON OF GOD

Man, the son of God, is powerless in the flesh, and free in the spirit

("Our Father")

JESUS in his childhood called God his Father. There arose in Judea, at this time, a prophet named John. John preached the coming of God upon earth. He said that when men should change their lives, when they should treat one another as equals, when they should cease to injure one another, and, instead of so doing, serve one another, then God would appear upon earth, and His kingdom would be established on earth. Jesus, having heard this declaration, withdrew from among men and went into the wild places, to meditate upon the meaning of human life, and upon his relations to that infinite source of all being, called God. And Jesus accepted as his Father that infinite source of being whom John had called God.

After passing days in the wild places without taking food, Jesus began to suffer hunger. Then he thought to himself, "I am the Son of God the Almighty; I ought, then, to be as He is. But now, I wish to eat, and no bread comes for my need; I am not, then, all-powerful." Then he said to himself, "It is true, I cannot make for myself bread out of stones; but I can overcome the want of bread. So that, though not all-powerful in the body, I am all-powerful in the spirit, and I can quell the body; and thus I am the Son of God, not through the flesh, but through the spirit."

Then he said: "But if I am the Son of the Spirit, I can free myself of the body, and do away with it." But to that he answered, "I am born as spirit, embodied in flesh. Such is the will of my Father, and I cannot set myself against His will."

"But if you cannot satisfy the wants of your body, and if you are no better able to free yourself from your body," he went on to himself, "you ought, then, to labor for the body, and to enjoy all the pleasures it gives you."

But to that he answered, "I cannot satisfy the wants of my body any better than I can rid myself of it; but my life is all-powerful, in that it is the spirit of my Father; and it follows that in my body I must serve the spirit, my Father, and labor for Him only! And becoming convinced that man's life is only in the spirit of the Father, Jesus left the wild places, and began to declare his teaching to men. He said that the spirit dwelt in him, that henceforth heaven was opened, that the powers of heaven were brought to men, that for men a free and boundless life was begun, and that all men, however unfortunate in the body, may be happy.

CHAPTER II

LIFE IN THE SPIRIT

Therefore man must work, not for the flesh, but for the spirit

("𝕸𝖍𝖎𝖈𝖍 art in heaben")

THE Jews, holding themselves orthodox, worshiped an external God, whom they regarded as Creator and Lord of the Universe. According to their teaching, this external God had made an agreement with them. According to this agreement, he had promised the Jews to help them, and they had promised to worship Him; and the chief condition of the alliance was the keeping of the Sabbath.

But Jesus said : " The Sabbath is a human institution. That man shall live in the spirit, is more important than all religious ceremonies. Like all external forms of religion, the keeping of the Sabbath includes in itself a delusion. It is impossible to do nothing on the Sabbath. Good actions must be done at any time ; and if keeping the Sabbath prevents good action, then the Sabbath is an error."

Another condition in this agreement with God, was the avoidance of the society of infidels. As to this, Jesus said : " God asks for no sacrifice to Himself, but only that men should love one another."

Still another condition related to the following of rules about washing and cleansing ; as to which, Jesus said : " God demands, not outside cleanliness, but only, pity and love toward men." He taught that all such external ceremonies were harmful, and that the church tradition itself was an evil. The church tradition causes men to neglect the most important acts of love, as, for instance, love to father and mother. Of all external ceremonies, of all the ritual of the old law, which had for object, as was held, the purification of men, Jesus said : " Know all of you, that nothing from outside can defile a man ; only what he thinks, and what he does, defiles him."

After this, Jesus went to Jerusalem, a town considered holy, entered the temple, where the orthodox believed that God dwelt, and there taught : " It is useless to offer God sacrifices ; man is of more consequence than a temple ; and the only duty is, to love one's neighbor, and help him."

And he taught, further : " Men need not worship God in any particular place, but they must worship Him in spirit and in act. The spirit cannot be seen or shown. The spirit is man's consciousness of his sonship to the Infinite Spirit. No temple is needed. The true temple is the society of men united in love." He said : " All external worship of the divine is not only false and injurious, as with the Jews, among whom it caused murder and admitted neglect of parents, but harmful, because one who goes through external ceremonials, thinks himself made righteous, and free from the need of doing what love demands." He said: "Only that man aims at good, and does good, who feels his own imperfection. To do good deeds, a man must think of himself as imperfect. But external acts of worship lead men into the delusion of self-conceit. All external ceremonies are unnecessary, and must be thrown aside. Deeds of love are incompatible with ceremonial performances, and it is impossible to do good in that form. Man is the son of God by the spirit, and therefore must serve the Father in the spirit."

CHAPTER III

THE SOURCE OF LIFE

The life of all men has proceeded from the spirit of the Father

("Hallowed be Thy Name")

JOHN's disciples asked Jesus what was meant by his "Kingdom of God." He said that the Kingdom of God as preached by him was also that preached by John; and that therein every man, however poor, might be blessed.

And Jesus said to the people: "John was the first who preached to men a Kingdom of God which is not of the external world, but is in the soul of man. The orthodox went to hear John, but understood nothing, because they know only those fictions of their own about an external God, which they preach; and they are astonished when no one pays heed to them. But John preached the truth of the Kingdom of God within men, and therefore he did more than them all. He did so much that, since his time, the law and the prophets, and all external forms of divine worship, are superseded. Since he taught, it is made clear that the Kingdom of God is in the soul of man.

"The beginning and the end of all things is in the soul

of man. Every man, in addition to his bodily life, to the fact which he knows as to his conception from a bodily father through a bodily mother, recognizes in himself a free spirit, intelligent, and independent of the body. This very Spirit, infinite, and proceeding from the infinite, is the origin of all, and is what we call God. We know Him only as we recognize Him within us. This Spirit is the source of our life, and must be ranked above everything; and to Him we must live. By making Him the foundation of our life, we gain the true and infinite life.

"The Father-Spirit, who sends this Spirit into men, cannot have sent Him to deceive men, so that, while conscious of Him, they might come to lose Him. This infinite Spirit being in man, He must have been given to the end that men, through Him, might have infinite life. Therefore the man who conceives of this Spirit as his life, has infinite life. The man who does not so conceive, has no true life. Men can of themselves choose life or death. Life,— in the Spirit; death, — in the flesh. The life of the Spirit is goodness, light. The life of the flesh is evil, darkness. To believe in the Spirit means to do good deeds; to disbelieve, means to do evil deeds. Goodness is life; evil is death.

"God, the Creator, external to us, the beginning of all beginnings, we do not know. Our conception of Him can only be this, that He sowed in men the Spirit; sowing, as a sower does, everywhere, not discriminating, over the field; and the seed, falling on good ground, grows, falling on sterile ground, perishes.

"The Spirit alone gives life, and men are responsible for keeping or losing it. To the Spirit, no evil exists. Evil is but an illusion of life. There are only the two conditions, of living and not-living. Thus the world presents itself to every man; and for every man there is in his soul a consciousness of the Kingdom of Heaven. Each one can, by his own free will, enter, or not enter, that Kingdom. To enter, belief in the life of the Spirit is necessary. He who believes in that life of the Spirit, has infinite life."

CHAPTER IV

GOD'S KINGDOM

Therefore the will of the Father is the life and welfare of all men

("𝕿𝖍𝖞 𝖐𝖎𝖓𝖌𝖉𝖔𝖒 𝖈𝖔𝖒𝖊")

JESUS pitied men because they did not know true blessedness; therefore he taught them. He said: "Blessed are those who have no property, no position, and who do not care for these; and unhappy are they who seek riches and position. Because such poor and oppressed people are in the Father's will; but the rich and acknowledged people seek only to make gain from men for this temporary life. To carry out God's will, one must not fear to be poor and despised, but must rejoice in this, while showing men what true happiness is.

"To carry out the will of the Father, which gives life and welfare, mankind must fulfil five commandments, namely:—

The First Commandment

To do no ill to any one, and to so act as to rouse evil in no one; because from evil comes evil.

The Second Commandment

Not to follow after women, and not to desert the woman with whom a union has once been formed; because desertion and change of wives causes all the world's dissoluteness.

The Third Commandment

To take no oath of any kind; because nothing can be promised, since man is in the Father's power; and oaths, when taken, are for bad ends.

The Fourth Commandment

Not to fight against evil, but to suffer wrong, and to give even more than men would exact from us; not to condemn, and not to use the law; because every man is himself full of errors, and cannot guide others. By taking revenge, we only teach others to revenge.

The Fifth Commandment

To make no difference between a fellow-countryman and a foreigner; because all men are children of one father.

"The observance of these five commandments is necessary, not to win praise from men, but for one-self, for one's own welfare; therefore there is no propriety in praying and fasting in sight of men.

"The Father knows all that men need, and there is no necessity to pray for particular things; it is simply needful to seek to be in the Father's will. And this is the will of the Father, that a man shall have no anger toward any other. To keep fasts is not essential, for men may fast merely to win praise from men, and such praise ought to be avoided. It is only necessary carefully to conform to the will of God, and the rest will follow of itself. While caring for the body, care cannot be given to the Kingdom of Heaven. Even though a man does not trouble about food and clothing, he will live on. The Father will give life. The needful thing is, at this present moment, to be in the will of the Father. The Father gives to his children what they need. We must desire only the power of the Spirit, which the Father gives.

"The five commandments mark out the road to the Kingdom of Heaven. This narrow path alone leads to eternal life. False teachers — wolves in the skins of sheep — always try to turn men astray from this road; they must be guarded against. False teachers can always be detected, because they teach evil in the name of good. If they teach violence and executions, they are false teachers. By the deeds they teach they may be known.

"Not that man does the Father's will, who calls on the name of God; but he who does good deeds. And he who fulfils these five commandments will have secure and true life, of which nothing can deprive him. But he who does not fulfil them will have an insecure life; one soon to be taken from him, leaving him nothing."

The teaching of Jesus filled the people with admiration and joy, because it offered freedom to every one.

The teaching of Christ was the fulfilment of John's prophecy that God's chosen one should bring light to men, overcome evil, and restore truth, by kindness, meekness, and goodness, but not by violence.

CHAPTER V

THE TRUE LIFE

The fulfilment of the personal will leads to death; the fulfilment of the Father's will gives the true life

("Thy will be done")

THE wisdom of life is, the recognition of one's own life as the offspring of the Father's Spirit. Men set before themselves the aims of the bodily life, and in pursuing these aims, they harass themselves and others.

In receiving the doctrine of the spiritual life, and in subjecting and making less of the body, men will find a full satisfaction in the life of the Spirit, in that life which is appointed for them.

Jesus said to his disciples: "The true food of man is the fulfilment of the will of the Father-Spirit. This fulfilment is always possible. Our whole life is a gathering of the fruits of the life sown within us by the Father. Those fruits are the good we are doing among men.

"We ought not to look forward with anxiety for anything. We ought, without ceasing our interest in life, to do good among men."

After this, Jesus happened to be in Jerusalem, where was a bath, beside which lay a sick man, doing nothing but waiting a miracle to cure him. Jesus came, and said to him: " Do not expect a cure by a miracle, but live your life according to your strength, and do not be deluded as to the purpose of life." The invalid obeyed Jesus, got up, and went away.

The orthodox, seeing this, began to reproach Jesus for what he said, and because he had, on the Sabbath, raised an invalid. Jesus said to them: " I did nothing new. I have only the power to act of our common Father, the Spirit. He lives, and gives life to men, and I have done likewise. And to do this is every man's business. Every one is free, and can live, or not live. To live, is to fulfil the will of the Father, which is to do good to others. Not to live, is to fulfil one's own will, not to do good to others. It is in every one's power to do this, or that; to gain life, or to destroy it.

" The true life of man is like this. A master apportioned to his slaves some valuable property, and told each one to work upon what was given to him. Some worked ; some did not work, but put out of sight what was given to them. The master demanded an account : and to those who worked, he gave yet more than they had ; but from those who did not work, he took away everything."

The portion of valuable property of the master is the Spirit of life in man, who is the son of the Father-Spirit. He who in his life works for the sake of the spirit-life, receives infinite life ; he who does not work, is deprived of what was given to him.

The true life is the common life of humanity, and not the life of the individual. Each one must work for the life of others.

After this, Jesus went to a desert place, and many people followed him. At evening, the disciples came, and said: " How shall we feed all these people? " Among the gathering were some who had nothing, and some who had bread and fish. And Jesus said to his disciples: "Give me all the bread you have." He took the loaves, and gave bread to his disciples, who gave to others, who did likewise. So all ate of others' bread, not consuming all there was, and all were satisfied. And Jesus said: "Act just in this way. It is not necessary that each one should get food for himself, but it is needful to do that which the Spirit in man demands, namely, that each shall share to others what supply there is. The true food of man is the Spirit of the Father. Man lives by the Spirit only. Everything in life must be made subservient to this; for life consists in doing, not one's own will, but the will of the Father of life. And that will is, that the perfect life of the Spirit which is given to men, shall remain in them, and that all shall cherish the life of the Spirit within them until the hour of death. The Father, the source of life, is Spirit. Life consists only in carrying out the will of the Father; and to carry out that will of the Spirit, one must surrender the body. The body is the food, the material for the life of the Spirit. Only in giving up the body does the Spirit live."

After this, Jesus chose certain disciples, and sent them everywhere to preach the doctrine of the life of the Spirit. In sending them, he said: "Preach the life of the Spirit, and, consistently therewith, renounce beforehand all fleshly desires, and have nothing of your own. Be ready for persecution, privation, suffering. Those who love the life of the body will hate you, harass and murder you; but do not fear. If you fulfil the will of the Father, then you possess the life of the Spirit, of which no one can deprive you."

The disciples went away, and when they returned, declared that everywhere the teachings of evil were conquered by them.

Then the orthodox told Jesus that his teaching, even if it conquered evil, was in itself an evil, because those who carry it out must of necessity suffer. To this, Jesus answered: "Evil cannot conquer evil. If evil is conquered, it can only be by good. Goodness is the will of the Father-Spirit common to all men. Every man has a knowledge of what benefits himself. If he does similar benefits to others, if he does that which is the will of the Father, then he will do good. Therefore the carrying out of the will of the Father-Spirit results well, even though it be followed with sufferings and deaths of those who fulfil that will."

CHAPTER VI

THE FALSE LIFE

Therefore, in order to receive the true life, man must on earth resign the false life of the flesh, and live by the Spirit

("On earth as in heaven")

To the spiritual life there can be no difference between members of one family and strangers. Jesus said that his mother and his brethren, as such, had no superior claims upon him; only those were near to him who fulfilled the will of the common Father. A man's life and welfare depend, not on family relations, but on the life of the Spirit.

Jesus said: "Blessed are those who retain their understanding of the Father. The man who lives by the Spirit has no home, for, being by the Spirit, he cannot own any special house." And he said that he himself had no fixed abode; that not being needed to enable a man to carry out the will of the Father, which can be done at all times, in all places.

The death of the body cannot be dreadful to a man who gives himself up to the will of the Father, because the life of the Spirit goes on despite the death of the body. Jesus said that he who believes in the life of the Spirit has nothing to fear.

No cares make it impossible for a man to live in his Spirit. When a man said that he would obey the teaching of Christ presently, but that he must first bury his father, Jesus answered: "Only the dead trouble about

burial of the dead; but the living live always in fulfilling the will of the Father." Cares about relations and
family affairs must not hinder the life of the Spirit. He
who troubles about the results to his bodily life from the
fulfilment of the Father's will, does as the plowman
does, who plows, looking not in front, but behind.

Cares for the pleasures of the bodily life, which seem
so important to men, are delusions. The only, the real
business of life, is the making plain of the Father's will,
attention to it, and fulfilment of it. To Martha's reproach, that she alone troubled about the supper, and
that her sister Mary did not help, but listened to his
teaching, Jesus said: "You blame her unjustly. Take
some trouble, yourself, if you need what comes of it, but
let those who do not need pleasures for the body attend
to the one essential business of life."

And Jesus said: "He who desires the true life, which
comes of fulfilling the Father's will, must first of all give
up his own personal desires." He must not only cease
to plan out his life to his own wishes, but he must be
ready at any moment to bear any privations and sufferings. One who seeks to arrange his bodily life to his
own desires, will wreck the true life of fulfilment of the
Father's will.

Most ruinous to the life of the Spirit is the love of
gain, of getting rich. Men forget that, however much
they acquire riches and goods, they may die at any
moment, and their property is not an essential of life.
Death broods over every one of us. Sickness, killing
by men, fatal accidents, may at any minute end life.
Bodily death is the unescapable condition of every
second of life. While one lives, one must regard every
hour of life as a delay granted by the kindness of
some power. This we must remember, and not say that
we do not know it. We know and foresee in regard
to all events of earth and sky, but death, which we
know waits on us every moment, we forget. But unless
we forget death, we cannot yield ourselves to the life
of the body, we cannot build upon it. To follow the
teaching of Christ, one has to count up the advantages

of serving the bodily life, of serving one's own will, and the advantages of fulfilling the Father's will. Only one who clearly takes account of this can be a disciple of Christ. And he who makes the calculation, will not prefer a visionary benefit and a visionary life to the true good and the true life. The true life has been given to men, and men know it, they hear its summons, but, always swept on by the cares of the moment, they are withheld from it. The true life is as though a rich man gave a feast, and summoned the guests. His call to them is the voice of the Spirit of the Father inviting all men to Himself. But of those invited some are busy in commerce, some in the household, some in family affairs, — none come to the feast. Only the poor, such as have no cares of the body, come to the feast, and gain happiness. So men, distracting themselves with cares for the bodily life, are losing the true life. He who cannot, and that altogether, decline the cares and gains of the bodily life, cannot fulfil the Father's will, because one cannot serve oneself a little, and the Father a little.

A man must calculate, whether it is better to serve the body, whether it is possible to arrange his life according to his own will. He must do as one does who would build a house, or who contemplates war. Such an one will reckon whether he has means to finish building, whether he has means to conquer. And upon seeing that he has not, he will not spend for nothing either labor or armies. Otherwise, he fruitlessly wastes, and will be a laughingstock to men. If one could arrange the bodily life to one's own will, then it might be well to serve the body; but as that is impossible, then better sacrifice the body, and serve the Spirit. Otherwise, one will gain neither one thing nor another; the bodily life will not be gained, and the spiritual life will be lost. So that, to fulfil the Father's will, the bodily life must be quite resigned.

The bodily life is involved in the world's false riches, which we are commissioned to manage in such a way as to gain the true and perfect riches.

If a rich man has a manager who knows that, however he may serve his master, the latter will dismiss him, leaving him with nothing, this manager will do well if, during his management of the other's riches, he treats people well. Then, even though his master dismiss him, those whom he has benefited will receive him and sustain him. So also must men act as to the bodily life. The bodily life is that wealth, not one's own, which is given to one to manage for a time. If men will rightly use this wealth, which is not their own, then they will gain true wealth, really their own.

If we do not give up our falsely held riches, then the true life will not be given to us. The illusory life of the body, and the life of the spirit, cannot both be served. One cannot serve property and God. What is honorable with men, is abomination before God. Riches are evil before God. A rich man is continually guilty, in that he eats abundantly and luxuriously, while at his door the poor starve. And every one knows that the property which one will not share to others is held in non-fulfilment of the Father's will.

Once Jesus was approached by an orthodox and rich ruler, who began to boast that he had fulfilled all the commandments of the law. Jesus reminded him that there is a commandment to love others as oneself, and that this is the Father's will. The ruler said he kept this also. Then Jesus said to him: "That is not true; if you desire to fulfil the Father's will, you would not have property. A man cannot fulfil the will of the Father, if he has a fortune of his own, which he does not give away to others."

And Jesus said to the disciples: "Men think it impossible to live without property, but I tell you, true life is in the giving up of one's own to others."

A man, Zaccheus by name, heard the teaching of Jesus, and believed it, and having invited Jesus to his house, he said to him: "I am giving half my fortune to the poor, and I will restore four times over to those whom I may have wronged." And Jesus said: "Here is a man who fulfils the Father's will; for the fulfilment of that will is not a matter of finding an opportunity, but the whole life must go in fulfilment."

Goodness cannot be measured in any way. It is impossible to say who has done more good, and who less, A widow who gives away her last farthing gives more than a rich man who gives thousands. It is also impossible to measure goodness by utility or inutility.

As an instance of how goodness must be shown, take the woman who pitied Jesus, and in her emotion poured upon him many pounds' worth of costly oil. Judas said she had done foolishly, because many people might have been fed on the price. But Judas was a thief; he spoke untruth, and in talking of the worldly value of the oil, he did not consider the poor. Not utility, not value, comes into the question, but the necessity of always, every minute, loving others, and giving up to them one's own.

CHAPTER VII

I AND THE FATHER ARE ONE

The true food of everlasting life is the fulfilment of the Father's will

("Give us our daily bread")

Answering the Jews' demands for proofs of the truth of his teaching, Jesus said: "The truth of my teaching is proved in the fact that I teach, not in my own name, but in the name of the common Father of all men. I teach that which is good in the sight of the Father of all men, and is therefore good for all men.

"Do as I say; fulfil the five commandments, and you will see that the truth is as I say. Fulfilment of these five commandments will drive away all the world's evil; therefore it must be that they are true and right. Clearly, he who teaches, not his own personal will, but the will of Him who sent him, will teach the truth. The Mosaic law teaches the fulfilment of men's own wills, and is therefore full of contradictions; but my teaching is to fulfil the will of the Father, and therefore in it all is harmonious."

The Jews did not understand him, and looked for external proofs as to whether he himself were the Christ written of in the prophecies. On this he said to them: "Do not inquire who I am, whether it is of me your prophecies speak, but attend to my teaching, to what I say of our common Father. It is not necessary to inquire about outside matters, as to whence I come; but my teaching must be followed. He who will follow my teaching will obtain true life. There can be no proofs of my teaching. It is the light itself, and as you cannot illuminate light, so you cannot prove the truth of truth. My teaching is light; he who sees it has light and life, and has no need of proofs. But he who is in darkness must come to the light."

But again the Jews asked him who he was, as to his bodily personality. He said to them: "I am, as I told you from the first, a man, the Son of the Father of life. Only he who will so regard himself (this is the truth I teach), and will fulfil the will of the common Father, only he will cease to be a slave, and become a free man. Because we are slaves only through the error which considers the bodily life as the real life. He who will understand the truth, that life consists only in the fulfilment of the Father's will, only he will become free and immortal. Just as a bond-servant in a master's house is not there for ever, but the son does remain, so the man who lives the life of a slave of the flesh does not remain in life for ever; but he who in spirit fulfils the Father's will, remains in life for ever. To understand me, you must understand that my Father is not that which is your Father, what you call God. Your Father is a God of the flesh; but my Father is the Spirit of life. Your Father, your God, is a God of revenge, a murderer, one who executes men; but my Father gives life. Therefore we are children of different Fathers.

"I am following the truth, and you wish to kill me for that, to please your God. Your God is the devil, the source of evil; and in serving him, you serve the devil.

But my teaching is, that we are the sons of the Father
of life, and that he who believes in my teaching shall not
see death."

The Jews asked: " How can a man not die, when all
the most God-pleasing men, even Abraham, are dead?
How, then, can you say that you, and those that believe
your teaching, will not die?" To this Jesus answered:
" I speak not by my own authority. I speak of the one
source of life, whom you call God, and who is in men.
This source I know, I cannot help knowing, and I know
His will, and I fulfil it; and of this source of life I say,
that it was, and is, and shall be, being deathless."

The demand for proof of Jesus' teaching is like a
demand made upon a once-blind man, to give proofs of
how and why he sees light. The blind man whose
sight was restored, still the same man he was before,
can only say, he was blind, but now sees. Just this, and
nothing else, can one answer who formerly did not
understand the meaning of life, but now does understand. Such a man will say that he did not, before,
know the true good in life, but now he knows. The
once-blind man, when told he is cured not according to
rule, and that he who cured him is the evil-doer, and
that he must be cured in another way, can only reply,
that he knows nothing as to the correctness of the manner of cure, or as to the faultiness of his healer, or as
to their being a better way of cure, but that he knows
only, he was blind, and now sees. And just so, he who
grasps the meaning of this doctrine, that the true good
is to fulfil the Father's will, can say nothing as to the
regularity of the teaching, or as to the possibility of
gaining something better. He will say: "Formerly I
did not see the meaning of life; now I see. I know no
more."

And Jesus said: "My teaching is the awakening of
the life which has so far slept; he who will believe my
teaching, shall awaken to eternal life, and continue to
live after death. My teaching is not proved in any way,
except that men give themselves up to it, because it
alone has the promise of life for men.

"Sheep follow the shepherd, who gives them food and life; and in the same way, men accept my teaching because it gives life to all. And as the sheep do not follow the thief who climbs over into the fold, but throw themselves aside from him, so men, also, cannot accept the doctrines which teach violence and putting-to-death.

"My teaching is a door to the sheep, and all who will follow me shall find true life. As those only are good shepherds who own and like the sheep, and devote their lives to them, while the mere hirelings, who have no liking for sheep, are bad shepherds; so, also, only that teacher is true who does not look after himself, and he is bad who cares only about himself. My teaching is, that a man shall not look after himself, but shall yield up the life of the body for the life of the spirit. This I teach and fulfil."

Still the Jews did not understand, and persisted in looking for proofs as to whether or not Jesus was the Christ, to determine whether they should believe in him or not. They said: "Do not torment us, but tell us frankly, are you the Christ, or not?" Then Jesus answered them: "Belief must be given, not to words, but to deeds. By the deeds I teach you may know whether I teach truth or not. Do as I do, and do not trifle over words. Fulfil the will of the Father, and then you will all join with me and with the Father, because I am a Son of Man, and at one with the Father. And I am that which you call God, and I call Father. God and I are one. Even in your own writings it is said, that God said to men, 'You are gods.' Every one, by his spirit, is son of this Father. And if a man lives fulfilling the will of the Father, then he becomes at one with the Father. If I fulfil the will, the Father is in me, and I am in the Father."

After this, Jesus asked the disciples how they under-stood his teaching as to the Son of Man. Simon Peter answered him: "Your teaching is that you are the Son of the God of life; that God is the life of the spirit in man." And Jesus said to him: "Not only I am a son, but all men are; and this is revealed to men, not

by me, but by the common Father of men. Upon this
knowledge is based the true life of man. To this life
there is no death."

CHAPTER VIII

LIFE IS NOT TEMPORAL

Therefore true life is to be lived in the present

("𝔗𝔥𝔦𝔰 𝔡𝔞𝔶")

DEALING with the disciples' question as to the recompense for surrendering the life of the body, Jesus
said : " To him who enters into the reality of this teaching, no further recompense can be given ; because,
first, when a man yields up friends and goods for the
sake of this teaching, he gains a hundred times more
friends and goods ; and second, a man who seeks such
recompense wants to have something over and above
others, which is entirely contrary to the fulfilment of the
Father's will." In the Kingdom of Heaven there is
neither great nor small ; all are equal. Those who look
for something extra as reward for their goodness, are
like the laborers who claimed a greater payment than
that for which they had agreed with their employer ;
merely because, in their opinion, they were more de-
serving than other laborers. There are no rewards,
punishments, degradations, or exaltations, for him who
understands this teaching. No one can be higher or
lower, more or less important, than another, according
to the teaching of Jesus.

All can equally fulfil the Father's will. Therefore,
in so doing, no one becomes superior, truer, or better,
than another.

Kings and those who serve them, they only are measured by such standards. By my teaching, said Jesus,
there can be no superior rank, because he who would
excel must serve everybody ; for the teaching is, that
life is given to man, not that others may serve him,

but that he may give his whole life to serve others; but
he who will not do this, but seeks to exalt himself, shall
fall lower than he was.

To get rid of all ideas of rewards and of one's elevation, the meaning, purpose, of life must be understood.
That lies in fulfilling the will of the Father; and the
will of the Father is, that that which He gave shall be
returned to Him.   As a shepherd leaves his flock, and
goes to look for the lost sheep, as a woman will search
everywhere to find a lost penny, so also the Father's
continual work is manifested to us in His drawing to
Himself that which pertains to Him.

We must understand the true life, what it is.   The
true life is brought to light always in the lost being
brought back to where they belong, in the awakening
of those who slept.   People who have the true life,
who are restored to the source of their being, cannot,
like worldly men, take account of others as better or
worse; but, being sharers of the Father's life, they can
take delight only in the return of the lost to their
Father.   If a son, who has gone astray and left his
father, should repent, and return, how then could the
other sons of the same father grudge at the father's joy,
or themselves not rejoice at the brother's return?

To lead us to believe the teaching, and to alter one's
way of living, and fulfil the teaching, we need, not external proofs, not promises of reward, but a clear understanding of what the true life is.   If men think they
are complete masters of their own lives, and that life is
given them for bodily enjoyment, then clearly, any sacrifice made for another will seem to them an act worthy
of reward, and without such payment they will yield
nothing.   A man demands rents from tenants who
have forgotten that their ground is theirs on condition
that they give up the fruits to the owner; and when he
demands the rent again and again, they seek to kill him.
So with the men who think themselves masters of their
own lives, not discerning that life is given by true
understanding; men who demand the fulfilment of
their own wills.

Both belief and action are necessary, to learn that a man can do nothing of himself, and if he give up his bodily life to serve goodness, he deserves neither thanks nor reward. We must understand that, in doing good, a man only does his duty, does what he must necessarily do. Only by so understanding his life, can a man have faith to enable him to do deeds of true goodness.

Precisely in such an understanding of life, the Kingdom of Heaven consists. This Kingdom is invisible; it cannot be pointed out as identified with this or that place. The Kingdom of Heaven is in the human understanding. The whole society of the world goes on living as of old; men eat, drink, marry, trade, die, and along with this, in the souls of men, lives the Kingdom of Heaven. It is the understanding of life, growing from itself, like a tree in the spring.

The true life of the fulfilment of the Father's will is not in the life of the past, or of the future, but it is the life of now, the life which all must live at this instant of time. Therefore one must never relax the true life in them. Men are set to watch over life, not of the past or the future, but the life now being lived; and in that, to fulfil the will of the Father of all men. If they let this life escape them, by not fulfilling the Father's will, then they will not receive it back again; just as a watchman, set upon a night-long watch, does not perform his duty if he fall asleep even for a moment; for in this moment a thief may come.

Therefore a man must concentrate his strength in the present hour, for in this hour only can he fulfil the Father's will. And that will is life and blessing for all men. Only those live who are doing good. Good done to men, now, in this hour, is life, life which unites us with the common Father.

CHAPTER IX

TEMPTATIONS

The illusions of temporal life conceal from men the true life in the present

("𝔉𝔬𝔯𝔤𝔦𝔟𝔢 𝔲𝔰 𝔬𝔲𝔯 𝔡𝔢𝔟𝔱𝔰 𝔞𝔰 𝔴𝔢 𝔣𝔬𝔯𝔤𝔦𝔟𝔢 𝔬𝔲𝔯 𝔡𝔢𝔟𝔱𝔬𝔯𝔰 ")

MAN is born with knowledge of the true life of ful-filment of the Father's will. Children live by that knowledge; through them we may see what the Father's will is. To understand the teaching of Jesus, one must understand the life of children, and be like them.

Children always live in the Father's will, not breaking the five commandments. They would not come to break them if their elders did not mislead them. In misleading children to break those commandments, men ruin the children. In misleading them, men are doing as they would do by fastening a millstone to a man's neck and throwing him into the water.

If there were no temptations, the world would be happy. The world is unhappy by them only. These temptations are wrong-doing which men enact for imaginary gain to the life in time. Temptations ruin men; therefore it is necessary to give up everything rather than fall into temptation.

Temptation against the first commandment leads men to consider themselves in the right against others, and others as in the wrong, debtors to them. To avoid this temptation, men must remember that all men are always infinitely in debt to the Father, and they can only clear themselves of this debt by forgiving their brother-men.

Therefore men must overlook injuries, and not be de-terred though the offender again and again injure them. However many times a man may be injured, he must forgive, and still forgive, not remembering the wrong. For the Kingdom of Heaven is forgiveness.

If we do not forgive, we are doing as the debtor did. This debtor, greatly owing, came to him in whose power he was, and began to ask for mercy. The other forgave him all. The debtor went away, and began himself to squeeze a debtor, who owed him but a little. Now, to gain life, we must fulfil the Father's will. And we pray the Father to forgive us, that we have not duly fulfilled his will, and we hope to be forgiven. What, then, are we doing, if we do not ourselves forgive? We are doing to others what we dread for ourselves.

The will of the Father is well-being, and evil is that which separates us from the Father. Why, then, should we not strive to quench evil right away, when evil ruins us, and takes our life?

Temptation against the second commandment is, to think that woman is created for bodily pleasure, and that in leaving one woman and taking another, heightened pleasure is gained. To avoid this temptation, we must remember that the Father's will is, not that man should amuse himself with woman's charms, but that every man, with his wife, should be one body. The Father's will is, for every man, one wife; for every wife, one husband. If one man keep to one wife, then there is wife or husband for each one who needs. Therefore he who changes the woman he lives with deprives her of a husband, and tempts some other man to leave his wife and take the deserted one. A man may do without a wife, but he must not have more than one, because if he does, he goes against the will of the Father, which is, that one man unite with one woman.

Temptation against the third commandment is, for men to create, for the protection of the temporal life, authoritative powers, and to demand from each other oaths, pledges, to do the deeds those powers demand. To avoid this temptation, men must remember that they are not indebted for their life to any power but God. The claims of authority must be regarded as violence; and, following the commandment regarding the non-resistance of evil, men must yield what the authorities demand, namely, their goods and labor; but they cannot, either by oaths or promises, pledge their conduct. Oaths, being imposed, make men bad. He who recognizes life in the will of the Father cannot bind his actions by pledges; because for such a man there is nothing more sacred than his own life.

Temptation against the fourth commandment is, for men to hold that, by giving themselves up to animosity and revenge, they can exterminate evil from among themselves. If a man injure another, men think he should be punished, and that justice lies in human judg· ments. To be free from this temptation, we must re member that men are called, not to judge, but to save each other. To judge of another's injustice is impossible for men, as they themselves are full of wickedness. The only thing open to them is to teach others by example of goodness, forgiveness, and purity.

Temptation against the fifth commandment is, for man to think there is a difference between one's own countrymen and men of other nations; and that it is therefore necessary to make defense against other nations, and to injure them. To avoid this temptation, it is necessary to know that all the commandments are summed up in this one, of fulfilling the will of the Father who gives life and well-being to all men; and therefore it is necessary to do good to all men, without distinction. Even though others still make such distinctions, and though nations who look on each other as aliens are at war, nevertheless, everybody who would fulfil the Father's will must do good to all men, even to those who belong to another nation which is at war.

To avoid falling into any delusions of men, we must not think about bodily affairs, but about spiritual. To him who has understood that life consists in being, at this moment, in the Father's will, neither deprivations, nor suffering, nor death can be dreadful. Only he obtains true life who is, at every moment, ready to give up his bodily life in order to fulfil the Father's will.

And that all may understand the true life to be one in which there is no death, Jesus said: " Eternal life must not be understood to be like this present life. For the true life in the Father's will, there is neither space nor time. Those who are awakened to the true life, live in the will of the Father, for which there is no space nor time ; and they live with the Father. Though they die to us, they live to God. Therefore one commandment includes in itself all others ; the commandment, namely, to love, with all our strength, the source of life ; and consequently to love all men, each of whom bears in himself this same original."

And Jesus said : "This source of life is that very Christ which you await. The comprehension of this source of life, which knows no distinction of persons, no time, no place, is the Son of Man which I teach. Anything which hides this source of life from men is temptation. There is the temptation of the scribes, bookmen, and of the materialists ; do not yield thereto. There are the temptations of authority ; do not yield thereto. And there is the most terrible temptation, from the teachers of religion who call themselves orthodox. Beware of this last more than of all others ; because just they, these self-ordained teachers, by inventing the worship of a false God, decoy you from the true God. They, instead of serving the Father of life by deeds, substitute words, and they teach words, while they themselves do nothing. Therefore you can learn nothing from them but words. But the Father requires deeds, not words. And they have nothing to teach, because they themselves know nothing ; but for their own gain they must parade as teachers. But you know that no man can be the teacher of another. There is one teacher for all — the Lord of life — understanding. And these self-assuming teachers, thinking to teach others, deprive themselves of true life, and prevent others from the understanding of it. They teach that their God will be pleased with external ceremonies ; and they think they can bring men to serve religion by vows. They are concerned with appearances only. An outward assumption of religion suffices them, but they do not care what is in the hearts of men. Therefore they are like elaborate coffins, very nice outside, but within full of repulsiveness. They give honor, in words, to saints and martyrs, but they are themselves just the very men who have murdered and tortured in the past, and who murder and torture the saints of to-day. By them come all the world's temptations; because, under the guise of good, they teach evil. The temptation they create is the root of all others, because they defile that which is most sacred. For a long time yet they will not be changed, but will continue their deceptions, and increase evil in the world. But there shall come a time when all the temples will be ruined, with all the external God-worship; when all men will understand, and unite in love, to serve the one Father of life, by fulfilling His will."

CHAPTER X

THE WARFARE WITH TEMPTATION

Therefore, not to fall by temptation, we must, at every moment of life, be at one with the Father

("Lead us not into temptation")

THE Jews saw that the teaching of Jesus would destroy their state, religion, and nationality, and at the same time they saw they could not controvert him; so they decided to kill him. His innocence and justness stood in their way, but the high priest Caiaphas discovered a reason for killing Jesus, though innocent. Caiaphas said: "We need not consider whether this man is just or unjust; we have to determine whether our Jewish people shall remain a separate nation, or whether we shall be broken up and dispersed: the nation will perish, and the people be scattered, if we leave this man alone, and do not put him to death." This argument settled the matter, and the orthodox sentenced Jesus to death. They instructed the people to seize upon him as soon as he might appear in Jerusalem.

Jesus, although he knew about this, nevertheless, on the feast of the Passover, came to Jerusalem. His disciples entreated him not to do so; but he said: "What these orthodox can do to me, and all that other men can do, cannot alter the truth for me. If I have the light, I know where I am, and which way I am going. Only he who does not know the truth can fear anything, or can doubt anything. Only he who cannot see, stumbles." And he went to Jerusalem, stopping on the way at Bethany.

When he left Bethany, and went to Jerusalem, crowds of people met and followed him. This still more convinced the orthodox of the need to kill him. They only wanted an opportunity to seize him. He knew also that the lightest incautious word from him at that time, spoken against the law, would be a reason for his execution; but notwithstanding this, he entered the temple, and declared again that the worship of the Jews, with their sacrifices and libations, was false, and he declared his teaching. But his teaching, based on the prophets, was such that the orthodox could not yet find a palpable breach of the law which would justify them in putting him to death; the more so that the greater part of the lower class was with Jesus.

At the feast were certain heathen, who, having heard of the teaching of Jesus, wished to talk with him about it. The disciples, hearing of this, were afraid, fearing lest Jesus, in talking with them, should betray himself, and excite the people. At first they would not bring Jesus and these heathen together; but afterward they resolved to tell him these men wanted to see him. Hearing this, Jesus was disturbed. He well knew that his speech to the heathen would clearly show his antagonism to the whole Jewish law, would turn the crowd from him, and would give the orthodox a reason to accuse him of being in league with the hated heathen. Jesus became disturbed, knowing this; but he also knew that his mission was to make clear to men, the children of one Father, their real unity, despite differences of religion. He knew that the step he was about to take would end his bodily life, for the sake of giving birth to spiritual results. He said: " He who holds fast to the bodily life is deprived of the true one; and he who is not careful for the bodily life obtains the true life. I am troubled by what is before me, but I have only lived that I might reach this hour; how, then, can I fail to

now do what I must do? So let the Father's will be
shown through me now."

And turning to the people, heathen and Jews, Jesus
declared openly what he had only privately told to Nicodemus. He said: "Men's lives, with all their various
religions and organized powers, must be wholly changed.
All power and authority must disappear. It is only
necessary to understand the nature of man as the son of
the Father of life, and this understanding abolishes all
division among men, and all ruling power, and makes
men one."

The Jews said: "You wholly destroy our religion.
Our law looks to the Christ, but you speak only of the
Son of Man, and say that he must be set up. What do
you mean?" He answered them: "To set up the Son
of Man means to live by the light of the understanding
which is in men, to follow this light into more light.
I teach no new faith, only that which every one may
know within himself. Every man knows he has life,
given to him and to all men by the Father of life. My
teaching is only this, that man must live the life given
by the Father to all."

Many of the humbler kind of people believed Jesus.
But the notable and official classes disbelieved; because
they did not want to consider the universal basis of
what he said, but only its immediate and temporary
bearings. They saw that he turned the people from
themselves, and they wished to kill him; but they were
afraid to seize him openly, and did not seek to do so in
Jerusalem and in the daytime, but secretly elsewhere.

And one of the twelve disciples, Judas Iscariot, approached the authorities, and him they bribed to take
their emissaries to Jesus when he should be away from
the people. Judas promised this, and went again to
Jesus, awaiting a suitable opportunity to betray him.

On the first day of the feast, Jesus and his disciples
kept the Passover. And Judas, thinking Jesus was not
aware of his treachery, was with them. But Jesus
knew Judas had sold him. And as they all sat at table,
Jesus took bread, broke it in twelve pieces, and gave a

piece to each disciple, including Judas with the rest. And not mentioning any name, he said: "Take, eat my body." Then he took the cup with the wine, passed it to them, for them all, including Judas, to drink from, and said: "One of you will shed my blood. Drink my blood."

Afterward Jesus got up, and began to wash the feet of all his disciples, including Judas. And having finished, he said: "I know that one of you will betray me to my death, and shed my blood; but him I have fed, and given to drink, and washed his feet. I have done this to show you how you must act toward those who do you harm. If you will act in this way, you shall be blest." And the disciples went on to ask who the betrayer was. But Jesus did not give his name, so that they might not turn on him. And when it had grown dark, Jesus showed that it was Judas, and at the same time told him to go away. Judas got up from the table and went off, no one hindering him.

Then Jesus said: "This is the meaning of setting up the Son of Man. To set up the Son of Man is to be like the Father, good; and that, not only to those who love us, but to all men, even to those who do us harm. And therefore do not argue over my teaching, do not pick it to pieces as the orthodox did, but do as I have done; do as I have done under your eyes. This one commandment I give you: Love men. My whole teaching is, to love men always, and to the last."

After this, fear came over Jesus, and he went in the dark with his disciples to a garden, to be out of the way. While walking, he said to them: "You are all wavering and timid; if they move to take me, you will all run away." To this, Peter said: "No, I will never leave you; I will defend you even to death." And all the disciples said so. Then Jesus said: "If that be the case, then get ready for defense; take provision, because we must hide, take weapons, to fight for ourselves." The disciples said they had two swords.

When Jesus heard this about the swords, anguish came over him. And going to a vacant place, he began to pray, and entreated his disciples to do the same. But the disciples did not understand his state of mind. Jesus said : " My Father, the Spirit, end in me this struggle with temptation. Strengthen me to the fulfilment of Thy will. I do not want my own way. I do not want to defend my bodily life. I want to do Thy will, in not resisting evil."

The disciples still did not understand. And he said to them : " Do not consider the concerns of the body, but try to rise into the spirit ; strength is in the spirit, but the flesh is powerless." And a second time he said : " My Father, if suffering must be, then let it come. But even in suffering, I want one thing only : that not my will shall be fulfilled, but thine." The disciples did not understand. And again he struggled with the temptation ; and at last conquered it. Coming to the disciples, he said : " It is settled now ; you can be at rest. I shall not fight, but shall surrender myself into the hands of the men of this world."

CHAPTER XI

THE FAREWELL DISCOURSE

The self-life is an illusion which comes through the flesh, an evil. The true life is the life common to all men

("Deliver us from evil")

JESUS, finding himself prepared for death, went to give himself up. Peter stopped him, and asked : " Where are you going ? " Jesus answered : " I am going where you cannot go. I am ready for death, and you are not yet ready." Peter said : " No, I am even now ready to sacrifice my life for thee." Jesus said to him : " A man cannot promise anything."

And he said to all his disciples : " I know death is before me, but I believe in the life of the Father, and therefore am not afraid of it. Do not be distressed over

my death, but believe in the real God, in the Father of
life, and then my death will not seem dreadful to you.
If I am united with the Father of life, then I cannot be
deprived of life. It is true, I do not tell you what and
where my life will be, after death, but I point out to you
the way to true life. My teaching does not reveal what
that life is to be, but it reveals the only true way of life.
That is, to be in unity with the Father. The Father is
the source of life. My teaching is, that man shall live
in the will of the Father, and fulfil His will for the life
and well-being of all men.

"Your teacher, when I am gone, will be your knowledge of the truth. In fulfilling my teaching, you will
always feel that you are in the truth, that the Father is
in you, and you are in the Father. And knowing in yourselves the Father of life, you will experience a peace of
which nothing will deprive you. And therefore, if you
know the truth and live in it, neither my death nor your
own can trouble you.

"Men think of themselves as separate beings, each
with his own power of will in life; but this is only an
illusion. The only true life is that which recognizes the
Father's will as the source of life. My teaching reveals
this oneness of life, and represents life, not as separate
shoots, but as one tree, on which all the shoots grow.
Only he who lives in the Father's will, like a shoot of a
tree, only he lives; and he who wishes to live by his own
will, dies away like a torn-off shoot.

"The Father gave me life to do good, and I have
taught you to live to do good. If you will fulfil my commandment, you will be blessed. The commandment
which sums up my whole teaching is no more than this,
that all men shall love one another. And love is to
sacrifice one's own bodily life for another's sake. Love
has no other definition. In fulfilling my commandment
of love, you will not fulfil it like slaves, who follow the
orders of a master without understanding them; but you
will live as free men, as I am, because I have made clear
to you the purpose of life, which follows from the knowledge of the Father of life. You have adopted my teach-

ing, not from accidental choice, but because it is the only truth by which men are made free.

"The teaching of the world is to do evil to men; but I teach that men love each other. Therefore the world will despise you, as it has despised me. The world does not understand my teaching, and therefore will persecute you, and do you evil, thinking thereby to serve God. Do not be astonished at this; you must understand that it is necessarily so. The world, not understanding the true God, must persecute you; but you must affirm the truth.

"You grieve because they will kill me; but they kill me for declaring the truth. And therefore my death is necessary for the declaration of the truth. My death, in facing which I do not go back from the truth, will strengthen you, and you will understand the nature of untruth and of truth. You will understand that untruth lies in men's belief in the bodily life, and their disbelief in the life of the spirit; that truth consists in unity with the Father, from which results the victory of the spirit over the flesh.

"Even when I shall not be with you in the bodily life, my spirit will be with you. But you, like all men, will not always feel within you the power of the spirit. Sometimes you will relax and lose strength of spirit; and you will fall into temptation; and at times you will again awaken to the true life. Hours of bondage to the body will come upon you, but for a time only; you will suffer, and again be restored to the spirit, like a woman who suffers birth-pangs, and then has joy because she has brought a human being into the world. So will your experience be, when, after falling under the power of the body, you rise again by the spirit. You will then feel such joy, that nothing will be left for you to desire. Know this, then, beforehand; and in spite of persecution, in spite of internal struggle and casting down of spirit, know that the spirit lives in you, and that the only true God is the knowledge of the Father's will, as I have revealed it."

And addressing the Father, the Spirit, Jesus said:

"I have done that which Thou hast commanded me; I have revealed to men that Thou art the source of everything. And they have understood me. I have taught them that they all come from the source of infinite life, and therefore they are all one; and that as the Father is in me, and I am in the Father, so they, too, are one with me and the Father. I have revealed to them also, that, like Thee, who in love hast sent them into the world, they, too, shall with love live in the world."

CHAPTER XII

THE VICTORY OF THE SPIRIT OVER THE FLESH

Therefore, for him who lives, not the self-life, but a common life in the will of the Father, there is no death. Bodily death is for him union with the Father

("𝔗𝔥𝔦𝔫𝔢 𝔦𝔰 𝔱𝔥𝔢 𝔨𝔦𝔫𝔤𝔡𝔬𝔪, 𝔭𝔬𝔴𝔢𝔯, 𝔞𝔫𝔡 𝔤𝔩𝔬𝔯𝔶")

WHEN Jesus had ended his discourse to the disciples, he rose, and, instead of running away or defending himself, he went on the way to meet Judas, who was bringing soldiers to take him. Jesus came to Judas, and asked him why he had come. But Judas did not answer, and a crowd of soldiers came round Jesus. Peter threw himself forward to defend his teacher, and, drawing his sword, began to fight. But Jesus stopped him, and said to him, that he who fights with a sword must himself perish with the sword, and ordered him to put up the sword. Then Jesus said to those who had come to take him: "I have up to now gone about among you alone, without fear, and I do not fear now. Do as you choose."

And while all the disciples ran away, Jesus was left alone. The officer of the soldiers ordered Jesus to be bound, and led before Annas. This Annas was a former high priest, and lived in the same house with Caiaphas, who was then high priest. Caiaphas it was who provided the reason upon which they decided to

kill Jesus; namely, that if he were not killed the nation
would disappear.

Jesus, feeling himself to be in the will of the Father,
was ready for death, and did not resist when they took
him, and was not afraid when they led him away. But
the very Peter who had just promised Jesus that he
would not renounce him, but would die for him, this same
Peter who wished to protect him,— now, when he saw
that they were taking Jesus for execution, and being met
with the door-keeper's question, Whether he was not
with Jesus? gave up, and deserted him. It was only
afterward that, hearing the cock crow, Peter brought to
mind all that Jesus had said. Then he understood that
there are two temptations of the flesh, fear and fighting;
and that it was with these that Jesus struggled when he
prayed in the garden, and asked the disciples to pray.
And now he, Peter, had fallen before both these temptations of the flesh, of which Jesus had forewarned him;
he had wished to fight against evil, and to defend the
truth, he had been about to strike and to do evil himself;
and now he could not endure the fear of bodily suffering, and had renounced his teacher. Jesus had yielded
neither to the temptation to fight, when the disciples got
ready two swords for his defense, nor to the temptation
to fear before the men of Jerusalem, first, in the case of
the heathen, and now before the soldiers, who had bound
him and led him to trial.

Jesus was taken before Caiaphas. Caiaphas began
to question him about his teaching. But knowing that
Caiaphas was examining him, not to find out what his
teaching was, but only to convict him, Jesus did not
answer, but said: "I have concealed nothing, and now
conceal nothing. If you wish to know what my teaching
is, ask those who heard and understood it." For saying
this, the high priest's servant struck Jesus in the face,
and Jesus asked him why he so beat him. But the man
did not answer him, and the high priest continued the
trial. Witnesses were brought, who deposed that Jesus
had boasted that he made an end of the Jewish religion. And the high priest interrogated Jesus; who,

seeing they did not examine him to learn anything, but only to make a show of a judicial trial, answered nothing.

Then a priest asked him : "Tell me, are you the Christ, the Son of God ?" Jesus said : "Yes, I am the Christ, the Son of God ; and now, in torturing me, you will see how a Son of Man is like to God." And the priest was glad to hear these words, and said to the other judges : "Are not these words enough to condemn him ?" And the judges said : "That is enough ; we sentence him to death." And when they said that, the people threw themselves upon Jesus, and began to beat him, to spit in his face, and insult him. He was silent.

The Jews had no power to punish men with death, and for that needed permission from the Roman governor. Therefore, having condemned Jesus in their court, and having subjected him to ignominy, they took him to the Roman governor, Pilate, that he might execute him. Pilate asked why they wished to kill Jesus. They said, because he was a criminal. Pilate said that if he was so, they must judge him by their own law. They said : "We want you to put him to death, because he is guilty before the Roman Cæsar ; he is a rebel, he agitates the people, he forbids payment of taxes to Cæsar, and calls himself the Jewish king."

Pilate summoned Jesus before him, and said : "What is the meaning of this ; are you the Jewish king ?"

Jesus said : "Do you really wish to know what my kingdom means, or are you only asking for form's sake ?"

Pilate answered : "I am not a Jew, and it is the same to me whether you are the Jewish king or not ; but I ask you, who are you, and why do they call you king ?"

Jesus said : "They say truly, that I call myself a king. I am indeed a king, but my kingdom is not of earth, but of heaven. The kings of the earth war and fight, and have armies ; but as for me, — you see they have bound and beaten me, and I did not resist. I am king from heaven : my power is of the spirit."

Pilate said : "Then it is indeed true that you think yourself a king ?"

Jesus answered: "You know this yourself. Every one who lives by the spirit is free. I live by this only, and I only teach by showing men the truth, that they are free by the spirit."

Pilate said: "You teach the truth, but nobody knows what truth is, and every one has his own truth."

And having said this, he turned his back on Jesus, and went again to the Jews. Coming out to them, he said: "I find nothing criminal in this man. Why, then, put him to death?"

The priests answered: "He ought to be put to death, because he incites the people."

Then Pilate began to examine Jesus before the priests; but Jesus, seeing it was only a mock inquiry, answered nothing. Then Pilate said: "I alone cannot condemn him; take him to Herod."

At Herod's tribunal, Jesus again answered nothing to the accusations of the priests; and Herod, thinking Jesus to be a common fellow, ordered him, for mockery, to be dressed in red clothes, and sent back to Pilate.

Pilate pitied Jesus, and began to entreat the priests to forgive him, if only on account of the feast. But the priests did not consent, and all — the people with them — cried out to crucify Christ. Pilate tried a second time to persuade them to let Jesus go; but priests and people cried out that he must be executed. They said: "He is guilty of calling himself the Son of God." Pilate again summoned Jesus, and asked him what he meant by calling himself the Son of God. Jesus answered nothing.

Then Pilate said: "Why do you not answer me, seeing that I have power to execute you or to set you free?"

Jesus answered: "You have no authority over me; authority only comes from on high."

And Pilate a third time began to persuade the Jews to set Jesus free. But they said to him: "If you will not execute this man, whom we have exposed as an enemy to Cæsar, then you yourself are not a friend, but an enemy, to Cæsar."

And hearing these words, Pilate gave way, and ordered the execution of Jesus. They first stripped him and flogged him; then they dressed him again in a ridiculous way. And they beat him, mocked him, and insulted him. Then they caused him to carry the cross, and led him to the place of execution, where they crucified him.

And as Jesus hung on the cross, the whole populace mocked him. But to this mockery Jesus answered: "Father! do not call them to account; they do not know what they are doing." And then, as he was now drawing near death, he said: "Father! I yield my spirit into Thy care."

And bowing his head, he breathed his last.